THEY CALL IT
HYPNOSIS

The Emperor's New Clothes
(Alternate Version*)

Once upon a time there was an emperor, a real cool king, who loved new clothes and spent all his money on them. He was always showing off his fashionable duds and he had a different set for every day of the week. One day two swindlers came to the castle and told the king they had the finest cloth in all the world—cloth so fine that it would become invisible to everyone who was unworthy to look on it. They said that for a pot of gold they would be happy to make the emperor a new set of clothes of this material. The king said, "That's for me, boys. I can not only look swell but at the same time separate the good guys from the bad guys in my kingdom."

So the two crooks happily went to work. They set up looms and pretended to weave. A few days later, wanting to know how the weavers were doing, the emperor sent his right-hand man, an old minister, to have a look. The old minister could see nothing—not the threads, the cloth, or the garments—but he was afraid to say so because it would make him seem unworthy. So the old minister told the emperor the costumes were beautiful. Then the emperor sent more of his subjects to see the clothes being made. They too, for fear of being thought unworthy, said that the coat and colors were gorgeous. Finally, the emperor himself took a look, and seeing nothing on the looms, paled and panicked. He said to himself, "Since I can't see anything, I must be unworthy. I must lie and tell everyone the clothes are marvelous to behold." And he did.

Eventually, the swindlers said the garments were ready. The emperor stripped to the buff and donned the new invisible clothes. All the king's courtiers and all the king's men bowed and scraped and said the new clothes were beautiful. Then the king set off down the avenue in his see-through

*Adapted, with a few variations, from *Fairy Tales* by Hans Christian Andersen.

garments to head up the weekly parade through the village. All of the grown-ups along the way shouted, "Look, look at the emperor's new clothes!" Everyone was afraid to tell the truth for fear they would be thought unworthy.

Finally, some street urchins took a look at the emperor and shouted, "Hey, king, I hate to tell you—but you're nude as a jaybird!" As soon as the children said this, all the grown-ups acknowledged they were correct. Thereupon, the people threw a blanket over the real cool* king, and drove the swindlers out of the kingdom.

---

*It was a wintry day.

This book is dedicated to all of those who have long maintained that the emperor is nude, in particular: Theodore X. Barber, Kreskin, Graham F. Wagstaff, Peter Blythe, Nicholas P. Spanos, Irving Kirsch, William C. Coe, and Theodore R. Sarbin.

Special recognition is also accorded to Frank A. Pattie, the Hilgards—Josephine and Ernest R.—and Andre M. Weitzenhoffer, who have never relented in their efforts to subject the tailor's work and the seamstress's claims to the most rigorous scientific scrutiny.

Contents

Introduction

Many people believe that a hypnotic trance is an invariant state with definite signs, and that an expert can detect whether or not a subject is truly hypnotized. They also believe that it is a dichotomous situation—that a subject is either hypnotized or not. Finally, they believe that it is this special "altered state of consciousness" that produces all of the phenomena commonly associated with hypnosis. All of these ideas are inaccurate.
—Roy Udolf, *Forensic Hypnosis*, 1984

Another book on hypnosis? What else can possibly be said about it that hasn't already been said over and over a thousand times? In many ways the topic is like a toddler's torn and tattered security blanket. It has been pulled and ripped asunder so many times by so many authorities, experts, and know-it-alls that nothing is left except a few ragged strings. To say that the subject is controversial is an understatement. It is often said that every user and practitioner of the hypnotic art "knows what it does but can't tell you what it is," that hypnosis is "a source of great embarrassment to those who do practice it and a source of great confusion to the public, since there is a lack of agreement as to exactly what hypnosis is," that it is "an altered or changed state of awareness, concentration, or perception," that it is "nothing but relaxation," etc., etc., ad nauseam.

Some authorities say there is no such thing as hypnosis, that the entire process is a delusion; others say that everything—everything we are aware of and perceive—is hypnosis. Then the same authorities say that both points of view are correct.

Any intelligent nonbiased observer has the right to ask the very simple and straightforward question: Is there a real, observable, reproducible state of hypnosis, an actual phenomenon we can pin down and agree on? They deserve to receive a simple, straightforward answer: yes or no. To provide this answer is not, however, as easy as it would appear. The answer will depend upon which expert is asked the question. For the past twenty years I have been asking experts of all sizes, shapes, and convictions this simple question and have received just about every possible and conceivable answer. On many points the experts agree; on other points the disagreement is sharp and acerbic. Nevertheless a large body of experimental, empirical, and practical evidence has been accumulated over the past twenty years that is beginning to clear up the confusion and misunderstanding surrounding the concept of hypnosis and the "hypnotic mystery." This book is an attempt to bring this evidence together and solve the puzzle of hypnosis.

In many ways the concept of hypnosis is analogous to some other mysteries that have confused and confounded scientists in the past—such as phlogiston, the ether wind, and "N-rays."

Lavoisier, who was also a member of King Louis XIV's team that investigated mesmerism, was responsible for demolishing the so-called phlogiston theory, dear to the scientific community of his time. As set forth by G. E. Stahl, this idea was that in all combustible substances and metals there was an invisible substance—a handy all-purpose ingredient—that could be used to explain all sorts of chemical reactions. For example, the reason why a substance crumbled to ash when burned was that the phlogiston had left it; the reason why a metal oxide in the form of a soft powder resumed its metallic form when heated with charcoal was that it "took up" phlogiston from the charcoal. For years scientists accepted the existence of the ghostly phlogiston, until chemists began to argue that on certain occasions phlogiston could have weight, while on others it remained weightless or even took on "negative" weight. It was over this difficulty that the theory finally broke down. Lavoisier, using highly accurate balances which could measure very tiny amounts of material, in a series of experiments with precisely weighed quantities of tin and lead discovered what he called an "atmospheric principle." After Joseph Priestley told him about heating mercuric oxide, using sunlight and a magnifying glass, to liberate a new gas that Priestley labeled "dephlogisticated air," Lavoisier recovered this "air" in a new experiment. He found it to be the atmospheric principle he was looking for—a principle responsible for both combustion and calcination, and for the respiration of all living things. When he found that it had acid-forming properties, he named it "oxygen," after the Greek word for acid, oxys, adding the suffix gene. Following other experiments he formulated the principle that the total weight of the products of a reaction exactly equals the combined weight of the reactants from which they were formed. Chemical changes, in other words, caused no loss of mass. With this finding the concept of phlogiston was gone forever.

Again, in the nineteenth century, scientists thought that light waves were carried by an invisible medium they named ether, and that the movement of the earth through this medium created an "ether wind." They believed light was affected by this wind just as a boat is by a water current—it moved faster with the wind than against it. In an attempt to prove ether's existence, Albert Michelson and Edward Morley performed an experiment with an interferometer in which a beam of light was split and the two portions first sent in different directions and then caused to reunite. If the ether wind existed, it would have affected the two beams differently, and they would have been out of phase when they reunited. But clearly they were not. Thus, the ether theory was doomed.

In 1896, Roentgen startled the world with his discovery of X-rays. Shortly thereafter, in 1902 a distinguished French physicist by the name of Blondlot announced the discovery of a new ray, the N-ray, named after its place of discovery, the City of Nancy, which interestingly was the home of Liebault, a hypnosis pioneer, and also of Emile Coué, the father of "suggestion." While working with X-rays, Blondlot found that the brightness of a small surface made phosphorescent by a coating of calcium sulphide significantly increased when a beam of light, refracted through a prism, fell upon it. From this minuscule effect Blondlot argued for the existence of another type of ray. As confirmation, other similar effects were noted: a tiny electric spark became brighter, a blue flame from a gas jet became whiter, etc., and curiously enough, all of these effects occurred only in dark rooms where they developed slowly and then slowly faded away. Many observers could not detect them at all. Convinced, however, that the N-rays were real, Blondlot proceeded to investigate their properties. Careful research revealed that,

> Aluminum, wood, dry or wet paper, and paraffine do not enjoy the property of storing N-Rays. Gold, however, heightens the glow and an 18th century tool, an heirloom, was found to emit N-Rays. Also a knife found in a Gallo-Roman tomb—only the blade—also emitted N-Rays thus showing the N-Rays could remain active for over twelve centuries. Blondlot also found them in sun rays. Bits of rock exposed to the sunlight all day spontaneously emitted N-Rays. Vegetable earth has no N-Rays because the thinnest layer of moisture arrests the rays. (Jastrow 1935)

A chisel is N-ray active, but it becomes inactive when the temper is taken out of the steel. Finally, according to Blondlot, N-rays "are reflected and polarized, and possess well-defined wavelengths which I have measured."

Poor Blondlot, without realizing it, had discovered what is well known to all students of vision: N-rays originate in the retina of the eye. The play of color and the fluctuations in brightness in the feebly stimulated retina was the cause of his N-rays. Blondlot even discovered the conditions that favored seeing them. He told others to focus their eyes a little to one side of the phosphorescent strip and a bit out of focus. Incredible as it may seem, a number of physicists confirmed the effects and even added to them, finding N-ray reactions in compressed rubber, in ivory and celluloid, and in ice at near zero temperatures. Some even proposed that the N-ray test be used for the diagnosis of disease. The majority of physicists, however, who repeated the experiments failed to observe the effect, and they became even more skeptical when they noted the less than rigorous conditions under which Blondlot experimented. Professor Wood, from Maryland, surreptitiously removed the prism essential to the effect, yet many subjects reported they continued to see N-rays. This caused Faure, a French physicist, to remark that all physicists should be trained in psychology. As Jastrow notes, "The N-Ray confronted the established position of psychology; its refutation was prompt and decisive" (Jastrow 1935).

Although hypnosis has not had a Lavoisier, a Michelson and Morley, or even a Professor Wood to lay its ghost to rest, it has had a steady stream of acute observers and experimenters, such as Theodore X. Barber, Graham F. Wagstaff, Nicholas Spanos, Kreskin, Theodore R. Sarbin, William C. Coe, and a number of other psychologists from the social-cognitive-behavioral school. Rather than hypnosis being a special, altered state of consciousness, Sarbin in 1950 argued that hypnotic responding should be viewed as role enactment, that is context-dependent and determined by the subject's willingness to adopt the hypnotic role and do what is expected of him or her in that role as he or she follows the hypnotist's suggestions. Barber in 1969 also explicitly rejected the notion that hypnosis required an explanation in terms of an altered state of consciousness. In a concatenated series of experiments stretching over a period of nearly twenty years, he demonstrated convincingly that hypnotic responses were in no way extraordinary and that all such responses could easily be matched by the behavior of subjects who were wide awake and motivated to the same degree as the so-called "hypnotic" subjects. As Spanos and Chaves recently noted (1989):

> Special process views of hypnosis had long been sustained by the mystifying belief that hypnotic responding was extraordinary and, therefore, required the positing of extraordinary causes. Barber's extensive and systematic work was without a doubt the single most important factor in driving home the basic *ordinariness* of hypnotic responding, and therefore, its amenability to explanations that were framed in terms used to account for other "ordinary" social behavior.

Wagstaff, too, in 1981 published a long and brilliant work essentially agreeing with Sarbin and Barber, but pointing out the important roles that social compliance and belief play in the game we call "hypnosis." Wagstaff also suggested there is no such thing as hypnosis per se, and that all the phenomena subsumed under the rubric "hypnosis" can be explained by or accounted for in terms of simpler, well-understood psychological processes.

Kreskin's denial of the existence of any such thing as a "hypnotic trance" and his monetary challenge to anyone who thinks he can prove otherwise—in addition to his powerful demonstrations of the powers of suggestion and compliance in persons who are wide awake—are all contributing to the demise of the belief in a special state called "hypnosis."

Nevertheless, old ways of thinking and believing die hard. Many serious and respectable thinkers are still convinced that there is such a thing as hypnosis and that, after all the experiments, there are enough phenomena to constitute a solid basis for believing that some dramatic change takes place in the human subject that cannot be accounted for by relaxation, suggestion, and role-playing. And they are adamant in their position. Thus, there is no single topic in the history of psychology more controversial than hypnosis. From its beginning in the middle of the eighteenth century with Franz Anton Mesmer to the present, the phenomenon has been mired in controversy. For any graduate student assigned the subject of hypnosis for his thesis or dissertation, one can only feel pity. The research literature surrounding the topic is a veritable quagmire of disagreements, pro and con experimental results, claims and counterclaims. If there is any path leading out of the current swamp it is difficult to find. Much of what has been published on the subject is neither reliable nor valid. In fact, one of the most respected scientists and students of hypnotic phenomena in our time has stated emphatically:

> modern research has contributed very little new to our understanding or utilization of hypnosis. . . . Today, some 200 years after the discovery of artificial somnambulism, researchers are divided on even such basic issues as the veridicality of hypnotic phenomena and whether or not hypnosis exists as a state. . . . About the only point on which there seems to be a general consensus is that, if it exists, hypnosis is not sleep. (Weitzenhoffer 1985)

Curiously enough, the word itself is derived from the Greek word *hypnos*, meaning sleep. If one has had a little personal experience with hypnosis, it is easy to understand why sleep and the behavior called hypnosis are associated. On numerous occasions in my practice as a professional psychologist, when working with clients who have not had enough sleep the night before or who are not overstimulated with caffeine, the instant I suggested slow deep breathing and muscle relaxation, they fell asleep. Some even snored. To communicate with a client—and communication is the essence of the hypnotic relationship—quite frequently the hypnotist must insure that the client *is awake* and *is attending* to the therapeutic or experimental message. When people are asleep they are beyond the hypnotist's reach.

Although someone undergoing hypnosis appears to be asleep, merely having one's eyes closed and engaging in deep, regular breathing by no means insures that a person is asleep. In fact, it is so difficult to tell whether one's clients are or are not asleep, it is a good policy to perform periodic checks to insure that they are "still with you." Experienced hypnotists know quite well that many of their subjects may not be hypnotized, but are acting like they are, that is, simulating what they think is the hypnotic condition. It is difficult to tell whether a subject is playing along and merely complying with a request to go into some sort of a trance or is truly in some sort of an "altered state." It is so very difficult to tell the difference that some hypnotists doing research have required their subjects to sign a statement swearing that they were in a trance, *assuming, of course, that there really is a difference—though the greater part of the evidence leads to the conclusion that there is no difference.* One of the most inventive and creative researchers in the field, Dr. Frank A. Pattie, required his subjects to sign a form reading as follows:

> I, realizing that the experiment performed on me will probably be published in a scientific journal, solemnly declare that I was not faking or imitating the hypnotic trance but that I was genuinely hypnotized and do not remember the events of the experimental periods. (Pattie 1937, pp. 435–443)

Of course, there is another problem here, that many of the subjects may not have recalled the details because they *were* asleep and not in a trance at all.

Despite the claims of many that hypnosis is a trance-like, altered state of consciousness, hypnosis as we know it today in the laboratory and clinic is essentially nothing other than communication between an individual in the role of an authority figure calling himself the hypnotist and a second individual complying with the first individual's requests and suggestions, and calling himself "the client," "the subject," or "the person being hypnotized." Yet, because the process appears to produce such a number of strange behaviors and powers in the person supposedly under hypnosis, there are few aspects of psychology that have excited as much interest and have drawn as much attention from the public, the medical establishment, and behavioral scientists. Despite this widespread interest, only in the last few years has hypnosis been subjected to careful scientific scrutiny. The reason for this neglect has been due, primarily, to the long association of hypnosis with the occult, the magical, and the sensational. For this reason, respectable scientific scholars would not touch the subject with an eleven-foot pole. Moss (1965) pointed out that professional psychologists in the past were dissuaded from active inquiry into the phenomenon because of the serious "career risk" entailed in the suspicious attitudes of skeptical colleagues who saw in the study of hypnosis something associated with the abnormal or pathological as well as with stage magic and/or a personal neurotic need to manipulate and control others. Another, but seldom ever verbalized, factor was the danger to the male experimenter of exposing himself to sexual assault charges from female clients.

Strictly speaking, every time the word "hypnosis" is used it could be placed in quotation marks. This is because *there is no such thing as hypnosis.* The point and purpose of this book is to convince the reader that the phenomenon called "hypnosis" does not exist, has never existed in the past, and will not exist in the future. What is commonly called and referred to today as "hypnosis" is a fallacy, that is, a false and mistaken idea handed down from generation to generation since the time of Mesmer by individuals with little or no understanding of simpler psychological principles, or by individuals with pet theories and axes to grind that have blinded them to the fact of multiple causation.

Over the years one expert or another has defined "hypnosis" as simply: relaxation, compliance, role-playing, an altered state of consciousness, suggestion, cognitive restructuring, or response expectancy. Depending of course upon which aspect of the behavior is studied, the experimenter and theorist finds what he or she expects to find. The search for the explanation of hypnosis can be likened to the story of the blind men and the elephant.

With regard to multiple causation, in a recent book Wagstaff (1981) wrote:

> Having spent some years studying the literature on hypnosis, I had to admit that no single "mundane" concept seemed capable of explaining *all* hypnotic effects. In fact, it appeared doubtful whether any single concept could account for the multitude of contradictions and anomalies to be found in this area. . . . After puzzling over these problems for some time it occurred to me that perhaps the reason why no investigator has been able to find an acceptable solution to this mystery is that *there is no central mystery to solve* [italics mine]. Instead, we might have a collection of phenomena, bound together in name only by the term "hypnosis," but which demand a number of different explanations.

Wagstaff goes on to compare this situation to the conclusion reached by Lawrence Kusche in his investigation of the Bermuda Triangle mystery. Kusche (1975) noted:

> It is no more logical to try to find a common cause for all the disappearances in the Triangle than, for example, to try to find one cause for all automobile accidents in Arizona. By abandoning the search for an overall theory and investigating each incident independently, the mystery began to unravel.

Similarly, we are all indebted to those theorists and investigators who reached the conclusion that there is no mystery regarding hypnosis, since hypnosis does not exist. These researchers have brought the topic into the mainstream of psychology.

The claim that there is no such thing as hypnosis is by no means novel or original. It, too, has a long history, dating back to the year 1784, when Louis XVI of France, at the urging of the French Academy of Science, appointed a distinguished committee to investigate the healing powers of Mesmerism or "animal magnetism." This committee, composed of people like Benjamin Franklin, the American ambassador; Bailly, the astronomer; Lavoisier, the father of modern chemistry; Dr. Guillotine, inventor of the guillotine; and other distinguished citizens, concluded after an investigation extending over a seven-year period that there was no evidence for the existence of "animal magnetism" or for the theory that disease was due to an improper distribution of the body's "magnetic fluids." With regard to Mesmer's purported "cures," the committee decided his results were due entirely to "excitement of the imagination." A second committee report pointed out that Mesmerism was not in the best interests of public morality. In short, the committee concluded, there was no such thing as either "Mesmerism" or "animal magnetism." Instead, the phenomena were due to people's overwrought imagination. Curiously, these findings and conclusions with regard to Mesmerism are equally applicable to what today we call "hypnosis." Araoz, in his foreword to A Clinical Hypnosis Primer (1984), stressed that

> suggestions work to the extent that they produce an image in the patient's mind. . . . Other authors writing on hypnosis state that imagery prepares the mind to accept suggestions. That imagery is suggestion is especially important in view of what Watzlawick and his colleagues of the Mental Research Institute have taught us about the function of the right hemisphere and its activity in the process of human change.

The important point here is that *suggestion* is the key to hypnosis, and essentially the only tool the clinician has to work with when he uses hypnosis. For the most part, hypnosis has centered around the use of suggestion. Hypnosis came into being mainly as a way to enhance suggestibility. Both Hull and Weitzenhoffer have defined "hypnosis" as a state of enhanced suggestibility. And of course the most effective method of suggestion is through imagery. According to Sheehan (1979), responsiveness to hypnosis appears to be related to the ability to fantasize and use the imagination, and hypnotic suggestions are most effective when they are conveyed in the form of images. According to Sheehan, suggestions work to the extent that they produce an image in the individual's mind.

A second theme of this book is that imagery or imagination is universal and is a human being's way of thinking and processing information. Even though some individuals insist they lack the ability to visualize, this is not true. Everyone dreams, and the predominant sensory modality of dreams is visual, although imagery can be experienced in other sensory modalities as well. Moreover, like many human skills, our ability to imagine can be improved with practice. It is, after all, the use of imagery in the form of suggestions that the clinician uses to prevent or heal disease and other mental disorders or alter negative behavior patterns, or that the experimental psychologist uses to improve performance or increase creativity—all under the name of hypnosis. In fact, it will be maintained in this book that the greater or better the individual's powers of imagination or fantasy, the easier it is for the individual to become hypnotized and to demonstrate all of the behavior others normally associate with or attach to the phenomenon of hypnosis.

There are a few individuals—approximately six percent of the entire population—whose imaginative powers and skills are such that they have difficulty discriminating the real from the imaginary. These individuals we refer to as "fantasy-prone," and one of their most distinctive traits is the ease with which they are hypnotized. This makes sense if imagination and hypnosis are related. It is assumed that the ability to become imaginatively involved is normally distributed in the population. At the upper and extreme end of the distribution of imaginative involvement are a few individuals—perhaps no more than one percent of the population—who are able to retreat so far from the reality around them that they appear to be *somnambulistic*, i.e., in a sleepwalking state. Although outwardly to all appearances deeply asleep, such individuals are readily influenced by verbal communications and are capable of being active and moving about. Moreover, this "state" seems always to be accompanied by a spontaneous amnesia with regard to all events transpiring during its occurrence. Such individuals appear to be truly in a trance, i.e., a profound and prolonged sleep-like condition or state of mystical absorption. Weitzenhoffer (1985) believes that such examples are the only cases of "true hypnosis," and that this condition is rarely encountered in the average laboratory or clinic. In his words, "The proper study of hypnosis . . . should focus on this group rather than on the much larger group of suggestible but nonsomnambulistic subjects, as has been the case in recent times." Other authorities doubt that any such true cases of somnambulism exist and that if an individual is influenced at all by verbal communications from the external world, the individual is conscious and aware, not in a hypnotic trance. There is an extensive body of evidence that casts grave doubt on the existence of any sort of so-called "hypnotic trance." This evidence will be presented in full in a later chapter.

To find our way through the morass of claims and counterclaims with regard to hypnosis, it is of paramount importance that we trace, albeit briefly, the historical pathway leading to the present understanding of the fallacy we call "hypnosis." In so doing we will not only look at hypnosis but at a number of other fallacies related to and associated with people using their imaginations and processing internal information as they call up memories—both accurate and confabulated—comply with and yield to the social demand characteristics of the situation, undergo past-life regressions, converse with extraterrestrials, and cure themselves of fears, phobias, and neuroses.

Not long ago when the legendary Milton Erickson was asked to provide his definition of "hypnosis" by Stephen and Carol Lankton, who were prepared to take extensive notes, Erickson looked at them and replied, "It's concentrating on your thoughts, values, memories, and beliefs about life." In his book *The Answer Within* (1963), Lankton said, "We wrote it down expecting a more scientific version would follow. But there was no more. His short definition seemed inadequate at the time but later came to mean more and more until now it says far more than any well chosen bit of psychological jargon" (p. xvii). The remarkable thing about Erikson's definition is that it is so thorough and so complete.

All experienced people working with others in the alleged "hypnotic situation" know very very well that all hypnosis is self-hypnosis, and that when we relax and turn inward and use our imagination to think about things in our lives we are doing what others have called "hypnosis" and are playing the hypnosis game.

Many individuals are such excellent players at the game that they sometimes have great difficulty separating their internal world of fantasy and memories from the everyday world of stark reality. Moreover, such individuals are never quite sure what is meant by "reality." Many things in our world that seem the most real are creations of our imagination. Bugs Bunny, Casper the Ghost, Superman, Indiana Jones, Captain Kirk and The Enterprise, Sam Spade and Spenser are all real creations of the human imagination. So are the Greek gods—Zeus, Hera, Prometheus, and the rest—ghosts, fairies, spirits of the dead, and in our own time, UFOs, channeled entities, past lives, and alien abductors. All are mental creations of the fertile human imagination. Many people who find it difficult to separate fact from fiction, and if given the choice, prefer fiction, are also prone to engage in flights of fancy, and when given the opportunity, use the phenomenon called "hypnosis" as a rationalization for erasing borders between the "real" and the "imagined."

In the final chapters of this book we will study such personalities and their imaginary worlds and look at the supposed relationships between hypnosis and pain, hypnosis and trance states, hypnosis and the supernatural, as well as at other common fallacies surrounding hypnosis. We will look at a number of directions for future investigations and at the relationship between mind and body and other problems of the human mind that have yet to be resolved.

1.

Popular Misconceptions of Hypnosis

The dictionary which I have on my desk defines hypnosis as "a sleeplike state in which the mind responds to external suggestions and can recover forgotten memories." Having provided that definition the next thing to do is to immediately forget it, because the startling truth is that there is no such thing as hypnosis. This statement, coming from someone like myself who has used hypnosis for years, has taught its use to hundreds of doctors, dentists and therapists, and has written about it extensively, may appear to be incredible. Many may suspect that I am in urgent need of hypnotherapy to overcome the mental aberration afflicting me. Nevertheless the fact remains that the so-called hypnotic state does not exist when it is put under the microscope of objective investigation.
—Peter Blythe, *Self-Hypnotism*, 1980

Difficult as it may be to believe, Blythe is correct, and he is joined in his opinion by a growing number of scientists, doctors, dentists, psychiatrists and psychologists, and others who have examined and studied the phenomenon of hypnosis objectively.

This book was written because the misinformation and mystique surrounding this topic has prevailed long enough—almost 200 years. Hypnosis was originally thought to be some sort of magnetic force that could be radiated by any living thing. Then it was believed to be due to spirit possession; then it was thought to be due to hysteria or pathology; then it was considered a form of sleep; then a form of trance, and so on and so on. Even in our own day many believe it represents an altered stated of consciousness—a detachment from reality, like dreaming. Others insist it is nothing but relaxation, while others say it is nothing but suggestion. Others maintain it is *none* of these things, and others argue it is *all* of these things. So the question remains: just what is this mysterious thing called "hypnosis"? Just what is it about this phenomenon that has caused such conflict and disagreement? And there has been conflict aplenty. Thousands of scientific papers and treatises and hundreds of books have been written arguing hypnosis is this instead of that, and that all other views are wrong.

Another purpose of this book is to attempt to bring order out of chaos, and show how the misunderstanding about hypnosis came about and what we have learned about the phenomenon over the past 200 years. It also attempts to show that all of what we call "hypnotic behavior" can be accounted for by a number of much simpler sorts of psychological processes that are well understood. As for the claimed therapeutic effectiveness of hypnosis and the many seemingly miraculous cures and events apparently due to the effects of hypnosis, in reality, these are due to a number of external social factors such as suggestion and conditioning interacting with internal psychological variables such as relaxation and imagination.

This book also attempts to resolve the differences and disagreements between the modern "state" and "nonstate" hypnosis theories by showing that in certain situations with certain personality types dissociative behaviors occur that would lead one to assume the presence of an altered state of consciousness. However, such behavior is not due to or the direct result of hypnosis, which is a hypothetical condition for which no evidence exists.

When normal, human beings close their eyes, go into a sleep-like trance state, and do strange and unusual things, it is easy to see why the average observer would jump to the conclusion that something mysterious has been done to them and that they must be in some highly unusual state of mind to behave in such an unorthodox manner. Observers are totally baffled when a stage magician picks people from the audience, seemingly at random, brings them on the stage, and in only a few seconds causes them to become immobile, forget their names and addresses, be suspended horizontally between two chairs and remain rigid while others stand on their bodies, and pursue imaginary butterflies. Surely people who would do these things must be out of their minds or in that strange mental state called hypnosis. It is difficult to believe that they are not under the magical, God-like powers and control of the stage hypnotist. It is mind-boggling to learn that stage hypnotists have no special or magical powers, that the volunteers are merely complying with the hypnotist's requests, and that nothing other than suggestion and their own imagination is responsible for their behavior.

The media also contribute to the public's confusion about hypnosis. In a recent episode of the popular TV series "Murder She Wrote," hypnosis formed the basis of the plot, and the writers managed, in less than an hour, to propagate six separate fallacies about hypnosis. The plot hinged on the fact that while a hypnotist was hypnotizing a group of six people, one of them put ear plugs in his ears so he would not be hypnotized. He supposedly had to do this to avoid being hypnotized against his will. FALLACY: No one can be hypnotized unless he wants to be hypnotized. Later in the telecast, Mrs. Fletcher visits a college psychologist who hypnotizes her against her will. Moreover, she wasn't even aware it was happening. FALLACY: This can't be done, either. Furthermore, when the murder was committed it was carried out in front of five other witnesses who didn't see or hear anything because they were hypnotized. FALLACY: Most people when hypnotized are fully aware of what's going on around them, and if a murder were committed in front of them they would know it. The audience was also told that people in a trance could not be brought out of it other than by the one who put them into it. FALLACY: If, as in the story, the hypnotist was murdered while they were under hypnosis, they would not continue to sit frozen in place for hours. Instead, as soon as any bodily need appeared—fatigue, full bladder, tired muscles, etc.—the persons hypnotized would wake up, stretch, and go on about their business. Experiments have shown this is what does happen to subjects who are relaxed, given suggestions, and then abandoned. In the TV story an expert had to be brought in to free the six subjects from their trance. FALLACY: Anyone can arouse someone supposedly in a hypnotic trance. Finally, the audience was told that hypnosis can be used to permanently erase anything and everything from a person's memory. FALLACY: This is simply untrue. This notion is also perpetuated in the comic strip "Beetle Bailey" where Mort Walker has had Sarge use hypnosis on several occasions to attempt to control Beetle's behavior.

The matter is further complicated when we look at popular books and articles on the subject. We are subjected to statements such as the following: "People who are hypnotized enter a trance-like state which is fundamentally different from normal consciousness" (Hassan 1988). FACT: There is no such thing as a hypnotic trance. If you think there is and can prove it, you can collect $100,000 cash immediately from the magician Kreskin. Or the following from the same source: Hypnosis is "a sleep-like condition produced by the hypnotist in a subject who allows himself to accept and respond to certain specific suggestions." This is partially correct, except that hypnosis is *not* a sleep-like condition. One thing that nearly all experts agree on is that hypnosis is not like sleep (Caprio and Berger 1968).

Leslie LeCron and J. Bordeaux (1947) define "hypnotism" as "The uncritical acceptance of a suggestion by the patient in a trance." Others such as Andrew Salter (1944) see hypnosis as "nothing more than a conditioned reflex." Dr. S. J. Van Pelt (1954) defines "hypnotism" as "nothing more than a super-concentration of the mind." Surprisingly, the definition found in the Merriam-Webster pocket dictionary (1964) is closer to the truth than most of the more formal definitions provided by the so-called experts. It defines "hypnosis" simply as "an induced state which resembles sleep and in which the subject is responsive to the suggestions of the inducer."

Actually, Beetle Bailey is very responsive to suggestion.

What Beetle should have said is: "It's impossible to hypnotize anyone without his consent!" *(Reprinted with permission of King Features. Strips appeared originally on 14 April 1985 and 9 April 1989 respectively.)*

In a truly remarkable bit of candor a few years ago, an editorial in the January 1985 issue of the *American Journal of Clinical Hypnosis* asked in all seriousness: "Are Hypnotherapy Patients Hypnotized?" and then proceeded to suggest that they were not. The editorial also reported that, as far back as 1962, Arthur Kuhner argued that we would soon be doing "Hypnosis without Hypnosis," and raised the possibility that suggestions, images, and a positive "mind set" of the patients—not hypnosis per se—were the critical items in such psychotherapy. In the final paragraph the editor summed up his dilemma with regard to the use of hypnosis in treatment:

> All of us, as clinicians, know that hypnosis is a valuable facilitator of psychotherapy. However, when the use of hypnosis in psychotherapy is reported it is often difficult to know if the patient was hypnotized and, if so, if being hypnotized was an important factor in the therapeutic result. As the health care dollar shrinks (no pun intended), a sound concept of clinical hypnosis and its contribution to therapeutic change may be necessary to justify compensation for its use. (p. 152)

The important point here is that even the so-called experts, including many trained people who use hypnosis every day to help their clients, are uncertain about exactly what it is they are doing when they do hypnosis. No wonder then that the average citizen who encounters the phenomenon only rarely is even more mystified. And, as we have noted earlier, the media have been of little assistance in helping the general public understand what's going on. A recent episode, for example, of the ABC hit show "Perfect Strangers" revolved around the visit of a hypnotherapist to a party put on by Larry and Balki. While trying to hypnotize Larry and make him believe he was Elvis Presley, the therapist accidentally put Balki into a trance. From then on, every time Balki heard a bell of any sort he went into an Elvis act. Efforts on Larry's part to snap Balki out of it failed miserably. The show became hilarious as Balki went in and out of his act everytime a bell rang: one ring *into* the trance and the second ring *out of* the trance. Larry told the therapist that he could not be hypnotized because he had such a strong will, and this piece of misinformation was never corrected. To get Balki out of the trance the therapist returned several days later and snapped his fingers and Balki was his old self again. When Larry asked "Why didn't he come out when I snapped my fingers?" the therapist replied, "Well, it was my voice that does the trick." Of course, the truth of the matter, that will power has nothing to do with hypnosis and that Balki's condition was impossible, would have ruined the comedy. Thus, hypnosis and hypnotic phenomena were again misrepresented and the public misinformed.

In view of the large number of other fallacies about hypnosis, however, the foregoing misrepresentations were small sins indeed. Just about every conceivable aspect of hypnosis has created at least one misconception, and most aspects more that one. Hypnotic fallacies are as numerous as ants at a picnic and much harder to get rid of. Some of the more common, popular, and often-repeated are the following:

1. A hypnotist is one who has unusual, Svengali-like powers—mysterious and magical abilities which he uses to control people and make them do as he wishes against their will.

2. The hypnotist can make people commit immoral and illegal acts—even murder—while under hypnosis, and they would not even be aware of it.

3. Hypnotists can hypnotize people at long distances—even over the telephone or by telepathic means—and can put someone in a trance any time the hypnotist wishes.

4. A skilled hypnotist can hypnotize anyone at anytime anywhere and under any circumstances—even against the person's will.

5. Many people are so strong-willed and have such strong minds they cannot be hypnotized. Weak-willed and less intelligent people can be easily hypnotized.

6. People in hypnotic trances may not be easy to awaken and they may remain in that state for a long time. Some people may never wake up!

7. Once a person is hypnotized, only the person who hypnotized them can wake them up, and this is a reason why hypnosis is dangerous. If the person who hypnotized you were to drop dead of a heart attack you would be in a trance forever!

8. While hypnotized you are apt to do anything—good or bad—the hypnotist asks; you are like a slave who must obey his master whether he wants to or not.

9. Hypnosis can effect a cure for just about anything in only one or two sessions, and the power of the mind is such that under the influence of hypnosis just about any ailment can be cured.

10. To be helped by hypnosis you must be in such a deep stage of hypnosis that you are in touch with your unconscious.

11. When you are hypnotized you are asleep and unconscious and totally unaware of your surroundings, i.e., you are in an altered state of consciousness. In other words, being hypnotized means you are in a state of unconsciousness.

12. Hypnosis is dangerous! Unskilled and inept hypnotists can cause people to lose their minds and go crazy and hurt themselves in terrible ways. Moreover, hypnosis is really the practice of medicine, and stage and amateur hypnotists are using their hypnotic skills as an illegal means of entering medical practice by the back door!

13. Hypnosis is an anti-Christian practice, like demonology. It is the work of the devil, and while you are in hypnosis your soul can be possessed by devils or demons or both.

14. Hypnosis is merely a "symptom swapper," i.e., if hypnosis clears up one symptom, a different symptom will soon appear. For example, if

you use hypnosis to get rid of a headache, then you will get a toothache or a stomachache.

15. Hypnosis and sleep are the same thing; hypnosis is a form of sleep and vice versa.

16. Hypnosis and meditation—Zen, yogic, or any other type—are the same thing; hypnosis is a form of meditation and vice versa; all forms of mind-altering practices are one and the same thing.

17. People cannot in their normal state remember what happened while they were hypnotized; in other words, hypnosis causes amnesia.

18. Under hypnosis people's memories are improved and they can accurately recall everything that has happened to them in the past. Conversely, hypnosis can permanently erase the memory of anything that has happened in the past.

19. Losing yourself in a book or play or movie, becoming enraptured while listening to music, becoming so absorbed in a task that you lose all track of time, being transported by prayer, or listening intently to a charismatic speaker and agreeing with everything he says—are all forms of hypnosis. Also, falling asleep while driving on monotonous roads or listening to monotonous sounds is hypnosis.

20. Hypnosis can increase clairvoyant ability as well as telepathic powers, psychokinesis, precognition, and other types of extrasensory perception.

21. Under hypnosis a person can be made to tell the truth, i.e., a person is unable to lie while he is in a hypnotic trance.

22. Once hypnotized, a person can be kept in a hypnotic trance for several hours or even days or weeks.

23. Hypnotized subjects can do things in the hypnotic state they could not possibly do while wide awake, e.g., have needles stuck through their skin, assume a board-like rigidity, be operated on without anesthetics and feel no pain. Moreover, hypnosis endows the person hypnotized with other extraordinary skills and abilities he does not possess in the waking state, e.g., enhanced muscular power, increased sensory acuity, improved memory, and improved control over the autonomic nervous system.

24. Hypnosis, like dreams, provides us with a royal road to the unconscious and all the material uncovered through its use should be accepted as veridical, i.e., true.

25. When a person is hypnotized he or she is in an altered state of consciousness, i.e., in a trance or a special and unique state of awareness.

These are twenty-five of the most commonly parroted mistaken notions and ideas about what we call "hypnosis." Each of these false ideas will be discussed at length and in depth in the chapters that follow.

Confessions of an Unwitting Hypnotist

Like many other psychologists, my first acquaintance with hypnosis came about vicariously through reading about it in textbooks and watching a demonstration in a classroom. At the time I was impressed with its dramatic qualities and with the seeming god-like powers of the hypnotist. Afterwards I gave it little or no attention, until many years later while working for the U.S. Army doing research on attention and watch-keeping (monitoring). Then it occurred to me that the problem of human vigilance was primarily one of motivation. If paying attention was recognized to be a matter of life and death, then the human watch-keeper, i.e., the soldier on guard duty, the airman watching a radar scope, the sailor looking for enemy subs, etc., would have no trouble performing these tasks. From reading the journals I remembered that hypnosis and post-hypnotic suggestions had been shown to influence people's level of motivation and thus, indirectly, their subsequent performance. Why not hypnotize our soldiers and give them post-hypnotic suggestions that detecting infrequently occurring signals would be the easiest thing on earth to do, and then they would regard such boring tasks as guard duty and watch-keeping as wonderfully exciting and fulfilling?

Since I myself knew nothing of hypnosis at the time, I called in a well-known and reputable hypnotist from a nearby university to hypnotize our soldier subjects. Taking the young soldiers one at a time, the elderly distinguished-looking hypnotist had no problems with the first few men. Then, a young red-headed eighteen-year-old came in and in spite of everything the hypnotist tried, the young man continued to remain wide-awake, trembling, and bug-eyed. Finally, the hypnotist came over to me and said, "I'm sorry but I just can't do anything with him. Some people, you know, are just not susceptible to hypnosis." I told him not to worry, we'd just replace him with a man who was hypnotizable. Despite what the venerable hypnotist said, it was obvious to me that the young redhead was terrorized. I pulled him aside and asked, "What's the problem, son?" Stammering his reply, he said, "Dr. Baker, I don't want to be hypnotized. I'm scared. My mother told me that as soon as you're hypnotized the devil will steal your soul!" I reassured him that he didn't have to worry, and told him to return to his barracks. But what impressed me most was his fear and his refusal to comply, which obviously interfered with his relaxing and his capability of being hypnotized.

Years later, I more fully appreciated the young man's problem. Browsing through the university library, I came across a book titled *Hypnosis and the Christian* by Martin and Deidre Bogan (1984). According to the Bogans,

Hypnosis has been an integral part of the occult. Therefore, a Christian would not allow himself to be hypnotized for any reason. The promises of help through hypnosis are very similar to the promises of help through other occultic healers. The Christian has another spiritual means of help: The Lord God Himself! . . . Hypnotism is demonic at its worst and potentially dangerous at its best. At its worst it opens an individual to psychic experiences and satanic possession. . . . Satan transforms himself into an angel of light whenever necessary to accomplish his schemes. If he can make an occult practice (hypnosis) look beneficial through a false facade (medicine or science), he will. It is obvious that hypnosis is lethal if used for evil purposes. However, we contend that hypnosis is potentially lethal for whatever purpose it is used. The moment one surrenders himself to the doorway of the occult, even in the halls of science and medicine, he is vulnerable to the powers of darkness. (pp. 52–53)

Throughout their totally unbelievable book the authors give case histories of people whose behavior changed dramatically after an "innocent" exposure to hypnosis. Even innocent hypnosis, the authors claim, places the soul in a passive receptive state, and even when the hypnotist has no such intention, this opens the door to morbid spiritual influences that may bring on oppression that lasts for years.

After I had studied and practiced hypnosis for many years, it became very clear to me that the major difficulty most hypnotists have with getting their subjects to relax and follow their suggestions is due to fear. To most people, being hypnotized means they are going to become unconscious or be placed in some strange and altered state of awareness from which they might never recover. They expect something highly unusual is going to happen to them. They believe they are going to lose their minds, or at least have them taken over by someone else. Over the last twenty years that I have been using and studying hypnosis, I have encountered only a handful of individuals that could not be hypnotized. In each and every case I quickly discovered that their refusal to comply, i.e., their refusal to relax and follow my suggestions, was due to fear and misunderstanding about what was going to happen to them and what they were going to experience.

My first noncooperative subject was a very religious young lady who had heard the same sort of stories the Bogans told. She absolutely refused to relax until I promised her faithfully that I would not hypnotize her but would only get her to relax. Once I had gained her trust, she became one of the best subjects I have ever had. Anyone and everyone who can relax and concentrate can play the game of hypnosis with any hypnotist.

My second experience with hypnosis came years after my Army experience when I began teaching a course in Humanistic Psychology at the University of Kentucky in 1969. Learning how to deal with stress was an integral part of the course and teaching the students how to relax was essential. I had a minor in physiology at both the master's and doctoral levels, and I was very partial to Edmund Jacobson's progressive relaxation procedures—especially a shortened and compressed version that takes approximately thirty minutes and involves tensing, holding, and then relaxing various muscle groups. Beginning with the toes, and proceeding to the feet and ankles, calves, everything below the knees, thighs, buttocks, stomach, chest, shoulders, biceps, forearms, hands and fingers, neck, head, facial muscles and tongue and eyes, the individual sequentially tenses and relaxes all of the muscle groups in the body. Starting with the toes, a muscle group is tensed for fifteen to twenty seconds, relaxed for thirty seconds or so, and then tensed again, and then the next group is added, until all the muscles in the body have been tensed and then relaxed. After this exercise is repeated once or twice, the student is physically fatigued and is very ready and willing to physically relax.

For a period of twenty years I taught two sections of this course, with approximately eighty students in each section, two semesters each year. I taught the course in an air-conditioned, carpeted room without windows, and so had control over the lighting and could black out the entire room. My procedure involved having the students move their chairs, lie down on the floor, engage in deep breathing exercises, and then perform the Jacobson relaxation exercises until they were physically exhausted. Then, without warning, I extinguished all the room lights and told them,

> Now that you are physically relaxed, let's get mentally relaxed. I want you to imagine that you are lying on a beach in Florida in your bathing suit. It's about 2 o'clock in the afternoon, the sun is blazing hot in a deep blue cloudless sky, and you're lying on your back on your beach towel with lots of suntan lotion so you don't have to worry about sunburn. You can feel the warm sun on your arms, legs, and face, and you can feel the warmth of the sand underneath your towel, and your whole body is like a warm sandwich. You take a deep breath and you can smell the ocean. There's no smell on earth like the smell of the ocean. You can feel a cool, cool breeze blowing across your face and hair, coming from the water. Take slow deep breaths and just lie there and enjoy that warmth and the cool breeze. You don't have a care in the world. You have all the time in the world to just lie here and relax and enjoy the sun and sand and ocean breeze. Just sink down, down, down in that warm soft sand and let your body float away.

After a few more repetitions of these images every student in the room was deeply relaxed and following every word and every suggestion. I always wore a watch and carried a small pocket flashlight so I could control the time, monitor the relaxed bodies, and find the light switches on the wall when necessary.

As you might expect, on occasions over the years some of the students would grab at each other, play games, and giggle. When this occurred I told them to consider the others in the room, and then I proceeded to use deepening procedures such as,

All of a sudden you hear the sound of people talking on your left and the clink of glasses. You look to your left and there is a man and a woman sitting at a table under a big beach umbrella. They have a large bottle of wine or champagne sitting in an ice bucket on a tray with four glasses. The woman sees you looking at them and she smiles and beckons you over. You get up, dust off the sand, and walk over to the table. She pushes out a chair for you and has you sit down and she says, "You look thirsty. Here have some wine." She takes the bottle out of the ice bucket, wraps the towel around it, and pours some of the cold, icy champagne into one of the four glasses in front of you. Boy, does it look good. You pick it up and the bubbles are jumping out of the glass and tickling your nose. You take a sip and it practically melts in your mouth. It's nice and cold until it starts down your throat and then it becomes nice and warm. You take another sip and then another, and then it's gone. The woman asks would you like another glass, and you want to refuse but she insists. So you wait till she refills your glass and you sip again, and again. This is really delicious wine, the best you've ever had. Finally, you thank the man and woman and go on back to your beach towel and lie down again. Now you are warm on the bottom, on the top, and you are now warm and drowsy inside as well. Very warm and drowsy, very warm and . . . drowsy.

By this time every student in the room is totally relaxed and silence reigns. After this I tell them to go ahead and fall asleep and have a nice little dream and that I will wake them up after a while. After approximately twenty minutes I announce in a loud voice,

In a few minutes I am going to slowly count to ten, and when I reach the count of five you will start to get feeling in your arms and legs and face again, and when I reach the count of ten you will be wide awake, but you won't open your eyes until I say the word "blue." When you wake up you will feel like you've had a good night's sleep. You'll be in a good mood, and you'll feel full of energy and vim, vigor, and vitality, and you'll look forward eagerly toward the rest of the day.

Then a few minutes later I count slowly to ten and repeat the same phrases, and then after the count I turn on the lights and say the word "blue."

Without exception, all of the students over the years have found this to be a very pleasant and enjoyable exercise and they have looked forward eagerly to a repetition the following week. Most of the students in each class reported falling asleep, especially when told to do so, and some of them even snored. Many remained awake and responsive throughout the entire session, but were relaxed and fully caught up in the fantasy.

When I first began this exercise it never entered my mind that what I was doing and so-called hypnosis were even remotely connected. Then, as I began to read hypnosis literature in the late '60s and early '70s, I suddenly realized to my horror that I had been hypnotizing hundreds of innocent students over the past few years without even knowing it. Moreover, after reading several of the textbooks and articles by Dr. Harold Rosen and Dr. Herbert Spiegel warning of the grave dangers of hypnosis, I actually began to believe that I was and had been committing a crime and possibly inflicting great harm on all of my naive and innocent students. For a time, I even seriously considered giving up the stress reduction exercises. Then, however, as my reading about hypnosis broadened, I discovered that misinformation was common in this area, and that one should never accept uncritically anything he reads or hears about the topic. As a result, I became fascinated with the topic and decided to do some empirical research of my own.

I began investigating various hypnosis induction techniques and soon discovered that one was as good as another and that with most subjects, once you have obtained their trust and confidence, most any technique would work—eye fixation, hand levitation, suggestions for sleep, indirect methods, direct authoritarian methods, permissive suggestive and analgesic suggestive techniques, etc. Most any relaxation technique or any repetition of monotonous, rhythmical, sensory stimulation to promote fixation of attention will do. However, it is extremely important that every student, client, or subject be queried at the outset as to what they think hypnosis means. Then they need to be made aware of the many fallacies with regard to this subject and reassured that they are not going to be knocked out, made unconscious, made to do things that are ridiculous and embarrassing, encounter demons or monsters, wake up with a headache, not ever be able to wake up, etc.

Early during the time of my experiments with hypnosis I attended workshops and training sessions, and also helped to establish a local hypnosis society in hopes of not only learning more about hypnosis but of improving my skills as a hypnotist. The workshops, unfortunately, were uneven in quality and were often conducted by individuals who were very poorly informed about hypnotic phenomena and knew even less than I did about the process. Our local hypnosis society, however, proved to be very helpful. Most of its members were and are practicing clinicians who were not only eager to learn and share what they knew but were also open to experimentation and new ideas.

Since I was a licensed experimental psychologist (as well as a faculty member very concerned about publication), I followed religiously the protocols for doing hypnosis research as set forth in the two major experimental journals: *The American Journal of Clinical Hypnosis*, and *The International Journal of Clinical & Experimental Hypnosis*. Since many of the investigators reporting their work in these journals used hypnotic susceptibility scales to select the subjects used in their studies, I also began to use the scales as prescribed. To my dismay I soon discovered this sort of screening was of no value—useless. Neither I nor my fellow researchers found the tests to be discriminatory. First of all, we never encountered anyone who was so resistant that they could not be hypnotized. Next, we found that nearly all of our subjects scored almost exactly alike—near the top—on the Stanford Hypnotic Susceptibility Scales, forms A, B, and C. After several years of using the scales simply because the journal editors seemed to require their use, I abandoned them entirely. Later, after talking with my clinician friends, I discovered most of them never used the scales at all or have ever thought of doing so.

For my first research efforts I also religiously followed standard induction techniques. One of my first research studies was concerned with past-life regression. With each of my experimental regression subjects I spent anywhere from thirty to forty-five minutes, relaxing him or her, using deepening techniques, testing for all possible signs of hypnosis, etc., before beginning the regression procedures and questioning. I had collected data on five or six subjects when one of our clinical society members offered to assist me with my research, since she had been working on this same problem informally for some time. I was delighted with her offer and proceeded to brief her on my procedures to insure that all subjects were treated alike, asked the same questions, and so forth. When she saw my induction procedures, she was appalled that I spent so much time in this manner. "It never takes me more than ten to twenty minutes to get my subjects under and back into a another lifetime," she said.

"But how could they be hypnotized in such a short time?" I asked.

"Well, I don't know how deep you want them to go, but I can get them where you want them very quickly, and you can get all the data you could ever use."

"Show me," I demanded.

She did. I turned my student subject pool over to her and sat with her as she began to work with subject after subject, never spending more than ten minutes with any one and getting all the information it had taken me an hour to get. Live and learn.

Years later, I was to learn that what my colleague had shown me is called the "Christos procedure" or "Christos phenomenon." In 1971 the Australian author G. M. Glaskin read a magazine article called "Windows of the Mind: The Christos Experience," by Jacquelin Parkhurst. Parkhurst developed a method for the induction of lucid dreams in which it was claimed that the subject might also relive part of one or more previous lives. Glaskin was so taken with Parkhurst's method that he proceeded to write several books (Glaskin 1974, 1978, 1979) telling in detail how he had used the Christos procedure to induce people to experience former lives. The use of the term "Christos" (i.e., Christ) in this context has no specifically Christian significance, but refers to the center of the forehead, where, according to occultists, we have a "third eye," an organ of psychic vision.

The Christos procedure for producing the past-life experience is quite simple.

The subject lies on his back on the floor, or a couch or a cot, eyes closed, without shoes, and with his head supported by a cushion. The experimenter uses the edge of his clenched hand or the heel of his hand to massage the lower center of the subject's forehead with a vigorous circular motion for about two or three minutes. At the same time, a helper should massage the subject's feet and ankles. The subject is then told to imagine himself growing two inches taller through the soles of his feet, then shrinking back to his previous height. The process is repeated several times. The stretching and shrinking is next applied to the head. The exercises are then repeated with the stretching extended to twelve inches, then to twenty-four inches. The subject is next asked to imagine himself expanding like a giant balloon in every direction. Then he is told to visualize his own front door and describe it in detail. Next, the subject visualizes himself on the roof of his house and describes everything he can see. Next he ascends 500 feet into the air, alternately by night and day, and describes the scene below. The subject is then asked to fly through the air and descend when he is ready. When he lands, the Christos experience proper can be said to begin.

The subject is now asked to look down and describe himself and what he is wearing. By this time he will have changed. According to Glaskin, his feet may be bare, his legs black or brown, his height, age, and personality different, his sex may have changed, and his clothes will be different. The landscape may be unfamiliar or remind him of one far away that he has known or journeyed through. He may find himself in another life, in another age. Nevertheless, he will remain aware of the experimenter's voice and answer his questions. Glaskin claims that the Christos procedure "makes it possible to dream while one is fully awake and . . . possibly even reveal past lives and/or future events" (Glaskin 1979). Also, as sometimes happens in dreams, the subject is aware of himself both as an observer and a participant.

There are a number of variations on the Christos procedure. Instead of having the person ascend into the air, he may be told to go stand in front of the building where he lives and describe the scenery, and then change it to another time and place. Or ascend into the air and when he descends come down in another lifetime and another place. The idea is to induce a fantasy or a dream of another lifetime, and to do it fairly quickly. The average time for subjects to complete these exercises is between ten and twenty minutes. If the subject is highly imaginative and one to whom fantasies come easily, less time will be required. In this regard, both Dr. Helen Wambach and Dr. Morris Netherton have reported they never bother with hypnosis at all for many of their clients undergoing past-life regression. All that is necessary is the idea or suggestion, a couch or chair, and having them close their eyes—and immediately they are off, reliving prior incarnations.

Startling as this may sound, hypnotizing someone or getting someone to play games such as hypnosis, past-life regression, stage hypnosis, and so on, is actually quite easy and very simple. It requires little or no skill or technique or even specialized knowledge. As mentioned earlier, there are literally hundreds of induction procedures or ways in which a willing and compliant volunteer can be induced to cooperate and go along with your request to relax, close their eyes, and use their imagination. Sometimes a simple direct command, "Go into hypnosis!" or "You will now go into a trance!" is all that is required.

A few years ago, for instructional purposes, I made a short videotape illustrating the compliance phenomenon. From one of my classes I picked several student volunteers and asked them to report to the university television studios the following afternoon. The next afternoon, when I found myself a few volunteers short, I asked some of the studio personnel to fill in. Just before we started to shoot the tape I told the group of eight men to sit down in the chairs facing the camera, relax, close their eyes, and follow my directions and to do exactly what I told them. All eight behaved in such a manner that no one in the viewing audience was able to distinguish the fill-ins from those who had undergone a lengthy formal induction procedure. All eight "simulated" or "complied with" my requests for limb catalepsy, inability to open their eyes, inability to clench and then unclench their hands, inability to lower their hands once they were raised, deep relaxation, and simulated sleep. After being awakened, all left their seats in response to the earlier suggestion that their seats were burning hot. All of this was accomplished even with the strangers who had simply been requested to appear in a television tape about hypnosis and then requested to follow my directions. The social and psychological demand characteristics of this situation were exactly the same as for the stage magician who is also, ninety-nine percent of the time, equally successful in hypnotizing his volunteers.

Whether or not any induction procedure at all is needed depends, of course, upon the personality of the individual subject. Most people coming to a therapist for hypnosis are already in an agreeable or compliant mood. When appearing for hypnosis—especially for therapy—the typical hypnotic subject or client is socially conditioned to do everything exactly as the therapist asks him/her to do it. When the typical patient is requested by a physician to remove his or her shirt or dress for a routine physical exam, it is highly unlikely he or she would refuse or put up a fight to keep it on. Similarly, when the hypnotherapist says, "Close your eyes, relax and think of a rose," it is the rare client indeed who would tell the therapist, "Hell no, I won't close my eyes, I won't relax, and I prefer to think of geraniums!" Therefore, most any request from the hypnotist—as long as it is not immoral, illegal, or fattening, and is within reason—is likely to be honored.

Though over the years I have used a number of different induction techniques, most of the time I use the simplest and shortest ones possible. Since slow, deep breathing helps the relaxation process, I encourage this at the beginning of each session. Then I suggest eye closure and relaxation of the arms and legs. I watch closely for any signs of muscular tension, and if I detect its presence I then include suggestions for the relaxation of other major muscle groups: feet, calves, thighs, stomach, chest, biceps, forearms, shoulders, neck, face, mouth, and eyes. If there is any reason to suppose that any tension remains, I move to another simple, sure-fire technique. I tell the client:

Imagine that I am screwing a light bulb—the kind we use in our lamps— right into the center of your head. These bulbs put out both heat and light. We will use the light from the bulb to illuminate the various muscle groups of your body, and we'll use the heat from the bulb to melt the tension out of the muscle groups—just like a hot knife melts butter. All right, I am screwing the bulb into your head and turning it on. Now you can see the light shining on the muscles behind your eyes and you can feel the heat from the bulb melting all of the tension out of these muscles. In fact, they ache a little as all the tension flows out. Just let those muscles go soft and loose and limp. Now the light is moving down behind your nose. You can feel the light behind your nose and at the back of your throat. Now the heat and the warmth are melting all of the tension out of these muscles. Now the light is moving down into your throat and you can feel the heat and warmth inside your mouth, at the back of your throat, on your tongue, warming and relaxing the face muscles. Let them go soft and loose and limp. Now your entire face feels warm, relaxed and comfortable. Now the light is moving further down into your throat, warming and relaxing as it goes. . . .

In a similar fashion, the light is moved slowly through every major muscle group in the body, proceeding from the toes of the right foot over to the toes of the left, and then slowly up the left side, warming and relaxing everything in its path until it is back where it started. If the client still shows any tension at all I continue to deepen the relaxation by suggesting floating through the air to the top of a tall building, then down an elevator, counting down floor by floor, and then when the basement is reached moving to either deep relaxation in an easy chair or to a sunny summer beach by the ocean. Once deep relaxation has occurred, then the therapeutic or experimental procedures can begin.

Though these combined approaches are somewhat time-consuming, I have never had a client that has resisted the effects of them. Of course, I have always made sure from the outset that all confusions and misunderstandings have been cleared up about what hypnosis is and is not. Once this is done and relaxation has been obtained, compliance and cooperation is guaranteed. From then on, it is all up to the skill of the therapist to meet and deal with the client's problem or problems.

Anyone and everyone can relax and benefit from the effects of positive and helpful suggestions, provided that the efforts are, as Peter Blythe phrases it, "client-centered rather than hypnotist-centered" (Blythe 1980). What is required is that the client fully understands what is meant by the term "hypnosis," that any and all fears of the hypnotic session have been dispelled; and that he is prepared to cooperate, to let things happen naturally. In addition, he must have a legitimate reason for seeking out the hypnotist and must want the therapist's help himself, rather than be pressured by others into seeking help. Finally, the therapist and the therapist's techniques and approaches must be compatible with the client's own personality. If all these conditions prevail, both the relaxation and the suggestions are likely to be beneficial. In fact, just about everyone—other than psychotics or very young children with limited verbal ability—can benefit from these sorts of ministrations.

In all candor I must admit that early in my pursuit of information about hypnosis I found myself as confused and baffled as the proverbial man in the street. Much of the information published in the professional journals was unreliable and contradictory. Information obtained from so-called "experts" proved to be faulty or incorrect. For example, one of the biggest disappointments was over the matter of so-called "suggestibility tests." When I first began to use them, my colleagues and I, on the basis of our initial testing, divided our student volunteers into two groups: Pass and Fail. Curious about those individuals who on the basis of the test results were supposedly "unhypnotizable," I took each of them aside and discussed hypnosis with them at length. After clarifying their misconceptions and misunderstandings, and using various induction techniques, every one of the so-called "unhypnotizables" turned into a compliant, cooperative, and easily relaxed and highly suggestible, i.e., "hypnotizable," subject. While there have been over the years one or two "hard cases," I have yet to encounter a "normal," i.e., not psychotic, retarded, or drugged, individual who cannot be "relaxed" or who is not "suggestible" or even cooperative. For the hard cases—people who had extreme difficulty relaxing—I did resort to the use of placebos (sugar pills) that I told them were tranquilizers in order to calm them down. The rest, without exception, could be "seduced," "taught," "trained," or could "learn how" to play the game of hypnosis.

Many investigators have gone so far as to argue that there is a difference between "clinical hypnosis" and "laboratory hypnosis." This may well be true if the laboratory workers sort a naive, heterogeneous group of volunteers into one or more categories based upon some hypnotic susceptibility test and refuse to go further. As Gill and Brenman (1959) wrote:

> So-called suggestibility tests as instruments for predicting hypnotizability are highly successful in so far as they are actually small attempts to hypnotize the subject. In short, such tests lead to the less than remarkable finding that if you can hypnotize a person, he is probably a good hypnotic subject.

Others have argued that the only true measure of whether or not an individual is hypnotized is how he feels about his condition. In many situations it is quite likely that neither the subject nor the experimenter knows what is happening, since they do not have a definition of hypnosis in common. Our language is notoriously deficient in words that adequately describe interpersonal feelings and emotions, as well as subjective or affective states. Little wonder that Frank Pattie required his experimental subjects to sign a statement swearing that they were "really hypnotized." This, too, however, is obviously inadequate. People would vary in their responses depending upon what they did or did not consider to be the characteristics of "being hypnotized."

Over the years as I began to investigate other problems and issues in the area of hypnotic phenomena, I became more distrustful, more skeptical about what I was reading in the textbooks and journals. The more I read, the more I began to suspect that hypnosis per se did not exist. The research literature proved to be of little help. As Moss (1965) stated the case precisely,

> Because so few unequivocal facts have been established about hypnosis *per se*, investigators who employ hypnosis as a research instrument are in the vulnerable position of studying one unknown (the subject of experimental inquiry) by means of a second unknown (hypnosis).

Weitzenhoffer (1978) was even more melancholy. As he saw the situation at that time, he concluded:

> Hypnotism has been a topic of intensive scientific study for over 135 years. Consciousness has been a topic of study for even longer. Perhaps the complexity of these topics is such that nothing better could have been accomplished in that period of time. Considering the advances made in other disciplines in that period, I doubt it. Speaking only of hypnotism research done during

the last forty-five years, I find that much of it and the associated writings have been of low scientific caliber. There has been far more pseudoscience than science in it. Except for a small minority, investigators in this area have been on the whole a pretentious and opinionated lot, basically ignorant in spite of their academic training, and frequently poorly grounded even in their very chosen field of inquiry. They have been prone to shallow thinking, the overuse of technical jargon, the abuse of statistics, and various forms of unintentional and intentional intellectual dishonesty. They have been far more concerned with convincing others, frequently with evangelistic fervor, of their beliefs and convictions and with winning academic and professional laurels than with ascertaining the truth. In this process, they have preferred the easier and more expeditious path of selective rediscovery, replication, disconfirmation, and demonstrations of the obvious, the already known, and the inconsequential to the more arduous path of judicious building upon past findings. I am also led to reflect that what an investigator does is very much influenced by the necessity of satisfying the stated and unstated demands of academia or of the organization he works for, those of his professional peers, of the scientific community at large, of society, of grant-giving agencies and their representatives—not to mention those of the editors of scholarly journals and their referees. And, while the existence of these forces does not excuse such features as poor workmanship, ignorance, and dishonesty, in all fairness they must also be held to account for their deleterious effects upon scientific progress.

In 1963 Weitzenhoffer also expressed a concern

that many would-be "serious" investigators of hypnotic phenomena are prone to make inferences with regard to the nature of hypnosis and hypnotic behavior much too prematurely in terms of the actual and of experience they have had in this area. . . . Unfortunately many investigators have boldly stepped into it without sufficient preparation. Many have had no other background of experience than hearsay information, and often very limited at that. . . . But even running several hundred subjects within the *highly constraining* atmosphere of a controlled, statistically well-designed laboratory experiment is actually no better guarantee that an individual is better prepared to talk about what the nature of hypnosis and hypnotic behavior might be. . . . Too limited actual and vicarious experience with hypnotic phenomena is, in my opinion, one of the main faults of current would-be theorists in the area of hypnotism. (Weitzenhoffer 1963a)

Weitzenhoffer's point is well taken. Just about anyone with a modicum of common sense can hypnotize people, that is, obtain their compliance and have them follow suggestions. To do this is certainly no great feat, and unfortunately too many naive and/or unscrupulous individuals are doing this daily, reinforcing people's fantasies that they have been molested by

Satanists or kidnapped and violated by UFO inhabitants, or helping them believe that they have lived before. In no way are such amateurs to be considered knowledgeable or "experts" in the use of hypnosis. On the other hand, many people that Weitzenhoffer would not consider qualified to voice an opinion have done as much as anyone, if not more, to take the subject matter of hypnosis out of the Dark Ages and into the twenty-first century.

One individual that comes to mind in this regard is the stage mentalist George Kresge, now officially known as Kreskin. Kreskin and a number of other stage magicians, performers like Franz Polgar, Ralph Slater, Howard Klein, and C. A. George Newman, for example, contributed methods and techniques that were adopted by medical scientists such as Milton Erikson and others. Moreover, when it is considered that an august member of the medical establishment such as Dr. S. J. Van Pelt, a former editor of the *British Journal of Hypnotism*, president of the British Society of Medical Hypnotism, and a fellow of the Royal Society of Medicine, stated publicly that "Hypnosis is an important method for growing hair on a bald person's head," it is difficult to take all physicians seriously. While it is true that some stage performers did make wild and unverifiable claims about their powers and the powers of hypnosis, as noted above, similar exaggerations have been made by members of the medical establishment. We have good reason to be wary of those with heavily vested interests.

In fact, if Weitzenhoffer's attitude were to prevail, it could easily mean the death of science as we know it. That is, if only those with years of supporting a particular point of view and with substantial vested interests were permitted to speak, do research, and publish on a subject, it is unlikely we would ever learn anything new. How often have you read or heard a scientific luminary write or pronounce, "Sorry folks, I was mistaken. My entire theory is wrong!" Throughout the history of science it has been clear that progress has been made by the dedicated rebels and amateurs, those who swam against the stream and challenged the prevailing paradigm. Moreover, there is good reason to believe that the power and prestige of the academic establishment with its ingrained practices and procedures has, in many instances, retarded the flow of information and the gaining of knowledge. In the field of psychology, Mahoney (1977 and 1978) documented a number of such cases, as did Andrewski (1972) in the field of sociology. See also the many cases cited in the recent work *Profscam: Professors and the Demise of Higher Education* by Charles J. Sykes, published in 1988. If we were to exclude or deny comment from those without years of experience in hypnosis, then all of the members of King Louis XVI's commission—even Benjamin Franklin—would be silenced, as would half of the published writers in this specialized field. Certain established academic practices such as the unwillingness of journals to publish negative results, academic "publish or perish" policies, journals' refusal to publish many opposing points of view, etc. are some of the sociopolitical factors that have also worked against the advance of our knowledge about the understanding of hypnotic behavior (see Chapter 3).

According to Weitzenhoffer's criterion, we could not possibly entertain or accept the validity of any contributions coming from "amateur" sources such as stage magicians or scientific newcomers.

To reassure Weitzenhoffer and other possible skeptics about my own credentials, I have had over twenty years of experience in hypnotizing individuals in free and controlled situations, and I have read extensively and widely in the literature of the field. Although I have not published as much as many others, I have carried out a number of laboratory studies and have worked with students, friends, and others in Kentucky hypnotizing, i.e., using relaxation and suggestion techniques, to help them overcome addictions to food, alcohol, and tobacco, ease birth pains, lose weight, overcome bulimia (overeating) and anoxeria, avoid panic reactions and shed phobias of various sorts, deal with hallucinations of a nonpsychotic variety, reintegrate their multiple or supposedly multiple personalities, stop nail-biting, overcome writer's block, reduce pain from a partially severed spinal cord, overcome insomnia, locate lost objects of various sorts, overcome intense migraine attacks, pursue past and future lives, recover forgotten memories, and learn to relax and reduce stress. My best estimate is that I have "relaxed" approximately 5,000 individuals during this time. This background, I hope, gives me the right to express some opinions on the topic. In the past, other commentators with less experience, training, and background in the area of hypnosis have not been disqualified from doing so.

Before leaving the topic of hypnotic misinformation we would be somewhat remiss if we failed to take note of the role that fictional literature has played in these conceptions and misconceptions. The aura of mystery surrounding the topic of hypnosis has always intrigued the public and has fostered many fantasies about this strange "mental state." In 1962 the psychiatrist Dr. Arnold M. Ludwig published a fascinating review of the role that hypnosis and hypnotists have played in various literary works over the years. Beginning with George du Maurier's *Trilby*, published in 1894, the prototype for the use of hypnosis in fiction, Ludwig examines the basic ideas, attitudes, and concepts held by writers dealing with the subject. Their ideas and concepts, we can be sure, pretty much reflect the views and conceptions also held by the general public at the time.

And, most certainly, the works themselves did much to mold and shape public opinion. *Trilby* is the story of Trilby O'Ferrall, an artist's model with ambitions to become a singer, even though she is tone-deaf. By chance she falls under the spell of a villain named Svengali. When Trilby's engagement to a young artist is broken up by the artist's mother, she flees, and after five years becomes "La Svengali" a world-famous singer. However, she can

In the novel *Trilby*, the evil Svengali hypnotizes the beautiful but unfortunately tone-deaf young lady, transforming her into a talented singer.

only perform after being hypnotized by staring into Svengali's eyes. When Svengali dies of a heart attack during one of her performances, Trilby is left on stage tone-deaf and confused. Though rescued by her artist friends, Trilby grows ill. But just before dying, she comes upon a picture of Svengali and bursts into beautiful song. The theme of an older man using hypnosis to dominate a younger woman was common in fiction at this time. In Alexander Dumas's six novels about Marie Antoinette, this theme is found on several occasions, particularly in the first of the series *Memoirs of a Physician*, published in 1879. Count Dracula also hypnotizes his intended victims, usually young naive females, prior to sucking their blood. In his 1899 short story "A Story of the Days to Come," H. G. Wells tells of a father who employs a hypnotist to produce amnesia in his daughter concerning her love for a young man. A variation of this theme is found in Ralph Milne Farley's *The House of Ecstasy*, published in 1942, where a hunchback keeps a beautiful young girl in a trance state of bondage and hypnotizes young men to make love to her while he watches. He then induces amnesia in the young men and sends them away. In A. M. Ludwig's words,

All these stories tend to depict a sweet, guileless female virtually seduced through hypnosis into love and bondage by a crafty, much older, Simon Legree type of villain. While in this state, she is powerless to resist his wishes and commands. However, by submitting to hypnotic control, she herself acquires certain preternatural powers, such as a voice change, heightened mental faculties, or an "Un-Dead" state. Any attempt to dissolve the bond usually leads to disaster for the heroine. (Ludwig 1963, p. 73.)

The hypnotic trance is thus used as a literary device to relieve characters of responsibility for their actions and thoughts, e.g., young women can gratify their forbidden love impulses toward the father figure, and the father figures obtain special powers that allow them to compete with younger men in strength and virility.

As Ludwig notes, fiction also tends to attribute all sorts of supernatural powers to the hypnotic trance. In two of Edgar Allen Poe's short stories we encounter this notion. In "Mesmeric Revelation," published in 1871, Poe defines hypnosis as a state resembling death in which the subject possesses exalted mental faculties. In a second tale, "The Facts in the Case of M. Valdemar," also published in 1871, Poe's plot revolves around the idea that mesmerism can delay death and death is not possible while in a state of hypnosis. Edward Bellamy in his utopian novel *Looking Backward: 2000–1887*, published in 1888, uses hypnosis as a means of transcending time and achieving a state of suspended animation. The hero, Julian West, calls in a mesmerist to relieve his insomnia, and after being placed in a trance, West awakens in 2000 A.D. In Arthur Conan Doyle's story "The Great Keinplatz Experiment," published in 1890, an old professor maintains the theory that the soul is separated from the body under hypnosis. The professor then hypnotizes himself and a young colleague in the hope that their minds or souls will change places. They do, and many humorous episodes ensue, until the two remeet, enter into a hypnotic trance again, and put their souls back in the proper bodies. Other fictional accounts describe such powers as clairvoyance, mental telepathy, precognition, and so on, as common features of the hypnotic trance. Why are all these miraculous powers attributed to hypnosis? According to Ludwig, the release of the soul during hypnosis not only assures us of an existence after death, but also promises us the omniscient and ubiquitous powers many strive to obtain. Since hypnosis has always been viewed as a mysterious, mystical, and inexplicable phenomenon, "it has provided fiction writers with an excellent vehicle for the expression of man's megalomania and desire for immortality" (Ludwig, p. 76).

Also common is the theme of the use of hypnosis as a means for dominating and controlling and the hypnotist's love of power. In T. H. White's *The Master*, published in 1975, an old, power-crazed man uses mesmerism to dominate his subjects. He also plans to eventually conquer the entire world. In John Buchan's novel *Three Hostages*, published in 1924, Dominick Medina subjugates three hostages through hypnosis as a first step in his master plan to dominate the whole British Empire. In Ambrose Bierce's *The Realm of the Unreal*, published in 1946, Dr. Dorrimore hypnotizes the principal character against his will, and in H. R. Wakefield's *He Cometh and He Passeth By!* published in 1944, Oscar Clinton uses his great hypnotic powers to dominate men and even cause their death. Finally, in a short story by Edward Bulwer-Lytton called "The House and the Brain," published in 1944, Mr. Richards uses both mesmerism and magic to produce an "Odic" force which can traverse space to produce terrifying hallucinations in anyone who dares to enter a certain haunted house. In nearly all such instances the hypnotist is seen as brilliant but deranged, with fierce passions, extremely strong-willed, and well-versed in many fields of occult knowledge. In contrast, the hypnotic subject is young, naive, moral, humble, and guileless—a simpleton who wouldn't and couldn't hurt a fly. As to the hypnotist's physical features, there is only one common feature in nearly every story—the eyes— and it seems likely this emphasis comes from mythology, folklore, and demonology, where frequent references are made to the "evil eye" and where the idea is common that eyes show a person's basic character. Most fiction writers, who write about hypnotism seem to think that the hypnotist either enjoys power for its own sake or attempts to deny his own sense of impotency by dominating others. They also see that the possession of the power of hypnosis has its serious drawbacks. Fictional hypnotists, it seems, pay for their megalomaniacal ambitions either by death or by being socially rejected. Ludwig finds that death is the most common fate of fictional hypnotists. In his view, the reason for the severity of this punishment is that

> there is no more frightening a fantasy than the thought of being complete-ly dominated or controlled by another against our will. If someone possessing this sort of power were allowed to emerge triumphant, this would endanger all our partially deluded beliefs in our own individuality and mental freedom. Perhaps for this reason, we feel it necessary to sacrifice anyone possessing super-natural powers, whether they be witches, sorcerers, or hypnotists. (p. 79)

One of the most successful and entertaining novels dealing with the topic of hypnosis and post-hypnotic suggestion and control since World War II was Richard Condon's *The Manchurian Candidate*, published in 1959. Condon based his story on the so-called "brainwashing" techniques employed by the Chinese and North Koreans during the Korean War. Using mind-altering techniques such as hypnosis and drugs on a captured American soldier, Raymond Shaw, the communist psychologist Yen Lo programmed Shaw to return to the United States and at a later date, whenever they commanded him to do so, assassinate key political figures. Shortly after it was published the novel was made into a movie starring Laurence Harvey as Raymond, and Frank Sinatra as Raymond's buddy Marco, and supported by Angela Lansbury and Janet Leigh. Both the novel and film were very popular and the film has become something of a "cult classic."

Once
Unbelievable

Now
Unthinkable

The
Chilling
Classic

Frank Sinatra
Laurence Harvey
Janet Leigh

The
Manchurian
Candidate

Co-starring

Angela Lansbury

Henry Silva   James Gregory

Produced by
GEORGE AXELROD and JOHN FRANKENHEIMER   Directed by JOHN FRANKENHEIMER
Screenplay by   Based upon a Novel by   Executive Producer   Distributed in Association with
GEORGE AXELROD   RICHARD CONDON   HOWARD W. KOCH   FRANK SINATRA

Richard Condon's novel *The Manchurian Candidate* was also made into a highly successful film. The story is of a captured American soldier who as a prisoner of war is transformed through drugs and hypnosis into a human killing machine.

Fortunately, the scenario described in the novel could never happen. Years of experimentation by the CIA has shown this sort of programming simply does not work and never will.

Another novel in a similar vein is *The Holland Suggestions,* by John Dunning, published in 1975. In this story, Jim Ryan, a middle-aged divorcé raising a teenaged daughter on his own, receives a photograph in the mail. It is a picture of a mine entrance with a Maltese cross carved in the rock nearby. A few days later he receives another photograph, this one of a trail that apparently leads to the mine. While looking at the photos he begins to doodle, and scratches out the numbers 90-52-12, apparently road routes, and for some strange reason is impelled to follow them. They lead him to a fabulous gold mine, into danger, a brush with death, and to the solution of a fifteen-year-old double cross. It seems he was hypnotized fifteen years before and given a post-hypnotic suggestion to seek out the gold mine. The hypnotist was a scientist who was dying and was using Ryan as an experimental subject to prove that long-term post-hypnotic suggestions were possible. As Ryan's reward, if the experiment worked, he would inherit the gold mine.

In Cornell Woolrich's novel *Nightmare,* published in 1956, a man dreams he has killed someone and pulled a button off the victim's coat. When he wakes he finds the button still in his possession. Was the killing real? It seems that a neighbor hypnotized him the previous night and took him, in a trance, to a house where he was forced to kill the neighbor's enemy in self-defense.

Hypnosis has proved to be very useful to mystery novelists. In 1976 Marc Lovell published a mystery tale titled *The Blind Hypnotist.* The plot revolves around a hypnotist named Jason Galt whose stage career is on the decline until he hatches an ingenious scheme. The scheme involves kidnapping Elsie Vanetti, a famous star of stage and screen, using hypnosis to erase her memory of the event, and then releasing her in a state of amnesia. Then Galt hires himself out to her as a "psychic consultant" in order to stage a dramatic, news-making revelation. Unfortunately for Galt, however, the star's fan club puts up a very attractive reward that prompts Galt's accomplices to renege on their deal. Meanwhile, the actress's husband is using the kidnapping to help his own career. Then Galt discovers that there is more to Elsie than he had bargained for and begins to have a startling change of heart. Once again, however, to hypnosis are attributed powers it does not possess.

In 1981 mystery novelist Barbara Paul published a novel with the title *Your Eyelids Are Growing Heavy,* also concerned with hypnosis. In this Crime Club selection, a young woman, Megan Phillips, is awakened on the four-teenth hole of a golf course by the groundskeeper, who assumes she is drunk. She is not drunk, however. Rather, she is a very well-controlled businesswoman at the top of her profession, but she has no idea where she has been for the past forty-eight hours. Neither her neighbor nor her psychiatrist is able to help her remember the past day and a half. As her memory gradually comes back, she recalls having been with someone who hypnotized her and told her to do something she cannot remember. She only knows that it is imperative that she find him and kill him. It seems that rival drug companies are trying to outwit each other to reap huge profits, and are using Megan to sabotage another rival's efforts while she is hypnotized and unaware of what she is doing. Assumptions about hypnosis throughout the novel are totally bizarre and implausible as well as simply untrue. Both the story and the assumptions about hypnosis are entertaining fictions, however.

Of course, many other plays, television dramas, movies, and so forth, have used hypnosis as a central theme. A typical story is of an unhappy wife and her lover, who, unfortunately, is desperately poor. The only obstacle to their happiness ever after is the presence of the doddering but rich old husband. Hypnosis is the answer. The lover wins the old man's confidence and gets the old man to allow the lover to hypnotize him. Once the old man is hypnotized, the lover plants the hypnotic suggestion in his mind that when he receives a certain signal over the telephone he will do exactly as the hypnotist commands. A few night's later the lover calls the old man and orders him to go to his bureau drawer, take out his revolver, and shoot himself. The old man complies, and the lovers would have lived happily every after had not the hypnotist made the mistake of having the left-handed old man hold the gun in his right hand. A fine story, but it is purely fiction.

Another theme involves sexual seduction. In the classic situation, an evil old man hypnotizes a beautiful young girl and has his way with her. Again, despite what some supersalesmen would like us to believe (see illustration) no young lady will willingly surrender unless she wants to. In such cases, hypnosis would provide a useful alibi. The hypnotic trance is the result of the subject's willingness to be hypnotized, not the result of the hypnotist's powers. Moreover, it is not the command strength of the instructions which causes the subject's compliance, but rather the "cue quality," that is, the communication that, regardless of appearances, it is perfectly safe and proper for the subject to comply. Thus, when a hypnotized subject picks up a supposedly loaded revolver and fires it at an attacker, or when the subject throws acid at the experimenter, or when the student steals a watch or a set of examinations, or indecently exposes himself, or commits any immoral or illegal act—in every one of these cases the subject is well aware that someone is taking full responsibility for his behavior. A few years ago, William Coe facetiously remarked that if a person really wanted someone to help him in an antisocial act, he should try to convince the subject that he is participating in an experiment. We have

Learn hypnosis and become a sexual success! Unfortunately, this advertisement promises more than hypnosis can deliver.

known for a long while that laboratory crimes are possible only because the perpetrators are in a completely safe and protected situation and that the entire performance is never anything more than make-believe. But as we have noted, the better one is at make-believe or in using the full power of one's imagination, the better a hypnotic subject he or she becomes.

2.

A Brief History of the
Concept of Hypnosis

Far from being a modern practice, the use of hypnotic-like procedures to modify human behavior dates back to prehistoric times. Suggestion and monotonous stimuli were used by many of the world's most ancient civilizations. These practices were usually linked with belief in magic and the occult. Inducing a sleep-like state in others was familiar to the priest-physicians of ancient Egypt and the practice was also prevalent in the sleep temples of classical Greece, where worshipers went to invoke Hypnos, the god of sleep, who brought them prohpetic dreams.

In China, the father of Chinese medicine, Wang Tai, in 2600 B.C. wrote about a medical procedure that involved using incantations and mysterious passes of the hands over the patient that leaves no doubt about its hypnotic nature. The Hindu Veda, written around 1500 B.C., mentioned the use of hypnotic-like techniques and procedures, and the Ebers papyrus, known to be over 3000 years old, describes a suggestive method amazingly similar to what hypnotherapists do today.

Chaldean priests were also aware of the power of suggestion to heal the sick. Among the early Celtic inhabitants of Britain, the priestly sect of the Druids, who were also physicians, would often place the ailing in a condition of artificial or "Druidic Sleep" in order to cure them. Accounts of phenomena that we would now call hypnotic can be found in the Bible, the Talmud, and on 3,000-year old Egyptian stone steles. The use of a lighted lamp in what seems to have been a self-hypnotic procedure is described in a document referred to as the Demotic Magical Papyrus now located in museums in London and Leiden. Descriptions of so-called "trance states" and reports of miraculous healing reported by the Greek oracles, the Persian

Franz Anton Mesmer, inventor of "mesmerism" and "animal magnetism." *(From the picture collection of The Institute for the History of Medicine, Vienna)*

magi, the Hindu fakirs, and Indian yogi all attest to the use of hypnotic-like procedures. Similarly, the healing power attributed for many centuries to the "royal touch" of kings and princes may also be seen as having its basis in the power of suggestion and strong belief. The achievements of healers who used their hands, religious or mystical objects, or exorcism and prayer to cure the sick also tapped these same psychological sources.

In Europe during the sixteenth century attempts were made to provide a more scientific explanation for the existence and the cure of diseases which until then were assumed to be due to supernatural or metaphysical causes. One of the first of such theorists was Paracelsus (1493–1541), a Swiss-born physician and alchemist who believed that magnets and the heavenly bodies—the sun, moon, and stars—had healing effects on the human body. From then on a number of similar notions influenced the thinking of various physicians, astronomers, physicists, and healers of the sick. A Scottish physician, Gul Maxwell, in 1679 proposed that a universal and vital force or spirit inhabited and affected all human beings. Even Isaac Newton attempted to identify natural laws that underlay all living systems. This effort led Richard Mead, an eighteenth-century English physician, to study the universality of life itself. And around 1771 Maximillian Hell, a Viennese Jesuit, became famous for cures he obtained by applying a steel plate to the bodies of the sick. In 1774 Hell met a Viennese physician named Franz Anton Mesmer and showed him the healing powers of his magnetized steel plates.

Mesmerism, Somnambulism, and Animal Magnetism

Although the history of hypnosis is often considered as beginning with Mesmer, the relationship of hypnosis to mesmerism more closely resembles that of chemistry to alchemy or astronomy to astrology. The former grew out of the latter piece by piece and bit by bit over a period of several hundred years. Mesmer developed the theory of "animal magnetism" and postulated there was a universal magnetic fluid present in all objects that produced disease when it was out of balance in the human body. Mesmer developed techniques that he believed would restore the balance of the magnetic fluid and thus cure disease. Before he received his medical degree, Mesmer studied philosophy, theology, and law, and developed a great interest in music and astrology. It was his interest in astrology that was largely responsible for his theory of animal magnetism and disease. Mesmer believed that perfect health depended upon the individual having a correct relationship with the heavenly bodies.

After he was shown the powers of the magnet by Father Hell, Mesmer became convinced that the same powers that held the sun and moon and planets in place regulated human health. When a magnet was brought into

This drawing shows patients in an early group therapy session around one of Mesmer's *Baquets*.

contact with a patient, the subtle and mysterious fluid exuded by the magnet entered the body of the patient and healed him of his complaint. "Animal magnetism" was the name Mesmer gave this fluid. His doctoral thesis, written in 1766, was titled *On the Influence of the Planets*. It is now known that most of it was lifted bodily from an earlier work (Pattie 1989). Nevertheless, the thesis earned him his degree and allowed him to begin the practice of medicine in Vienna in 1768. Soon thereafter, Mesmer married a wealthy widow and took up residence in a fashionable part of the city. Thousands of patients soon began coming to him to be healed by his magnets.

To cure such problems as urine retention, toothache, earache, depression, and paralysis, Mesmer began to make passes with magnets over the bodies of his sick patients to enhance the balance of their fluids . Often the patients improved. Along with the cures came honors and awards. The Bavarian Academy of Sciences made Mesmer a member and his reputation spread across Austria and all Europe. Mesmer's success, however, aroused feelings of jealousy among a number of his professional colleagues. Matters came to a head when Mesmer was asked to treat a case of hysterical blindness in a young pianist who was a protegé of the Empress Maria Theresa. Because of her blindness, the young woman received a regular pension from the queen. Mesmer proceeded to treat the girl, and apparently, for a while at least, her vision was restored. But the young pianist soon had a relapse, perhaps related to the possibility that if she were cured her pension would cease. Mesmer was summarily removed as the physician in the case, providing his jealous colleagues opportunity to ridicule both him and his theories. As a result he left Vienna for Paris in 1778.

In Paris, where he was treated more kindly than in Vienna, Mesmer became bolder and practiced even more theatrical techniques. He began to dress in long, flowing, colorful robes and carried out his cures to the accompaniment of piano music. He passed long iron rods over his swooning female patients, and most were apparently cured after two or three sessions. Soon Mesmer had so many patients it became impossible to treat them on an individual basis. Accordingly, Mesmer devised his famous "baquets," which allowed a number of patients to be treated at a time. The baquets were large oak tubs containing water, iron filings, and powdered glass. From the tubs projected long iron rods which were grasped by the patients, who joined hands so that they could receive the healing virtue of the magnetic fluid and pass it around from hand to hand. The "magnetic hysteria" theory gained so much popularity among the Parisians at this time that a rumor that one of the oak trees in the Bois de Boulogne was magnetic caused hundreds of citizens to rush to the tree and hug it fervently, expecting to be cured thereby.

Through the influence of a physician friend, Mesmer gained the attention of Queen Marie Antoinette, and with the queen's permission Mesmer and his friend founded a clinic in Rue Montmartre. For a period of five years animal magnetism was the rage of Paris and hundreds of the sick and merely curious were treated at the clinic. Such goings-on were bound to be questioned by a number of skeptics. Primarily because of opposition in the scientific and medical communities, in 1784 the French government under Louis XVI established a commission, presided over by Benjamin Franklin, to look into and report upon the truth about animal magnetism. After an investigation that extended over a seven-year period, they concluded that the phenomenon was due to an "excitement of the imagination" rather than the activities of any mysterious magnetic fluid. The commission also prepared a second, secret report for the king in which they argued that mesmerism was also a menace to public morality in that many ladies could be easily seduced while under its influence. One member of the commission had noted that many of the magnetizers achieved their greatest success by pressing their hands and fingers upon the patient's abdomen, "an application often continued for a long time—sometimes for several hours" (Mackay 1869, Wagstaff 1981). The commission also noted that many of Mesmer's clients were agitated and tormented with convulsions as a result of the treatment, and some—especially the women—ran around hugging and kissing each other. It is ironic to note that Louis XVI, who ordered the investigation, was a strong believer in the healing power of the "royal touch." Traditionally, the French and English believed that kings and queens had the ability to heal certain diseases—particularly scrofula or tuberculosis of the glands of the neck—by merely touching the afflicted area with their hands. This was considered evidence of the divine power and right of kings. Queen Anne was the last of the English sovereigns to practice this form of cure, but it was revived briefly in France in the nineteenth century.

Mesmer's "Grand Crisis"

Mesmer frequently walked around his clients and touched them with a wand, urging them to yield themselves up to the magnetic fluids that surrounded them. He exhorted them that they would be cured if only they could focus on the heavenly powers within their sick bodies. Some of his patients went into a trance-like state and would sit or stand in place apparently unseeing and unhearing for extended periods. But he would continue to exhort others to "reach further into your mind." Through his persistent pressuring he would drive many of them to reach what he called "a grand crisis," something that today we would call a grand mal convulsive seizure. Mesmer was convinced that this "grand crisis" was responsible for the cures that many of his clients reported. In their secret report to King Louis, the investigating committee reported that this "grand crisis" was probably habit-forming and dangerous to one's health. Furthermore, they told the king, women seemed to be particularly susceptible to this "grand crisis," and could easily be seduced while undergoing it.

E. M. Thornton, in a fascinating book called *Hypnotism, Hysteria and Epilepsy* (1976), argues that the source of the behaviors we now attribute to hypnosis resulted from the misdiagnosis of the ancient malady epilepsy.

In 1981 Wagstaff raised the question:

> How did Mesmer's writhing, convulsing patients come to be classified along-side subjects responding to suggestions for body sway and arm levitation, lifting weights, experiencing hallucinations, committing antisocial acts, falling into a state of profound relaxation and so on?

According to Wagstaff "many of these phenomena are related by historical misjudgment and error, rather than by some central unique 'hypnotic' property" (p. 214). Many of the convulsive fits of Mesmer's patients turned out to be quite violent and showed "precipitate and involuntary motions of all limbs of the body, by a contraction of the throat, by sudden affections of the hypochonders and epigastrium. . ." (Thornton, p. 8). Moreover, these crises were often preceded and followed by a comatose state. Mesmer believed that such crises were necessary to bring the disease to a climax, and that shortly thereafter recovery would take place.

Due to the strong similarity of such states as the grand mal and petit mal and Jacksonian seizures to epileptic seizures, Thornton concluded that in many cases the disease of the nervous system that Mesmer was treating was epilepsy. The techniques used by Mesmer to bring the crisis about are also the exact same techniques known to produce convulsions in epileptic patients. Well-documented is the use of light (photogenic epilepsy), sound in the form of music (musicogenic epilepsy), and touch (tactile precipitation).

Citing the work of Lennox (1970), Thornton also points out that there are three main groups of epileptics: psychomotor, automatic, and subjective. For the psychomotor subgroup, symptoms include rigidity of the muscles with unconsciousness and amnesia, periods of excessive muscular activity, and periods of immobility that involve staring, stupor, and sleep-like states. For the automatic subgroup, symptoms include full consciousness but with confusion, impaired speech, and amnesia. For the subjective subgroup, symptoms include dream states, feelings of unreality, illusions, and hallucinations of sight, hearing, smell, or taste. And although the patient may be aware of what is being said and done, he cannot participate or speak. Moreover, these seizure patterns vary from time to time and from patient to patient, and one person may have more than one pattern. Students of epilepsy have also reported that many clients subject to very light seizures may carry out entire sequences of complex behaviors in a state of apparent unconsciousness or delirium. Thornton reports that many patients during attacks of temporal lobe epilepsy will follow the instructions of others in robot-like fashion, and that "a discharge from the temporal lobes to the nearby sensory cortex in the Rolandic area would bring about diminished bodily sensations, a feature of both temporal seizures and hypnotism" (p. 38). In summing up the close relationship between the epilepsies and hypnosis as performed by the Mesmerists, Thornton concludes, "We can thus identify the condition they produced and which they called 'somnambulism,' which later generations named 'hypnotism' or nervous sleep, as a psychomotor or temporal lobe epileptic seizure" (p. 39).

Even today epilepsy is difficult to define and to detect, and contrary to popular belief, it is not a specific disease but a group of symptoms caused by a number of different conditions. We also know that, neurophysiologically, it is a condition characterized by seizures stemming from excessive neuronal discharges caused by a variety of central nervous system disorders, e.g., cortical lesions, tumors, strokes and other circulatory problems, and inflammation. In some patients heredity appears to be an important predisposing factor, while in others, a head injury creates a scar on the cortex that becomes a source of electrical irregularity. Temporal lobe epilepsy is also most quixotic and difficult to diagnose, and it may well be that among the one percent of the population Weitzenhoffer identifies as true "hypnotics" and the classical somnambulists we may also find an undiagnosed case of epilepsy, since the behavior Weitzenhoffer calls "hypnotic," the epilepsy authorities call "epileptic."

According to Thornton (1976), the history of magnetism, from which hypnosis arose, "is a comedy of errors" (p. 43). Since the Mesmerists had only a rudimentary understanding of the nervous system, it is easy to understand why this comedy of errors occurred and why, as Wagstaff stresses, "if a magnetizer could produce such dramatic, convulsive and trance-like results, perhaps he should be able to make his subjects perform paranormal feats of levitation, elongation of body, and mental telepathy" (Wagstaff 1981, p. 217). It is also sad to note that the association between the mystical state of mesmerism and the occult and magical claims of the paranormal still exist— even today in our scientific age. Moreover, as Wagstaff has stressed:

We now have a term "hypnosis" which relates to *mimicking* of these clinical symptoms, and the bizarre range of extrapolations and exaggerated effects that accompanied and developed from them, by *normal* people (i.e., non-sufferers from pathological illnesses such as epilepsy). In blunt terms, when "normal" subjects are given modern hypnosis scales they are being asked to perform, to the best of their ability, what really amounts to a parody of epileptic symptoms. The contradictions of hypnotic phenomena could not become clearer. Supposing we take two epileptic symptoms, muscular rigidity and a trance-like stuporific appearance. In the epileptic the two symptoms are not incompatible, they are accompanied or followed by an electrical discharge which is identifiable on EEG records. However, in a "normal" person a stuporific trance-like appearance might best be produced if the subject is told to *relax* and appear to be sleepy. However, deep relaxation, which [is confirmed] in terms of an abundance of alpha waves, is incompatible with muscle tonicity which occurs when the normal subject has to try to hold his body or his arm rigid in a distinctly *unrelaxed* state. These contradictions may thus exist in hypnosis because different methods have to be employed to mimic different epileptic symptoms. . . . One way of viewing the situation would be to say that, in many respects, the modern hypnotic subject plays the "game" of hypnosis, according to the rules laid down by the hypnotist, our cultural notion of "hypnosis" and his individual attitudes and preconceptions. If he is a good subject he will play very hard, but he will not know that what he is really doing is employing a variety of strategies in order to mimic, in many ways the tragic condition of epilepsy. The epileptic may look in a trance, so the hypnotic subject relaxes and tries to mimic this; the epileptic may suffer spontaneous hallucinations, so the hypnotic subject tries his best to imagine things which are not present; the epileptic may suffer spontaneous amnesia so the hypnotic subject "pretends" he cannot remember, or engages in a number of strategies such as thinking about something else in order to mimic amnesia. Fortunately, the modern hypnotic subject no longer has to mimic the more violent and more distasteful aspects of a "grand mal" seizure, such as convulsions and foaming at the mouth, but he may have to mimic behaviors appropriate to the myths that grew from the early misunderstandings of the nature of epilepsy, and the "powers" of those who seemed able to evoke the fits in others. (pp. 218–220)

Disillusioned and embittered by the rejection of his work, Mesmer left France just before the outbreak of the French Revolution and retired to Switzerland. It was reported that he returned to Paris for a short while in 1801 to receive a small pension in compensation for his loss of property during the Reign of Terror. Though animal magnetism was discredited, Mesmer's role was critical in the history of hypnotism, for it was he who initiated the movement that was later taken up and modified by others.

During Mesmer's lifetime, one of his pupils, the Marquis de Puysegur, a French landowner, stumbled upon somnambulism, which excited considerable interest and led to a renewed interest in mesmerism, especially in Germany. One day in 1784 Puysegur magnetized a peasant by the name of Victor Race. Instead of falling into convulsions as expected, Race appeared to doze off, yet Puysegur found that he could still communicate with him. Because of the similarity of this state to sleepwalking, Puysegur called it "artificial somnambulism." Puysegur proceeded to put other patients into the magnetic state, which he saw as characterized by deep sleep followed by amnesia. Also continuing his experiments with Race, Puysegur now claimed

This old engraving shows dotted lines of magnetic force from the mesmerist to his patient. *(From an engraving in Ebenezer Sibly's* Keys to Physics and the Occult Sciences, *1790.)*

he could communicate with Race on a soul-to-soul basis, without the use of any physical means whatever. Puysegur claimed his patients also gained supernatural powers while in the magnetic state, and that they could detect the diseased body parts of another patient by merely passing their hands over his clothes. Miraculously, they could also see into the interior of the body. One day, in an orgy of enthusiasm, Puysegur magnetized an elm tree. Astonishingly, as he continued his work around this tree he found that not only did the minds of many of his patients remain alert, but many of them showed remarkable powers of thought transference, clairvoyance, and an increase in intelligence. Puysegur sincerely believed the magnetism from the tree affected his patients. Belief in the superior abilities of mesmerized patients was thus launched and rapidly became widespread.

During this same period, another Frenchman, the Chevalier de Barbarin, of Lyons, showed it was possible to produce artificial somnambulism merely by sitting at the patient's bedside and praying that he would be magnetized.

Barbarin also claimed he could cure almost any disease and that he and other proficient magnetizers could communicate with their patients from almost any distance, since they had the power of clairvoyance.

Both Puysegur and Barbarin were by now aware that magnets were no longer necessary to produce the mesmeric effects. But it is generally acknowledged that the individual most responsible for taking the magnetism out of mesmerism was the Portuguese priest Abbé Jose di Faria, who rejected the notion of a magnetic fluid and argued that the magnetized person was in a state of lucid sleep that was brought about by concentration. Faria, who gave public exhibitions in Paris in 1814 and 1815, produced this state of sleep by merely asking his clients to sit down, close their eyes, and focus their attention on sleep. When he was ready for them to wake up he would simply tell them to awaken. In fact, the Abbé's approach was amazingly modern and perceptive. In 1819 he published a book *De la cause du sommeil lucide ou étude sur la nature de l'homme*, in which he wrote that mesmeric phenomena depend upon the disposition of the subject and the state of his mind. Furthermore, he called attention to the social "demand characteristics" of the hypnotic situation by stating that when clients see what is required of them, "they immediately lend themselves to fulfilling these demands, and sometimes even in spite of themselves, by the power of conviction." For Faria any cures that resulted were not due to magnetism but to suggestion and the expectations and cooperation of the patients—elements now considered to be crucial to the therapeutic process. Faria was also well aware of the power of suggestion and used it in his treatments. In his book he says, "a glass of water swallowed with the notion that it is eau-de-vie completely intoxicates."

Crucial to the development of the study of hypnosis was the adoption of mesmerism by the medical community—particularly the surgeons who began performing major operations using mesmeristic techniques. Curiously, one of the first of these was the American surgeon Benjamin Perkins, who in 1798 began using a pair of metallic tractors to induce the magnetic state in patients prior to his operations. The discovery by others that wooden tractors painted silver were just as effective as Perkins's metallic ones contributed to the demise of the magnetic concept.

The man most responsible for this development, however, was the surgeon John Elliotson (1791–1868), a professor of theology and medicine at London University. An enthusiastic proponent of mesmerism, Elliotson believed that the progress of medicine should not be hampered by a rigid adherence to outmoded beliefs. Not only did he introduce Laennec's stethoscope into England, but he experimented with a wide variety of drugs and established the importance of potassium iodide in medical treatment and the use of prussic acid in the control of vomiting. After seeing demonstrations of mesmerism by the Frenchman Dupotet, Elliotson began to use it in the treatment of his patients and to demonstrate its use in the hospital wards. This led to friction between Elliotson and the hospital administrators, and in 1838, after Thomas Wakley, the founder and first editor of *Lancet*, carried out some tests of claims for mesmerism and found them wanting, Elliotson fell further into disfavor. When he delivered a lecture on magnetism to the Royal College of Physicians, he was criticized and denounced. And when the governors of the hospital declared that all mesmeric demonstrations within the hospital precincts should cease, Elliotson resigned his post.

With the help of his supporters, however, Elliotson started his own mesmeric hospital in Fitzroy Square and started a journal called the *Zoist* for the express purpose of promoting animal magnetism. The journal was quite successful, publishing articles by eminent writers, such as Herbert Spencer, and reporting numerous case histories of successful mesmeric cures. Phrenology, the science of diagnosing disorders by reading the bumps on the head, as well as clairvoyance, were also discussed in its pages. Undoubtedly, by emphasizing the usefulness of mesmeric practices in the cure of disease, and particularly by focusing attention on its use in the treatment of psychoneuroses and other functional disorders, Elliotson kept interest in the subject alive. Elliotson's book *Numerous Cases of Surgical Operations Without Pain in the Mesmeric State*, published in 1843, claimed that the positive results he and his colleagues had observed were due to mesmeric passes. Elliotson believed that mesmerism was a cure-all. He also made the highly dubious claim that in all of his practice with it he never had a failure. It is likely that many of Elliotson's so-called "painless" operations were not quite as painless as he claimed. Elliotson's writing tends to be rather rambling and hard to follow, so we are often unsure just what occurred in the examples he relates.

In the United States around the middle of the nineteenth century interest in mesmerism also was growing. Elizabeth Blackwell, one of our first women physicians, as well as authors Henry James and Edgar Allan Poe refer to it. Mary Baker Eddy, the founder of Christian Science, became acquainted with it through a physician named Phineas Quimby, who was the anaesthetist at the first surgical operation performed under hypnosis in the United States. In France in 1829, a Dr. Cloquet operated on a sixty-four-year-old woman with a malignant tumor of the right breast, using mesmerism but no drugs. During the surgical procedure this woman talked with the physician and showed no signs of pain. Earlier, while mesmerized, the woman had diagnosed herself as having a diseased liver. Three weeks after the breast surgery the woman died of pleurisy and an autopsy showed no evidence of a diseased liver. Since she was mistaken and may have even lied about her liver, a commission from the Medical Academy decided that she probably lied about feeling no pain. Meanwhle, in India the analgesic

This cartoon, which was published in Paris in the 1780s, depicts the animal magnetist as an ass and alternatively as various carnivorous beasts—and the client, too, as several types of animals.

and anaesthetic properties of mesmerism were being demonstrated in dramatic fashion by a Scottish surgeon, James Esdaile.

Over a seven-year period while working in Calcutta, Esdaile carried out over 300 major operations and thousands of minor ones quite painlessly, he claimed, with the aid of mesmerism. His specialty was the removal of scrotal tumors, but he also performed a large number of amputations as well. His work was recognized by the Bengali government, which established a special mesmeric hospital for him in Calcutta. An outstanding feature of his surgical operations was his low mortality rate and the rapid healing which followed. Many of his operations were written up and published in the *Zoist*, but most of the other medical journals refused to publish his work. Mesmerism still was too closely associated with superstition and quackery. And Esdaile did not help his own case. In describing one case, Esdaile reports that he tried unsuccessfully for four days to mesmerize the patient. Finally the patient fainted, upon which he proceeded with the operation. In his later years he stressed that mesmerism was a cure-all, not just of limited use as an analgesic agent. He also swears that he mesmerized clients in court by making mesmeric passes *behind their backs,* and then by putting them in a somnambulistic trance made them walk away and forget what had happened. There is reason to believe that many of Esdaile's operations were not as painless as he claims. As Wagstaff writes:

> Esdaile himself reported instances of patient responses which seem somewhat like responses to pain; he wrote, "She moved and moaned"; "About the middle of the operation he gave a cry"; "He awoke, and cried out before the operation was finished." (Wagstaff 1981)

Esdaile also reported a case in which he attempted over a period of eleven days to mesmerize some patients and finally had to give up. Moreover, an investigating committee looking into Esdaile's claims reported that three of the six patients they observed in surgery showed "convulsive movements of the upper limbs, writhing of the body, distortions of the features, giving the face a hideous expression of suppressed agony; the respiration became heaving with deep sighs." Two of the other patients showed marked elevations in pulse rate. Such evidence suggests that these patients did feel pain. Finally, the claim that so many of his successful cases had total amnesia and remembered nothing is highly suspicious. We now know that a complete spontaneous amnesia after a hypnotic induction is extremely rare. I will take up this issue again in a later chapter.

Braid and the Age of Hypnosis

The Age of Hypnosis can rightly be said to have begun with the work of James Braid, an Edinburgh surgeon who set up his practice in Manchester, England. On November 13, 1841, Braid witnessed a demonstration of mesmerism by a certain La Fontaine, a relative of the French fabulist. Braid's views at this time were skeptical with regard to the causes of the condition.

In fact, he was so unconvinced that he tried to expose La Fontaine as a fake and a charlatan. Braid was convinced that the girl on the stage was, indeed, in a trance, but he thought that she and others were unable to open their eyes during the mesmeric state due to ocular fatigue. Experimenting with his friends and relatives, Braid found that he could induce the trance state by the simple expedient of having them fix their gaze on a single point or a bright object such as his lancet case. He then concluded that the phenomena of mesmerism were wholly subjective in character, that they were not dependent upon any magical power possessed by the mesmerist, and that the French commission had been correct in rejecting the idea of a universal magnetic fluid or forces flowing from the operator's body. Braid was determined to do his utmost to put the subject on a proper scientific foundation. In 1842 he approached the Medical Section of The British Association in Manchester with an offer to read a paper on the new science of "hypnotism," a word he invented. His offer was refused, but later Braid was successful in getting a number of the association members to hear his lecture and witness his demonstrations.

Before Braid's time it was accepted that the proper way to magnetize anybody was to stroke the face, neck, and shoulders, and the entire body until the animal magnetism was transferred from the operator to the subject. Braid allegedly used this technique himself until one day one of his patients arrived early and had to wait for him in the waiting room. When Braid was ready for him he found the patient sitting at the table, his chin resting in his hands, looking into the flame of an oil lamp. When Braid said, "I'm ready for you now," his statement was ignored. As he walked to the center of the room, Braid noticed that the patient's eyes were glazed, something he had witnessed in magnetizing others. He was so captivated that he decided to test to see if the patient was in a premagnetic state. He said, "Close your eyes." The patient did. Braid then said, "Go to sleep," and the man appeared to comply. Following his discovery that it was not necessary to go through the stroking routine, Braid had all of his patients gaze into a bright light while he gave them suggestions of tiredness and sleep. Since he found this too time-consuming, Braid then started using his shiny scalpel case. He moved it up and down in front of the patient's face, at the same time making his client hold his head still and follow the case with his eyes only. Braid would then tell him to close his eyes. Not only was this successful, but many hypnotists still use a variant of this procedure today. In 1843 Braid published *Neurypnology, or the Rationale of Nervous Sleep*. In this book he proposed that the phenomena be called "hypnotic" rather than mesmeric. In the first part of the book he used the word "neuro-hypnotism" to denote a "condition of nervous sleep," because he believed that the term "neuro" would make the entire concept more scientifically respectable and acceptable. Later, he switched to "hypnotism."

Braid did not hesitate to modify his views of the phenomena as he gained better acquaintance with them. He thought at first that the phenomena were entirely subjective and were caused by an alteration inside the subject's mind. The external cause was, of course, a physical stimulus or behavior, such as gazing fixedly at a bright light or object. This induction technique used to be referred to as "Braidism." Later on, Braid tried, without success, to substitute a new term, "monoideism," or the influence of a single idea, for "hypnotism," which he now considered a misnomer, since it implied sleep. The best way to characterize the phenomenon, he thought, was the deep concentration by a person on a single dominant idea. Toward the end of his life Braid also came to realize that several ideas could be planted in a patient's mind at the same time. Although he was also aware of the influence of suggestion in causing the phenomenon, he did not consider this an adequate explanation of it.

In 1860, the year of Braid's death, Dr. A. A. Liebault of Nancy, France, a country general practitioner, took up the serious study of hypnosis. To test his views of its curative powers, Liebault offered to treat all of his patients free as long as they would permit him to use hypnotic methods. As you might expect, Liebault was soon overwhelmed with patients seeking his help. In spite of his heavy caseload, he also found time to write a book about hypnosis, his methods of treatment, and the outcomes of many of his cases. Although the work was meticulous in its attention to detail, it was generally ignored. Most of Liebault's colleagues regarded him as a fool. In 1882 Liebault gained both fame and respect when he managed to treat and cure a severe case of sciatica that the famous Professor Bernheim of Strasbourg had treated in vain for over six months. Bernheim then visited Liebault's clinic and was so impressed by what he saw and heard that he became Liebault's ardent admirer and supporter. In 1884 Bernheim published a book De la suggestion. Liebault's name became world-famous almost overnight, and medical men from all nations converged on Nancy in order to study his methods. Together Bernheim and Liebault founded what came to be known as the Nancy School of Hypnotism. The association between them was rather loose and they did not always agree. Nevertheless, the hallmarks of the Nancy school were its beliefs that the hypnotic state was caused by suggestion acting on and through the patient's own mind, and secondly, that the hypnotic state was a normal one.

This latter belief was the very antithesis of the opinion held by the famous Jean Marie Charcot (1825–1893), the greatest neurologist of his time, who began to investigate hypnotism at the Salpêtrière hospital in Paris. Charcot, who began convinced of the already outdated theory that magnetism explained hypnotism, on the basis of the treatment of a small number of carefully selected and well-rehearsed patients arrived at the conclusion that hysteria and hypnotic phenomena were virtually synonymous physiological states of the nervous system. During the 1880s the literature on hypnosis was dominated by the issues of whether hypnotism was physiological or psychological, and whether it was pathological or normal. Charcot and Bernheim were at the center of this heated controversy. It is a rather sad commentary on the state of medical science in his day that although Charcot's theory was patently false, his lectures on hypnotism were heralded far and wide and attracted physicians from all over the world. The fact that a man of such outstanding reputation worked on hypnotism did much to awaken and legitimize medical and scientific interest in it. Even though Bernheim replicated Charcot's results and even substituted a piece of paper for the supposedly essential magnet, Charcot's reputation was only slightly diminished. Eventually, Charcot's ideas about hypnotism were repudiated and Bernheim's adopted. The theories of Liebault and Bernheim became more generally accepted and were even officially endorsed at the International Congress of Hypnotism held in Paris in 1900.

Charcot was a rather pompous fool when it came to the subject of hypnotism. According to Thornton (1976), considerable evidence suggests that some of Charcot's patients who manifested hypnotic catalepsy were epileptics who had incorrectly been diagnosed as "hysteric." According to Charcot, who considered himself to be an expert on hysteria, there were four main phases of a major hysterical attack: first, the "epileptical phase which included convulsions; second, the phase of large gross movements; third, the phase of hallucinations; and finally, the phase of terminal delirium." Although Freud and Breuer (1950) also noted "hysterical" symptoms such as colonic spasm and cataleptic rigidity, they suggested that such convulsions could well be epileptic in nature. Thornton points out that epileptic fits are often followed by a temporary neurological deficit such as paralysis, or weakness of the limbs, numbness, blindness, or aphasia. He further suggests that physicians of the time diagnosed these deficits as hysterical because, due to their lack of knowledge of the nervous system, they did not appreciate that they were genuine neurological deficits. For example, they would label blindness after a fit "hysterical," because they did not know that the pupillary reaction to light could be preserved due to the separate innervation of this reflex. Thornton also reports that many physicians would scream at, stick pins in, and pinch and slap patients in abortive attempts to test hysterical paralysis and anaesthesia that followed fits of varying degrees of severity. At this time, diagnoses of hysteria were occurring in epidemic numbers.

Charcot merely added fuel to the flames with his wrong-headed notion that hysteria was related to the cerebral cortex and that its determinants were psychological. We are indebted to physician Axel Munthe for a detailed account of Charcot's various scientific crimes. In his popular *The Story of San Michele*, published in 1929, Munthe reported:

According to Charcot, the famous French neurologist, hysterical women made the best hypnotic subjects. *(From Le Salon de 1887, Paris)*

To me who for years had been devoting my spare time to study hypnotism these stage performances of the Salpêtrière before the public of Tout Paris were nothing but an absurd farce, a hopeless muddle of truth and cheating. Some of these subjects were no doubt real somnambulists faithfully carrying out in a waking state the various suggestions made to them during sleep—post-hypnotic suggestions. Many of them were mere frauds, knowing quite well what they were expected to do, delighted to perform their various tricks in public, cheating both doctors and audience with the amazing cunning of the hysteriques. They were always ready to "piquer une attaque" of Charcot's classical grande hysterie; arc-en-ciel and all, or to exhibit his famous three stages of hypnotism: lethargy, catalepsy, somnambulism, all invented by the Master and hardly ever observed outside the Salpêtrière. . . . Hypnotized right and left, dozens of times a day, by doctors and students, many of these unfortunate girls spent their days in a state of semi-trance, their brains bewildered by all sorts of absurd suggestions, half conscious and certainly not responsible for their doings, sooner or later doomed to end their days in the salle des agités if not in a lunatic asylum.

Munthe, although condemning Charcot's Tuesday performances as unscientific and unworthy of the Salpêtrière, did stress that some serious investigations of hypnotic phenomena took place, and he was involved in some of these experiments. The atmosphere at the hospital was so dominated by Charcot, however, that in Munthe's words, "to speak of the Nancy school at the Salpêtrière was in those days considered almost as an act of lèse-majesté. Charcot himself flew into a rage at the very mentioning of Professor Bernheim's name." Many of Charcot's patients and star performers were ex-prostitutes from the music hall stage and were skilled comedians and imitators, although they were essentially uneducated and naive. In an aborted attempt to rescue one of them from Charcot's clutches, Munthe's efforts to restore her to her parents were discovered, and Charcot, in a towering rage, banished Munthe from the hospital forever. Munthe points out that,

Almost every single one of Charcot's theories on hypnotism has proved wrong. Hypnosis is not, as he said, an artificially induced neurosis only to be encountered in hysteria, in hypersensitive, weak-minded and ill balanced people. The contrary is the truth. Hysterical subjects are as a rule less easily hypnotizable than well balanced and mentally sound people. . . . The therapeutic value of hypnotism in medicine and surgery is not negligible as Charcot said. On the contrary it is immense if in the hands of competent doctors with clear heads and clean hands. . . . I have often obtained marvelous results by this still misunderstood method of healing. . . . The great benefit derived from hypnotic anesthesia in surgical operations and childbirth is now admitted by everybody. Even more striking is the beneficial effect of this method in the most painful of all operations, as a rule still to be endured without anesthesia—Death. . . . Outside the Salpêtrière I have hardly ever come across Charcot's famous three stages of hypnosis so strikingly exhibited during his Tuesday lectures. They were all invented by himself, grafted on his hysterical subjects and accepted by his pupils by the powerful suggestion of the Master. The same affirmation holds good in regard to his special hobby, his grande hysterie then rampant all over the Salpêtrière, ward after ward full of it, now almost extinct. The fact that all these experiments in hypnotism were done on hysterical subjects, is the only possible explanation of his inability to understand the true nature of these phenomena. If the statement of the Salpêtrière school that only hysterical subjects are hypnotizable was correct it would mean that at least eight-five percent of mankind was suffering from hysteria.

It is highly unlikely that the disease of "hysteria" or the "wandering womb" disorder ever really existed. As described in the earliest accounts, of the Egyptians and the Greeks, the symptoms appear very similar to forms of epilepsy. Moreover, as the result of better diagnosis and better understanding of the epilepsies, organic pathologies, and psychological disorders, cases of the sort described by Charcot, Freud, and Breuer are increasingly rare.

Charcot was not, however, without his defenders. In 1888 Alfred Binet, the father of the intelligence test, coauthored a book, *Animal Magnetism*, that reported a series of experiments supporting Charcot's claims. Reviewing this work years later in his classic work *Hypnosis and Suggestibility* (1933) Clark Hull stated:

There has rarely been written a book containing a greater aggregation of results from unrelated experiments, all put forward with loud protestations of impeccable scientific procedure and buttressed by the most transparent sophistries than this work of Binet and Fere. (p. 16)

One of the positive aspects of Charcot's work was his demonstration that hysterical symptoms could be induced and eliminated through hypnotic suggestion. This discovery played an important role in the development of psychiatry and in the growing recognition that psychological factors play a significant role in mental illnesses. One of the first to recognize this fact was Freud. In 1889 Freud visited Liebault's clinic in Nancy and watched both Liebault and Bernheim carry out their "astonishing experiments." It was here that Freud first entertained the possibility that "there could be powerful mental processes which nevertheless remained hidden from the consciousness of men" (Freud 1925). Working with Breuer, another Viennese physician, Freud began to use "hypnosis" to encourage patients with hysterical symptoms to talk, and in doing so discovered that long-repressed experiences somehow or other seemed to be the cause of the symptoms. Moreover, the emotional catharsis provided by the verbalization led, in many cases, to the elimination of the symptoms. In 1895 Breuer and Freud together published their classic *Studies in Hysteria*. Not only does this work provide a detailed account of Freud's first efforts as a psychotherapist, but many of his significant discoveries are foreshadowed here. Using hypnosis, the two investigators were able to demonstrate the causal connection between hysterical symptoms and unpleasant childhood experiences. The patients' symptoms were also found to have a specific meaning which became very clear when the etiology was known. To their surprise, they found that the symptoms disappeared if they caused the recall of a highly traumatic memory with sufficient vividness. In their words, "Traumatic experiences must be repeatedly recalled until the emotional elements are exhausted." They also noted that the memories which caused the hysterical symptoms are preserved with remarkable fidelity, though they were not available to voluntary conscious recall. Forgetting in these instances was apparently not a passive process but an active one in which the painful memory was repressed or pushed out of conscious awareness.

Breuer had earlier stumbled onto this treatment technique in the celebrated case of "Anna O." During spontaneous autohypnotic states, Anna insisted on providing detailed autobiographical memories and fantasies that had the effect of temporarily calming and relaxing her. To facilitate this process, Breuer later induced hypnosis. When all of Anna's symptoms were eventually traced back to their origin, they permanently disappeared and the reason for the illness became vividly clear. Breuer was convinced of the validity of Anna's explanation because of their perfect inner logic and their consistency. Freud, impressed with Breuer's technique, used it to treat other patients. At first he used hypnosis in efforts to directly remove the annoying symptoms as well as the disturbing thoughts and memories. Finding this ineffective, Freud gave up the effort and resigned himself to merely listening and letting the patient talk. In the case of one Lucie R., Freud found he could not induce hypnosis at all. Having already noted that even in hypnosis some patients resisted frank discussion, Freud was forced to consider alternative approaches. Recalling Bernheim's demonstration that the subjects' recollection of their experiences while hypnotized is only apparently forgotten in the waking state and can be recovered if the hypnotist insists, Freud began to use more active measures on his patients. He would place his hands on the patient's head and loudly state with strong conviction, "through the pressure of my hands it will come to mind!" This simple maneuver, to his great astonishment, enabled many patients to produce much the same content he previously thought could only be obtained under hypnosis.

Freud called this "a trick," and after a short time discarded it and replaced it with the now familiar psychoanalytic couch routine, wherein the patient is asked to lie down, relax, and freely associate about his problems. Freud never returned to the use of hypnosis. There were a number of reasons for this. First, his use of hypnotic techniques was unusually crude. Originally he combined hypnosis with physical massage, and by his own admission he was not a successful hypnotist—being very impatient and easily discouraged by any resistance to induction. Another cause for his disenchantment with hypnotism was the eventual recognition that the forgotten experiences themselves did not constitute the core of the neurosis, nor their recovery into consciousness the cure. Instead, it was the patient's need to avoid the pain and anxiety that caused and kept the memories repressed that was the fundamental problem. For further discussion of Freud's avoidance of hypnosis, consult Milton V. Kline's *Freud and Hypnosis: The Interaction of Psychodynamics and Hypnosis* (1958). Years later, in 1919, Freud modified his rejection of hypnosis, and in one of his later works spoke of the need to blend "the pure gold of analysis plentifully with the copper of direct suggestion" (Kline 1958).

Unfortunately, Freud's early rejection of hypnosis slowed the development and understanding of hypnotherapy. Psychoanalysis became the rage, and hypnosis might have been neglected totally were it not for the interest of Pierre Janet (1859–1947), a French neurologist and psychologist who originally opposed the use of hypnosis but became one of its greatest advocates after he discovered its relaxing effects and their usefulness in promoting healing. Janet, along with Morton Prince in the United States, hypothesized that there were multiple layers of consciousness and hidden underlying causes for manifest pathological symptoms.

The growth of interest of psychoanalytic theory and the discovery of chloroform, ether, and other chemical agents to produce chemical anaesthesia resulted in a temporary decline in the medical uses of hypnosis. By the early 1900s hypnosis had faded from the scene, except for the work

A 1923 photograph of Emile Coué.

of a few investigators like Janet, and that of the "new Nancy school" and psychology of Emile Coué (1857–1926). Coué, who was born in Troyes and grew up there, studied pharmacy in Paris and in 1882 returned to Troyes and opened a drugstore. In 1884 Coué married a young lady from Nancy, and one day while visiting his wife's parents attended a lecture by Dr. Liebault at the Nancy School of Hypnotism. What Liebault said interested him greatly, but was not entirely satisfying. For the next few years Coué studied and practiced hypnotic suggestion according to Liebault's technique. As a pharmacist Coué also noticed that waking suggestions given along with medication brought about cures, whereas the medication alone was often quite ineffective. Coué studied and brooded over these matters for a number of years and after his drug business afforded him enough money to retire he turned to the study of hypnotic techniques full-time. Since his drug business automatically furnished him with subjects, Coué began to hold hypnotic clinics right in his store. He quickly discovered, however, that only about one tenth of his hypnotized patients were completely hypnotized. He also noted that certain drugs seemed to have a beneficial effect that could not be explained by the medical potency of the drugs themselves. In other words, it was apparent that the benefit must have been brought about through the mind of the patient and not through the drugs. He gradually came to the conclusion that hypnotism was not necessary. Moreover, many people were afraid of hypnotism and refused to subject themselves to it. Its usefulness was therefore limited.

Working and thinking along these lines, Coué gradually abandoned the use of hypnotism and for it substituted his own ideas about *suggestion* and finally *conscious autosuggestion*. As the hypnotist suggests to his patients while they are supposedly unconscious, Coué insisted that his patients give themselves suggestions while fully conscious, i.e., awake. In 1910 Coué and his wife moved to Nancy, built a home, and opened it, free of charge, to anyone needing help. People flocked to this "new Nancy school" in increasing numbers. By the beginning of World War I, Coué was treating as many as 15,000 patients a year. The psychologist Charles Baudouin was so impressed with Coué's work he wrote a book, *Suggestion and Auto-Suggestion* (1920), that brought both Coué and himself a measure of attention but did not have a great impact, and Coué's truly revolutionary ideas and insight were generally ignored by students of hypnosis, who failed to recognize in his arguments and ideas the answer to the mystery of the curative powers of hypnosis.

In his books *Self Mastery Through Conscious Autosuggestion* (1922) and *My Method* (1923), Coué even denies that the discovery of autosuggestion is his own idea. He says that Pythagoras and Aristotle taught it and in the Middle Ages Saint Thomas Aquinas stated: "Every idea conceived by the mind is an order which the organism obeys." The mind, Thomas added, can also engender a disease or cure it. Aristotle taught that

A vivid imagination compels the body to obey it, for it is a natural principle of movement. Imagination, indeed, governs all the forces of sensibility, while the latter, in its turn, controls the beating of the heart, and through it sets in motion all the vital functions; thus the entire organism may be rapidly modified. Nevertheless, however vivid the imagination, it cannot change the form of a hand or foot or other member. (quoted in Coué 1922, p. 8)

This, according to Coué, contains two of the fundamental principles of autosuggestion:

(1) The dominating role of the imagination, and
(2) The results to be expected from the practice of autosuggestion must necessarily be limited to those coming within the bounds of physical possibility.

Coué also argues that he is no healer and that all he can do is teach others to cure themselves and to maintain perfect health. How to do it? First, from our birth to our death, he says, we are the slaves of suggestion. It is an all-powerful tyrant over whom we must take command. To do this, we must first realize that our subconscious—a permanent, ultrasensitive photographic plate that nothing escapes and the source of creation and inspiration—is infinitely larger than our conscious part and dominates the conscious part. For example, Coué says, imagine sucking a lemon and your mouth instantly will start to water. What has happened is that under the influence of the idea your glands went to work just as if you had bitten into a real lemon. Thus, it is impossible to separate the physical from the mental, the body from the mind; not only are they dependent upon each other, they are really one. But the mental element is always dominant and our physical organism is governed by it, so that we actually make or break our own health according to the ideas at work in our subconscious. We can freely implant in the subconscious whatever ideas we desire. Moreover, the imagination dominates the will. Whenever imagination and will come into conflict, it is always the imagination that triumphs. Try to do something while at the same time saying, "I cannot do it," and you will see this truth confirmed. The mere idea of inability to accomplish a thing paralyzes the will power. This is the psychology of a baseball player's batting slump. In autosuggestion the exercise of the will must be strictly avoided—except in the beginning, when getting started. For example, suppose you are suffering from insomnia and try autosuggestion. Unless warned ahead of time, you might repeat to yourself phrases like: "I want to sleep; I will sleep; I am going to sleep." All the while you will be making desperate efforts to coax sleep. This is futile. The very fact of exerting effort will convert the effort into a force acting contrary to your original suggestion, with the result that you will toss and turn all night.

In other words, you should be quiet and passive and let the imagination do its work alone, unhindered. The imagination is more powerful than you know. For example, no one would have the slightest difficulty walking along a foot-wide plank placed on level ground. But put the same plank across the space between two forty-story buildings and few would be able to cross without falling to their death. No clearer proof to the power of an idea could be desired. Coué uses another example, of a cook who rushes into the middle of a large dinner party and announces she mistakenly mixed arsenic with the food. Several diners are immediately seized with stomach pains, which stop only when the cook comes back and reports a false alarm. Again, the power of the imagination and suggestion are supported. By such effects on our subconscious, we can help the curative powers of our body become more effective. Our physical organism is controlled by the subconscious self, which obeys every suggestion and sends it as an order to all parts of the body, and then the body reacts. Then the only obstacle to the accomplishment of the suggested operation is the intervention of the conscious will, or reason. But how can we acquire control of our subconscious self? The answer, Coué says, is so simple that people make fun of it. But its logic is irrefutable.

> All that is necessary is to place oneself in a condition of mental passiveness, silence the voice of conscious analysis, and then deposit in the ever-awake subconscious the idea or suggestion which one desires to be realized. (Coué 1923, p. 26)

Coué recommends that every night before dropping off to sleep one should murmur in a low, clear voice, just loud enough to be heard by oneself, this little formula: "Every day, in every way, I am getting better and better." Recite this phrase over and over twenty to thirty times or more. Don't worry if cynics scoff and think what you're doing is foolish and puerile. It is a mere suggestion, but it will set off some powerful internal forces. Moreover, a general suggestion of this nature is really more effective than specific ones, because our subconscious knows more than we ever can about our physical organism. Leave it to the subconscious and avoid all effort. Concentration is valuable and necessary when conscious reasoning must be performed, but fatal to the success of autosuggestion. There is no need to struggle to impose your suggestion. These precepts do not mean, however, that suggestion cannot be used for specific conditions like the alleviation of pain, insomnia, or stammering.

To cause pain to vanish, Coué recommends the following procedure:

Rub the affected spot lightly but rapidly with your hand, at the same time repeating in an undertone, so swiftly as to make of it a mere gabble the words "ca passe" (pronounced "sah pass"). In a few minutes the pain should disappear, or at the very least be considerably diminished. The reason for gabbling the words is to avoid the risk of any other extraneous or contrary thought slipping in through fissures which might result from a more distinct but slower diction. For the same reason I advise English-speaking people to stick to the French version; it being much easier to say "ca passe" quickly than the longer and more awkward expression "it is passing" or "it is going." (Coué 1923, pp. 30–31)

To cure insomnia, Coué has the sufferers proceed in another way:

Having settled themselves comfortably in bed they will repeat (not gabble) "I am going to sleep, I am going to sleep," in a quiet, placid, even voice, avoiding, of course, the slightest mental effort to obtain the desired result. The soporific result of this droning repetition of the suggestion soon makes itself felt; whereas, if one actually tries to sleep, the spirit of wakefulness is kept alive by the negative idea, according to the law of converted effort. Insomnia indeed affords a striking demonstration of the disastrous effect of the exertion of the will, the result of which is just the contrary of the one desired. (Coué 1923, pp. 31–32)

To eliminate stammering and lack of confidence, Coué asks:

What is the cause of stammering? Merely the fear or the idea that one is going to stammer. If you can substitute for that idea the conviction or the suggestion that you are not going to stutter, that if you can say ten words without stuttering there is no reason why you should stumble over the eleventh, then you are cured.

Nervousness, timidity, lack of confidence and still worse, nervous phenomena, can be eradicated by the practice of autosuggestion, for they are simply the consequences of self-suggestion of a wrong, unnatural character. Those who suffer from such infirmities must set up a different train of suggestions by saying, "I am not nervous; I am well and full of confidence; All is going well." In a fit of anger, try the effect of suddenly murmuring "I am calm," and you will be surprised. (Coué 1923, pp. 32–33)

Coué also indicates that many organic diseases can be influenced and many unpleasant symptoms can be eliminated, even when the disease may continue. Sciatica, gastric trouble, constipation, asthma, and headaches are all readily helped by autosuggestion. Even diabetes and tuberculosis can be influenced positively. In general, most any ailment of the body can be helped via autosuggestion, though not necessarily cured.

Within the history of hypnosis, Coué's work is significant in a number of respects. First, he emphasized that the presence of a suggester is not essential to suggestion; it is enough to have a subject. Second, by placing the major or primary emphasis on suggestion itself as the only truly significant factor in hypnosis, he focused attention where it belongs. Third, since the new Nancy method does not involve the induction of profound hypnosis, he demonstrated such induction is not necessary for either suggestions or suggestive therapy to be effective. In his own words, "Profound hypnosis suspends the voluntary activity which is impairing the chances of success." Fourth, he demonstrated very clearly and effectively that "without having recourse to the classical methods of hypnotic suggestion, we obtain results more remarkable than those secured by earlier hypnotists. So simple is the procedure that few can fail to master it" (Coué 1923). Thus, he established that autosuggestion can be and often is more effective than hypnosis. In fact, there is good evidence that all so-called "hypnosis" is self-hypnosis, i.e., autosuggestion. In Coué's words, "Induced suggestion is not a violation of the subject's individuality; it is a means of training the subject's powers of autosuggestion." Fifth, Coué was remarkably prescient in calling attention to the importance of purely psychological factors in hypnosis and getting rid of the older physiological concepts. Sixth, Coué also called attention to the fact that suggestion plays a significant role in amnesia, opinion and attitude formation, social contagion, hallucinations, and in social influence and the placebo effect. For example, amnesia, or memory loss, may, like the revival of memories, be the outcome of suggestion. Among hypnotists, a classical experiment suggests to the subject that he has forgotten his own name. But the hypnotism merely exhibits in an exaggerated form phenomena which occur in the normal state, and there is no essential difference between heterosuggestion and autosuggestion. A name we know as well as our own may elude us just when we want it the most. The harder you struggle to recover it, the more it eludes you. When you give up and leave your mind at rest, the name returns. The failure to remember is often due to an antecedent suggestion. Spontaneously and unconsciously you make an autosuggestion which aggravates the amnesia. Then the greater the effort, the more complete the forgetfulness. If this happens very often you begin to believe you are losing your memory. This idea now adversely affects your memory, simply because you think it and because your attention is now focused upon the idea of amnesia.

In the domain of opinion and attitude formation, the role of suggestion can also be disastrous. You hear an opinion stated and you are well aware that it is nothing more than an opinion. Time passes and you no longer think about it. Then one day you are called upon to decide the question and you discover that your mind is made up, you hold the very opinion you heard expressed before, although you never received any proof of it. Similarly, readers of newspapers read statements which are merely hearsay or even lies. However, the seed planted in them when they read germinates in the subconscious, and without realizing it their minds are made up, and they believe their opinion is based upon both reason and evidence. It is well known that by repeating tales to themselves and others, people come to believe and defend the tales, and thus are duped by their own falsehoods.

Coué also tells the story of a maniac who pricked a woman shopping in a dry goods store with a needle, injecting some liquid that caused the affected part to swell. The newspapers published a few lines about it, and the following day two or three similar cases were reported. On following days, the number of victims continued to grow, until over a hundred women reported similar attacks. While suggestion seems to have created more "prickers," autosuggestion seems to have created more victims, i.e., women were led by sheer imagination to believe themselves "pricked" and to feel the pain of a sudden jab. The authorities could, of course, find no evidence for many of these reported assaults.

Similar epidemics are reported in the annals of social psychology, i.e., mass psychogenic illnesses and disorders due to suggestion. One modern example is what is called "assembly line hysteria." This strange malady strikes suddenly and affects more women than men. It spreads so quickly that an assembly line or an entire plant may have to shut down within days or even hours of the first appearance of the disorder. One morning in an electronics plant in Ohio a woman assembly line worker began to feel dizzy, light-headed, and nauseous, and complained of muscular weakness and difficulty in breathing. In a matter of minutes some forty-odd other employees were being treated in the company's dispensary for the same symptoms. The illness spread quickly to the point that the plant had to close. Investigators at first thought the cause was something in the air—some chemical, gas, virus, or other infectious agent. However, physicians, toxicologists, and industrial hygienists conducted an intensive search and found nothing that would explain the disorder. They soon found that the phenomenon was due to suggestion and social contagion, with no physical cause whatsoever. Examples of such social contagion are reported quite frequently, year in and year out. Similarly, a report of a UFO sighting is immediately followed by a rash of other UFO sightings. Again, the same social phenomena of suggestion and autosuggestive contagion is at work.

Coué and his champion, Charles Baudouin, also stressed the fact that suggestion can not only create hallucinations or wholly imaginary sensations, it can also more easily and more frequently cause *partial* hallucination. That is, we often take real sensations and transform them until they correspond to one of our fixed ideas. For example, we take, from among our real sensations those which conform most closely to the image preexisting in our minds. Then, between the sensation and the image, a compromise takes place that becomes a more or less complete identification. If we are waiting for or expecting an attack, any noise at all, of the wind in the trees or of the settling of an old house, is mistaken for the enemy's approach. Hallucinations are rarer in the visual than in the auditory domain, undoubtedly owing to the fact that whereas a vision is often contradicted by the presence of external objects—I know that two objects cannot occupy the same space at the same time—the image of a noise is not absolutely contradicted by the sensation of a real noise, since they tend to blend. Though complete hallucinations are rarer in the visual domain, what Coué and Baudouin call "hallucination by compromise" is very common. Phantoms, for example, usually make their appearance in the night, when the outlines of objects are comparatively hazy and indistinct, so that forms are more elastic to the imagination. "A pillar, the white wraith of a fountain, the bright space between two trees—such things constitute the material substratum of a phantom, owing to the resemblance between their appearance and that of the imagined winding-sheet" (Baudouin p. 54). The phenomenon is even easier to understand when it is suggested during the process of hypnosis. Here a complete hallucination is by no means very rare, but it is interesting to note that the subject often prefers hallucination by compromise. The imagination, instead of inventing the delusion out of whole cloth, makes use of elements borrowed from "real" sensations. This is not only more economical but is also an example of the psychological law of least effort.

Finally, Coué anticipated very early the importance of indirect suggestion in medicine in the form of the placebo effect and "a good bedside manner." In his words,

If a doctor, after examining the patient, writes a prescription and hands it over without comment, the drugs thus ordered are not likely to do much good. But when the practitioner explains that this medicine or that must be taken in such or such conditions and it will produce such and such effects, the results thus described will rarely fail to occur. . . . In my opinion, whenever a patient consults a doctor, the latter should always order some drug or other, even if drugs should not be really indicated. For the ordinary patient goes to see a doctor in the expectation that the doctor will prescribe a drug which will cure. Only in exceptional cases does the patient know that hygienic measures are of the first importance, that he will be cured by following a regimen. These seem to him trifling matters. What he wants is a bottle of medicine.

Should the doctor merely prescribe a regimen and fail to order any medicine, the patient is likely to be discontented. He will be apt to say to himself that since he has not been given any medicine he has wasted his time. Very often he will seek other advice. I consider, therefore, that the doctor should always prescribe some medicine for his patient. He should avoid ordering advertised specifics, whose chief value is derived from the very fact of wide advertisement. He should write his own prescriptions, for the patient will have far more confidence in these than in X's pills or Y's powders, which can be bought from any druggist without a prescription. (Baudouin, pp. 324–325)

In this manner, suggestion can be methodically employed without the patient being aware of it.

Since the Age of Hippocrates, medical science has known about the mind-body linkage and the effects of suggestion in what we now call "the placebo effect" (from the Latin "I will please"), i.e., medications that are chemically inert, yet somehow achieve remarkable cures. Placebo medications, which are usually sugar pills, are thirty to sixty percent as effective as the real medicines they replace. What this means is that the placebos allow us to mobilize our body's capacity for self-healing. This is really what accounts for the impressive effectiveness of these ersatz medications. Sir William Osler, the "Father of American Medicine," referred to the placebo effect as "faith." In his words,

Faith in drugs and methods is the great stock in trade of the profession. . . . While we doctors often overlook or are ignorant of our own faith cures, we are just a wee bit too sensitive about those performed outside our ranks. Faith in the gods or saints cures one, faith in little pills another, hypnotic suggestions a third, faith in a plain common doctor a fourth. The faith with which we work . . . [is] the most precious commodity. . . . (quoted in Berger 1988, p. 289)

Osler's "faith," however, we now know involves a very complex network of glands in the brain, chemical messengers and hormones, the entire immune system, and hundreds of complex biochemical reactions. The physical effects of suggestion can be powerful indeed. Berger, in his bestseller *What Your Doctor Didn't Learn in Medical School*, reports on a Harvard Medical School study in which heart surgeons treated one group of angina patients by the standard surgical procedure of suturing in an internal chest artery to ease the burden on the heart, while for another group the surgeons only pretended to perform the operation, i.e., they gave anaesthesia, made a chest incision, then stitched up again without performing the full procedure. The surgeons intended to spare the patients in the second group a serious operation and use suggestion alone to relieve the symptoms. If suggestion failed, they could go ahead with the real procedure later. As the surgeons surmised, there was virtually no difference whatsoever in healing effects between the two groups. Patients in both groups showed a sixty to ninety percent reduction in pain, an enhanced quality of life, and improved performance on the electrocardiogram. According to the author, the real surgery produced "no greater benefit than the sham operation!" Another group of researchers repeated this experiment with another group of eighteen patients. Again, neither the doctors who judged the improvement nor the patients knew which operation had been done. Yet *all* of the patients with the sham operation enjoyed marked improvement. There are well over a hundred controlled experiments of this nature in the literature. All reported similar findings, underlining the power and potency of suggestion in bringing about positive physical effects.

About the same time that Coué and Baudouin were practicing at the new Nancy school in France, a German physician and student of Freud by the name of Oskar Vogt was carrying out studies of sleep and hypnosis and the clinical potential of some autosuggestive techniques. During his studies Vogt discovered that intelligent patients could induce certain autosuggestive states, and these states could be relaxing and refreshing, and they helped his patients call up psychoanalytically valuable material. Vogt also discovered that the smarter you are the easier it is to learn to relax and control your body. Stimulated by Vogt's work, another German physician, Johannes Schultz, in 1905 began to study under what circumstances normal people were able to hallucinate. He discovered that most of his subjects who were being hypnotized and given hallucinatory suggestions reported a similar sequence of subjective experiences, despite the fact that quite different hypnotic induction techniques were used. The most consistent self-observations were the experience of "a feeling of heaviness in the extremities," which almost invariably was followed by a sensation of warmth.

Schultz concluded that muscular relaxation (heaviness) and vasodilation (warmth) are the two basic factors responsible for bringing about a hypnotic state. His next step was to find out if the psychophysiological mechanisms responsible for inducing heaviness and warmth could be mobilized through autosuggestion, and thus a state of amplified relaxation similar to the hypnotic state would result. Following months of trial and error, Schultz worked out the essential features of what he subsequently called "autogenic training." For a period of twelve years Schultz applied his autogenic therapy to several hundred cases of patients suffering from a variety of psychosomatic and neurotic disorders. This therapy has been very successful in standing the test of time. Since its beginning in the 1920s, over 600 publications dealing with autogenic training and techniques have appeared, most of them in Europe, where it has been much more popular than in the United States. Schultz's *Das Autogenic Training* first appeared in 1932 and was in its twelfth edition in 1970, having sold well over a million copies in its various editions. The American edition, *Autogenic Training: A Psychophysiologic Approach in Psychotherapy* (1959) has sold well and is definitely in the tradition of Edmund Jacobson's *Progressive Relaxation*, published in the 1930s and still in print, and G. D. Read's classic *Childbirth Without Fear* (1984).

Schultz believed that the core of hypnosis is a "central shift" that can be activated either psychically or physically. He recognized that hypnosis really was the art of inducing the patient to make what he called a "self-hypnotic shift," and that it was important to make sure that the patient did not go totally to sleep. Schultz knew that if a patient takes a "long relaxing bath" an "organismic psychosomatic shift" occurs, and he wanted his patients to make this shift themselves. He knew this was possible because Vogt had shown that people could "place themselves in a hypnotized condition by means of a complete shift" (Schultz 1959). Schultz recognized that patients had to relax and then induce in themselves the feelings of heaviness and warmth. This led to six physiologically oriented steps which are the core of autogenic training. These six steps are to be carried out, effortlessly and passively, in the "dozing driver position," i.e., sitting up straight in a chair, forearms resting on one's thighs, head down, chin on chest. As you go through each of the steps, you give yourself verbal suggestions:

1. For muscular relaxation of the striate musculature

Repeat several times:
—My right arm is heavy
—My left arm is heavy
—My right leg is heavy
—My left leg is heavy

2. For vasoconstriction and vasodilation (coolness and warmth)

Repeat several times:
—My right arm is warm
—My left arm is warm
—My right leg is warm
—My left leg is warm

3. For cardiac regulation

Place hand over heart and repeat several times:
—My heartbeat is calm and regular
—My heart rate is slowing down
(This can be enhanced by a verbal description of how the heart's action is experienced)

4. For respiration

Repeat several times:
—My breathing is calm
—It breathes me
—My breathing is slow, calm, and regular

5. For abdominal warmth

Place hand over center of stomach and repeat several times:
—My solar plexus is warm
—My stomach is warm

| 6. For cooling of forehead, head, and face | Repeat several times:
—My forehead is cool
Imagine the wind is blowing over your forehead or that you are lying face down in the snow, or a piece of ice is on your forehead, and repeat several times:
—My head and face are cool |

Once the relaxed state is attained, the trainee then goes on to more advanced meditative and visualization exercises, physiologically oriented and organ-specific, all designed to meet a host of pathological problems. Schultz, and especially his coauthor and colleague Wolfgang Luthe, also have developed a number of intentional formulae designed to influence mental functions and mental deviations (Luthe 1969). Just as Coué emphasized, a strongly inhibiting element in learning autogenic therapy is the will. If the student tries too hard or puts out excessive effort, he cannot possibly succeed. This "principle of paradoxical intention" works in such a way that any conscious effort of the will stimulates and reinforces the opposite impulses. The person who can relax and "let go" and surrender himself to the moment will succeed. As a number of therapists have pointed out, the relaxation method inherent in autogenic therapy, i.e., concentrative self-relaxation, is made to order for the modern stressed and harassed individual suffering under the pressure of time.

With the advent of World War I and the need to treat hundreds of men suffering from battle neuroses, hypnotherapy became a valuable tool for physicians and psychiatrists. The work of Dr. William Brown and Dr. J. A. Hadfield was particularly noteworthy and should be remembered in this connection. Hypnotherapy was again employed successfully during World War II in numerous similar cases and was also widely used along with narcosynthesis. Here the hypnotic trance was used to treat veterans who had repressed traumatic battlefield emotions and to remove symptoms directly. Under hypnotherapy the soldiers remembered the traumatic situations and were then able to release the negative emotions surrounding them. In 1945 Louis Wolberg published *Hypnoanalysis*, a landmark study in which he combined both hypnotherapy and psychoanalysis.

In the early 1930s Clark L. Hull, then an experimental psychologist at Yale University, began a systematic series of precise, controlled experiments designed to determine the exact nature of hypnosis. Hypnotized and unhypnotized subjects were exposed to the same experimental conditions so that Hull could determine what differences were due to hypnosis or the induction process. In his book *Hypnosis and Suggestibility* (1933) Hull concluded that the only significant difference between the hypnotized and unhypnotized state lay in the fact that subjects under hypnosis were more suggestible, i.e., hypnosis is a state of hypersuggestibility. Hull's efforts laid the foundation for hundreds of other carefully controlled experiments in the laboratory and for the development of standardized, objective research procedures in this area. However, Hull himself was quite pessimistic about possible advances in the study of hypnotic phenomena. According to Hull, the difficulties of doing research in this area, the fundamental elusiveness of the phenomena involved, and the subtlety required in the experimental controls all work against the experimenter. In his words, "These difficulties are so great that to enter seriously on a program of investigation in this field is a little like tempting fate; it is almost to court scientific disaster. Small wonder that orthodox scientists have usually avoided the subject!" (p. 403). Prophetic words indeed, as subsequent research efforts have shown.

All sciences have descended from magic and superstition, but few have been as slow as hypnotism has been in shaking off the occult associations of its origin. Also, as Hull noted, from the beginning, "the nonphysical notions of the nature of mind fostered by metaphysical idealism probably favored hypnotism's mystical affinities, and mysticism is notoriously incompatible with controlled experiment" (p. 18). Moreover, from the beginning the dominant motive in this area has been the curing of human ills and the limitations of clinical practice often interfere with the requirements of experimentation. Historically, the result has been literally hundreds of case-history reports, pseudoexperiments, quais-experimental studies, and sloppy, poorly controlled, and irreplicable experiments that have consistently contradicted each other, as well as complicated and confused the picture to the point that—if one believes everything he reads in the literature—no explanation of any sort is possible.

Despite such problems, the interest in and study of hypnotic phenomena increased dramatically after World War II, and in 1949 the Society for Clinical And Experimental Hypnosis was founded here in the United States. A decade later it became an international society. In 1959 The American Society for Clinical Hypnosis was formed. For both these groups professional journals also followed. In 1955 the British Medical Association passed a formal resolution approving hypnosis as a valid therapeutic technique for treating psychoneuroses and for relieving pain in surgery and childbirth. Both the American Medical Association and the American Dental Association in 1958 made policy statements recognizing hypnosis as a legitimate form of treatment in medicine and dentistry and recommended training in hypnosis for students in these areas. In 1960 The American Board of Hypnosis in Dentistry was established to certify practitioners trained in the use of hypnotic suggestion, and at approximately the same time the American Psychological Association established two divisions dealing with hypnosis, one for experimental hypnosis and the other for clinical practice. Recently, the two divisions have joined into one, Division 30, the Division of Psychological Hypnosis. Today hypnotherapy is employed in general medicine, obstetrics and gynecology, dermatology, forensic medicine, clinical psychology, dentistry, and psychiatry, as well as in numerous other mental health and mental hygiene situations where the stress and strain of modern living has brought on a host of psychosomatic complaints.

Summary and Conclusions

The story of hypnosis has been one of human error and more of a tragedy of errors than the comedy that others have referred to. From its very beginning with Mesmer, the physician, the aim and ambition of nearly all the students of hypnotic phenomena was to find ways to heal and cure the sick and suffering. One might assume that after 200 years of the study and application of hypnosis just about everything there is to know about the subject would already be known, and all we would need to do nowadays is just apply this knowledge. Unfortunately, a great deal of what we currently think we know is false information, and a great deal of what we need to know has not been and is not now being researched. Fortunately, with regard to using hypnotic procedures to heal the sick, just about any method, technique, or procedure that is placed in the hands of someone calling himself a healer can, on occasion, if conditions are right and the disorder has a psychological basis, bring about if not an outright cure then at least an alleviation of symptoms. Mental factors influence the human body. Paralysis, deafness, blindness, constipation, indigestion, palpitation of the heart, etc., may and do occur as symptoms of disturbances which are purely psychological. If and when they are of this origin, they may be remedied, temporarily at least, *by any form of suggestion that inspires confidence.* Miracles of recovery have occurred by the mere touching of a holy relic: the lame have thrown away their crutches, the halt have walked, the blind have seen. Similar so-called miracles have been performed with medicinal substances, with metal rods, electrical appliances, sugar pills, mere philosophical discussions, even prayer. In fact, with any form of treatment that catches and holds the attention of the ailing one and somehow or other inspires a belief in recovery. But none of these sorts of things are miracles. The most striking symptom of any physical disease is pain and anxiety. Both of these are subjective and entirely mental. Any form of treatment in which the patient has implicit faith will relieve both pain and anxiety, but the mere treatment of symptoms does not get at the underlying disease, unless of course the symptoms are the disease. While the pain of a toothache can be stopped by suggestion, an abscess may form and systemic disease will follow, regardless of the presence or absence of pain.

Suggestion, i.e., hypnotherapy, thus has its limits. Ignorance of the self-reparative ability of the human body as well as failure to recognize the mind's influence on the subjective symptoms of the disease—as well as confusion about cause and effect—have misled the hypnotists of the past. In the past, when a person fell ill, a remedy was given or a course of treatment prescribed. In due time the patient's health was usually regained. Here were all the ingredients for an application of false logic: the person was ill, he or she was treated, they recovered; therefore, they recovered because of the treatment. Before the days of the controlled experiment, the recovery was taken as proof that the treatment cured the disease.

It is sad to say, but even today this same sort of false logic is still encountered daily in psychological clinics and psychotherapists' offices. An even greater logical error, however, is that of assuming that because one particular method of treatment or medication helped one patient, the same medication or treatment will help another patient, since the symptoms appear to be the same and all human bodies are alike! After all, what do you expect, we are practitioners not laboratory scientists, and we do the best we can. True, indeed, but so did the mesmerists, who were not experimental scientists, either. The moral is clear: no one today has any right to gloat over the mistakes and errors of his or her predecessors. Perhaps the only truly unforgivable sin is made by those who, knowing the truth, persist in error.

Several years ago Abraham Meyerson pointed out that while the soul, a metaphysical immortal part concerned with mind and consequently with madness, has pretty much disappeared from psychiatric concern, separation of the mind from the body still offers a formidable obstacle to scientific progress. While belief that the celestial bodies are somehow concerned with the individual's health, as well as the idea that an anthropomorphic god in an anthropocentric universe is concerned about the welfare of the individual and his conduct, have largely disappeared as active forces in the diagnosis and treatment of diseases of the body, the doctrine that mental abberations are punishment from God or the gods has persisted. Linked with this idea of punishment, we find the notion of supernatural possession—the idea that devils, demons, witches, and the like inhabit the bodies and minds of psychotics. Although one rarely sees or hears of patients who believe themselves inhabited by the souls of others, it is highly likely that such reports will now start to increase due to the fact that recently a number of psychologists and psychiatrists have published books supporting the idea of possession (e.g., Allison and Schwartz 1980; Crabtree 1985; Fiore 1987; and Guirdham 1982). The mentally ill also reflect the temper and opinions of their times. In the days of witchcraft, the schizophrenics believed they were persecuted by witches; in Mesmer's time magnetism was believed to be a favorite persecutory technique. Later on it was radio that the paranoiac believed was torturing him, then TV, and more recently, aliens

in flying saucers. Incredible as it may seem, the idea of witches and possession was so powerful among sixteenth-century physicians that Pope Innocent VIII appointed two Dominicans in Germany to undertake measures
to wipe out the crime of sorcery. The devastation which these ruthless clerics
wrought for the honor of the Church is mind-boggling. In the province
of Trier alone, 6,500 men, women, and children were put to death within
a short period of time. Luther and Melanchthon both attributed illnesses
of all kinds to demons and ghosts. Fortunately there were a few rational
souls who opposed such nonsense. John Wier (1515–1558), the father of
modern psychiatry, argued, "It is usually melancholy and hysterical women
with disordered power of imagination who start the rumors and ideas of
possession and witchcraft" (Myerson 1936, pp. 421–422). Weir was cas-
tigated severely for his view. Fortunately, after the sixteenth century the
ideas of possession and witchcraft waned—among physicians at least.

By far the greatest error in the history of hypnotic phenomena, we
believe, has been the very common one of taking a few natural facts, inflat-
ing them into a broad generalization, developing neat logical systems based
on the generalization, then blinding oneself to all contradictory knowledge
and experience, seeing only that which one wishes to see. Then, identify-
ing with his theory, the proponent becomes ego-involved and turns into
a specialist, an authority on the subject. He becomes dogmatic because his
supporters expect it; they need his expertise and convictions and confidence.
They cannot believe that he does not know everything there is to know
about his subject. The "expert" plays up to their expectations, talks with
conviction, authority, and logic, whereas in truth he has neither certainty,
truth, nor logic. The great Charcot was a prime example of this scenario.
The scenario was played out again with hypnotists from Mesmer on and
is still a prevalent pattern. Dr. William C. Coe (1989) published a fascinating
survey of contemporary research clearly illustrating the role of sociopolitical
factors—specifically the effects of power, prestige, and ego—in determining
the outcome of the controversy over the state/nonstate nature of hypnosis.
This issue will be discussed at length in the following chapter.

3.

Hypnosis: Recent and Contemporary Views

In his book *Hypnosis and Suggestibility* (1933), Clark Hull pointed to a number of what he termed "pseudo-difficulties" that have confused and confounded those interested in developing a theoretical understanding of hypnotic phenomena. In other words, one of the reasons that we have gone so long without fully understanding what is going on in hypnosis is that just about every kind of behavior remotely resembling the phenomenon has been called by this name. Catalepsy, for example, has never been an essential or inherent characteristic of hypnosis. It can be induced in hens, rabbits, toads, roosters, lizards, and other animals by nonviolent means and can be induced in humans by means of violent stimulation or physical restraint. Tonic immobility, in other words, can be caused by a number of things other than hypnosis. Hypnosis and suggestion effects generally show positive practice effects, whereas animal catalepsy shows negative practice effects. Whereas hypnotic abilities seem to be acquired, animal immobility seems innate and unlearned. Catalepsy is, therefore, anything but peculiar to hypnosis. We also know that hypnosis is not true sleep, and that hypnosis is not a pathological condition. Finally, Hull concludes,

> We have fairly good experimental evidence indicating that hypnosis is a state of dissociation neither in the sense that persons in that state can carry on two independent mental processes more effectively than when in the non-trance state, nor in the sense that persons susceptible to hypnosis can in the normal state carry on two independent mental processes relatively more readily than can persons who are not susceptible to hypnosis. It is true, however, that specific suggestions to that effect are able in hypnosis to make certain

memories inaccessible to voluntary recall, and to reduce to varying degrees the responsiveness of the organism to painful stimuli. These are, in a certain sense, dissociation phenomena, but by no means such in the sense of a dissociation into two independent "minds", one conscious and the other subconscious. These latter notions are probably survivals of an outworn metaphysics which conceived the mind as a kind of disembodied spirit which was associated with a living body only by reason of a kind of metaphysical coincidence. It seems fairly clear, however, that the dissociations observed are not inherent and essential to the hypnotic state, but are always the result of direct or indirect suggestion. Accordingly, they must find their explanation in the general theory of suggestion, rather than in the theory of hypnosis as such. (p. 390)

Not only were these words prophetic of arguments to come but they are also of great importance to our understanding of what hypnosis is all about. Hull concluded his work in this area with his definition of "hypnosis" as

Professor Clark L. Hull in his laboratory. *(From* Hypnosis and Suggestibility, *D. Appleton-Century Co., 1933.)*

a state of relatively heightened susceptibility to prestige suggestion. . . . The difference between the hypnotic state and the normal is, therefore, a quantitative rather than a qualitative one. Despite the widespread and long-standing belief to the contrary, the author is convinced that no phenomenon whatever can be produced in hypnosis that cannot be produced to lesser degrees by suggestions given in the normal waking condition. (p. 391)

This statement by Hull may well have been responsible for launching a long and varied series of experimental investigations by many researchers, comparing the performances of individuals in the alleged "hypnotic state" with the same and different individuals who were wide awake. Hull's work also launched the modern era of hypnosis theory and research using the controlled experiment as the paradigm. It would be pleasing to be able to say that the major issues and problems surrounding hypnotic phenomena were all resolved now that the emotional and subjective biases surrounding theoretical stands were brought into the cool objective atmosphere of the experimental laboratory. Unfortunately, this was not the case, nor has it been the prevailing condition in our own time, either. Any careful investigation representing one theoretical position was immediately challenged with another experimental investigation representing a second theoretical position, followed by a third experiment representing a third position, and so on. Then, following the experimental investigations, we had a number of position papers, i.e., critical reviews of the experimental procedures and deficiencies, justifying the theoretical position of the critic and denigrating the work of his adversaries. Typical of such exchanges was the in-print debate between J. P. Sutcliffe (1960), a theoretically neutral experimentalist (if such an animal exists), and Andre Weitzenhoffer (1963, 1964), who at that time was a strong advocate for and a believer in the viewpoint of hypnosis as a special and unique state of consciousness.

Prior to Hull's work and the work of P. C. Young (1926), methodological rigor was not characteristic of studies of hypnosis. In fact, most of the work prior to Hull's experimental approach was of the clinical "single case," anecdotal, or "naturalistic" variety, and what theory there was was based on such evidence. Rather than dignifying the many concepts and ideas as theory, it would have been more accurate to consider them as points of view.

Recently there have been a number of investigators who have looked for physiological correlates of the hypnotic state and by combining the psychological and physiological hoped to offer a viable theory of hypnotic phenomena. Kubie and Margolin (1942, 1943, 1944) used their subject's respiratory rhythms as conditioned sleep-inducing techniques to produce a state of partial sleep or hypnogogic reverie by which they could recover the client's repressed memories. At times they supplemented this technique with barbiturates, benzedrine, or bromides. They minimized the usual interpersonal contact between the client and the doctor and the use of suggestive manipulations on the doctor's part. In 1908 Sidis used monotonous stimuli such as reading, singing, and the rhythmic beats of a metronome to induce hypnoidal states in children. In 1909 Silverer used hypnogogic dreams to study subconscious symbology as a means for testing some of Freud's concepts. Both of these workers seemed to regard hypnosis as somehow related to sleep. Others seemed to see hypnosis as a product of physical changes in various parts of the brain. Pavlov, the father of the conditioned reflex, claimed that hypnosis was a complex conditioned reflex due to a spread of cortical inhibition built up over a period of time after exposure to soporific stimulation. In 1944 Salter, expanding upon the Pavlovian model, argued that from infancy on words like "sleep" serve as triggers for automatic reactions as a result of associative reflexes. Words, he argued, serve as the bells of conditioned responses. Individual differences in susceptibility depend upon how easily one is conditioned. Some aspects of the theory of Kubie and Margolin have a distinctly Pavlovian ring, in taking hypnosis to be the result of the creation of a focus of central excitation surrounded by other areas of inhibition. Hypnosis is considered a condition of "partial sleep" in which one or more channels of communication with the external world are kept open. It is generally agreed, however, that if any physiological correlaters of hypnosis exist, they have yet to be discovered. The search for them continues despite the mountain of evidence against their existence (Barber and Chaves 1974; Wagstaff 1981; Memmesheimer and Eisenlohr 1931; Barber and Hahn 1963; Crailsneck and Hall 1959; Edmonston and Pessin 1966; Gorton 1949; Sarbin and Slagle 1972).

Spanos, in his 1982 review of hypnosis and its physiological correlates, concludes as follows: "The available evidence indicates that reliable physiological correlates of hypnotic susceptibility have not been demonstrated." Another problem with the physiological evidence is that the changes that have been observed are not specific to hypnosis per se (Sarbin and Slagle 1972; Edmonston 1979). Moreover, many are due to the effects of relaxation alone, as Edmonston has shown.

Individuals who are said to be hypnotized cannot be differentiated from waking subjects on any normal or standard physiological measure, including heart rate, blood pressure, peripheral blood flow and volume, blood clotting, respiration rate, skin and oral temperature, skin resistance, palmar potentials, cortical potentials, electromyogram, electrooculogram, and EEG measures. Furthermore, subjects who have been hypnotized differ from each other on such physiological measures as much as they do from subjects who are wide awake. This does not mean, however, that relaxation—especially profound relaxation—can not and does not make a difference in these physiological parameters. Relaxation does reduce heart rate, respiration rate, tonic muscle tension, and skin conductance, and progressive relaxation is a wonderful way to bring about these desirable changes in the emotionally stressed.

And relaxation is more effective than hypnosis in bringing about the changes, since it is solely the relaxation in the hypnosis that has any effects of any kind whatsoever.

P. Davies (1988) in his review of some of the physiological effects of hypnosis emphasizes that all our behavior, including the decision to role-play, is a product of a brain which is a physiological structure operating on neurological principles. Even thoughts are physiological events. The real question, though, is "whether or not the process known as hypnosis may give rise to physiological or biochemical events which cannot be produced without hypnosis! The answer, in general, is almost certainly not" (p. 62).

Nevertheless, Davies finds it most difficult to admit defeat and closes with the lament that, "After all, if you cannot be certain your subject *is* hypnotized then you equally cannot be certain that he is not!" Were we to leave out the word "hypnotized," we would face no less a challenge. We would still have to explain how verbal instructions can mediate physiological change, including relaxation. Fortunately, Davies recognizes the existence of psychology and he concludes with the profound statement: "The underlying issue seems to be whether or not hypnosis is a special state. This is to miss a major point; namely, that a wide range of physiological responses can be modified without direct physiological or pharmacological intervention" (Davies 1988).

If physiology alone cannot account for hypnosis, what else may do so? Strange indeed have been the far-fetched explanations. The psychoanalyst Ferenzi in 1916 hypothesized that hypnosis was but a resurgence of the parent-child relationship, and he contrasted the persuasive versus the authoritarian methods of hypnotic induction, calling the former "mother hypnosis" and the latter "father hypnosis." In this regard, the personality theorist Robert W. White (1941) postulated that hypnotic susceptibility is positively correlated with deference, or the need to yield willingly to the wishes of a superior person, and is negatively correlated with the need for autonomy or dominance. White also sees hypnosis as "meaningful goal-directed striving." And the goal in this instance is to behave like a hypnotized person, as this condition is defined by the hypnotist and understood by the person being hypnotized.

White's ideas are important because of his motivational hypothesis and because of his influence on Theodore Sarbin, who not only extended the motivational approach but was also the father of the antistate, social-cognitive behavioral view of hypnosis. Sarbin sees hypnosis as a form of "role-playing" on the part of the subject. According to Sarbin, the introspective accounts of actors and hypnotic subjects are identical, and the stage director is doing the same thing that the hypnotist is doing. Sarbin argues that both the actor and the hypnotic subject must have some talent if they are to do the job adequately. In his view, hypnosis is nothing other than a culturally defined

Theodore X. Barber in his study. Dr. Barber's work has markedly advanced our understanding of hypnosis. He has devoted his professional career to experimental and clinical research in hypnosis and to training professionals in the use of hypnosis and self-hypnosis. He has also published over 180 articles in scientific journals on hypnosis and related topics as well as a number of books which have served as landmarks in the history of hypnosis and hypnosis research.

influence situation and there is no need whatsoever to postulate any kind of special state or any kind of trance phenomenon.

Sarbin's arguments were followed by Theodore X. Barber, who has spent the past thirty-some years attempting to establish that there is no such thing as hypnosis, i.e., there is no sort of special state or alternate or unique kind of reality that a subject "enters, goes deeper into, and comes out of as a result of suggestion." According to the traditional and orthodox views:

1. There exists a state of consciousness that is fundamentally different from the waking state and the deep sleep state. This distinct state is called "hypnosis," "the hypnotic state," or a "trance."
2. Hypnosis may occasionally occur spontaneously, but it is usually induced by certain kinds of procedures that are labeled "hypnotic inductions" or "trance inductions."
3. Hypnosis is not a momentary condition that lasts only for a few seconds. On the contrary, when a person has been placed in a hypnotic state, he remains in it for a period of time and he is typically brought out of it by a command from the hypnotist, such as "Wake up!"
4. There are levels or depths of hypnosis; that is, hypnosis can vary from light to medium to very deep.
5. As the person goes deeper into hypnosis, he becomes increasingly responsive to a wide variety of suggestions, including suggestions for anaesthesia, age regression, hallucination, and amnesia.

Barber and his associates Spanos and Chaves (1974) flatly and firmly reject all of the above assumptions and also reject any and all comparisons of the hypnotized person with a sleepwalker or somnambulist. Hypnotized people have normal EEGs, they are attentive to suggestions, they remember what occurred while hypnotized unless they are given suggestions to the contrary, and they think and imagine along with the suggestions being received.

The use of hypnosis for curing warts and other kinds of skin disorders has been offered as another proof that hypnosis contains some sort of magic ingredient not found elsewhere. Work by Barber, Wagstaff, and particularly the experimental work by Memmescheimer and Eisenlohr (1931) has shown that suggestion in the form of a placebo alone is equally as powerful as hypnosis in the removal of warts. Other studies, such as those by Barber, Spanos, and Chaves (1974) have failed to demonstrate that suggestion, hypnotic or otherwise, has any effect on warts. We must also take into consideration that all warts disappear in time—six weeks to six months. A good proportion of subjects given no suggestions also lost their warts. In general, all such attempts purporting to show physiological correlates of being hypnotized come to us in the form of case reports from individual clinicians involving one or two subjects or from the conclusions of poorly designed and controlled experiments.

Barber, Spanos, and Chaves (1974) point out that response to suggestions can be easily obtained without any hypnotic induction at all. In fact, "task motivational instructions" actually work better than standardized induction procedures involving suggestions of relaxation, drowsiness, and sleep. In motivation instructions the subjects are told: (1) your performance will depend on your willingness to try to imagine vividly and to experience those things that will be described to you; (2) previous subjects have been able to imagine vividly and to have the experiences that were suggested to them when they put aside the idea that this is a silly or difficult thing to do; (3) if you try to imagine to the best of your ability, you will experience a number of interesting things and you will not be wasting either your own or the experimenter's time. Through a series of experiments the authors found that there were eight separate variables which enhanced responsiveness to suggestions. They were:

1. Defining the situation as "hypnosis."
2. Removing fears and misconceptions about hypnosis.
3. Securing cooperation, i.e., making the subject want to comply or convincing the subject he couldn't resist.
4. Asking the subject to keep his eyes closed, i.e., removing visual distractions.
5. Suggesting relaxation, sleep, and hypnosis.
6. Elaborating and varying the wording and tone of suggestions.
7. Coupling suggestions with actual events to enhance suggestibility.
8. Preventing or reinterpreting subject failure to act in accordance with suggestions.

All of the above variables heighten or augment suggestibility because they give rise to positive attitudes, motivations, and expectancies toward responding to suggestions and to being hypnotized, which in turn give rise to a willingness to think and imagine along with whatever is being suggested.

By far the most impressive and convincing aspects of Barber's work has been a series of experiments over a period of a dozen years or more demonstrating that any human activity or behavior that has been attributed to hypnosis—particularly the unusual ones, such as anaesthesia, hallucination, enhanced muscular performance, amnesia, post-hypnotic effects, unusual perceptual effects such as deafness, blindness, color-blindness, etc., and physiological effects such as heart acceleration, curing warts, pain suppression, etc.—can be brought about in the normal waking subject without hypnosis just by direct suggestion. As Barber notes, thousands of books, movies, and magazine articles have woven the concept of "hypnotic trance" into the mainstream of common knowledge. Yet there is almost no scientific support for this concept. Since Mesmer's day it has been assumed the hypnotic trance state is real, i.e., that there is some reliable way to tell whether or not a person is hypnotized, some simple physiological measure such as brain waves, eye movements, pulse rate, etc. Yet no such physiological test exists, no way we can distinguish a hypnotized individual from an awake one. As Barber says, the notion of the hypnotic state is circular, i.e., state theorists say that a person obeys suggestions because he is in a hypnotic state. How do you know he is in a hypnotic state? Well, "because he obeys the suggestions."

The only reasonable challenges to Sarbin's and Barber's contentions have come from those state theorists who argue that hypnotized subjects are able to do things they would not or could not do while awake. It's hard to imagine that anyone could maintain his role-playing or even a high level of motivation while undergoing major surgery. Both clinical and experimental evidence clearly shows that the hypnotic induction procedure followed by suggestions for pain insensitivity is highly effective in diminishing reports of pain. Robert Sears, for example, found that people's reports of pain from a sharp point could be reduced by twenty-two percent under hypnosis when compared with waking controls. This ability to go through an ordinarily painful experience without reporting pain is so extraordinary that some theorists have suggested this as a test for the presence of hypnosis. Because of the importance of analgesia and the problem of pain we will take up the subject again at length in a later chapter. Suffice it to say here that it is not hypnosis per se that reduces the pain but the effects of relaxation and anxiety reduction, and suggestion and distraction serve as the active agents.

Regarding the other unusual or bizarre things that people do in hypnotic situations, Barber shows how wide-awake individuals accomplish the same things with ease. A standard stunt that nearly all stage magicians perform is to hypnotize a member of the audience and make his body so rigid that he can be stretched out like a plank, with his head on one chair and his ankles on another. It is assumed, of course, that in the ordinary waking state no one could do this. This is not true at all. Kreskin has shown how anyone can do the same thing while wide awake by just holding the body tense. The stunt is capped by having another person remove his or her shoes and then stand on the suspended person's chest. In such a case, usually the person playing suspension bridge has his shoulders on one chair and his calves on another. This simple stunt has nothing whatsoever to do with hypnosis.

While it is true that some people can be made to hallucinate under hypnosis, many people can be made to hallucinate without it. In Barber's laboratory at the Medfield Foundation, subjects were told to close their eyes and listen to an imagined phonographic playing of "White Christmas." Later, when asked what they had experienced, about half of them said they heard the music clearly. Similar results were reported when the subjects were asked to see a cat in their lap. Reports of the hallucination were the same no matter whether the subjects were hypnotized or were merely given task motivation instructions. Another amusing example comes from a series of experiments having to do with hypnotic deafness. After suggesting to the subject that he is deaf, the hypnotist then asks "Can you hear me?" Some of the subjects immediately respond, "No, I can't hear you," revealing that they can hear. If the hypnotist then says, "Okay, now you can hear again," and if the subject then responds normally, it is obvious that he was able to hear all along. There are, of course, other ways to tell if someone is really deaf. One way is to have a person with normal hearing read a paragraph aloud, record his words, and then delay them about half a second before playing them back. This built-in delay is very disconcerting and causes marked speech disruption, stuttering, and slurring of words. Subjects who are given suggestions of deafness and who then claim they are deaf will halt, stutter, and slur their words when subjected to the delayed playback, just as if they had normal hearing.

For years psychotherapists have claimed that with hypnotic regression their clients could summon long-forgotten memories and reexperience past events as if they were yesterday. Barber and his researchers carried out an objective test of this claim by having students learn a list of nonsense syllables at the beginning of the semester. Toward the middle of the semester the students were given suggestions to regress back to the time they had originally learned the syllables. Some of the subjects were given the regression suggestions after they were exposed to a hypnotic-induction procedure and others were given the regression suggestions under waking conditions. Neither the hypnotic-regressed nor the waking-regressed group differed significantly in their ability to recall the syllables from a control group who were simply asked to recall them without being given any suggestions about regression.

It has also been claimed that hypnotized subjects are remarkably more responsive than waking control subjects to suggestions that they will perform certain acts after an experiment. Barber has shown that in every study in which this assumption has been put to empirical test it has been disconfirmed. For example, when Damaser (1964) gave her subjects postcards with the suggestion they would mail these cards back to the experimenter one card each day, more cards came back from the subjects who were given the instructions while they were wide awake than from those who were given the suggestion under medium or deep trance states.

Another assumption is that upon waking from a hypnotic trance the individual is unable to remember what happened. In fact, the opposite is the case. Nearly all subjects remember the events that took place unless they are specifically asked not to remember. Even then subjects may claim they have forgotten, but the use of subtle detection measures shows they have not. Patten, for example, gave subjects practice in complex addition problems and then suggested they forget the practice sessions. All subjects said they had forgotten the practice. He then gave them new addition problems. If they had truly forgotten the practice sessions they would not show the improvement that typically comes with practice. His subjects did show improved performance, however, indicating that they had retained the skills learned during the practice sessions.

Barber also strongly objects to the use of the term "trance" and to acceptance of the hypnotic subject's report that "he felt like he was hypnotized" as evidence for the presence of hypnosis. Barber feels that whether or not a subject reports himself hypnotized depends on a host of very subtle variables such as the wording and tone of the questions asked, etc. Using the Stanford Suggestibility Scales, for example, Barber reports that when his subjects were asked, "Did you feel you could not resist the suggestions?" all subjects said "yes." But when similar subjects were asked the opposite, "Did you feel you could resist the suggestions?" over half still said "yes." Whether or not a person says he has experienced the hypnotic state also depends, says Barber, on what he thinks hypnosis is supposed to be. For instance, some subjects believe that hypnotized individuals are not aware of what is going on and are in a zombie-like trance. When they find that they do not lose awareness and do not become zombie-like when they are exposed to hypnotic induction procedures, they conclude immediately that they were not hypnotized, even when they responded to all of the hypnotist's suggestions. Other subjects think that hypnosis is a state of relaxation. If the subjects feel relaxed during the experiment, they report that they feel hypnotized, even when they are unresponsive to the suggestions. If subjects are told repeatedly that they are becoming relaxed, drowsy, and sleepy, they may appear to be in a hypnotic trance—they may look passive and lethargic, they may stare blankly when they open their eyes. But if the hypnotist tells them to sit up, act alert, and not look lethargic, they will appear normal while continuing to respond to suggestions. In other words, Barber insists, the way a person behaves under hypnosis depends in part on what he expects the hypnotic state to be like. Barber cites a demonstration by Martin Orne— one of the most distinguished experimenters and theorists in this area— who in a lecture to a psychology class gave the students a list of the typical effects of hypnosis, but also included an extra one, that under hypnosis one's dominant hand becomes cataleptic, i.e., it will stay in whatever position it is placed. Later, when he put these students under hypnosis, over half of the students showed catalepsy of the dominant hand. Accordingly, Barber insists that it is difficult to study hypnosis in adults because most of them already have their own idea of what hypnosis is. These conceptions have, unfortunately, been conditioned and shaped by the cultural mythologies we encounter in books and movies and on TV. We "know" that hypnotized people behave irrationally, Barber says, with glassy stares, zombie-like movements, and sluggish, mechanical speech. Therefore, when it is suggested we are under hypnosis, no wonder that we tend to behave exactly as expected.

Barber has also shown that simply by telling a subject that he is in a hypnosis experiment rather than in some other kind of study, one can increase his suggestibility. His suggestibility can also be increased by repeatedly telling him he is becoming relaxed, drowsy, and sleepy. But, as Barber has repeatedly shown, hypnotic procedures are not necessary to produce a high level of suggestibility. When Barber exposed his waking subjects to the task motivational instructions—i.e., when he exhorted them to cooperate and to try to think and vividly imagine the things to be suggested—they showed just as high a level of suggestibility as subjects exposed to the hypnotic induction procedures. Over a period of several years and a number of experiments, Barber has shown that both hypnotic subjects and waking control subjects are responsive to suggestions for analgesia, age-regression, hallucinations—both positive and negative—and amnesia, provided they have positive attitudes toward the situation and are motivated to respond. The subjects listen to the suggestions without analyzing them critically, and they allow themselves to think about and imagine the things that are suggested, i.e., that they are insensitive to pain, that they have returned to childhood, or that they hear music playing. Subsequent developments have clearly shown that imagination and an individual's ability to fantasize are important variables—if not the most important—in determining any and all of the behavior that has previously been attributed to hypnosis.

Barber's own personal experiences with pain has led him to be able to control it. Having his experimental subjects focus on the pain sensations and learn to think of them as merely sensations with their own unique and interesting properties, or thinking of themselves as numb and insensitive, or thinking of something very pleasant, turned out to be very effective not only in his laboratory subjects but for Barber himself when he visited his dentist. Interviewing his regression subjects, Barber found when they were given suggestions to regress to childhood, they tried to think of their bodies as small and themselves as children in specific situations they remembered from childhood. They also tried to inhibit contrary or negative thoughts— they refused to think about really being adults sitting in the lab. Barber and his experimenters found that they, too, could experience age-regression by doing the same thing as his subjects, i.e., thinking of themselves as children, inhibiting contrary thoughts, and vividly imagining childhood situations.

Barber's theoretical position is very clear: the idea that there is a state of consciousness called "hypnosis" is totally unnecessary. No test of any kind has ever been able to demonstrate the existence of the hypnotic state; therefore, there is no reason to assume there is such a state. Hypnosis, Barber believes, will eventually go the way of ether in physics or phlogiston in chemistry—concepts that were popular for a while but have long since been abandoned. Finally, Barber accuses the state theorists of using the term "hypnosis" to explain everything and thus explain nothing at all. When he reported (1964) that people were more suggestible when they were told it would be easy to respond than when they were told it would be difficult, the state theorists argued that the statement "it will be easy" produces a deeper hypnotic trance than the statement "it will be difficult." Had the data come out the other way, Barber says, the state theorists would have assumed that the suggestion that the task would be difficult produced a deeper trance. When Barber's experiments showed that his control task motivated subjects could also exhibit strong responses to suggestions of analgesia, hallucinations, amnesia, and so forth, the state theorists argued that Barber's controls had spontaneously slipped into hypnosis without knowing it. Since the state theorists believe that the hypnotic state is necessary to produce these effects, the fact that the effects occurred means that the subjects must have been hypnotized! Hypnosis can thus explain anything and everything.

Fantasy-Prone Personality

In the early 1980s Barber and a collaborator Sheryl C. Wilson uncovered a fascinating group of individuals whom they alternately termed "fantasy addicts" or "fantasy-prone personalities" (Wilson and Barber 1983). The first group of fifty-two women they interviewed in their search for good hypnotic subjects revealed twenty-seven that were excellent. With one exception, these excellent subjects also had a profound fantasy life in which their fantasies were as "real as real," even hallucinatory, and their involvement in fantasy played an important role in producing their superb hypnotic performance. According to Wilson and Barber, this study also led to the discovery that there is a small group of individuals—possibly four to six percent of the total population—who fantasize a large part of the time, and typically "see," "hear," "smell," "touch," and fully experience what they fantasize. These Barber and Wilson call fantasy-prone personalities primarily because their extensive and deep involvement in fantasy seems to be their basic characteristic. Their other major talents, i.e., their ability to hallucinate voluntarily, their ability to be easily hypnotized, their vivid memories of their life experiences, and their talents as psychics or sensitives, all seem to derive from or grow out of their profound fantasy lives. This fantasy-prone syndrome, Wilson and Barber suggest, has important implications for understanding such diverse phenomena as hypnosis, out-of-body, re-ligious, visionary, parapsychological, and near-death experiences, mind-body relations, and creativity. Most importantly, Barber and Wilson stress, these fantasy-prone subjects with a propensity for hallucinatory fantasy are as well-adjusted as the normal population. In fact, it appears that the life experiences and skill developments that underlie the ability for hallucinatory fantasy are independent of the kinds of life experiences that lead to psychopathology. Nearly all of the original groups of subjects studied by Wilson and Barber proved to be happy, popular, competent, and loving, with high self-esteem. Though some had adjustment difficulties, all fell within the broad average range of social adjustment. Of course, it may be that some individuals with psychopathology are also fantasizers. Wilson and Barber suggest that during the days of Charcot and Janet a substantial proportion of those diagnosed as hysterics were also fantasizers, and today some of those diagnosed as schizophrenics may also be fantasy-prone personalities. Some schizophrenics, however, even though they may "hear voices," do not otherwise have a profound fantasy life.

Follow-up research on such individuals by Lynn and Rhue (1988) and others using over 6,000 college students has furnished general support for Wilson and Barber's construct. Fantasizers were found to differ significantly from nonfantasizers on measures of hypnotizability, imagination, waking suggestibility, hallucinatory ability, creativity, psychopathology, and childhood experiences. They did find some differences between their subjects and Barber and Wilson's. They found less correspondence between fantasy-proneness and hypnotizability than Barber and Wilson. They found hypnotic responsiveness to be possible even in the absence of well-developed imaginative ability, and they found that not all fantasizers were highly hypnotizable. Fantasizers also recalled being physically abused and punished to a greater degree than other subjects did, and they reported experiencing greater loneliness and isolation as children. Lynn and Rhue also found much more diversity in the fantasy-prone personalities than Wilson and Barber surmised. It should also be noted that Wilson and Barber's work is largely derivative of and follows from the work of Josephine Hilgard at Stanford and her concept of "imaginative involvement," to be discussed later in this chapter.

Ernest R. Hilgard and the State Theorists

Among Barber's strongest and most vocal opponents have been the distinguished psychologist Ernest R. Hilgard and his wife Josephine. Hilgard must be considered—if anyone can be—the dean of American psychologists. For well over fifty years he has done as much as anyone to make psychology a respected and respectable science on the world stage. In 1949 he was elected president of the American Psychological Association, and after he came to Stanford University from Yale in 1933 he proceeded to make the Psychology Department there the best and most distinguished in the nation.

Ernest R. Hilgard and Josephine R. Hilgard met and married at Yale, where they earned their Ph.D.s in psychology. He moved to Stanford University in 1933 and was head of the Psychology Department from 1942 to 1951 and dean of the Graduate Division from 1951-55. He was president of the American Psychological Association in 1949. When he became emeritus professor in 1969, he held professorships in both psychology and education. She completed her M.D. at Stanford in 1940, and served as clinical professor of psychiatry from 1948 until her death in 1989. She worked closely with her husband in his hypnotic research laboratory and has collaborated with him on numerous articles and several books on hypnosis.

Over the years he has authored dozens of books and hundreds of articles in the fields of learning and education. Many of these are considered by professional psychologists classics and landmarks in their special fields. In the late 1950s, Hilgard developed a deep interest in the subject of hypnosis. In 1957 he developed a research program and an experimental laboratory devoted to its study. Josephine has also had a distinguished career in medicine and psychiatry, and she too developed great interest in hypnosis and its personality correlates. Together, the Hilgards ran the hypnotic research laboratory from 1957 until 1979. During this time they published hundreds of individual studies and a number of books on the subject. Best known perhaps are his *Hypnotic Susceptibility* (1965) and *Divided Consciousness: Multiple Controls in Human Thought and Action* (1977), her *Personality and Hypnosis: A Study of Imaginative Involvement* (1970), and their *Hypnosis in the Relief of Pain* (1975). The Hilgards feel strongly that people like Barber and the others who are skeptical about hypnosis have delayed our understanding of the phenomenon and have kept research in the field from attaining scientific respectability. In Hilgard's words:

> Those who today hold back hypnosis from advancing into a position of sound scientific respectability are of several kinds. There are those who exploit hypnosis for entertainment purposes, and thus give it a bad name as an area of serious interest. . . . Then there are the enthusiastic practitioners of hypnosis who claim too much for it. . . . Most troublesome are those with scientific creden-tials, fascinated enough by the problems of hypnosis to experiment and publish in the field, but making a special point of holding a skeptical, debunking attitude. Skepticism in science is a good thing. . . . But it is possible to turn this skepticism into a kind of sophistry, a "scientism" that feeds upon itself and gives the impression that all the answers are already known. . . . By an odd turn of logic it is the "skeptics" who now have a dogmatic, assured position, and all who think there are unsolved problems are the "credulous." (1971, p. 568)

Hilgard's criticism would be much more telling had not Barber and the other skeptics backed up their claims with experiment after experiment. Nevertheless, Hilgard has made some pointed and valid criticisms of the "nothing but" exposés, i.e., hypnosis is nothing but relaxation, nothing but suggestion, etc., and some staunch defenses of the state position. With regard to Sarbin's role theory, Hilgard argues that in many points it is nearly indistinguishable from classical hypnotic state theory. Individual differences in role-playing ability are clearly recognized and these are essentially the kinds of differences measured by the standard hypnotic scales. Moreover, there are some hints of unconscious role-playing, in which case the difference between a role theory and a conventional state theory are hard to find. With regard to Barber's antecedent variables, e.g., attitudes, expectations, motivation to cooperate, etc., Hilgard says these variables are intrusive in all psychological experiments and clever experimenters deal with them successfully. We know that if it is made very easy for subjects to respond, or if they are practically forced to respond affirmatively, they comply, but if the criteria are made more severe, positive responses become more limited in number. This sort of phenomenon is bothersome in all experiments, but it only means the experimenter has to discover some ingenious ways to overcome the "noise" in the system. In Barber's case, Hilgard argues, he has made the "noise" the major contributor and finds nothing substantial about hypnosis. What Barber fails to consider, Hilgard says, is individual differences. And if, as Barber claims, the motivational or other instructions were more important than the individual difference variables, we would expect the differences in the instructions to distort the correlations obtained between sets of scores under different, conditions—but they do not. Therefore, Barber's motivational variables are not as influential as the individual difference variables. And thus, in a field of study like hypnosis, in which the highly susceptible are in a minority and may respond quite differently than the less susceptible to experimental procedures, Barber's standard experimental design tends to underplay the role of hypnotic susceptibility, and so conceals as much as it reveals.

Hilgard places much credence in the use of hypnotic susceptibility scales such as his and Weitzenhoffer's Stanford Hypnotic Susceptibility Scales. These are essentially work samples of hypnotic responsiveness. The items for form A of the Stanford scales are shown below:

Suggested Behavior	Criterion For Passing (yields a + score)
1. Postural sway	Falls without forcing
2. Eye closure	Closes eyes without forcing
3. Hand lowering (left)	Hand lowers at least 6 inches by end of 10 seconds
4. Immobilization (right arm)	Arm rises less than 1 inch in 10 seconds
5. Finger lock	Incomplete separation of fingers at end of 10 seconds
6. Arm rigidity (left arm)	Less than 2 inches of arm bending in 10 seconds
7. Hands moving together	Hands at least as close as 6 inches after 10 seconds
8. Verbal inhibition (name)	Name unspoken in 10 seconds
9. Hallucination (fly)	Any movement, grimacing, acknowledgment of effect
10. Eye catalepsy	Eyes remain closed at end of 10 seconds
11. Post-hypnotic (changes chairs)	Any partial movement response
12. Amnesia test	Three or fewer items recalled

As Hilgard notes, when the number of items passed is totaled we find that the distribution of hypnotic susceptibility is not much different from other individual difference measures—scores for most subjects fall around the middle or average value. Of further importance is the fact that these susceptibility scores turn out to be quite stable over the years, i.e., childhood scores are about the same as adult scores for the same individuals.

Based on this finding, Hilgard is even more convinced that in hypnosis we are dealing with something that is fixed, permanent, and "real." In other words, there is indeed such a thing as hypnosis and hypnotizability. If so, then we ought to be able to relate the hypnotizability trait to other kinds of personality-relevant behavior. Josephine Hilgard looked into this possibility and found clear evidence that a history of imaginative involvement in childhood correlated highly with a later susceptibility to hypnosis.

By "imaginative involvement" is meant an absorption in some kind of fantasy so real that ordinary reality is set aside; the imaginary experience is felt as actually being lived, and is savored as such. This involvement differs from a pathological condition in that it is a temporary involvement, and reality ties are readily restored. The scientist who enjoys science fiction without any detriment to his career as a critical scientist furnishes an illustration of such flexibility. Moreover, the area of involvement differs from person to person.

This kind of imaginative involvement, in which the child departs from ordinary reality through fantasy, can be found in reading, dramatic viewing or participation, aesthetic interest in nature, adventure, religion, and some but not all forms of athletics. Activities requiring high degrees of alertness are not included, but activities like long distance running are. One of Josephine Hilgard's totally unexpected findings of considerable significance was the existence of a positive correlation between severe discipline or punishment in childhood and later hypnotizability. Many of the punished children, it seems, turned to imaginative escape as a way of dealing with the punishment. Such imaginative adventures made them, in later years, very easy to hypnotize. Two things are important to note: Josephine's finding are very much in line with Wilson and Barber's discovery of the fantasy-prone personality pattern, and are also relevant to the findings regarding the alleged "multiple-personality" cases that have emerged over the last few decades. In eighty to ninety percent of multiple-personality cases, severe abuse and mistreatment during childhood occurred.

The capacity to imagine vividly may also have something to do with hypnotic hallucinations and with the splitting of consciousness as in "automatic writing," in which a hand may write something while the person is carrying on a conversation or is otherwise unaware of what the hand is doing. This splitting is sometimes described as "dissociation," and is another way of thinking about aspects of hypnosis.

Of considerable relevance in this context is Hilgard's notion that hypnosis always involves processes of "dissociation" which occur in response to simple suggestions from the hypnotist. Dissociation is seen by Hilgard as a sort of "splitting" of the mind into voluntary and involuntary parts. Hypnosis involves the involuntary part, as simple acts that were performed voluntarily now become automatized or involuntary. In the Hildgards' book on the hypnotic relief of pain (1975) it is taken for granted that all hypnotic responding is involuntary. Also central to Hilgard's concept of hypnosis is his notion of a "hidden observer," a little man inside the passive and involuntarily responding hypnotized subject who is watching what is going on and taking notes. In other words, according to "neo-dissociation" theory, as Hilgard calls it, our cognitive or thinking systems become dissociated. At one level a person is unaware of the toothache pain, but at another level that the first level is unaware of, the pain is felt. When Hilgard puts his subjects into hypnosis during the induction period he tells them that

> When I place my hand on your shoulder (after you are hypnotized) I shall be able to talk to a hidden part of you that knows things are going on in your body, things that are unknown to the part of you to which I am now talking. The part to which I am now talking will not know what you are telling me or even that you are talking. . . . You will remember that there is a part of you that knows many things that are going on that may be hidden from either your normal consciousness or the hypnotized part of you. (Knox, Morgan, and Hilgard 1974, p. 842)

Since these instructions were given during an experiment on hypnotic analgesia, some fascinating results were obtained. The ordinary reports given by the subjects following the above induction instructions showed little evidence of pain, but when the hypnotist put his hand on the subject's shoulder it became clear from the "hidden observer" that the subject was experiencing a great deal of pain. In fact, in the case of one type of pain, the amount experienced was little different from the amount experienced with the subject wide awake. Superficially, this behavior smacks of some variation of Sarbin's role-playing, or in Wagstaff's words,

> a rather elaborate game that some subjects feel obliged to play in order to give the hypnotist what he wants. Perhaps at our present state of knowledge, genuine automatic talking, out of awareness, under hypnosis, could be viewed as no more likely on a priori grounds than an explanation of these results in terms of voluntary compliance on behalf of the subjects. (Wagstaff 1981, p. 181)

If compliance itself is not an all-or-nothing affair, some subjects might feel that they are really hypnotized and can pass the hypnotic scale items. But, Wagstaff argues, this cannot be used as an argument that the subject's analgesia reports are genuine or that he or she really can dissociate the "hypnotized" part from the "hidden" part, so that neither is aware of the other.

Hilgard also criticizes Barber on the grounds that his motivational instructions produce excessive demands for compliant behavior. Hilgard says the fact that under these demands some subjects complied more than without them does not mean that the changes observed under hypnotic instructions were brought about in the same way as those observed under the motivational instructions. Two roads from an initial to a final destination, Hilgard says, are not the same road merely because they get to the same place. Hilgard also argues that the controversy over the hypnotic state is largely irrelevant, and is like other controversies such as that over instinct versus learning, etc. As an investigator, Hilgard prefers to define a "domain" of hypnosis, which then becomes a field of investigation, and also saves the terms "hypnosis" and "hypnotic state" as terms of convenience, so that there is no need to defend such terms. Hilgard would also exclude certain behaviors from this domain, particularly those behaviors due to social suggestibility, gullibility, placebo effects, etc., which have been shown not to correlate with hypnotic responsiveness. Though suggestibility is clearly one aspect of hypnotic behavior, hypnotic suggestibility can be differentiated from the total domain of suggestibility.

By no means is Hilgard rigidly set in his position. He admits that the state concept is a difficult one, since it is hard to know even if a person is asleep. Sleep, we now know, is by no means a single, simple physiological state. Similarly, it is hard to know if and when a person is intoxicated by alcohol. Blood level alone is not a reliable indicator. In Hilgard's words,

> I can get along without a state concept, if it proves too troublesome, still investigating the domain of hypnotic-like behaviors. . . . There are genuine difficulties with the concept of the hypnotic state or trance. . . . For example a subject can be told, prior to terminating hypnosis, that his arm will remain in a raised position, but he will be unaware of it. Then he is aroused from hypnosis in the usual way, feels wide awake and refreshed and . . . will report himself as not hypnotized. What then can be made of his "dissociated" arm? Can an arm be hypnotized, when he is not? Obviously the concept of "state" is not very useful here, unless it is broken down to cover partial dissociated activities. I am inclined to believe that the notion of dissociation ought to be revived, and it may turn out to be more useful that the concept of state or trance. (1971, pp. 575–576)

Martin Orne: Confabulation and Trance Logic

Another very distinguished psychologist and psychiatrist (he has both M.D. and Ph.D. degrees) who falls in the state theory camp is Dr. Martin T. Orne. Dr. Orne is director of the Unit For Experimental Psychiatry, The Institute Of Pennsylvania Hospital, Philadelphia, as well as a professor in the Department of Psychiatry at the University of Pennsylvania School Of Medicine. Over the years Dr. Orne has made a large number of truly significant contributions to our understanding and use of hypnosis, particularly in the medical and forensic areas. For many years there has been a widely held belief that hypnosis is a very useful tool for helping people recover material from their past that has been forgotten. For at least the last two or three decades hypnosis has been used in a number of criminal cases to help improve the memory of victims and witnesses in order to gain information needed to solve a crime. While Martin Reiser has been a strong advocate of the use of hypnosis for such purposes (Reiser 1980, pp. 39–40), Orne has been opposed to such use of hypnosis and repeatedly has warned the courts of the dangers of misuse in this context.

Orne has consistently called attention to two characteristics or "by-products" of the hypnotic process that tend to work against a hypnotized subject's ability to remember accurately. The first is what Orne and others have called the "social demand characteristics" of the hypnotist-subject situation. By this is meant the strong desire of the subject to supply the information demanded of him by the hypnotist, which often causes the subject to supply information that is inaccurate or information the subject himself is not sure is true. To say it another way, the subject may be so eager to please that he will tell the hypnotist anything in order to make the hypnotist happy. An additional problem is the fallibility of normal human memory. Recent evidence regarding the nature of memory has shown that all human memories—no matter how accurate they might seem—are flawed to some extent (Bolles 1988).

These phenomena, coupled with the sometimes insistent demands of the hypnotist, may give rise to another very common phenomenon: the error of confabulation, in which the subject honestly tries to supply accurate information, but because of faulty memory is unable to do so, and so supplies inaccurate or misleading information. It is important to note that there is no attempt on the part of the subject to lie or misrepresent in this case. The mistake is wholly an honest one. The subject believes he has remembered accurately. Then, on the other hand, many subjects deliberately, for one reason or another, lie. For the above reasons, normal human memory is considerably more reliable than memories induced by the use of the hypnotic process, and Orne has shown this over and over in a series of excellent studies and well-controlled investigations over the past three decades.

In a recent survey of what is currently known about the use of hypnosis to reconstruct memories, Orne *et al.* (1988) state:

> It appears that the criminal justice system's traditional use of a jury as a trier of fact, of the adversarial process, and of cross-examination has served as the best available means of defining "truth." However, this process can

be subverted by a technique, such as hypnosis, that greatly facilitates the reconstruction of history, that allows an individual to be influenced unwittingly, and that may catalyze beliefs into "memories." The resultant testimony may then be presented under oath by an honest individual who is convinced of the accuracy of what may well be pseudomemories. Paradoxically, then, the same attributes of hypnosis that make it a useful adjunct to psychotherapy also create the greatest obstacles to its use in the forensic domain. At the present stage of scientific knowledge, we cannot distinguish between veridical recall and pseudomemories elicited during hypnosis without prior knowledge or truly independent proof. (p. 55)

Orne concludes with the observation that legal testimony based on hypnosis or on any other procedures that invite fantasy, diminish critical judgment, and increase the risk of pseudomemories, should be prohibited. Orne was also the principal author of a position paper by the American Medical Association's Council On Scientific Affairs, published in the Journal of the American Medical Association in 1985, reviewing the scientific status of using hypnosis to refresh the memory. This position paper is essentially the same as what Orne has said above.

With regard to the nature of hypnosis, however, Orne is convinced that there is "something there" beyond compliance, suggestion, and rapport. Orne accepts the fact, however, that the willingness of the individual to adopt the role of hypnotic subject and accept the hypnotist's suggestions uncritically are prerequisites to the use of this technique.

Along with Hilgard, Orne sees hypnotizability as a relatively stable and enduring trait with a near-normal distribution in the general population. Consequently, nearly everyone is capable of experiencing some of the effects of hypnosis—especially if it is carried out in some sort of facilitating context. Among the important "facilitators," Orne notes, are: the level of trust placed in the hypnotist by the subject; the subject's motivation to cooperate; and the kinds of preconceptions the subject has concerning the nature of hypnosis and its effects. Other critical aspects of the hypnotic situation are, according to Orne, the willingness of the subject to relinquish his normal, reality-monitoring activities; the subject's involvement in imagination or fantasy—he agrees with Sarbin and Coe's definition of hypnosis as "believed in imaginings" (Sarbin and Coe 1972); an increase in suggestibility, in part as a direct consequence of the subject's putting aside critical evaluative functions while hypnotized; the fact that individuals can successfully simulate being hypnotized and it is exceedingly difficult to detect such purposive simulation; the fact that subjects, even though deeply hypnotized, are still able to lie; and, finally, the fact that the subject's willingness to accept fantasy as reality during the hypnotic experience, together with the often dramatic vividness of recollections in hypnosis, may inspire great confidence in the subject that the recalled material is true. In the latter case, the subject's conviction that these memories are accurate, and the greater number of details reported subsequent to hypnosis, confer credibility by others in the subject's memory reports, regardless of their factual status.

In Orne's earlier view, one of the most persuasive facts about the hypnotic situation and the one that at the time convinced him the subject was, indeed, in some sort of altered state of consciousness, is what he refers to as "trance logic." Orne coined this term in 1959 because subjects who were judged to be deeply hypnotized stated they could see a hallucinated person sitting in a chair, and at the same time they could see the chair through the hallucinated person. Also, they could see an actual person standing in the room, and at the same time they could see a hallucination of the same person in another part of the room. Since the hypnotized subjects were showing a special type of logic, it appeared reasonable to Orne to assume they were in some sort of "special state of consciousness." Later research, however (see Johnson 1972; and Johnson, Maher, and Barber 1972), showed that nonhypnotic subjects gave similar illogical reports to the same extent as subjects who were judged to be deeply hypnotized. Though trance logic was found in some hypnotic trance subjects, it was found just as often in unhypnotizable subjects who were asked to simulate hypnosis, and in control subjects who were simply asked to imagine the hallucinated person.

More recently Spanos, de Groot, and Gwynn (1987, pp. 911–921) investigated the claim that both hypnotic "reals" and hypnotic "simulators" are exposed to the same "demand characteristics." This assumption led Orne to conclude that differences in trance logic responding between these groups were due to variables other than demands that were unique to the "real" subjects. Based on the same reasoning, differences between reals and simulators in post-hypnotic responding and source amnesia have also been attributed to hypnosis per se rather than demand characteristics. Results of experiments by Spanos, de Groot, and Gwynn, as well as of a number of other investigators, clearly indicate that the assumption of equivalent demands in hypnotic and simulation conditions is incorrect. On the contrary, differences in demand characteristics associated with these conditions seem to account not only for the differences in trance logic responding that emerge between the two groups, but also for differences between the reals and the simulators in post-hypnotic responding, source amnesia, and response to conflicting instructions. Contrary to Orne's belief, the simulation instructions do not equate with the demand characteristics; rather, they profoundly alter the demand characteristics. Consequently, performance differences between the reals and the simulators do not support Orne's assumptions and should not be used to make inferences about demand-free, counter-expectational, or "essential" aspects of hypnotic responding.

De Groot and Gwynn subjected Orne's trance logic claim and Hilgard's "hidden observer" postulate to a detailed analysis in terms of the existing experimental evidence and found them both wanting, i.e., both are more simply and easily explained in terms of simple everyday social behavior (de Groot and Gwynn 1989) than as some sort of altered state. The latter notion, as well as notions like "trance" and "dissociation," the authors claim, besides producing conceptual confusion, appear peculiarly inadequate to explain the many subtle variations in subjects' responding as a function of changes in the experimental context.

In short, Orne's observation about trance logic, i.e., that hypnotized subjects are characterized by a unique and special type of logic, which at first received considerable attention, is no longer held to be valid.

Orne is—as much as if not more than any investigator in the field of hypnosis research—extremely sensitive to faking and deception on the part of the hypnotic subject. He agrees with Sarbin and others that hypnotic age regression is nothing more than an extremely convincing form of role-playing, and that unhypnotized control subjects are much more successful in simulating age regression than are subjects in deep hypnosis. Orne also more than anyone else has provided sound and useful advice to any and all who wish to use hypnosis in an applied setting for practical benefits. His view, for example, of the potential uses of hypnosis in interrogation (Orne 1961) is still the best and wisest practical advice on this subject. It is a gold mine for anyone planning to undertake research in this area.

Orne's sensitivity to the faking of hypnosis came to the fore in the so-called Hillside Strangler Case in 1979, when Orne's trance logic indicators were used in court to evaluate the credibility of the defendant, Kenny Bianchi. Bianchi had been accused of the murder of several women in the Los Angeles area. The case is also important in that it furnishes a perfect example of how easy it is for a fairly clever person to simulate hypnosis and fool even so-called experts.

Although Bianchi was a psychopathic killer, his appearance and demeanor were those of a gentle, kindly, well-adjusted, normal person. Prior to his trial, Bianchi was counseled by a psychiatric social worker, who found it difficult to believe that the mild, sensitive Bianchi was also a multiple murderer. Since Bianchi claimed total amnesia for the time and events of the murders, the social worker felt that Bianchi might be suffering from a multiple personality disorder (MPD). He told Bianchi's defense attorney as well as Bianchi himself about his supposition. Both the attorney and Bianchi seized upon this way to build a defense based upon insanity, i.e., it wasn't the mild Kenny Bianchi that committed the murders but one of his alternate personalities. Prior to Bianchi's first psychiatric examination, by Dr. Donald T. Lunde of Stanford University, Bianchi had an opportunity to see the movie "Sybil," starring Joanne Woodward and Sally Field, and he had earlier read Thigpen and Cleckly's book about multiples, *The Three Faces of Eve*.

Lunde, however, did not focus upon the question of multiple personality. Instead, he concentrated on Bianchi's inability to remember and suggested the use of either drugs like sodium amytal or hypnosis. Bianchi, who was familiar with hypnosis and knew that one couldn't be hypnotized against one's will, preferred hypnosis and persuaded his attorney to call in a hypnotist.

Although it is generally agreed that multiple personality is an extremely rare phenomenon, the attorney brought in Dr. John G. Watkins, who believed it was less rare than most psychologists supposed. Moreover, he was aware that two years earlier in Ohio the rapist Billy Milligan had used MPD as a successful not-guilty-by-reason-of-insanity alibi. Dr. Watkins, a professor of psychology at the University of Montana, was also a diplomate of the American Board of Professional Psychology and well-trained in hypnosis. When Watkins first encountered Bianchi, he told him that he "felt that I can be of some help to you." Bianchi was well-prepared to play on Watkins's credulity and came across as an abused child with total amnesia for the distant past. The entire hypnotic session was videotaped. It became evident to impartial observers that, since Watkins believed beforehand that Bianchi was a multiple, he was able to confirm his own self-fulfilling prophecy by suggesting to Bianchi in unmistakable terms that Bianchi had an alternate personality. Bianchi, of course, played his role to perfection, and had Watkins believing he had not only hypnotized him but had found the evil side of his personality that committed the crimes. After watching this charade, the detectives who had broken the case and arrested Bianchi suggested that the judge should let Kenny off but give the evil alternate personality the chair.

Bianchi and his attorney also called in a psychiatrist, Dr. Ralph B. Allison, an expert on multiples and the author of a book about such cases, *Minds In Many Pieces* (1980). Since Allison, too, was an avid believer in multiples, Bianchi also succeeded in fooling him, even going so far as to give the alternate evil personality the name of Steven Walker—a name Bianchi had used earlier in a scam to obtain a college degree under false pretenses. Again, Bianchi faked hypnosis and had no trouble fooling Dr. Allison.

The prosecution felt that since Bianchi, by revealing the name he had used in the prior scam, revealed that he was a practiced con artist, it would be possible now to show that he also faked the hypnosis. To establish this, Martin Orne was called in as the prosecution's expert witness. After viewing the Watkins and Allison videotapes, Orne knew that his primary task was to determine whether or not Bianchi was or was not hypnotized. Here was the perfect place for his trance logic tests and Orne proceeded with the single and double hallucination tests, as well as suggested anaesthesia and source amnesia test.

Orne first asked Bianchi to imagine his lawyer was sitting next to him in an empty chair. Bianchi did so, pretending to talk to him. Orne then pointed to the real attorney at the back of the room. Bianchi explained that the hallucinated man was no longer there. Then Bianchi made a fatal mistake by overreacting and yelling about how it was impossible for the man to be in two places at once. If he had really been hypnotized, Orne argued, he would not have questioned the hallucination. Bianchi also got up and pretended to shake hands with the hallucinated lawyer—something only a simulator would attempt to do. Continuing to overact, Bianchi also asked the hallucinated lawyer whether he would mind being touched. Only someone faking hypnosis would do this.

In the suggested anaesthesia test, Orne drew an imaginary circle on the back of Bianchi's hand and told him he would feel pressure when touched outside the circle, but would feel nothing when touched inside the circle. Bianchi was told to say "yes" when touched outside the circle, and say "no" when touched inside the circle. Someone who was not hypnotized, using normal waking logic, since he supposedly felt nothing when touched inside the circle, would say nothing. Someone who was hypnotized, using trance logic, would feel the touch, but would suppose he felt nothing, and would say "no." Bianchi, trying to prove he was really hypnotized, said nothing. This was a serious mistake. Orne knew Bianchi was faking.

Although the source-amnesia test was inconclusive, Bianchi's responses to three of the four tests indicated he was faking being hypnotized. Orne also caught Bianchi faking amnesia. When his alter ego had been tearing up cigarette butts, Bianchi acted like he didn't remember, even though he had been told about it on several occasions.

Finally, Orne told Bianchi there was a problem with the multiple personality diagnosis in that it was very rare for there to be only two personalities. If Bianchi was faking the multiple personalities it is likely that he would soon come up with another one. Sure enough, when Orne then hypnotized Bianchi and summoned the alternate personality and asked if there were any more around, on cue, Bianchi came up with a third one. Thus, Orne showed that Bianchi was also faking MPD.

Although Dr. Watkins and Dr. Allison were fooled by Bianchi, they were in no way irresponsible or unprofessional. They simply did not believe that anyone who was not a professional could know that much about their specialty. Darcy O'Brien, in his excellent account of the Bianchi murders, trials, and convictions, *Two Of A Kind: The Hillside Stranglers* (1985), noted that

In truth they were being so thoroughly professional that what was obvious to the layman was not to them. The detectives saw the fraud at once; a BBC producer who was filming a documentary about Bianchi sensed the fakery after viewing the videotape of one session with Dr. Watkins; a writer who was doing a book about the Stranglers recognized the sham at once; the writer's daughter who was fifteen at the time and who knew nothing about the case, happened to see five minutes of a tape showing Bianchi playing Steve (the alternate personality) for Dr. Allison and commented of Kenny, "What a lousy actor!"

Shortly after his arrest and the accumulation of evidence, Bianchi implicated his cousin, Angelo Buono, in the crimes, and both were sentenced to life imprisonment without parole.

Thinking again of Hilgard's arguments and the neodissociation viewpoint, one would expect multiple personalities to emerge during hypnosis, since hypnosis facilitates dissociation and thus allows the various submerged personalities to surface. If the Hillside Strangler case prosecution's view of multiples is correct, however, then even the multiple personality syndrome itself is in line with a social-psychological, role-enactment view of all MPDs. Direct support for this viewpoint comes from a study by Spanos, Weeks, and Bertrand (1985) showing that most subjects who were instructed to role-play a defendant undergoing hypnosis displayed the main signs of MPD, even though they had no previous information about MPD nor any knowledge about its specific symptoms. Spanos and his collaborators argue that it is highly unlikely that anyone in Bianchi's position would really believe in his or her role enactments. In clinical situations, however, it is possible that some patients may begin to believe that they have multiple personalities. From the nonstate perspective, according to Wagstaff (1989),

the credibility of hypnotically elicited multiple personalities as a defense cannot rest on objective tests of whether the defendant is "simulating hypnosis" or whether he or she *has* multiple personalities. No such tests exist, and any claim that they do is likely to mislead the courts. Instead the important issues concern whether the court decides the defendant *believes* he or she has multiple personalities, and the implications of this for a defense of insanity on the grounds of a defect of reason or insane delusion. (pp. 350–351)

Wagstaff concludes with the cogent remark that one is tempted to ask how a man who deliberately committed brutal rapes and murders could be considered "sane," regardless of whether he faked multiple personalities or not.

Be that as it may, despite Orne's experience, knowledge, and acumen, the evidence is increasing that such phenomena as trance logic and hidden observer responding can be accounted for by considerably simpler and more conventional psychological concepts involving social conditions and the relationship between the hypnotiz r and the subject hypnotized.

Milton H. Erickson and the Ericksonian School

Milton H. Erickson, M.D. (1901–1980), was considered by many to be one of the world's greatest medical hypnotists as well as one of the world's greatest psychotherapists. Not by all, however. Despite the fact that for well over forty years Erickson wrote about, practiced, researched, and studied hypnosis and was considered by many to be somewhat of a deity, today he has almost as many detractors as admirers. What is it about the man and his work that has made him so controversial? First, many people have questioned the accuracy of calling his psychotherapy "hypnotic."

Although he was one of the acknowledged leaders in medical hypnosis, Erickson used a formal trance induction in less than ten percent of his cases. According to Erickson, hypnosis is "communication," and this communication between the patient and the therapist takes place at all levels of the personality, particularly within the client's unconscious. The forces by which unconscious processes guide our everyday thoughts and actions are also at work when we are given therapeutic suggestions. In Erickson's view, "it is the task of the therapist to achieve rapport with all of these levels so portrayed" (Beahrs 1971, 73–74). The therapist may achieve rapport at all of these personality levels by giving recognition, by acceptance, and by participating at these levels. This may sometimes involve hypnotic trance induction and at other times merely speaking to the patient on his own terms, but at all times it means accepting the patient's behavior as a potential tool for growth. As Erickson sees it, the boundary between waking and hypnotic techniques often becomes blurred and unimportant. He gives the example of a rebellious two-year-old who refuses to do anything he is asked. Erickson challenges him, "I'll bet you can't lie down quietly and go to sleep!" The child's response is, "Can too!" and immediately he lies down and falls asleep. Although definitely not hypnotic, this technique still used the power of suggestion. These sorts of indirect methods were very characteristic of Erickson's therapeutic style. Erickson justified this approach and his reluctance to use direct therapeutic suggestions on the basis that he believed that most psychological disabilities involve an inability on the patient's part to communicate directly. Erickson managed to "get around" these defenses by interspersing therapeutic suggestion with irrelevant small talk and social chatter. When directness was used, it was done when least expected. The suggestions still reached the patient's unconscious and got there most effectively because all the defenses had been sidetracked. Erickson used partial remarks, remarks with implications, subtle double-minds, pauses and hesitations timed to create the maximum expectancy, unexpected interruptions and diversions, and many other techniques. He engaged the patient's curiosity and made him think about topics he formerly avoided.

Although Erickson was very accepting of the patient's behavior, his technique was also powerfully directive and manipulative. The therapist must find out how the patient thinks and meet him where he is, and then modify the patient's behavior and gain control over it. This emphasis on control applies to both hypnosis and therapy. Since Erickson believed that no suggestion would be accepted if it was incompatible with the unconscious needs of the patient, he thought most hypnotic techniques based on direct suggestion would fail. Therefore, why use direct suggestion?

In Erickson's view, most hypnotists advocating direct suggestion have been academic experimentalists who focused on the hypnotist's power rather than the hypnotist-subject relationship. Such a focus has led to the conclusion that hypnotizability is a normally distributed trait in the population, that it is stable, and that some people have it and some do not. Success or failure is attributed to the subject, and the hypnotist is not important. There are major problems with this approach, as we have noted earlier, e.g., there are many ways to induce a subject into trance, and the therapist's task is to find the induction technique best for his particular client. Hypnotic susceptibility scores are influenced by a variety of factors, including various induction strategies. Many people erroneously believe they are not good subjects or even hypnotizable, and so on. While standard tests can tell us what a person can do with ease, they do not tell us what an individual is intrinsically incapable of doing. As Stephen Gilligan says, "a high score on a susceptibility test generally means that the subject will be responsive to just about any hypnotic instructions; a low score suggests that a different strategy by the hypnotist or more training is needed" (Gilligan 1987).

Besides his disagreement with the authoritarian view, with its emphasis on the hypnotist's power and the subject's susceptibility, Erickson also differed from the traditionalists in a number of other ways. First, in his belief that each person is unique. Since Erickson himself was color-blind, tone deaf, twice paralyzed with polio, and also dyslexic, he very early learned to sympathize with others and appreciate individual differences. Second, hypnosis in Erickson's view is an experiential process of communicating ideas. Thus, effective hypnosis taps ideas already in a person's repertoire. Third, every individual has the built-in inner resources sufficient not only to heal himself but to lead a happy and satisfying life. Related to this is the fourth belief, that the hypnotic trance can break a person away from rigid self-defeating sets of mind and help him restructure and reorganize his inner resources in an effective and positive way. Fifth, hypnotic trance experiences are not separate from a person's normal pattern of behaving. Trance experiences are naturalistic. They are like reading a novel, daydreaming, or watching television. In the hypnotic trance, the personal involvement is only intensified. Sixth, Erickson's approach was focused on the here and now rather than on the past, and it emphasized self-development rather than the correction of past mistakes. Seventh, people are not only unique, they are unique at different levels of their personality, and a person's unconscious processes can support and complement his conscious ones. Moreover, the unconscious can operate independently of the conscious and can bring about major changes in thinking and feeling. In Erickson's words, "Your conscious mind is very intelligent but your unconscious is a lot smarter" (Beahrs 1971, p. 81).

With regard to the hypnotic trance per se, Erickson's view is in full agreement with Barber on these points: 1) that everyone is capable of being hypnotized, 2) suggestions can be equally effective if given outside the trance, 3) the trance is naturalistic, and 4) stress on the importance of motivational and interpersonal variables. Nevertheless, Erickson falls into the state camp because he agrees with those who argue that the hypnotic trance is qualitatively different from role-playing or imaginative involvement. In his view, trance is an important concept and hypnosis is an experientially absorbing inter-actional sequence culminating in an altered state of consciousness, or in other words, hypnosis is a relationship between a hypnotist and a subject that produces trance and trance-like phenomena. Trances come about because the therapist employs techniques that grab the subject's attention and shape his ways of thinking by using the subject's own patterns of self-expression. The Ericksonian therapist must be both an observer and a participant in the hypnotic process if he expects to do his clients any good.

As you might expect, many therapists have tried Erickson's techniques with their own clients and have had some failures. Others find the entire process too confusing and too time-consuming, and they either give up hypnosis entirely or use other, simpler methods that are easier to understand and apply. Erickson did not think that client "insight" was necessary for changes to occur, because the unconscious would effect the changes auto-matically, whether the conscious mind of the client knew it or not. Most of Ericksonian therapy is indirect, and the primary vehicle for the indirect approach is the *anecdote*, or, as the Ericksonians say, the "therapeutic meta-phor." Therefore, anecdotes are used to induce trance, facilitate specific trance phenomena, and suggest resolutions to problems and the underlying unconscious dynamics—without encouraging or promoting insight. Inter-spersal approaches, i.e., sticking in words or phrases to build new associations and thinking patterns, confusion methods, i.e., creating a state of uncertainty and disrupting the client's usual patterns of thinking, and reframing tech-niques, i.e., turning the client's usual or customary was of looking at things around and putting the scene in a new frame, a new way of looking at the situation, are specific approaches to helping the client. All are consid-ered indirect forms of suggestion.

Some of Erickson's friends and colleagues, while admiring and respect-ing his talents and accomplishments, tend to see him in a more human light than others. According to D. C. Hammond, one of his students and friends,

> I believe that many myths are being perpetuated about Erickson . . . I have the highest respect for Erickson, but this does not restrain me from seeing him as human. He made therapeutic errors and he certainly failed with some patients. There were also shortcomings and limitations in his writings and research (Hilgard 1984). But accepting his humanness does not stop me from acknowledging his exceptionally creative contributions and positive attributes. . . . He was not a "hypnotist" who believed in hypnosis or any other method as a panacea. Hypnosis was just one part of his work. He was an exceptional model of eclecticism, willing to use almost anything that might be helpful. He always attempted to individualize treatment to suit the patient's needs rather than attempting to fit the patient into the mold of the therapist's theory or favorite method. He was concerned with what worked and not with what fit or didn't fit this or that model of therapy. He was also uniquely dedicated to the patients he worked with and cared enough to devote enormous amounts of time to thoughtful treatment planning and introspective analysis of his own behavior. He was persistent, and resistance was not perceived as a problem of the patient, but as a challenge to his creativity and flexibility. I consider these to be qualities of excellence. (Hammond 1986, p. 235)

And so do we all. These are the kind of things we hope to find in all those that call themselves physicians.

Interestingly enough, one of Erickson's cleverest and most innovative students, Dr. Steven Heller, although he was one of the first to present what was to become known as "Ericksonian hypnotherapy," parts company with the master on the issue of hypnosis as a trance state. In his book *Monsters and Magical Sticks: There's No Such Thing as Hypnosis?* (1987), co-authored by Terry Lee Steele, Heller argues that hypnosis "doesn't really exist except in people's minds." He goes on to point out that the major problem in discussing or writing about hypnosis is that over the years so many definitions have been promulgated about what hypnosis is or is not that people now have preconceived notions and ideas that make it very difficult to communicate with them about the process. In Heller's words,

> It might be said that they have been hypnotized into believing whatever it is they believe about hypnosis. . . . If, however, hypnosis means a special state in which a person is put into some deep mystical state and then loses volition over their being because another person, called a hypnotist, creates such powerful, overwhelming suggestions that the victim or subject is helpless to resist, then there is no such thing as hypnosis. If that "power" existed, I would not be writing this book nor working at my profession. (p. 3)

Agreeing with Erickson that hypnosis is, essentially, nothing more than communication, Heller says that if you consider hypnosis as a specific state that always includes a deep trance, then there's no such thing as hypnosis. On the other hand, if you use "hypnosis" as a generic term to include anything and everything that alters our perception or causes changes in our consciousness, then hypnosis is nothing but a word like meditation, fantasy, or relaxation. In other words, according to Heller, anything that causes an individual to temporarily become unconscious of the external world and turn inward and have an experience that becomes more profound or more important than outer consensual reality is what we mean by hypnosis. He has noted that it is sad to realize that people use this hypnosis phenomenon "that doesn't exist" to convince themselves that their freedom to select among choices doesn't exist.

Heller has, perhaps unwittingly, put his finger on the crux of the matter: the term "hypnosis" is being used to refer to any and all psychological reactions of turning inward, away from the external world to a private, individual world. If every thought, every private psychological act is hypnosis, hypnosis differs hardly at all from the medieval notion that "everything is God." Such concepts are unusually deficient in explanatory power. We will discuss this semantic problem more fully in a later section dealing with the idea of a trance.

Graham B. Wagstaff: Hypnosis as Compliance

In 1981 Graham F. Wagstaff, an English psychologist who teaches at the University of Liverpool, published a brilliant study of hypnosis titled *Hypnosis, Compliance and Belief*. The book is a well-written and successful attempt to explain all of the various kinds of phenomena that are attributed to the mysterious and elusive phenomenon called "hypnosis." In the preface, Wagstaff says that it always struck him as very odd that people who are able to tolerate surgery under hypnosis are not necessarily the same people who were hypnotically susceptible by criteria such as hypnotic tests. Also, it seemed odd to him that subjects judged by the hypnotist to be in a deep somnambulistic trance strongly denied feeling the slightest bit hypnotized. Even stranger, he reports, is the fact that some hypnotized subjects reported they were hypnotized because they felt lethargic and drowsy, while others given similar suggestions were quite alert, managed to lift enormous weights, carry out complex tests and tasks, and act like clowns. After giving these problems considerable thought, Wagstaff concluded that,

> perhaps the reason why no investigator has been able to find an acceptable solution to this mystery is that there is no central mystery to solve. Instead,

we might have a collection of phenomena, bound together in name only by the term "hypnosis," but which demand a number of different explanations. My conclusion seemed similar to that arrived at by Kusche (1975) following his investigation of the infamous "Bermuda Triangle." He says: "My research which began as an attempt to find as much information as possible about the Bermuda Triangle, had an unexpected result. After examining all the evidence I have reached the following conclusion: *there is no theory that solves the mystery.* It is no more logical to try to find a common cause for all the disappearances in the Triangle than, for example, to try to find one cause for all automobile accidents in Arizona. By abandoning the search for an overall theory and investigating each incident independently, the mystery began to unravel" (p. 251). Given this impression, I wondered whether many of the mysteries of hypnosis might be, at least, partially, unravelled by reference to a number of possibly related areas of mainstream psychology; and this book represents my attempt to find commonalities between the phenomena subsumed under the term "hypnosis" and other phenomena more familiar to psychologists and physicians, and hopefully, the layman. (pp. 9–10)

Needless to say, his attempt succeeds admirably. Following a brief review of the history of hypnosis, Wagstaff devotes considerable time to a discussion of the role of the importance of compliance in the hypnotic relationship. Studies of obedience, conformity, and demand characteristics all point to their role also in the hypnosis situation. Many people have suggested that hypnosis is a form of obedience behavior and that in stage hypnosis it is more embarrassing for a volunteer to refuse to cooperate than to agree to go along with the show. In the hypnosis situation, the expectations of the hypnotist are very explicit, and this alone is sufficient to pressure the subject into complying with any reasonable request. Most hypnotic suggestions are also given as directives, and since it would be embarrassing for the subject to fail to comply, most subjects behave as they think they ought to behave.

In studies comparing the performance of hypnotized and task-motivated groups, Wagstaff sees the task-motivated controls as critical. If no differences are found between the controls and the hypnosis groups, it remains to be demonstrated that the responses of the hypnotized subjects reflect anything other than high motivation and compliance. The task-motivated control groups are only irrelevant if one assumes that the hypnotized groups are experiencing something uniquely hypnotic that accounts for their responsiveness. This is the crux of the argument: if task-motivated subjects can do what hypnotized subjects do, then we do not need the assumption of something unique about hypnosis to explain what the hypnotized group is doing. The burden of proof lies on the state theorists to demonstrate that the experiences and behaviors of the hypnotized subjects are qualitatively or quantitatively different from those of the task-motivated subjects.

Wagstaff enumerates example after example of compliance in hypnosis research, particularly in studies of blindness, deafness, feats of strength, and other sorts of esoteric performances that humans are capable of. In every case, compliance seems to be the simplest and most efficient explanation of the behavior. With regard to the state theorists' argument based on the subject's report that being hypnotized "feels different" from being awake or asleep, Wagstaff remains highly skeptical. He notes that subjects' reports of their experiences under hypnosis vary widely. Some report being blacked out and remembering nothing. Others report being aware of everything but feeling like they were entering a cave or a well. The mere fact that people don't always agree upon what it feels like to be hypnotized tells us very little.

We know that people, generally, have difficulty describing internal experiences, and Wagstaff notes that many subjects confuse the mere feeling of relaxation with hypnosis. In this regard, he cites a report by a researcher who in the process of measuring hypnotic susceptibility using biofeedback equipment discovered that for the majority of subjects without prior hypnotic experience, the feedback from a skin-resistance meter alone quickly produced a trance-like state of relaxation in which post-hypnotic suggestions were highly effective. The researchers called it "psychocybernetic hypnosis." The phenomenon is similar to "non-hypnotic hypnosis," according to Wagstaff. The semantic problems in communicating about internal states are obvious.

Compliance, and belief on the part of the subject that there is such a thing as the hypnotic state, and that if he tries hard enough he can experience it or did experience it, seem to be sufficient to explain the subjects' feelings and behavior. With regard to special feats, Wagstaff dismisses the claim that these can occur only after a hypnotic induction has been performed. He does stress that even though hypnosis can be ruled out as the necessary agent, by no means have we adequately explained how various waking suggestions prove to be so effective in changing and influencing behavior.

Concerning the issue of individual differences in hypnotic susceptibility, Wagstaff argues that there is no need to postulate anything particularly weird or wonderful to account for alleged differences between subjects with high and low ratings on the hypnotic susceptibility scales. The differences probably arise because of normal and natural differences in responses that subjects make to the instructions they are given and to their interpretation of the situation in which they find themselves. All of the work on measuring and changing susceptibility is complicated by a large number of interacting factors: compliance and related attitudes; differences in the procedures employed; differences in the capacity to experience genuine sensations such as "unconscious mimicry," etc. Though some of the correlations between imaginative experiences, alpha production, eye movements, and hypnotic susceptibility at first look impressive, these relationships are complex and inconsistent. Also impressive are some of the correlations between acquiescence and imaginative experiences, influenceability and body sway suggestibility, and acting ability in "faking" suggestions and hypnotic susceptibility. Since all of these factors interact, however, it is impossible to determine which are most responsible for individual differences and variations in scores on the hypnotic susceptibility scales. According to Wagstaff, we are obviously not looking at a unitary phenomenon; different tests may require different skills and be influenced by different personal factors in the subjects who take them.

With regard to therapeutic effects, Wagstaff again emphasizes it is not necessary to assume that any unique property of hypnosis is responsible for the benefits coming from hypnotic induction. The effects may occur through perfectly normal processes such as relaxation. Or the warm, encouraging manner of the therapist may be the key ingredient. Or the client's ability to imagine may be the essential element. In this connection, Clawson and Swade (1975) successfully treated a case of warts by using hypnotic suggestion to restrict blood supply, while Ewin (1974) had equally effective results with hypnotic suggestions to increase blood supply. Wagstaff even invokes the famous Hawthorne effect to explain the effectiveness of hypnotherapy. This term came from the studies carried out in Western Electric Corporation's Hawthorne, Illinois, plant in the 1930s by Roethlisberger and coworkers. Looking for factors which influenced production, they found that by increasing workroom illumination, production went up. However, when they decreased workroom illumination, production again went up! In fact, everything they did caused a production increase. The attempt to change conditions introduced novelty and boosted morale; illumination was irrelevant. Giving and taking away special privileges also increased production. If the company had hypnotized the workers once a week, they might have concluded it was hypnosis that increased the working efficiency. In the clinical situation, Wagstaff notes, the Hawthorne effect may also be at work. Hypnosis is a novel procedure that is perceived to be so much better than those dreary old pills. For some individuals, Wagstaff suggests, even "standing on one leg" therapy or "putting your fingers in your ears" therapy might be effective.

Similarly, Wagstaff is not terribly impressed by the claims of the state theorists with regard to hypnotic analgesia and hypnotic dissociation. In the former case, he notes, there is a wide range of individual differences with regard to pain tolerance. Many people are not as sensitive to pain as others. Some patients seem to be able to tolerate major surgery without either drugs or hypnosis, while others faint at a paper cut. Part of the problem is that any psychological technique used to alleviate pain is now labeled a "hypnotic technique." Most researchers in this area use relaxation, suggestion, and distraction, and none of these are hypnosis. Moreover, the proportion of patients selected for surgery with hypnosis is very small. As for hypnotic dissociation, Hilgard argues that under hypnosis cognitive systems become dissociated, i.e., at one level a person may not be aware of the pain, but at another level, which the first level is unaware of, the pain may be experienced. However, Wagstaff sees compliance rather than a hidden observer at work, and the entire business as a rather elaborate game some subjects feel obliged to play in order to give the hypnotist what he wants. Compliance may not be an all-or-none phenomenon. Compliant subjects might also genuinely feel they are hypnotized, but this cannot be used as evidence that their analgesia reports are genuine or that they can dissociate the hypnotized part from the hidden part so that neither is aware of the other. Other problems with the dissociation studies include the fact that none of them used waking suggestion controls to see if the hypnotic induction was necessary to produce the effects, and none of the hidden observer pain studies used independent groups of waking controls, i.e., simulators, to set independent baseline performance levels and to measure the possible effects of demand characteristics.

Because of the importance of the pain and hypnotic analgesia issue to the state versus nonstate argument, we will take up this issue in detail in a later chapter.

Finally, in connection with the state-nonstate issue, although Wagstaff (1981) sees a great deal of agreement between the two positions, he comes down firmly on the nonstate side. In his words,

> Although many of the interpretations of hypnotic behaviors put forward in this book could possibly be conceptualized within the boundaries of either state or non-state theories, my own view is that the notion of hypnosis as an altered state of consciousness could be somewhat misleading, and the attempts by some to identify both schools of thought with the concept of imaginative or organismic involvement could be equally misleading if both oversimplify the diversity of processes which contribute to the various hypnotic phenomena. The first problem is that it has not been conclusively demonstrated that all subjects who respond to hypnotic suggestions are experiencing a high degree of imaginative or organismic involvement, i.e., compliance can easily disappear by default in this kind of analysis. (pp. 211–212)

Added to this problem is the semantic problem of the concept of trance. Wagstaff feels that it will take some time before the notion of a hypnotic trance as a state of profound insensibility similar to sleep will be erased from our culture. It is very misleading to both subjects and patients for investigators to continue to use the term "trance" as an explanation or description of what happens as a result of the hypnotic induction procedures. People unfamiliar with the scientific literature still conceive of a hypnotic trance as a sleep-like state of insensibility, in which the individual loses his will power and responds like an automaton to the commands of the hypnotist. The continued use of words like "trance" and "somnambulism" only perpetuate this mistake. With regard to an alternate state of consciousness, Wagstaff feels that to describe a hypnotic subject as in an altered state of consciousness suggests that he is in a single particular state. But just when does a normal state of consciousness become an altered state? Many believe there is an altered state of consciousness associated with relaxation or with meditation or yoga. If the altered state of consciousness, contingent upon suggestions for relaxation, is achieved following hypnotic induction, then in this case the hypnotic subject would indeed be in an altered state of consciousness. If we wish to go further, Wagstaff suggests, and label this state a "trance," in the same way that meditators and yogins are said to be in trances, then the hypnotic subject could be accurately described as in a trance. There is, however, no real basis at present to believe that the achieved state is relevant to general responsiveness to hypnotic suggestions. It presumably disappears when relaxation disappears. Yet unrelaxed subjects are still considered hypnotized.

If any experience outside the normal is considered to be an altered state, then even deep concentration could be so considered. But then anyone caught up in a book, or captured by the television screen, or engrossed in a movie would have to considered hypnotized, and these conditions are often so designated. This would be logically consistent, too, except for the fact that people in such conditions are not always in a state of profound relaxation. Thus, we now need to distinguish two states or hypnotic trances —one for relaxation and one for concentration. In his obedience studies, Milgram talked about his subject becoming "agenetic," i.e., an agent captive to the will of others and blindly obeying orders, like concentration camp guards in Nazi Germany. Such agents have been referred to as "hypnotized by those they obey" (Milgram 1974). If obedience is considered to be an altered state, and since it doesn't require either relaxation or concentration, we would now have to distinguish three states.

In other words, Wagstaff argues, while it might seem logical to say that a hypnotic subject may be in altered states or trance states if he is relaxed, obedient, or concentrating, if we say that the communications used during hypnotic induction make the versions of these states unique to hypnosis, we would also have to propose unique, discrete altered states of awareness or trances for Yoga meditation, Transcendental Meditation, obeying the Pope, obeying the boss, watching television, etc., because each would have its own unique system of communications. Since people do not usually talk about "TV trances," "book trances," or "boss trances," one really cannot blame them for thinking that a hypnotic trance must be a lot more than just deeply relaxing, concentrating very hard on something, and doing what someone says.

William Edmonston: Hypnosis as Relaxation

William Edmonston's position on hypnosis evolved, he says, out of a grow-ing awareness that in experiments the responses of subjects to a variety of stimuli while under hypnosis did not differ from their responses while simply relaxed. Edmonston says he was slow in coming to this conclusion because in reading about the history of the phenomenon he became con-vinced there was something peculiar and unique about hypnosis that made it a special state. The more research he carried out, the clearer it became to him that there was no difference between responses made in hypnosis and in nonhypnotic relaxation.

In his book *Hypnosis and Relaxation: Modern Verification of an Old Equa-tion* (1980), Edmonston traces the twenty-four-century-old notion of hyp-nosis as sleep and concludes that down through the ages virtually everyone connected with hypnosis has taken note of the sleep-like, relaxed appear-ance of most hypnotic subjects. Moreover, the history of hypnosis is re-plete with associations with ideas of sleep, inhibition, and relaxation. As for induction procedures, the instructions themselves link relaxation and hypnosis. Since subjects and patients do what they are told, when they are told to relax they do so, and then they are hypnotized. In Edmonston's words, "to relax is to be hypnotized. If they are told not to relax, as we will see, they are not hypnotized" (p. 45). In a discussion of "the relaxation response," as described by Herbert Benson (1975), Edmonston sees little or no difference between this and hypnosis, and in fact refers to both as "the relaxation-hypnosis equation."

Edmonston also argues that the induction of hypnosis produces various physiological changes that strongly mimic the changes that occur in relaxa-tion and sleep. While there are a few discrepancies between hypnosis and relaxation, the differences are negligible. Most of Edmonston's colleagues would respond to his proposition that neutral hypnosis is relaxation with the question: What about the alert trance? or Doesn't the alert trance dem-onstrate that hypnosis is not relaxation? Edmonston meets this challenge by arguing that virtually all studies show that whether the measures used are motivational, cognitive, physiological, or behavioral, alerting instructions produce a condition that is different from traditional hypnosis. As for the question: Doesn't the alert trance demonstrate that hypnosis is not relaxa-tion? the answer is simply no. The alerting instructions always produce a modified condition in the human listener, but they do not produce hypnosis in the traditional sense, and hypnosis in the traditional sense—historically, clinically, and experimentally—is basically and fundamentally relaxation. In Edmonston's words,

Hypnotic phenomena are producible through relaxation, whether it is designated hypnosis or not and whether the individuals involved perceive the relaxation to be hypnotic or not. Neutral hypnosis is not a two-step phenomenon. There is but one step, the relaxation. All else is secondary to that one fundamental characteristic. (1980, p. 212)

Edmonston makes some interesting points in further support of his argument. First, he notes the impossibility of simulating or role-playing relaxation. Recognizing that no precise line can be drawn demarcating sleep from wakefulness, that there is a series of gradations between these two states, individuals can pretend to be asleep. Individuals who are asleep, however, cannot pretend to be awake. Not only can they not feign wakefulness to the satisfaction of an observer, they cannot do it at all! Sleep is so overpowering, the pretense of wakefulness is out of the question, short of actually becoming awake. So it is, Edmonston says, with relaxation. When you are relaxed, you are relaxed; no amount of feigning, pretending, or simulating will help you gain the condition of wakefulness short of actually becoming awake. Once neutral hypnosis or relaxation has occurred, the credible simulation of a more alert condition is out of the question.

Edmonston's second point concerns a potential ethical dilemma. Suppose a patient refuses hypnosis as part of his treatment. Is it ethical then to substitute relaxation techniques? Is it ethical for the practitioner to say to his patient, "All right, I won't use hypnosis in your treatment; I'll just teach you how to relax." Edmonston asks,

Has our knowledge of the relationship of relaxation to hypnosis placed us in the ethically awkward position of having to deceive, "for their own good", patients who are resistive to the use of hypnosis? Are we now forced to an "end justifies the means" position, in which the practitioner must live with a sin of omission (not informing the patient of the relationship between the treatment refused—hypnosis—and the treatment proposed—relaxation) in order to benefit the patient? Of course not. The problem is one of education and nomenclature, not ethics and legalities. (p. 215)

Although Edmonston would solve all of the problems by changing the word "hypnosis" to a word he feels is a more accurate descriptor, "anesis" —which is the noun form of the Greek verb *aniemi*, meaning to relax or let go—it should be obvious that this suggestion has not caught on. Nor has Edmonston's main thesis, that hypnosis and relaxation are equivalent, caught on. While everyone agrees as to the importance of relaxation to hypnosis, the proposal that hypnosis is nothing more than relaxation seems a little extreme. As Wagstaff remarks, there is a big difference between a relaxed hypnotic subject sitting comfortably in an easy chair, breathing deeply with eyes closed and a human plank, or an individual acting like an infant, or throwing acid in someone's face, or performing complex cognitive tasks. To say that subjects could perform these energetic tasks while in a drowsy state of "complete relaxation" seems somehow absurd (Wagstaff 1981).

As Barber and others have noted, all induced relaxation seems to immediately disappear when suggestions are given that require a subject to become active. Even when the relaxation is not present, many subjects still show a high level of responsiveness to suggestions. In one study, subjects were successfully hypnotized while riding a bicycle ergometer under loaded conditions with their eyes open and at the same time receiving suggestions of alertness. Barber, Spanos, and Chaves (1974) showed that as long as it is made clear to the subjects that they are in a special situation in which they are expected to respond to suggestions, the administration of suggestions for relaxation and sleep is unnecessary to elicit a high level of hypnotic responsiveness. These researchers believe that most likely the reason repeated suggestions for sleep and relaxation tend to result in responsiveness to hypnotic suggestions is not primarily because they induce relaxation or a special state, but because they define the situation as "truly a hypnotic one," i.e., a situation in which the subject is expected to respond to the suggestions.

Social-Cognitive Theorists: Spanos, Kirsch, and Coe

Nicholas P. Spanos, currently a professor of psychology at Carleton University, Ottawa, Ontario, Canada, is another brilliant researcher and theorist who has worked closely with Barber over a period of many years and shares his views with regard to the nature of hypnosis and what hypnosis is and is not. According to Spanos, though he was never formally one of Barber's students, Barber became sort of an adopted mentor. Although Spanos collaborated closely with Barber at the Medfield Foundation and coauthored a book with him, Spanos has also made a large number of independent contributions of his own, extending, elaborating, and clarifying what has come to be known as the cognitive-behavioral perspective in hypnosis research. Spanos has published over a hundred original scientific papers on the subject of hypnosis and related topics, and this impressive body of work has done more perhaps than the work of anyone else (except Barber himself) to discredit the special process or state theories of hypnosis. Study after study and paper after paper authored by Spanos and his collaborators have systematically eroded and undermined the special process or altered state of consciousness viewpoint.

Sarbin also had a profound influence on Spanos's thinking both through personal contact and through his writings. Although Sarbin reformulated hypnosis in terms of role-enactment, he conducted relatively little empirical work in the area. His ideas did, however, have a tremendous influence on the thought of Barber and Spanos, who carried out voluminous experimental work over the last three decades.

The special process views of hypnosis have long been sustained by, in Spanos's words, "the mystifying belief that hypnotic responding was extraordinary and, therefore, required the positing of extraordinary causes" (Spanos and Chaves 1989). The systematic and extensive work of Barber and Spanos has, beyond all doubt, eliminated this belief and shown how very ordinary—i.e., like other kinds of ordinary social behavior—hypnotic responding really is.

Over the last two decades Spanos and his students and associates have carried out a number of in-depth studies of discrete hypnotic phenomena dealing with auditory and visual hallucinations, suggested amnesia, suggested pain reduction, hidden selves, past-life regression, glossolalia, and other sorts of unusual special state phenomena. They have also carried out a series of studies challenging the traditional view that individual differences in hypnotizability should be thought of as due to some fixed trait or cognitive skill. Rather than inferring a stable trait, they feel, we need to emphasize the stable nature of the test situation and the stable attitudes, interpretations, and preconceptions the subjects bring to the situation.

Overall, Spanos's position on hypnosis is very clear. He argues that, despite widespread belief to the contrary, hypnotic procedures do not greatly augment responsiveness to suggestions. Nonhypnotic control subjects who have been encouraged to do their best respond just as well as hypnotic subjects to suggestions for pain reduction, amnesia, age regression, hallucination, limb rigidity, etc. Hypnotic procedures, he says, are no more effective than nonhypnotic relaxation procedures at reducing blood pressure and muscle tension or affecting other behavioral, physiological, or verbal report indicators of relaxation. Hypnotic procedures are no more effective than various nonhypnotic procedures at enhancing imagery vividness or at facilitating therapeutic change for such problems as chronic pain, phobic response, cigarette smoking, etc. The available scientific evidence that Spanos and his collaborators have compiled fails to support the notion that hypnotic procedures bring about unique or highly unusual states of consciousness or that these procedures facilitate responsiveness to suggestion to any greater extent than nonhypnotic procedures that enhance positive motivation and expectation.

Spanos also notes that hypnotic suggestions do not directly instruct the subject to do anything. Instead, they are usually phrased in the passive voice and imply that something is happening; for example, "Your arm is rising," instead of "Raise your arm." The passive phrasing communicates the idea that the suggested effects are occurring automatically. In other words, the hypnotic suggestions are really tacit requests to the subject to become involved in a make-believe activity. Good hypnotic subjects understand this and use their imaginative abilities and acting skills to become absorbed in the make-believe activities. Spanos notes that the method actor who throws himself into the role is the analogue of the good hypnotic subject who throws himself into generating the experiences relevant to his role as someone who is hypnotized and responsive to suggestions.

Spanos and his collaborators have looked closely at hypnotic age regression and have demonstrated that regressed subjects do not, in any real sense, take on the cognitive, perceptual, or emotional characteristics of actual children. Instead of behaving like real children, age regressed subjects behave the way they *believe* children behave. To the extent that their expectations about how children behave are inaccurate, their age regression performances also are off the mark. Simply put, age regression suggestions are invitations to become involved in the make-believe game of being a child again. People who accept the invitation do not, in any literal sense, revert psychologically to childhood. Instead, they use whatever they know about real children, whatever they remember from their own childhood, to temporarily become absorbed in the fantasy of being a child again.

Just as subjects can be given suggestions for age regression, amnesia, or pain reduction, Spanos says they can also be led to believe that they possess "hidden selves." When Hilgard's good hypnotic subjects were told that they possessed hidden selves they normally were unaware of—but to which the experimenter could talk when he gave the proper signals—many of them, when the signals were given, acted as if they did have alternate egos. Hilgard interpreted this as indicating that good hypnotic subjects carry around unconscious hidden selves with certain intrinsic, unsuggested characteristics. Spanos counters this by pointing out that the evidence shows these so-called hidden selves are neither intrinsic to hypnotic procedures nor unsuggested. On the contrary, hidden self-performances—like other suggested responses—appear to reflect attempts by motivated and imaginative subjects to create the experiences and role-play the behaviors called for by the instructions they are given. By the experimenter varying these instructions, the subjects can be easily led to develop hidden selves with whatever characteristics the experimenters desire. Depending upon the instructions given, good hypnotic subjects will act out hidden selves reporting very high levels of pain, very low levels of pain, or both high and low levels of pain in succession. Subjects can also be led to act as if they possess hidden selves that can remember concrete but not abstract words, or the opposite; or they can report seeing stimuli accurately, seeing them in reverse, or not seeing them at all, as the experimenter wishes. In short, the subjects are acting out a fantasy which is initiated by the suggestions of the hypnotist. Then the fantasy is imaginatively elaborated upon and sustained by the subject and his interactions with the hypnotist.

Spanos has also carried out studies of past-life regression, and in agreement with the findings of other researchers, his work indicates that past-life reports from hypnotically regressed subjects are fantasy constructions of imaginative subjects who are willing to become absorbed in the make-believe situation implied by the regression suggestions. As expected, subjects who responded well to other hypnotic suggestions were also most likely to respond well to regression suggestions. Those with the most practice at vivid daydreaming and everyday fantasizing, i.e., the fantasy-prone, created the most vivid past-life fantasies. In the same manner as childhood regressees, past-life reporters construct their fantasies by interweaving information given in the suggestions with information gleaned from their own life experiences and from relevant material they have read and heard. Just as age-regressed subjects incorporate misinformation into their enactments of being children, so past-life reporters incorporate historical misinformation into their past lives. Those who from the outset believed in reincarnation thought their past lives were true rather than imaginary. A lengthier discussion of this topic and other paranormal hypnotic beliefs will be found in a later chapter.

By no means, however, does Spanos see the problem of hypnosis as solved. New knowledge leads us to new unknowns and in the well-known and pronounced effects of suggestion on the human body there are many unsolved problems. The suggestion-induced disappearance of warts, for example, is just such a dilemma. Spanos's own work has shown that neither a hypnotic induction nor preliminary instructions for relaxation add to the effectiveness of imagery-based suggestions in producing wart regression. Nor can the effects of suggestion be accounted for simply in terms of enhanced expectancies. Subjects given placebos and those given suggestions reported equivalent expectations of treatment success, but the suggestions were much more effective than the placebos in producing wart regression. The suggestions, however, were not effective with all the subjects. They were most effective, Spanos reports, with subjects who had multiple warts rather than single warts. Those who rated their suggested imagery as especially vivid also had better results. Spanos concludes that

> subjects' active involvement in suggestion-related thinking and/or imagery activates or strengthens systemic (as opposed to region-specific) physiological processes that can lead to eventual wart remission. The more vivid subjects' suggestion-related imagery (which perhaps in part reflects their degree of absorption in or commitment to the suggested task), the greater likelihood that the relevant physiological processes will become strengthened or activated. Also, the greater the amount of wart virus in the system (as reflected by multiple as opposed to a single wart), the greater the likelihood that the strengthened or activated physiological processes will make contact with and kill the virus. (Spanos and Chaves 1989, p. 446)

Obviously, more work remains to be done before the mechanisms are fully understood through which the mind influences the body and aids it in the conquest of disease and in the making of repairs.

Irving Kirsch and Response Expectancy in Hypnotic Behavior

Irving Kirsch, a professor of psychology at the University of Connecticut, has traced the link between expectancy and hypnosis all the way back to the experiments carried out by the French Royal Commission in 1784 (Kirsch 1985). But what does the term "response expectancy" mean? The French commissioners discovered that an individual's belief or expectation that he or she was being magnetized was all that was necessary to get them to fall into a swoon, faint, or go into a "mesmeric trance."

In the latter part of the nineteenth century, Albert Moll argued that hypnotic behavior was determined by two basic principles: 1) people have a certain proneness to allow themselves to be influenced by others through their ideas, and in particular, to believe much without making conscious logical deductions; 2) a psychological effect tends to appear in a person if he is expecting it. Moll also was able to cause his blindfolded subjects to hallucinate when he told them they were being mesmerized.

Moll's giving expectancy a role in the production of hypnotic phenomena anticipated Kirsch's thinking that response expectancies cause the individual to have internal subjective experiences which then cause behavior. A very clear example of this is the placebo effect. When the patient is given a sugar pill but is told or believes it is a powerful pain killer, miraculously, because of his expectancies, the pain goes away! As for hypnosis, according to Kirsch, the occurrence of a hypnotic response is a function of the subject's expectancy that it will occur. Once the subject has learned how a hypnotized subject is supposed to react and what he can expect to happen when he is hypnotized, then the hypnotic responses occur automatically, i.e., without conscious effort on the subject's part. Emotional reactions—fear, sadness, sexual arousal, pain—are good examples of automatic responses. Acrophobics, for example, will avoid tall buildings, cliffs, ferris wheels, etc., because of their expectancy that not doing so would result in a panic attack.

Various other evidence is available to demonstrate that automatic responses can be brought about by the mere expectancy of their occurrence. Both hypnosis and placebos are effective in treating pain, skin conditions, and asthma, and it seems reasonable to assume that the same mechanism, namely, response expectancy, produces these responses in both hypnosis and the nonhypnosis situations. Telling subjects they have received a psychedelic drug that will produce hallucinations causes about half to report visions, even though no drug was given. Subjects who are told that hypnotized subjects can't move their dominant arm are likely to experience this effect when hypnotized, and being told that inability to remember, i.e., spontaneous amnesia, is characteristic of hypnosis significantly increases the likelihood of its occurrence. When subjects were told that either the ability or the inability to resist responding to suggestions was characteristic of deep hypnosis, they responded accordingly.

Besides affecting overt responses, role perceptions are an important determinant of self-reported experiences of altered states of consciousness. In a number of studies it was shown that the degree of change in state of consciousness subjects expected to experience significantly predicted the number of unsuggested alterations in experience they subsequently reported. Moreover, the data from these studies indicate that no particular state of consciousness can be labeled a "hypnotic trance." Rather, a variety of changes in experience are interpreted by the subject as evidence of trance when experienced in a hypnotic context. Some of these are directly suggested in typical hypnotic inductions—relaxation, for example—whereas others occur as a function of the subject's preconceptions. How the subject perceives the situation pretty much determines how effective the situation will be in producing hypnosis. Just hearing the words, "You are becoming very, very relaxed," is enough in our culture to make most people think of hypnosis. Glass and Barber (1961) a few years ago set up a highly credible clinical environment and told subjects an inert pill was a powerful hypnotic drug which would produce a state of hypnosis. In this setting the pill was as effective as a standard hypnotic induction procedure in effecting the subject's responses to suggestion.

A particularly important aspect of Kirsch's response expectancy theory is concerned with the state of consciousness argument. The common belief that hypnosis involves a special state of consciousness affects people's responses and beliefs in the following way:

> Prior to experiencing hypnosis for the first time, people are likely to have weakly held expectancies about their own responsiveness. They may expect to be very responsive, but they do not hold that expectancy with very much conviction. If, in addition, their subjective criteria for concluding that they are hypnotized include very profound changes in conscious experience, their expectations of experiencing a "trance" are likely to be disconfirmed. When these weakly held expectancies are disconfirmed, their expectancies for response to suggestions are lowered, which in turn reduces their responsiveness. Others who hold less extreme expectancies about the nature of hypnosis are more likely to have their hypnotic response expectancies confirmed and thereby strengthened. (Spanos and Chaves 1989)

According to Kirsch's theory, the probability of occurrence of a nonvolitional response varies directly with the strength of the expectancy of its occurrence and inversely with the magnitude or difficulty of the expected response.

Trance induction procedures are, of course, typically designed to increase the subject's expectancies for responding to suggestions, and in the Ericksonian approach the hypnotist tailors his induction to the characteristics and ongoing behavior of the client. Kirsch sees most hypnotic induction procedures as merely expectancy modification procedures.

Kirsch's response expectancy theory is generally consistent with the nonstate theories of Sarbin, Barber, Wagstaff, and Spanos. All agree that hypnotic responses are best seen as compliance, belief, and imagination, and that the hypnosis experience occurs when people voluntarily play the role of hypnotic subject. One key difference between Kirsch's theory and others is that his response expectancies are the *immediate* causes of the hypnotic response. Rather than having goal-directed images enhancing hypnosis, as Barber suggests, Kirsch has shown that the imagery enhances responsiveness by virtue of its effects on expectancy. Kirsch has also shown that not all so-called hypnotic phenomena are under a subject's will power or self-control. Warts, for example, can be affected both by placebos and by hypnosis, and such changes in skin conditions are not under one's voluntary control. Kirsch notes that one could offer subjects a substantial sum of money to make their warts disappear, but it is highly unlikely that many subjects would be able to do so.

This phenomenon also clearly shows the commonality between hypnosis and placebo effects. Both are examples of the nonvolitional nature of response expectancy effects. Kirsch's observation raises another point of significance—the fact that we must realize that not everything that happens to the human being as a result of external stimulation is or should be considered hypnosis! Suggestion is a very powerful influence on human behavior and it can influence human behavior in many different ways, only a very few of which we would or should designate as "hypnotic."

William C. Coe and the Dangers and Politics of Hypnosis

One of the most inventive and creative investigators in the field of hypnosis research today is Dr. William C. Coe, professor of psychology at California State University at Fresno. For many years Coe has been a critic of the concept of hypnosis as an altered state of consciousness, and has challenged the utility of the trance concept for nearly a decade. From the time of his early work with Sarbin, Coe has considered the idea that hypnosis is some sort of a special consciousness state to be unnecessarily mentalistic and misleading. In close agreement with Spanos, Coe sees Hilgard's neodissociation theory, i.e., the postulation of involuntary cognitive processes as the basis of hypnotic responsiveness, as redundant. Nothing happens in the hypnosis situation that cannot be easily and readily accounted for as the result of social-psychological interactions involving the hypnotist, the subject, and the context.

In a recent and fascinating review of the different approaches taken by the state and nonstate theorists over the past few years (Coe 1989), Coe noted that special state concepts were used primarily in one of two ways: either in clinical case reports or in a limited number of experimental articles. In the former instance, state terms were employed solely for the purpose of showing that the procedures used were really different from relaxation, guided imagery, or some of the other common therapeutic techniques that are applied without hypnosis. In the latter instance, the authors seemed to be using them out of habit and as a procedural shorthand to show that their subjects were hypnotized. Coe concludes that,

> It seems clear that the vast majority of clinicians prefer using special state concepts in vague ways, perhaps naively, or perhaps to mystify purposely. It seems equally clear that the vast majority of experimental investigators avoid using special state concepts, and even when they do, they appear to stand for a procedural shortcut. The evidence therefore appears, at least on the face of it, to indicate that the special state position has won the day with clinical hypnotists and that the social psychological position has won the day with experimental hypnotists. (1989, p. 422)

There are, of course, advantages for clinicians when an altered state metaphor is accepted. It makes what the hypnotherapists do unique and different from what other therapists do. Their special talents and skills as hypnotists as well as psychotherapists makes their services even more desirable. On the other hand, the experimental scientists have as their goal the discovery of new knowledge, simple explanations, and an objective understanding of the world we live in. The less mystery the better! Thus, simple social psychological concepts are much more desirable.

Coe also emphasized that most people who are hypnotized these days in either the laboratory or the clinic do not show the kind of behavior historically associated with deeply hypnotized or somnambulistic subjects. This is another reason why special state or trance concepts are not useful. Most investigators agree that ninety to ninety-five percent or more of the behavior of the typical hypnotized subject nowadays can be accounted for adequately with social-psychological concepts. The idea of a special state is simply not necessary. Nevertheless, a sizable number of workers in the area of hypnosis are strongly supportive of the special state position. To try to find out just why people still support this idea, Coe surveyed numerous officers, editors, and members of the three major hypnosis societies, The American Society of Clinical Hypnosis, the Society of Clinical and Experimental Hypnosis, and Division 30, The Hypnosis Division of the American Psychological Association, querying them about their position on this matter, as well as about their honors, awards, elections to offices, editorial positions, and the like. The results of Coe's surveys are embarrassingly clear. Since clinical practitioners make up the large majority of the members of the first two societies, they are the ones most likely to hold the power to determine status-enhancing positions in these societies. Neither of the two societies have recognized any of the five leading social-psychological investigators to the degree that their scientific contributions would seem to warrant. In other words, they honor their own—the state theorists. The third group, Division 30 of the American Psychological Association, which includes a much larger percentage of social-cognitive types, is much less discriminating than the other two groups. Coe's results show that being friendly to the special state position helps one's chances of gaining status in the clinical and academic hypnosis community. This sociopolitical climate has made supporting special state concepts more attractive, despite the fact that the nonstate position provides a broader, better, and more accurate understanding of what hypnosis is and what it is not.

Though someone reading Coe's remarks about hypnotherapists might jump to the conclusion that he is hostile toward them, this is not true. On the contrary, any therapist considering the use of any sort of suggestive approaches to bring about therapeutic change in his clients is urged to read and study Coe and Buckner's survey of hypnosis and other suggestive techniques in Frederick H. Kanfer and Arnold P. Goldstein's *Helping People Change* (1975).

Coe has also dispelled the mystery surrounding the phenomenon of post-hypnotic amnesia, which he has shown to be most easily understood in terms of role enactment on the part of subjects who want to fulfill their roles as good hypnotic subjects. Finally, he has done much to destroy the idea that hypnosis is dangerous. Only a few years ago when the concern for the safety of human subjects involved in scientific research was at its peak, the U.S. Department of Health, Education, and Welfare listed a number of procedures that it considered as having the potential for creating stress or bodily harm sufficient to warrant careful scrutiny before being employed with human subjects. The procedures were called "at risk," and difficult as it may be to believe, hypnosis was one of them. It was listed along with public embarrassment, humiliation, deception, shock, excessive heat, *et al.* To lay to rest the claim that hypnosis is dangerous, Coe and one of his students carried out a massive experimental study with a large number of undergraduate college students (Coe and Ryken 1979). Using form C of the Stanford Hypnotic Susceptibility Scale, Coe and Ryken compared the aftereffects of its administration with the aftereffects of participating in a learning experiment, taking a college exam, attending a college class, and college life in general. The results, in terms of anxiety and emotional upset, showed that hypnosis was no more bothersome than any of the other activities and not as bothersome as the exam. In another context Coe emphatically made the point that:

> Because of the public and professional prejudices against hypnosis its greatest danger is probably *to the hypnotist*, not the subject! Even though there is no definitive evidence that hypnosis is harmful, it may be used as an explanation for unfortunate complications. Hollow arguments are often proffered by professionals against the use of hypnosis simply on the basis of their own misinformation, their naive beliefs, or their fears. For example, one anti-hypnosis psychiatrist made the claim that patients under hypnotic therapy commit suicide. But, the percentage of suicides is equally high, or higher in patients under the care of general psychiatrists or psychoanalysts. Such claims are as ridiculous as the statement that hospitals are dangerous because many people die there. (Coe and Buckner 1975, p. 42)

Coe concludes with the observation that most of the untenable claims made for hypnosis spring from the belief in some special inner state which makes the hypnotized person somehow different from other persons. Therefore, the hypnotized person's behavior must be explained by special propositions, and as a consequence, almost any behavior that would normally be accounted for on more rational grounds is now seen as due to some mysterious inner agent.

Because of the importance of the idea that hypnosis is somehow or the other dangerous, we will take up this topic again in a later section.

Stage Hypnosis, and Waking Hypnosis

In an 1883 lecture, Bernheim claimed that all hypnotic phenomena, including amnesia, paralysis, contractures, illusions, hallucinations, analgesia, and anaesthesia could be produced in subjects never before hypnotized, while they were wide awake. Following up on this, in 1923 Dr. Wesley R. Wells, at a meeting of the American Psychological Association, showed how all the behavioral phenomena called hypnotic could be produced in alert, wide-awake students, and used for instructional purposes in the classroom. Wells called these demonstrations waking hypnosis, which is, obviously, a contradiction in terms. Wells is not the only student of hypnosis who has had trouble with nomenclature. Recall that Braid in 1847 attempted to get rid of his own creation, "hypnosis," after he discovered that sleep was not essential to the phenomenon. Wells also looked into the work of Coué and Baudouin and followed their suggestive techniques very closely in order to produce inability to open the eyes, unclasp the hands, remember one's name, etc., as well as automatic writing and amnesia for what recently transpired—all as a result of direct suggestion—while his student subjects were wide awake. Unusual? Startling? Actually, it is far from being either.

Nearly all experienced hypnotherapists know that the type of induction procedure used is not half as important as the mental set of the subject when he comes to the hypnotic session. When an experimental subject— a student, a patient, or client—comes to a hypnotist for hypnosis, he has already committed himself and has agreed to cooperate in the procedure. Moss (1965) reports that on several occasions he has used the nonsense word "phoz" instead of the word "sleep" while carrying out the induction procedures and found it to be equally as effective as "sleep" (p. 17). Moss also reports that in giving demonstrations of the hypnotic process before professional organizations, he frequently has a volunteer come up on stage and asks him if he is willing to be hypnotized. When he replies in the affirmative, Moss says, "All right then, please sit over there in that chair and go into hypnosis." This is all he does before resuming his lecture to the audience. Almost invariably, Moss reports, the subject sits down quietly and in a second or two is hypnotized, i.e., he is playing the role of a person in hypnosis! Does this sound suspiciously like stage hypnosis? Certainly it does. And what Moss was doing in the above example and what Wells did in his demonstrations of "waking hypnosis" are exactly the same methods and techniques used by the stage hypnotists who have fascinated and entertained audiences for years. They are using suggestion, prestige, and the demand characteristics of the social situation to elicit cooperation and compliance from willing volunteers. But is there really any difference between what skilled professional psychologists like Moss and Wells do and what the stage performers do? The answer is: very little. Let's look at how the stage hypnotist works.

Stage Hypnosis

Stage hypnotists, like successful trial lawyers, have long known their most important task is to carefully pick their subjects—for the stage as for a jury—if they expect to win. Compliance is highly desirable, and to determine this ahead of time, the stage magician will usually give several test suggestions to those who volunteer to come up on the stage. Typically, he may ask the volunteers to clasp their hands together tightly and then suggest that the hands are stuck together so that they can't pull them apart. The stage hypnotist selects the candidates who go along with the suggestion and cannot get their hands apart until he tells them, "Now, its okay to relax and separate them." If he has too many candidates from the first test, he may then give them a second test by suggesting they cannot open their mouths, move a limb, or open their eyes after closing them. Those volunteers who fail one or more of the tests are sent back to their seats, and those who pass all the tests are kept for the demonstration. Needless to say, not only are they compliant, cooperative, and suggestible, but most have already made up their minds in volunteering to help out and do exactly as they are told.

For the tyro stage hypnotist, there are a number of excellent books to help him succeed. McGill's *The Encyclopedia of Genuine Stage Hypnotism* (1947), and R. A. Nelson's *A Complete Course In Stage Hypnotism* (1965), as well as Kreskin's *The Amazing World of Kreskin* (1973) all provide specific hints and instructions for putting on a successful stage demonstration of hypnosis. If all else fails, the stage hypnotist can use the typical induction method, and those who do not show relaxation, drowsiness, and appear sleepy can be sent back to the audience. Though sleep suggestions are really unnecessary, many stage hypnotists use them because the subjects expect it and the audience is impressed, and since nearly everyone associates hypnosis with sleep and immobility, this clearly defines the situation as "hypnotic."

Barber (1986) and Meeker and Barber (1971) have summarized the typical procedures used by the stage hypnotists to secure their subjects' cooperation and to fool and entertain the audience. Most of their material, however, is taken from the professional literature mentioned above. Borrowing tricks and techniques from professional stage hypnotists and magicians to improve one's clinical skill with patients is certainly nothing new or unheard of. Nor is it to be discouraged. Some of Milton Erickson's most successful suggestive techniques were borrowed from the stage hypnotists Ralph Slater and Franz Poldar. Most clinicians could learn a great deal from the tactics and techniques employed by the stage magician to get quick and effective results with any and all sorts of individuals.

Once the volunteer or volunteers have been selected, the performer can then give them direct requests or commands without qualms. They will nearly always obey without question for a number of reasons. First, since they have been carefully selected for their willingness to go along—anyone who is opposed to doing so has already been eliminated. Second, since the audience believes the hypnotist is effective and competent, he has strong expectations working for him. And the subject, of course, believes this, too. Third, since the subject is facing an audience expecting him to respond as he is asked to, he would have to be negativistic indeed to resist the demands of both the audience and the hypnotist. Most subjects find it very difficult to refuse. This would make them appear to be real "party poopers." Moreover, most subjects quickly get into the act and go along with the fun because whatever happens they have a perfect shield to hide behind—after all, they were hypnotized!

All of these social-psychological pressures are found in the stage situation, and as McGill points out in his *Encyclopedia of Genuine Stage Hypnotism,* the volunteer is, in every sense of the word, an actor under the control of the stage director (the hypnotist). He holds the attention and the expectations of the audience, and when he receives his cue from the hypnotist-director, he must perform, i.e., act out his role. While the volunteer is on the stage he is tense and expectant, and the lights, music, curtains and other elements that create the dramatic atmosphere compel him to perform. McGill says that even though some subjects simulate hypnosis, it comes not from a desire to deceive but instead from a strong desire to help out and "put on a good show" for the audience.

The stage hypnotist, of course, has other advantages. The audience doesn't hear everything the performer says to the subject, and if the hypnotist says to him, "When I snap my fingers, go sit down in that chair and act like you're playing the piano," the audience is in the dark about it. What they do hear is the hypnotist speaking into the microphone and saying "Now you are Vladimir Horowitz, the concert pianist." Thus, the audience is misled into believing the subject is hypnotized and thinks he is Horowitz, whereas the subject is merely responding to the hypnotist's direct request to imitate the artist. What happens if the volunteer refuses? Simple, the hypnotist can whisper to him politely, "Please sit down and do what I ask. Close your eyes and help me out." More than likely the subject will comply with this direct and polite request, and if he does, the hypnotist will loudly announce, "You are going into a deep, deep and dreamless sleep." Then, when the subject closes his eyes, the audience believes the hypnotist has hypnotized him. It is rare indeed for any volunteer to refuse this sort of polite request. If the subject still refuses, the hypnotist can dismiss him and turn to another volunteer—having made sure there is always more than one on hand.

Stage hypnotists are also very careful not to challenge their volunteers. Instead of telling them they "can't do something" like bend their arm, unclasp their hands, or open their eyes, he suggests it cannot be done. This technique is usually effective in keeping the subject occupied testing the suggestion, and if it is effective for only a few seconds or so, the audience is convinced that it is the hypnotist's doing and that the suggestions were effective, when in reality they were never tested.

Most stage hypnotists supplement their stage performance with a number of other hypnotic feats that, although they are startling and impressive, have really nothing to do with hypnosis. One of these tricks is to have one of the volunteers go into a cataleptic trance, and then to suspend the subject's body between two chairs—one chair beneath the subject's head and neck and the other beneath his ankles. The performer then tells the audience that the subject is deeply hypnotized and in a cataleptic trance, and has become "a human plank." To further impress the audience, the hypnotist removes his shoes and steps up on the volunteer's body as the orchestra plays a crescendo. As every trained stage hypnotist knows, this trick has nothing whatsoever to do with hypnosis. It is a simple physical fact that practically anyone at anytime can hold their body rigid and easily remain suspended between two chairs. No special effect is required, and for maximum comfort, make sure that your subject's head and shoulders as well as his ankles and calves are on the padded part of the chairs. Common sense should also be used. Instead of having a 98-pound woman suspended and a 300-pound man stand on her midriff, make sure the man is the one suspended. Moreover, don't prolong the trick for more than a few minutes, because after two or three minutes the neck muscles begin to tire and maintaining the rigidity becomes uncomfortable for the subject. The average man can support up to 300 pounds in this suspended state with little or no discomfort. Also, make sure the standee removes his or her shoes—spike heels can be very painful! A similar trick of this nature is to place a large rock on the chest of a suspended subject and smash it with a sledge hammer. The trick, of course, is to use a block of sandstone and a felt pad under the rock next to the suspendee's skin. The subject feels a slight jar at the most; the force of the blow is absorbed by the sandstone and the felt pad.

Another trick that is often used to accompany so-called demonstrations of hypnosis and that again has nothing to do with hypnosis is a demonstration of hypnotic anaesthesia. While the volunteer is supposedly hypnotized, the hypnotist has him stretch out his hand and arm. The hypnotist announces to the audience that since the subject is deeply hypnotized he will have no feeling in either the hand or the arm. Taking a cigarette or a cigarette lighter the hypnotist places the flame close to or upon the subject's out-stretched palm and moves it slowly back and forth. Though impressive, the subject is in no danger of being burned as long as the flame keeps moving. All the subject feels is a little heat. The hypnotist next pinches the fleshy part of the subject's outstretched arm and rams a long pin right through the folded skin. Amazingly, the subject shows little or no response. Because of hypnosis? No, siree. When the hypnotist pinches the fleshy part of the arm, this numbs the area where the pin is inserted. While the finger-tips and the hand are very sensitive to being stuck, the fleshy part of the arm is not. Moreover, if the subject is distracted or is also told to make a fist and squeeze his fingers together with maximum force and concentrate as hard as he can on doing this while keeping his eyes closed, it is unlikely that he will feel the pin at all. If he does feel it, the feeling will be so slight that he will hardly notice it. The trick's effect is further enhanced if the hypnotist uses a long fine needle with a large colorful head.

The fascinating thing about all of these tricks is that carefully selected volunteers, compliance, and a gullible audience unaware of the various capacities and abilities of the human body are all that is necessary for an effective and entertaining performance of stage hypnosis, wherein hypnosis plays no part whatsoever.

Unfortunately, many many people have long associated the stage hypnotist's performance with fakery and assume that all of his subjects are confederates "in on the performance" and "putting on an act." Difficult as it may be to believe, some stage magicians used to look for subjects who would become cataleptic and fall into the epileptic-type trance with a loss of consciousness and muscular rigidity. They would then employ them as confederates on their barnstorming tours. After the magicians learned a little bit about human anatomy and human behavior, they became aware that anyone could serve the purpose and confederates were not necessary. In using confederates, not only did the magician run the risk of being discovered, but the confederate had to be paid or at least fed. Once the performer learns that any volunteer will do—provided the volunteer can be made to feel that the success of the act weighs on his shoulders and that the hypnotist depends on him—he will never be anxious again. He now has a failsafe personal weapon and has learned the secret: it is not necessary to hypnotize subjects to get them to act as if they were hypnotized!

Peter Reveen, a highly successful stage hypnotist, in his book *The Superconscious World* (1987), argues that the term "superconsciousness" should be substituted for the word hypnosis. In fact, Reveen argues, most volunteers who help out the stage hypnotist are motivated to cooperate in a situation wherein no adverse real-world consequences are involved. Such subjects feel a strong inner compulsion to go through the motions of obeying any demand or request, even when the only way they can do so is by simulating whatever effect they think the operator expects. According to Reveen, not enough attention has been given this "pleasing the operator" element of the phenomenon.

Kreskin, Suggestion, and Autosuggestion

Although most stage hypnotists and magicians are very careful not to reveal their secrets nor the ways in which they are able to con or trick their audiences, there is one outstanding exception to this rule, a man who has taken the art of legerdemain into a new and different realm and who has now become a public educator and benefactor as well. This is the very popular and well-known mentalist called Kreskin (né George Kresge). Not only is Kreskin a superb entertainer and performer, he is also a masterful practical psychologist, and for many years has been a student of so-called hypnosis. Kreskin's knowledge of and skill in using suggestion and auto-suggestion has made his performances across the nation, around the globe, and on television demonstrations of applied psychology that no one interested in human behavior can afford to miss. Along with Barber, Spanos, Blythe, and others, for well over two decades Kreskin has been trying to educate the public about the hypnotic fallacy, and has done much to demonstrate that hypnosis per se does not exist and that all the so-called hypnotic phenomena can be accounted for and demonstrated as due to the operation of simpler psychological processes.

My personal encounter with Kreskin came after I had just completed a long and intensive investigation of the effects of hypnosis on memory (Baker, Haynes, and Patrick 1983). While reading a copy of *Omni* magazine, I came across Kreskin's letter to the editor concerning the use of hypnosis in the courtroom. In Kreskin's words:

> In the past few years I have been a consultant on, and involved in, at least 74 law-enforcement investigations, mostly dealing with serious crimes. In each case I acted, not as a self-styled psychic, but as a person interested in the development of techniques that could dramatically utilize the mind to achieve a higher degree of productivity. I have successfully aided many witnesses in recalling in greater detail crimes that they had witnessed or been victims of. In many cases the recall of details of such experiences has been truly dramatic. At no time have I employed any formal hypnotic techniques or the induction of any hypnotic trance at all. Indeed the next monumental step in recall of traumatic or crime-oriented memories may be techniques of taping such memories that do not involve hypnosis at all. What law-enforcement investigators largely are not aware of is that people who have been exposed to crimes are not really suffering from any amnesia in the true sense of the word but have consciously or unconsciously forced the material from their thinking for any of a number of reasons.
>
> People, today, are less willing to volunteer testimony in a criminal case. They feel threatened. Our laws and our courts do not protect witnesses. Too many potential witnesses are aware that a criminal may be let out the day after he is indicted. Furthermore, a witness is questioned about the crime soon after it has taken place, and this is a period of great anxiety. He is questioned not only by the investigators but by friends, and during such a period it is very difficult to recall details clearly. Each attempt to recall the details of the crime only makes the witness even more confused. So he begins to convince himself that he really can't remember. Consequently, he simply locks away the material, without realizing he is doing so.
>
> Whether so-called hypnotic techniques really aid in the recall of material is a moot point. I doubt that hypnosis has anything at all to do with it. I believe hypnosis is a waste of time.

The amazing Kreskin—one of the most likeable and mystifying "mentalists" in modern show-business. Kreskin has for many years used suggestion and persuasion to amuse and entertain audiences. He has written several books discussing his techniques and experiences and has long denied the existence of any such thing as either hypnosis or hypnotic trance. He has also offered a prize of $100,000 to anyone who can scientifically prove the existence of the latter.

What impressed me most was my conviction that Kreskin was absolutely correct. Over the years I have helped a number of people locate lost articles, remember details of forgotten experiences, etc. Moreover, my own study of the role of hypnosis in memory (Baker, Haynes, and Patrick 1983) also supported Kreskin's assumptions. To help people remember, all that is necessary is to have them sit down, relax, close their eyes, and think back to the time of the forgotten event. With all of the anxiety and trauma absent, forgotten details emerge quite easily and naturally. In the case of lost objects, I have the client remember back to the time when he was last in contact with the lost object, and I then have him "walk through," in step-by-step fashion, every movement and action until we reach the point that the object disappeared. Without fail, we always discover the fate of the missing object. Nothing resembling a trance is ever involved.

After reading the letter, I began a correspondence with Kreskin. In our exchange of letters I discovered that we saw eye to eye on the subject of hypnosis, and that Kreskin's experiences mirrored my own. A master of suggestion, Kreskin uses it over and over in his stage performances, and at some point or other in his show he usually discusses his belief that there is no special state of hypnosis, and no need for fabricating a sleep-like trance. Kreskin admits that at one time, he, too,

> practiced what I believed to be so-called "hypnosis," and ardently fostered the trance concept. I now tell the audience that my references to "hypnosis," both historically and as I practiced it, are in the framework of the past. This is also why I use quotation marks when dealing with the subject. (Kreskin 1973)

Kreskin then explains to the audience how powerful a force is suggestibility, in which no known trance is involved, and how everyone is extremely prone to its influence. In somewhat the same way as we get imaginatively carried away with the story and action of a good movie, Kreskin causes members of his audience to respond to suggestion alone.

In a typical performance, such as his nationwide television appearance on a "Larry King Live" show in the spring of 1989, Kreskin invites volunteers from the audience for a demonstration of suggestibility. Though most stage hypnotists invite a dozen or so, hoping to find one or two who will be extremely responsive, Kreskin may invite fifty to sixty people on stage, even though there are only twenty to twenty-five chairs to be filled. Since the psychological conditioning has already occurred, in asking for large numbers he fulfills the apparent encouragement factor of "safety in numbers." After filling the twenty to twenty-five chairs, he asks the other volunteers to remain standing on stage, rather than sending them back to their seats.

Though many hypnotists, for example, Edmonston, believe the subjects must be relaxed before they can respond to suggestion, Kreskin demonstrates otherwise. While it seems highly improbable that, in a matter of a few seconds, someone can cause strangers to forget their names, not be able to open or close their mouths, or hands, or eyes, or even stand up or sit down, Kreskin does it daily and has done so for over thirty years. Typically, Kreskin asks the volunteers, "Are you wide awake?" "Yes," they answer. "Are you in a trance?" "No." Then Kreskin will pause and subtly change his voice tone to emphasize the suggestion he wants to plant, and say, "You know, we can forget things in everyday life quite easily." He then passes his hand in front of the volunteers' faces. The volunteers know there is some significance to what he has said, and something unusual about his hand gesture, but they don't know exactly what it is. Thus, the suggestion is planted.

Kreskin then asks a few questions, such as, "Where do you live?" or "Where do you work?" Then, after a pause of three or four seconds he asks in a meaningful way, carefully spacing the words, "By the way, what is your name?" Amazingly, the subjects cannot remember it. They have been keying back to the planted suggestion. They have been waiting for the question and they have obeyed the suggestion, and they are all wide awake! In Pittsburgh a few years ago Kreskin put on such a demonstration with a volunteer who, when he couldn't remember his name, reached into his coat pocket for his wallet so he could read his name off his license. Kreskin then turned to the volunteer and said, "Your hand is locked in that pocket. You can't remove it." And for a moment the man's hand was paralyzed and he couldn't pull it free. Why people respond so readily to such irrational suggestions is a very good question that we will address in a later chapter.

Kreskin has gone on record as stating there is, in his opinion, no such thing as hypnosis. In his own words, "I am now convinced that no person under 'hypnosis' has ever been asleep unless sent to that nontrance happy state by the lullaby drone of the guide. I am convinced that there is no such thing as a specific state, condition, trance—call it anything with any twist of semantics—that can be considered 'hypnosis' " (Kreskin 1973). Since, like James Randi, Kreskin is a man who "puts his money where his mouth is," in the early 1970s Kreskin offered $25,000 to anyone who could prove conclusively the existence of the "hypnotic trance." His challenge was accepted a few times in the '70s, but the attempted proofs were abandoned after Kreskin used both the EEG and the polygraph to show that the supposed trances resulted in no difference in brain waves and that the people supposedly in a trance were really wide awake. In the 1980s Kreskin upped his offer to $50,000 and successfully met a challenge in 1983. In 1985 Kreskin was challenged in a legal case. The case was dropped, however, when the attorney for the plaintiff (challenger) decided he had insufficient evidence to warrant continuing the case. The following year, after Kreskin raised his offer to $100,000, a second court trial was held. In this trial I appeared as a witness for Kreskin, but the case was thrown out of court because no basis for a case was found. For those who are interested in challenging Kreskin and collecting the $100,000, here is Kreskin's challenge verbatim:

I now offer $100,000.00 to any Psychologist, Psychiatrist or Hypnotist who can conclusively prove under scientific conditions, that I shall clearly outline and define, a specific condition, trance or state called "hypnosis".

Secondly, the challenger must clearly demonstrate that what can be done in the so-called state cannot be reproduced without that state. Yours truly knows of no such special phenomenon.

After going through legal ramifications of what was a pending trial, it is only justice that in the future, aside from the claimant meeting the conditions that I shall specify, they will also agree to sign a statement that should they fail to prove, and fail to win the $100,000.00 they must pay all expenses incurred by me in the legal preparation of such a challenge. This, I feel, is only justice.

At the trial I had the good fortune to meet Dr. Stephen P. Abelow, an orthopedic surgeon, the official orthopedist for the American Olympic Ski Team, and a former president of the American Society For Ethical Hypnosis, who also was appearing as an expert witness for Kreskin. Dr. Abelow confided that while he was a student, both as an undergraduate at Columbia University and in medical school, he followed Kreskin around for a period of eight years watching his demonstrations and trying to figure out his hypnotic techniques. Although Kreskin assured him there were none, he still couldn't believe people were that compliant and suggestible until he perfected his own stage act while finishing his medical training. I pointed out that I, too, had exactly the same experience and learned only through trial and error that hypnosis does not exist. Kreskin maintains that since we have no ready explanation for what causes us to respond to suggestion, therefore, it must be called "hypnosis" or it poses a threat to our reasoning. Again, in Kreskin's words,

The battle of semantics may be waged for years, but I firmly believe that what is termed "hypnosis" is, again, a completely normal, not abnormal, response to simple suggestion. But for many reasons, not the least financial, it will be mystically mined for a long time to come. (1973, p. 160)

Following on the work of Bernheim, Coué, and others, Kreskin has described and explained in great detail exactly how the power of suggestion and autosuggestion works in the so-called "hypnotic trance state." Any careful reader of his book would be left with few if any questions about how or why suggestion and autosuggestion is so effective in influencing human behavior or in bringing on the behavior we call "hypnotic," as it is commonly used on the stage. Unfortunately, this eye-opening book has been badly neglected by the general public as well as the scientific community. It is a book anyone interested in hypnotic phenomena should read. Hypnotherapists, in particular, should study it, since it offers a number of clues for improving the client-therapist relationship.

Suggestion, Kreskin notes, has always been the keystone of hypnosis and it is something we all use everyday of our lives in all of our human contacts. Citing Maskelyne and his book *Our Magic*, published in 1911, Kreskin points out that once we have induced a condition of mental receptivity in another person, that person is wide open to most any suggestion we create. By "suggestion" we mean the human ability and willingness to accept an idea, whether verbally or nonverbally communicated, and respond to it almost automatically. It is a very normal response in most people, and people who are more intelligent, creative, or artistic seem to respond more quickly. Most people respond easily, as can be demonstrated by simply suggesting to them that their nose is red and looks like it must be itching. Nearly anyone would then rub his or her nose and scratch it. In Kreskin's words, "Using only suggestion, tapping nothing but the waiting imagination, I've had subjects seeing flying saucers or shivering in polar cold within two minutes and audiences of six hundred dancing Irish jigs. I doubt that . . . any of them . . . were abnormal" (Kreskin 1973). Suggestion, Kreskin adds, is also the reason for the effectiveness of so many of the professional magician's tricks. This plus the individual imagination enables the stage magician to have members of the audience "put on daydreams like a cloak" and act out the otherwise most preposterous of charades.

> If a group of closely knit people play charades for about an hour, suggestibility usually increases to the point that when a scene or idea is projected by the person doing the pantomime, he or she will function automatically, submerging into the role and expanding it without great thought. I have observed charades that have come close to telepathy, although the players were completely unaware of having crossed over into another form of communication. (Kreskin 1973)

Kreskin admits that he not only once practiced what he believed to be hypnosis but ardently espoused the trance concept—until he learned through experience that he could get individuals to respond to suggestion without a trance induction.

Not only will people respond instantly to reasonable suggestions, they will even respond to irrational ones. Kreskin believes that it is the imagination triggered by suggestion that controls our physical behavior. Moreover, according to Kreskin, when the imagination and the will are in conflict, the imagination will usually win. Kreskin is also careful to point out that suggestion is a powerful force in all walks of life. It is a tool used very effectively by charismatic leaders—people like Hitler and Castro—as well as television evangelists who are attempting to arouse people emotionally. Emotions, of course, lend themselves to suggestibility.

Kreskin notes that a handful of books written in the 1880s and 1890s still have a great deal to teach us about social reactions to suggestion and the power of various suggestive techniques when used on large groups of people. Boris Sidis's *Psychology of Suggestion* (1910), Hippolite Bernheim's *Suggestion Therapeutics* (1886), and Albert Moll's *The Study of Hypnotism* (1889) are three classics dealing with mass human reactions and suggestion. The information in these books is as timely today as it was when they were written. Current advertising, promotions, and publicity campaigns of every type employ suggestive techniques day in and day out. We also know that suggestion plays a dominant and significant role in nearly every aspect of medical treatment. It is obvious in the placebo effect and equally obvious in every hospital and clinic where it is used daily by doctors and nurses to reduce anxiety and pain.

Autosuggestion is also something that everyone can learn to use for his or her own benefit, Kreskin says. Autosuggestion should be preceded by auto-conditioning, i.e., a series of mental relaxation exercises patterned somewhat as follows: first, after getting yourself in a passive frame of mind, you mentally melt and give your imagination free rein. Then follow these steps in sequence:

1. Sitting in a deep chair, or lying down, make yourself comfortable.
2. Reflect for a few seconds on some time and place where you were very deeply relaxed—a quiet afternoon on a beach, falling asleep in front of a fireplace after a walk in the snow, lying in deep shade on a riverbank. Recall as vividly as you can the total experience.
3. Close your eyes and think of a soft, mellow color like blue or green, or the pink hues of roses.
4. After a few seconds take three deep breaths; hold the third and the deepest, and mentally repeat the color image three times.
5. Exhale and let your entire body go limp. Make no effort to move a muscle. Simply stay relaxed and count backwards, mentally, from fifty to zero—very slowly. When you reach zero count forward from one to three. Then open your eyes.

This routine, according to Kreskin, consumes about five minutes and gets you in the proper mood for autosuggestion. Not only is it simple, but it also corresponds very closely to Herbert Benson's formula for bringing on the relaxation response (Benson 1975). Benson's four-step method includes: 1) a passive attitude; 2) a comfortable position; 3) a quiet environment; 4) an object to dwell upon or a mental device, e.g., counting. It should be noted that Kreskin's formula preceded Benson's by several years and was developed long before Benson achieved notoriety with his book. Neither of the two men is concerned about priority, however, since the techniques for meditation and relaxation were known thousands of years ago. Kreskin's emphasis, however, is on setting up conditions so that autosuggestion can become maximally successful. The foregoing procedures must be practiced two or three times a day for the first two weeks, and at least twice a day for the weeks following. Relaxation can be learned even by the most hyperactive individual, and once the body is relaxed, the mind also relaxes, and vice versa. In fact, a fail-safe method to insure mental relaxation is to systematically relax all of the muscles using Edmund Jacobson's progressive relaxation technique (Jacobson 1929) or one of the many variations on Jacobson's original method.

A streamlined version that I favor is to begin with the toes and tense them as tight as possible and hold them tightly for approximately twenty seconds and then let them relax. Wait for about thirty seconds and then tense the toes, ankles, and calves together for another twenty seconds and then let go and let them relax for another thirty seconds. Next, add the thighs and buttocks—every muscle below the waist—tense them for twenty seconds then relax for another thirty. Next, add the stomach muscles to the buttocks, thighs, calves, ankles, and toes. Then add the chest; then the shoulders, biceps, forearms, and fists; then the neck and face muscles, squinting the eyes and gritting the teeth—until every muscle group in the body has been tensed up and held and then relaxed. The last step, involving all the body's muscles, should be repeated two or three times before beginning mental relaxation suggestions. After completion of the foregoing exercise, the average individual will be thoroughly fatigued and eager to relax. The individual will also be maximally suggestible and ready for suggestions whether supplied by a therapist or by oneself, which is autosuggestion.

The use of autosuggestion is no different from receiving direct suggestions from another person, with the exception that, because of social conditioning, we tend to place more credence in suggestions coming from others than in suggestions from ourselves. Nevertheless, self-suggestions having to do with rising at certain times in the morning without an alarm, remembering certain material from a book, overcoming a bad habit, etc., are stored in the mind, and if the suggestions are constructive and positively worded and otherwise acceptable, they can be motivational and often are. On many occasions we have the need or the desire to accomplish certain things but lack that little motivational push to do so. In such instances, autosuggestion can furnish the needed extra push. There is considerable power in positive thinking, as every baseball player who has ever broken a batting slump knows.

Although, as Kreskin notes, autosuggestion cannot remove pain, it can serve to deaden it somewhat and make it feel "detached." Just as suggestion can convert the mere touch of a finger into a sharp shooting pain, so can suggestion be employed in some circumstances to temporarily alleviate severe agony, even though it cannot remove it. And despite the claims of some psychiatrists, the use of autosuggestion for pain removal is in no way dangerous; the worst that can happen as a result is that the sufferer may delay getting needed medical attention. The only real danger from autosuggestion, Kreskin notes, is that people may expect too much from it.

By Kreskin's estimate, over the years he hypnotized more than 35,000 people before he discovered that the only person he was hypnotizing was himself. Once he got over the delusion he was putting people to sleep and entrancing them, he discovered he could do exactly the same things with wide-awake subjects through the use of a developed form of suggestion. In his words,

> I slowly realized that the possibility existed that the "sleep trance" was an invention passed along from Mesmer's days. I went back to Bernheim's writings and suddenly "hypnosis" began to reek. I now realize that as a teenager I submerged doubts while working with Anna Piukutowski. I had been told that when a good subject entered a deep trance, the "rapport" would be so strong that (1) the subject could not hear anyone except the "hypnotist," (2) the subject would ignore any directions and even the physical presence of outsiders. With Aunt Anna deep in an apparent trance, I would impress on an audience her complete separation by having people come up to say, "Aunt Anna, wake up." Each time I noticed that she would begin to stir, moving her head, I'd quickly end the test. Obviously, I was afraid she would awaken, and also afraid to admit she could hear other voices. Plainly, she was never asleep. . . . At first, possibly because I wasn't certain that it could be done, I had many failures. But as the months went by, I began to improve on my techniques. As a showman, I had learned how to get attention and the trust of my audience, a prerequisite for accomplishing anything by "suggestion." It is also one explanation why medical "hypnosis" has never been very productive. Very few doctors are skilled at it and are unable to work with it constantly.

With audience volunteers, complete strangers, I edged into it by first attempting to read their thoughts. This was mainly a crutch for me, and had little to do with their later response. After that, I finally succeeded in doing everything previously labeled "hypnotic" by simply getting their attention:

freezing, at my suggestion, in an awkward position; seeing things that weren't there; imitating well-known entertainers; finding their hands spinning, one around the other. It took two years to perfect. . . . I'm now convinced that no person under "hypnosis" has ever been asleep unless sent to that non-trance happy state by the lullaby drone of the guide. I am convinced that there is no such thing a specific state, condition, trance—call it anything with any twist of semantics—that can be considered "hypnosis". . . . One by one each manifestation of so-called hypnosis' has been discredited.

(1) The sleep trance has been discredited

(2) The unconscious state has been discredited

(3) Regression has been discredited

(4) The hysterical state has been discredited

(5) The conditioned-reflex state has been discredited. (Kreskin 1973)

It is also important to note that Kreskin was one of the first to question the existence of the so-called "trance" state, but was also one of the first to emphasize the important role that imagination plays in suggestibility. According to Kreskin, "Everything is within the person" (1973, p. 161). Most people do not need to assume some sort of unnatural state to use their mental capabilities, whether for fun, for reducing mental tension, for suppressing pain, or for improving themselves. Kreskin notes that if a subject is suggestible and has the mental capacity to accept an idea, if he is properly motivated and willing, and if he has any imagination at all, he can be persuaded to do everything that is currently done under the guise of entranced hypnosis.

Kreskin tells the story of how he "bridged" Johnny Carson between two chairs on one of the "Tonight" shows. Carson, of course, was wide awake. And then Kreskin had Bette Midler sit on Carson's stomach. Interestingly, this demonstration brought about allegations that Carson was hypnotized before the show and that Kreskin then gave Carson "secondary suggestions." Most of the accusatory mail came not from the general public but from professional hypnotists. Incredibly, Kreskin is not permitted to perform hypnosis on live television because a few years ago two very naive psychiatrists, Dr. Harold Rosen and Dr. Herbert Spiegel, succeeding in abolishing formal demonstrations of hypnosis from live televison because of its purported "dangers" to the general public. On this idiocy, Kreskin commented,

I appreciate the fact that some medical doctors are alarmed at the prospect of an intrigued public attempting to bridge chairs as a result of a demonstration or indulge in "self-hypnosis" after seeing a TV show. The likelihood of either experiment succeeding is in the same ratio as shooting a hole in one after watching Arnold Palmer, and involves about the same hazard. As to the effects on children, I'd rather have them experiment with *suggestion* than watch most of TV's murder and mayhem. . . . The safety factor in "self-hypnosis" is that it doesn't work. No one has ever learned how to go into so-called "deep trance" after reading a how-to book. In a prime example, I've tried to "hypnotize" myself on hundreds of occasions. Nothing has ever happened. It has always bothered me that I could put thousands of people into "hypnosis" but not myself. I'm not alone. Harry Arons, a professional in the field flatly states that "no one can learn self-hypnosis from a book." (pp. 163–164)

Kreskin has also elaborated on a number of the other common hypnotic fallacies, particularly the notion that people can be hypnotically programmed to commit murder. A book by Robert Kaiser some years ago theorized that Sirhan Sirhan was hypnotically programmed to assassinate Robert Kennedy in the manner depicted of the novel *The Manchurian Candidate.* If people commit crimes, the crimes cannot be blamed on hypnosis. No one will comply with any request unless he or she wants to do the thing requested. To illustrate, on several occasions Kreskin has tried to get "good hypnotic subjects" to harm him, without any success. In a Bloomfield, New Jersey, demonstration, for example, Kreskin gave a compliant volunteer

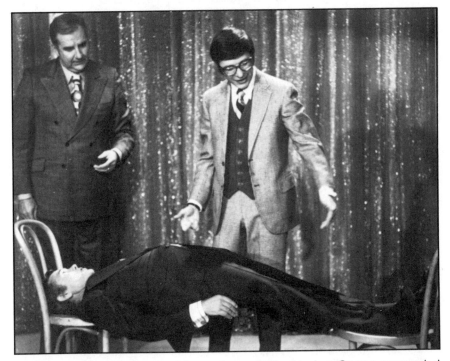

On the "Tonight Show with Johnny Carson," Kreskin has Carson suspended between two chairs as Ed McMahon looks on. Shortly after this picture was snapped, Bette Midler sat on Carson's stomach.

orders to leave the stage and after a five-minute delay to return, pick up the butcher knife on the table on the stage, and plunge it into Kreskin's back. The man did return to the stage and pick up the butcher knife, and even raised it over Kreskin's back, but then he dropped it and shuddered. Since the act was contrary to the subject's will, he refused to carry out the command. This will always be the case, unless somehow the subject is led to believe or is convinced that his life is in danger, and then and then only will use a weapon to defend himself. Experiments carried out years ago by the CIA had subjects pick up a revolver and fire it at an attacker while they were hypnotized. All this series of experiments proved, however, was that if people are led to believe their lives are in danger they will defend themselves. This has nothing to do with hypnosis.

Ridiculous as it may seem, many so-called experts in hypnosis claim they can even hypnotize animals and birds, and "prove" it with roosters. Yet nearly every chicken farmer knows that if you force the rooster's beak down to earth and focus his eyes on a long white line in front of him, he will remain motionless for a minute or so. Others have claimed that the snake charmer hypnotizes the cobra. As every herpetologist knows, however, it is the movement of the charmer's body and nothing else that fascinates the snake. Some hypnotists have even claimed that hypnotizing the Thanksgiving turkey before its beheading will make the meat more tender!

Although such silliness is hard to top, many other equally outlandish claims have been made for the wondrous effects of hypnosis, including its ability to cure most of the body's physical ills, as Dr. William J. Bryan Jr. of The American Institute of Hypnosis claimed a few years ago. He even stated that hypnosis could be used to set an athelete's broken leg or sprained limb almost immediately after injury, in which case there would be practically no pain or swelling and the recuperative time would be shortened through "subconscious control of the autonomic nervous system." Would that it were that simple and easy.

Preposterous claims about the powers of hypnosis reached their zenith, perhaps, when Dr. Bryan, in his book *Religious Aspects of Hypnosis* (1962), boldly claimed that the fact of hypnosis offered the long-sought proof of the existence of God. In his words,

The size of our soul can be likened to a balloon small and empty until through the use of hypnosis it is filled by the breath of God which gives it greater and greater power. Its size, therefore, depends on the amount that our soul is filled up with God. . . . Through hypnosis we have proved many times that mind power of phenomenal proportions exists. . . . In the same manner we can then prove the existence of God (something scholars and theologians have been trying to do for centuries). If we admit that the soul is a storehouse of spiritual power within us, a storehouse which comes with us when we are born and which leaves us when we die, a storehouse which is given power as our faith comes into being through hypnotic techniques, a storehouse which receives power (God) as our minds become concentrated and hypnotized, obsessed with and possessed with the acceptance of Christ as our personal savior. . . . It is easier to prove this through the use of hypnosis since it is also dependent upon the concentration of energy and it is the key to satisfying religious experience whether one calls it by the name of Hypnosis, Mono-ideaism, Prayer or by still another name. (pp. 69–71)

Bryan is, however, rational enough to admit that his attempt is "a rather clumsy and primitive proof of the existence of the Universal Mind and the Universal Soul. . . ." Bryan is correct on both counts.

Unfortunately, the only therapeutic agents the hypnotist has going for him are the effects of relaxation and the power of suggestion. Although the latter is, indeed, a potent force, it has definite limits. As Kreskin remarks, it has never lived up to the wild and foolish claims made for it and never will. Kreskin has also stated that, in his opinion, more knowledge about hypnotism has been unwittingly contributed over the years by the lowly stage hypnotist than by medical scientists. No one familiar with the facts and the history of hypnosis could disagree.

Before leaving the topic of stage hypnosis it might be of interest to look at one bit of stage magic that has, in the past, been associated with hypnosis. I am referring, of course, to the trick of having someone in the audience hide some object such as a ring while the stage magician or hypnotist is out of the room or securely blindfolded. Then, after the magician's return, while still blindfolded, he moves unerringly to find the hidden object. This he does through his ability to "mind-read" or "thought-read." Ability to perform this trick is due simply to what is called "idoemotor action," i.e., small unconscious muscle movements made by the audience member or volunteer who is totally unaware that he or she is giving the secret away. Clark Hull describes it in detail in Chapter Two of his *Hypnosis and Suggestibility* (1933):

Muscle Reading

Demonstration I. A number of young people have assembled for a demonstration of thought reading. I inquire if there are any persons present who have been successful in operating the "Ouija" board. Several have tried it and Miss X seems to have been quite adept. She even intimates that "Ouija" has made some interesting revelations. I decide that I shall try to "read her thought." I go out of the room and am thoroughly blindfolded. Meanwhile Miss X carefully secretes a finger-ring. I am led back to the room. I know nothing about where the object is hidden, or even what the object is. Miss X meets me at the door. I direct her to grasp my right wrist firmly with her thumb on the lower side and the tips of her four fingers on the back. I tell her to think constantly and intently of where the object lies hidden, and that I will try to read her mind and locate the object with my right hand. I hold my hand about ten inches from my body and slightly below my chest, forearm horizontal. I keep the arm and hand flexed just as much as possible so as to attain the maximum of sensitivity to slight unconscious movement of the person whose mind I am trying to read. I wait for a time for some leading movements but feel none. I begin to move slowly away from the door, at the same time reminding the subject to think intently of where the object is. Presently I pause and try again for signs. I make gentle movements in various directions, but find that the subject's hand makes a slight resistance in all directions except towards the right. I therefore begin moving slowly towards the right, watching intently for signs of resistance or of leading. After going some feet I pause again for further signs, but am unable to distinguish anything. I make tentative movements in several directions, but to no avail. Once more I admonish the subject to think intently. I hold my arm perfectly still for some minutes, waiting for an indication. At length I detect a faint pulling of my hand forward and somewhat to the left. I follow the lead slowly and tentatively. By moving carefully I can feel that slight pulling nearly all of the time now. It leads me around the corner of a table. At length I feel my hand touching the shoulder of a man's coat. I start to move my hand upward, thinking the object may be lying on top of the man's head, but encounter marked resistance from my subject's hand, which presses downward. I completely relax my arm and the subject quite definitely moves my hand down the front of the man's coat and pauses at a pocket. I reach into the pocket, feel the ring, and pull it out. Here the audience applauds and I know I have been successful. I remove the blindfold and ask Miss X if she intentionally led me to the ring. She vigorously denies leading me either intentionally or otherwise. (pp. 23–24)

Kreskin's variation on this trick is to have some member of the audience or his employer hide his paycheck for the performance while he is out of the room. Upon his return Kreskin will lightly hold or touch the arm of his guide and within a few minutes track down his paycheck. Kreskin is so adept at this bit of "mind reading" that he has failed to collect his fee and has had to watch it go to charity only twice out of hundreds of attempts. Kreskin is so skilled at "reading people's minds" that, on occasions, it is not necessary for him to use any physical contact at all. Nevertheless, he still discovers the hiding place. Such skill is, indeed, extraordinary *sensory* perception and represents an unusual refinement of the classical ideomotor technique. Ideomotor movements are also responsible for the spelling out of words on the "Ouija Board" and the so-called "unconscious writing" with the planchette used by spiritualists. The planchette, an offspring of the tipping table, is a polished board on rollers resting on a pencil in a socket at the apex. The medium places his hand on the board, and when the board moves, the pencil leaves markings on the paper placed beneath. Thus the medium communicates with the dead spirits!

Summary: Imagination, Imaginative Involvement, Absorption, and the Fantasy-Prone

As has been noted throughout the present chapter, one of the major reasons state theorists and the public in general have failed to understand what is happening in the hypnotic process is the focus they have placed upon the hypnotist, his techniques, and his imaginary powers, rather than upon the person being hypnotized, i.e., upon the personality of the subject. If the individual is a stable, hard-nosed, literal-minded, externally focused, here-and-now type, unimpressed with status, fancy titles, and overblown egos, and one who is innately distrustful and resentful of people who "want to mess with his mind," and M.D.s and the medical establishment in general, no hypnotist on earth will ever be able to obtain either his cooperation, relaxation, or compliance. He is the type that is usually considered unhypnotizable and ranks at the extreme or low end of the imagination or imaginative-type continuum. If the individual is at the other end of the continuum, however, the polar opposite of the individual just described, little or no effort at all is required to obtain all of the behaviors usually associated with the ideal or highly hypnotizable subject—the type that most of the laboratory research we find written up in journals uses as subjects. It is curious to note that we have come full circle: from the conclusion of King Louis's special commission in 1791 that the hypnosis phenomenon was due to "an excitement of the imagination" rather than any form of magnetism, to our contemporary realization almost 200 years later that imagination is the key to the entire hypnosis business.

People who are mentally stable and healthy, who are reality-centered, hard-driving, aggressive, ambitious, successful, and busy very seldom show up in mental health clinics or ever have recourse to psychiatrists or clinical psychologists. Only a fool who had good regular bowel movements would ever start gulping down laxatives. Similarly, mentally sound people seldom come in contact with members of the mental health professions or have need of their hypnotic services. If and when such individuals do contact a psychological helper, most would not be diagnosed as "fantasy-prone." This is not to say that hard-driving, successful entrepreneurial types are devoid of imagination, or are unable to relax, or are better able to resist powerful suggestions than the average. Rather, it is to stress that the human ability to become imaginatively involved (i.e., to be hypnotized) is normally distributed, and the people just described would not be at the high end of this distribution. It must also be noted that nearly all of our so-called scientific knowledge of hypnotic phenomena is based upon studies of late adolescent college students, who make up the majority of subjects of experiments, or of people who are mentally disturbed, i.e., patients and clients in hospitals and clinics.

For many years I have been intrigued by the fact that many of my clients and experimental subjects are so compliant and suggestible that hardly any effort at all is required to get them imaginatively involved in the hypnosis game. Others, even though very cooperative, show unmistakable signs of muscular tension and resistance to any and all forms of suggestion. These more literal-minded souls require a great deal of persuasion and wheedling before they are ever able to relax and begin to use their imaginative powers. A few years ago I carried out a small demonstration (I hesitate to call it an experiment, since the outcome was obvious) in hypnotic age progression (not regression). I took two groups of ten volunteers each one hundred years into the future. One of the groups—the experimental group—consisted of avid science fiction fans. These subjects scored in the upper quartile of a modified version of Tellegen's absorption scale (a measure of ability to immerse oneself in nonordinary reality). The second group—the control group—was made up of economics and business school majors. These subjects scored in the lower quartile of the absorption scale.

The experimental procedure consisted of relaxing each subject, putting them on a time machine, moving them 100 years into the future, and then requiring them to describe what they saw and experienced. As expected, the science fiction fans—without exception—described fantastic cities, vehicles, planet colonization, trips to distant stars, exotic creatures, magical human powers, etc. On the other hand, it was like pulling eyeteeth to obtain any information at all from the members of the control group. Many reported they were unable to see anything at all, while those who did envision a future reported one pretty much like our present world, except more crowded, more polluted, and with faster means of transportation. Three members of the control group focused on their grandchildren and their lives and jobs, and sports figures and records, in a world pretty much like the one we inhabit today. Four members of the control group had tremendous difficulty seeing anything at all, and only after much coaxing reported things like people in park-like settings wearing tunic-like clothing—men, women, and children clothed alike, as in "Star Trek"—and people living in domed cities with climate control, working in robot-controlled plants and offices. In terms of fantasy, the content of the visions of the two groups was dramatically different and reflected expected personalities, concerns, and interests of the group members.

While the power of suggestion to arouse and influence our internal image-making ability should never be discounted or minimized, it should also be clearly recognized that by temperament some individuals require little or no encouragement from external sources to exercise considerable imaginative powers. Such individuals are known as "fantasy-prone personalities," and when we find them in the role of hypnotic subjects we can expect (and we will receive) all the extreme behaviors formerly attributed to hypnosis alone in so-called "good" subjects, i.e., positive and negative hallucinations, somnambulism, amnesia, insensitivity to pain, etc.

Although one could be accused of using a conundrum to explain an enigma by arguing that hypnotic phenomena is all a matter of personality differences, this is, nevertheless, the best available explanation. Only those personalities capable of high imaginative involvement show the dramatic aspects of what has formerly been attributed to the mysterious force of hypnosis.

While the study of human personality is one of the most interesting and fascinating aspects of psychology, it is also one of the most complex and frustrating. Not only are personality disorders difficult to describe and explain, but there are even debates about what constitutes a healthy or an unhealthy personality. There is disagreement about the treatment of personality disorders and whether treatment is possible. Nevertheless, Josephine Hilgard, Daniel Araoz, Steven Starker, Jacob Stattman, and others have recognized the important role that personality attributes—particularly the attribute of imagination—play in the phenomenon of hypnosis.

According to Araoz, the concept that "suggestions work to the extent that they produce an image in the patient's mind," is of such significance that it can and should modify the clinician's entire approach to the use of hypnosis in general and suggestions in particular (Araoz 1984). And from the work of J. Hilgard and J. P. Sutcliffe (1965) we know that self-reports of vivid imagery and imaginal experiences correlate significantly with greater hypnotic susceptibility. Individuals extremely lacking in reported imagery turned out to be nonhypnotizable. Those who reported that their vivid imagery experiences were triggered by environmental stimuli were the best hypnotic subjects. More recent studies, by Tellegen and Atkinson (1974), Spanos and McPeake (1977), and Barrett (1979) have confirmed the earlier findings.

In summary, as Fromm and Shor have stated in *Hypnosis: Development, Research, and New Perspectives* (1979), hypnosis is essentially a "profoundly compelling imaginal fantasy." Both the state and nonstate theorists agree on this position. State theorists argue that: (1) there is a special state of awareness called the hypnotic trance; (2) this state is marked by increased suggestibility, and enhancement of imagery and imagination, including past visual memories; and (3) the state also involves a decrease in the planning function, a reduction in reality testing, and a number of reality distortions such as false memories, amnesias, and positive and negative hallucinations. Cognitive-behavioral theorists argue, on the other hand, that: (1) differences in response to hypnotic suggestions are not due to any special state of consciousness, but rather to the individual's attitudes, motivations, and expectancies; (2) concepts such as "trance" or "dissociation" taken from abnormal psychology are misleading and fail to explain the behavior, in other words, responsiveness to suggestion is a normal psychological reaction; and (3) all of the phenomena associated with hypnotic suggestions are within normal human abilities. Both the state and cognitive-behavioral positions agree that subjects are responsive to hypnotic suggestions to the extent that they think aloud and become imaginatively involved with the suggested scenarios, and both acknowledge the importance of imagination as the necessary ingredient for the production of any phenomena associated with the use of hypnosis.

With regard to points of disagreement, the more careful and refined the experimental investigations into the nature of the behavior, the more evident it is that the postulation of some sort of vague, will-o-the wisp, undefinable and undefined, unmeasurable and unmeasured, mental state known as "hypnosis" is both unnecessary and unwarranted. Our knowledge of human cognition, of human social behavior, and of aberrant and abnormal human behavior has advanced and will continue to advance at a steady pace without the assumption of the existence of a special state of consciousness or awareness called the "hypnotic trance." It is arguable that our understanding will proceed more rapidly if we discard all such unnecessary assumptions. The history of science is strewn with the corpses of discarded concepts, concepts such as ether and phlogiston, for example, that not only outlived their usefulness but also served to delay and impede the progress of knowledge. It is high time that we also rid ourselves of the useless concept of "hypnosis." Traditionalists will argue that a term or a word is needed to describe and characterize what we currently do. They are correct. But why not "call a spade a spade." If suggestion is what all hypnotherapists use, why don't we call it suggestive therapy, which is an accurate description, rather than hypnotherapy, which implies sleep is involved—and which all authorities agree is an inaccurate description? But perhaps it is expecting too much to assume that rationality is preferable to tradition.

4.

What Hypnosis Is, What Hypnosis Is Not, and What It Does and Doesn't Do

Perhaps because of the association of hypnosis with medicine and healing, for a long time interest was focused on the hypnotist and his methods and techniques rather than on the nature of the hypnotic subject. When the focus shifted to studying the person being hypnotized it began to dawn upon a number of investigators that there was and is a wide range of individual differences in the way human beings react to the ministrations of the hypnotist. As we have seen, a number of investigators and theorists dismissed some of their recalcitrant or resisting subjects as simply unhypnotizable, while embracing those who quickly retreated into a behavioral state resembling somnambulism. These "good" or "ideal" subjects seemed to be in some sort of altered state of consciousness similar to entrancement—the same sort of state that is brought on by drugs, monotonous and repetitive stimulation, physical exhaustion, and so on. The characteristics of the hypnotic state and the drugged state were apparently so similar that many hypnotic theorists adopted the term "trance" to describe all hypnotic states, and once the term was in use, made the assumption that the hypnotic state and all other altered states were, if not identical, alike enough that differences were negligible. The Eriksonians, in particular, have been prone to use the term "trance" with abandon and to consider even the entire human behavioral repertoire a form of trance. This glib use of the word to deal with every aspect of human response and to gloss over critical and significant differences in both internal and external reactions is totally unacceptable; it has led to confusion and misunderstanding on all sides. Because the use of the term "trance" is so widespread and so often and so heatedly defended, let us digress from our main theme for a moment and look at both the use and misuse of this term.

The Concept of Trance

The dictionary definition of trance is "a daze or a stupor, a prolonged and profound sleep-like condition or a state of mystical absorption." As used by many writers and theorists, it turns out to be a term embracing a number of widely differing psychological states. The states range from a cataleptic coma to an ordinary daydream in which a person ignores the immediate world around him. Trances come in various sizes and shapes: the Yogic trance of the Hindu mystic, the ecstatic trance of the shamans or religious visionaries, the somnambulistic trance of the sleepwalker, and the so-called hypnotic trance of the hypnotized subject. What they have in common is the subject's temporary unawareness of his immediate physical environment.

Trances also on occasion may be accompanied by mental dissociation and what is known as automatism, i.e., activities performed without the conscious awareness of the individual, or with the individual will in abeyance. We also find on occasion a mild form of trance involving wishful thinking, self-deception, and autosuggestion due to the subject's neurotic desire for attention. Drugs may also produce a type of trance in which the individual's will appears to be sapped and the individual seems half asleep and not aware of what he or she is saying and doing. People on tranquilizers often seem to be in a trance. People who are neurotic or have milder forms of psychosis also often appear to be and act like they are in a trance. Finally, we have the fake trances that the professional mediums and channelers exhibit at will. Many modern channelers can go into a trance instantly—even faster if you flash a few dollar bills.

Our concern here is with individuals in a so-called "trance state" of abnormal suggestibility engendered by hypnotic methods. Unfortunately, the confusion surrounding the term "trance" as used by many people in the hypnosis business is mind-boggling. Jay Haley's description of the problem is classic:

> The trance is sleep, but it isn't sleep. It is a conditioned reflex but it occurs without conditioning. It is a transference relationship involving libidinal and submissive instinctual strivings, but this is because of aggressive and sadistic instinctual strivings. It is a state in which a person is hypersuggestible to another's suggestions, but one where only auto-suggestion is effective since compliance from the subject is required. It is a state of concentrated attention, but is achieved by dissociation. It is a process of role-playing, but the role

is subjectively real. It is a neurological change based upon psychological suggestions, but the neurological changes have yet to be measured and the psychological suggestions have yet to be defined. Finally, there is a trance state which exists separately from trance phenomena, such as catalepsy, hallucinations, and so on, but these phenomena are essential to a true trance state. (Haley 1965)

Other notions with regard to trance are equally confusing. Roy Udolf, for example, states, "Once subjects have experienced 'hypnosis,' their reactions in subsequent trances tend to be very similar to the initial ones unless something contrary is suggested. *In fact, people enter trance states spontaneously in everyday life (in the absence of any hypnotist), and these spontaneous trance states are rarely recognized for what they are* [italics mine]. (Udolf 1984). Udolf notes that Spiegel has made the point that witnesses subject to the stress of questioning by police may slip into such a state as a way of defending themselves from a traumatic situation. Thus, trances are all around us all of the time. As Udolf defines it, "a trance is simply a response to a set of trance-inducing suggestions, as is any other phenomenon obtainable under hypnosis" (Udolf 1984, p. 4).

Others, like Hilgard, use the word "trance" not as an explanatory construct but merely as a metaphor. Another reason often given for using the word is that it corresponds to the subjective experience of the person entering hypnosis, i.e., these people feel like they are in a daze or stupor. Perhaps some individuals do, but certainly not all, and in fact those who do are likely few in number. This notion stems from the older idea that all hypnotized subjects are unconscious or in a sleep-like state, when in fact the opposite is the case, i.e., the great majority are aware of everything going on around them, they never lose control of the situation, nor do they surrender their volition to the hypnotist. In no way, while people are playing the game of hypnosis, are ordinary principles of human behavior suspended. The so-called subject is complying, role-playing, and he can come out of the game any time he chooses.

Although Udolf favors usage of the term "trance," he clearly recognizes the social-cognitive character of the trance condition and notes, "There is nothing that can be accomplished by using hypnosis that could not be done by using some alternative procedure" (Udolph 1984, p. 3). Dr. Jeffrey K. Zeig, an Ericksonian clinical psychologist, gives workshops around the country specializing in "Ericksonian hypnotherapy without trance," a clear example of semantic desperation.

Dr. Stephen Gilligan (1987), another Ericksonian, has written an entire book about the trance state. He sees the hypnotic trance as merely one of a number of trance states, all of which are naturalistic and all of which have been found since the beginning of time and in all human cultures.

Gilligan sees the trance state as biologically essential for all human beings. According to Gilligan, not only is trance experienced in many situations—daydreaming, dancing, listening to music, reading a book, watching television—but it is also induced in many many different ways. The trance can be induced through rhythmic and repetitive movement (dancing, running, rocking, breathing exercises, etc.); through chanting, meditation, prayer, group rituals, etc.; by focusing attention on an image, an idea, the sound of someone's voice; through relaxation, massage, warm baths, etc.; and through drugs such as alcohol, cannabis, or tranquilizers. All of these methods tend to decrease the cacophony of conscious awareness with its discontinuous patterns of stimulation. Anthropologists have noted that trance rituals can be found in nearly every culture on the planet, and they have been around for centuries.

Gilligan also sees trance as playing an integral role in the balance between biological and psychological systems. Going into a trance, he says, can help the individual maintain his sense of self-identity. Going into a trance by means of meditation, group chanting, etc., increases one's sense of security. A severe threat to survival can also bring on a protective trance involving complete withdrawal from consciousness through shock, catalepsy, or fantasy. Primitive tribes use the trance to affirm deeper connections to the environment. For example, the American Indian rain dance serves such a purpose. Most significant perhaps is that trance phenomena are the basic processes by which psychological experience is generated. In Gilligan's view, certain other phenomena frequently show up associated with a hypnotic trance, such as: regression into the past, progression into the future, improvements in memory, i.e., hypermnesia, amnesia or selective forgetting, perceptual distortions, and perceptual dissociations, i.e., positive and negative hallucinations. These phenomena are not common to all trance states, of course, and they may well be artifacts arising from our own culture's values and biases. While these phenomena at first appear unusual, they are actually entirely naturalistic.

Gilligan sees trance phenomena as the basic psychological processes by which experience is generated and maintained. Gilligan maintains that the phenomenological experience is intensified and amplified in trance states, which makes them appear spectacular or otherwise unusual. Phenomenologically, the experience of deep trance subjects is remarkably similar to that of psychotics. Both are characterized by perceptual and sensory alterations, dissociations, regressions, and amnesias. The quality of the experience, however, is radically different: it is painful and harrowing to the psychotic but usually pleasant or enjoyable to the subject in trance. While the form of the experience is the same, the context is radically different.

Where Gilligan makes his most important contribution is in his discussion of the phenomenological characteristics prominent in the trance

experience. He lists the twelve most common phenomenological characteristics of the trance experience as follows:

(1) *Experiential absorption of attention*—Becoming fully immersed in one
particular experience for a sustained period and able to resist irrelevant stimuli and distractions.

(2) *Effortless expression*—Things just seem to happen and flow without
any effort on the subject's part. One doesn't have to try to do
anything or plan ahead.

(3) *Experiential, non-conceptual involvement*—Thought processes typically
become less critical, less evaluative, and less verbal and abstract;
concurrently, they become more descriptive and image-based, more
sensory, and more concrete.

(4) *Willingness to experiment*—Often described as suggestibility. The entranced subject is usually quite willing to do unusual things he is
asked to—as long as they are congruent with the subject's personal
values.

(5) *Flexibility in time/space relations*—People in trance relate to time and
space in many different ways. They can age regress or progress,
distort time, condense or expand time, and positively and negatively
hallucinate.

(6) *Alteration of sensory experience*—Changes occur in most of the sensory systems, perceptual distortions of body parts may develop, and
visual and auditory alterations are also common.

(7) *Fluctuation in involvement*—Subjects may develop a deep trance, shift
to a medium one or a light one, and then arouse from trance altogether
before again dropping into a deep state.

(8) *Motoric/verbal inhibition*—Subjects usually do not feel like moving
or talking, they can if they want to, but consider such external
behaviors as irrelevant.

(9) *Trance Logic*—Subjects tend to find nothing bizarre about finding
themselves in two different places at the same time or in exploring
fantasy worlds whose rules violate real world constraints.

(10) *Metaphorical processing*—Trance subjects have a tendency to relate
all communications in a self-referential fashion. Everything happening to others also happens to them.

(11) *Time distortion*—The experience of time is often quite different for
the hypnotized subject. Many speak of trance as having a "timeless"
quality to it.

(12) *Amnesia*—Subjects often arouse from trance and remember little
(partial amnesia) or nothing (total amnesia) of what happened while
they were in trance.

It is important to note that all of the above experiences reported by
so-called hypnotized or entranced subjects are events that could be engendered

by suggestions from the hypnotist himself, by role-playing on the part of the subject, or as responses elicited by the demand characteristics of the hypnosis situation. Since study after study has shown that there are really no verifiable subjective or objective criteria to determine when hypnosis is or is not present, interesting and intriguing as the above twelve characteristics are, they do not tell us very much about the nature of trance. No individual ever shows all twelve characteristics in any one hypnotic session, and most so-called hypnotized subjects never show any of them at all. With regard to characteristic number 4, willingness to experiment, few hypnotists other than entertainers and stage magicians are going to ask their entranced subjects to do things that are weird or bizarre. Therapists are most unlikely to do this.

The major problem with the concept and use of the term "trance" lies in its being applied to every type of self-referent or internally directed cognitive behavior. Weitzenhoffer (1985) notes that so-called authorities have made statements such as "almost everyone goes into a trance in an elevator," or "one person's normal state may be another person's trance," or to the effect that obtaining a personal history from a patient automatically produces "a series of trances." If I become involved in reading a novel, then I am in "a novel-reading trance." If I concentrate on figuring my income tax, then I am in "an income tax trance." If I focus on keeping my bowling ball on the lane, then I must be in "a bowling ball trance." There is, of course, no factual basis for any of these statements and to use the term "trance" in this way removes all semblance of meaning from it and utterly destroys its usefulness.

We ought to be very clear about the use of the term "trance." If there is such a thing as a hypnotic trance, it is most likely, as Weitzenhoffer suggests, only one member of a larger class of trances, and they in turn are only one type of a broader class of altered states of awareness. Weitzenhoffer notes that hypnosis can be distinguished from other trances on the basis of its two-person interactional character (Weitzenhoffer 1985).

It is important to note, however, that the semantic problem is far from new or recent. Rawcliffe in the 1930s called the term "trance" vague and unsatisfactory, and noted that the concept which the term expresses originally rose in connection with the primitive belief that a person who shows any of the symptoms referred to earlier, e.g., stupor and automatic behavior, has had his soul drawn away from his body. The idea that the soul temporarily leaves the body is a universal one that has existed since the beginning of humanity and unfortunately is still around today.

We also know that hypnosis does not manifest any unique properties, nor do hypnotized or entranced subjects reveal any unique abilities. As noted, we have no reliable way of proving hypnosis or a hypnotic state exists except to accept the highly unreliable statements of the hypnotic or entranced subjects themselves.

What Hypnosis Is and Isn't

Hypnosis, as Peter van der Walde reminds us (1965), seems to be more a frame of mind than an independent state of consciousness. Van der Walde has been among the few to return our attention to the significance of the subject in the hypnotist, hypnotic induction procedure, subject triad. He argues that the essential prerequisite to a hypnotic reaction is unquestionably the subject's motivation. In his view, hypnosis is a goal-oriented phenomenon wherein the subject is out to achieve some desired end. Moreover, he says, the motivation of the subject's participation in the hypnotic reaction is highly individualistic and depends upon a variety of needs and desires. Unacceptable wishes, van der Walde says, are most often gratified in the hypnotic situation, and the subject gets his gratification either from the hypnotic relationship or as a result of hypnotic behavior. It is the subject—not the hypnotist—who prescribes the extent and the expression of the wishes that are gratified. Therefore, *hypnosis must be viewed, first and foremost, in terms of the subject and his motivations.*

The hypnotic situation does nothing but help the subject get what he wants under conditions that seemingly allow this to be done safely. The hypnotist is important only as a transference figure. This is obvious, since we have so many successful hypnotists and responses to the hypnotist are completely unrelated to the hypnotist's ability or to his grasp of hypnotic induction procedures. Furthermore, in many instances subjects can be hypnotized by listening to a recorded induction procedure. If the hypnotist were necessary for the hypnotic trance, this wouldn't be possible. The subject's response to the induction procedure, therefore, is determined more by the subject's preconceived notion of what a hypnotist should be and do than by what the hypnotist really is and does.

The hypnotist is a culturally approved authority figure upon whom many fantasies involving omnipotence are projected. And the subject strives to gratify this fantasized, omnipotent figure. The hypnotist, of course, allows this to happen, because hypnosis is supposedly caused by the hypnotist. Both hypnotist and subject place full responsibility for all that occurs within the hypnotic trance at the feet of the hypnotist. Responsibility for all that happens as part of the hypnotic situation is projected onto a supposedly omnipotent figure, who, because of his omnipotence, does not have to answer to anyone for what happens. As a result of this allocation of responsibility, the subject is relieved of the need to answer for his actions. Because of the large variety of successful induction procedures, the type of hypnotic induction used is obviously only a secondary part of the hypnotic phenomenon (van der Walde 1965, pp. 438–47).

Meditation Is Not Hypnosis and Vice Versa

When we meditate, we focus our thoughts on something, we reflect on something, or we contemplate something. Or, if we follow the Zen Buddhist religion, we attempt to keep our minds free of all thought—like an empty mirror. If we are able to "empty our minds," we also find that we gain in the process a significant reduction in tension and usually bring on what Benson calls "the relaxation response." After studying all of the various forms of both Eastern and Western meditative practices, Benson discovered that they had four requirements in common: a quiet environment, a comfortable position, a passive attitude, and a mental device, for example, a word or phrase which continuously repeated serves to prevent or block the normal flow of thought or the normal stream of consciousness.

When one is playing the game of hypnosis with a hypnotist, one is engaged in following the images and the thoughts and the suggestions supplied by this external source—the hypnotist. Whereas, in meditation one is internally focused and tries to reduce or eliminate the thought flow or tries to concentrate fully on only one thought or idea. Because of the apparent similarity of the two events—meditation and hypnosis—it is very important that the reader fully understand that the two phenomena differ significantly. Although some writers have insisted that the contemplation and self-absorption characterizing meditation and prayer are practically identical with self-hypnosis, both depend upon the motivation of the subject, and the motivations of individuals inducing self-hypnosis and of individuals engaging in meditation differ widely.

There is good reason to believe that very few attempts at self-hypnosis are successful unless such attempts have been preceded by heterohypnosis. This points to the social-interactional character of classical hypnosis. On the other hand, many mediational practices and prayer are solitary practices that do not require the presence or participation of other individuals.

The problem is that we have so few words and descriptive phrases to apply to the many and varied states of consciousness and mental activity that we tend to see any and all kinds of behavior that involve closure of the eyes, stillness of the body, and slow rhythmic breathing as identical and representing the same state of consciousness—despite the fact that the trances brought about by exposure to rhythmic chanting, monotonous visual stimuli, self-emptying of the mind and thought, the ministrations of a hypnotherapist, common fatigue and sleep deprivation (sleep) are all psychologically and phenomenologically different. Lumping these various reactive states into the same basket and regarding them as indiscriminable is not only a serious mistake in psychological terms but is one of the major reasons we have failed to develop any clear understanding of how hypnotic phenomena develop and how the human mind functions. It has also led to years of superficial research and the asking of trivial, insignificant questions about the nature of human consciousness and mental activity. If every state of consciousness in the human mental repertoire other than wide-awake alertness is considered a trance, and all trance states are identical, we might as well throw in the proverbial towel and abandon our search for further progress or understanding. Needless to say, by calling it "trance" we remain as ignorant as we were before we named it.

Many people have great difficulty in gaining and maintaining a state of relaxed but focused attention, i.e., a state of mental calm. Whereas meditation teaches one how to discipline one's mind through the control of attention, hypnosis is concerned with achieving and holding one's attention on ideas supplied by an outside source, i.e., the hypnotist. Although most hypnotists have done little in the way of training their clients in the skill of attentional focusing, teaching them to use some of the meditative, cognitive-centering techniques can go a long way toward making any application of hypnotherapy more efficient and more effective. Hypnosis is not meditation and meditation is not hypnosis, despite their superficial similarities.

Highway Hypnosis Is Not Hypnosis

So-called "highway hypnosis" and "laboratory (or clinical) hypnosis," although superficially similar in some ways, are also quite different from each other. The major difference, obviously, is that the altered state of awareness in highway hypnosis is brought about by an unvarying pattern of visual stimuli over a prolonged period of time. The laboratory or clinical form of hypnosis is brought on by the monotonous sound of the experimenter's or therapists's voice over a long period of time.

Nearly everyone who has ever driven an automobile on a modern highway has suffered at one time or another from the symptoms of this interesting form of trance. Typically, you have planned your trip weeks in advance and you are full of vim, vigor, and vitality, and are raring to go motoring. Strangely, however, after only a few hours on the road, and despite the fact that you had a good night's sleep the night before and aren't on any sort of drugs or medication (and definitely you have not had anything alcoholic to drink!), you nevertheless find yourself unaccountably sleepy and lethargic. You find it almost impossible to keep your eyes open and focused on the road ahead, and you long for a bed—any bed at all, anywhere. The most fascinating aspect of this experience is the fact that it is a sleep-like condition, or better, a condition of sleepiness brought about by the nature of the automobile, the highway, and the monotony of the stimulation you receive from the environment. If you are alone and unable to resist the forces that are impinging upon you and lulling you into a stupor and a state of automatic movements and behavior, your awareness disappears and you find yourself—if you are fortunate enough to awake in time—driving off the side of the road or following the car ahead of you into a turnoff you had no intention of making. If you are unfortunate, you never wake up and become just one more automotive fatality among the hundreds occurring daily.

Psychologically and phenomenologically there are some very interesting aspects to this everyday situation. Were you asleep? Well, no, I had my eyes open. Maybe yes, I wasn't aware of what I was doing when I followed the truck in front of me onto the off ramp, and I probably would have plowed into his rear if my hitting the pothole hadn't jarred me awake. Uh, oh. I must have been asleep then! The most puzzling aspect of this sort of phenomenon is the fact that the driving behavior continues automatically even though awareness has long since fled, and the driver's eyes remain open even though they may be somewhat glazed over. If the driver has a companion, sometimes the companion is ignored, or if the driver is asked a question he probably doesn't respond—thus alerting the companion something is amiss. In every way the driver appears to be hypnotized, or asleep with his eyes open and behaving as if he is in a trance. And, indeed, he is. If we were to define "hypnosis" as a "a sleep-like condition or sleep brought on by prolonged patterns of unvarying visual and auditory stimulation," it would be both appropriate and accurate with regard to this sort of situation. More than likely this is true hypnosis and the only kind of hypnosis there is, since it is a state of sleep, whereas laboratory and clinical hypnosis, authorities agree, is not a state of sleep (Weitzenhoffer 1953).

That people can be asleep with their eyes open is fairly well known and something that I, personally, experienced during World War II. During the invasion of Southern France it became necessary for my unit to establish radio communications for infantry and air units moving up the Rhone Valley. Building the radio station and putting it into operation required that we work continuously for approximately eighty hours without rest. On many occasions during this sustained work period I found myself blanking out, with no memory of having completed the task I had just performed or of giving and receiving orders from other members of my team. On one occasion after about sixty hours of enforced wakefulness I ate an entire meal without remembering it and was moving to the mess hall to eat again before a friend reminded me I had already eaten. During my college days I had a roommate who had a permanent sleep deficit problem. Despite all of my efforts to arouse him, he would fall asleep with his eyes open in front of the mirror shaving. On one occasion we caught him leaving the house for class without his trousers on—eyes open and moving, but dead to the world. Such experiences are in no way bizarre, rare, or highly unusual. Individuals who are deprived of their normal cyclical eight hours rest period due to job, combat, emergency, or whatever situation may show similar sorts of being asleep on their feet.

Although G. W. Williams demonstrated that automobile driving can be successfully carried out by subjects in a so-called hypnotic trance (Williams 1948, 1949), these demonstrations tell us very little. His subjects were awake and compliant, were not foolish enough to kill themselves or other motorists, and after the motoring was over they followed the prior instructions for amnesia and reported they did not remember the drives. We can be quite certain that if Williams's subjects had truly been asleep or were suffering from highway hypnosis, they would have had much more difficulty than Williams reported (Williams 1963). Again, we need to make a clear and separate distinction between the trance of highway hypnosis and the trance of clinical and laboratory hypnosis. Moreover, since the trance of sleep has in the past so often been confused with the trance of hypnosis, perhaps we should take a brief look at the two and the differences between them.

Hypnosis and Sleep and Dreams

The most interesting aspect of all so-called trance inductions is their reliance on the same conditions that ordinary people use everyday to bring on that very normal state of unawareness we call sleep. Both monotony and visual stimulation that tend to fatigue or tire the eyes are used to bring on the so-called hypnotic trance. The subject is told, "Your eyes are growing tired, your eyelids are heavy, you are getting sleepy . . . and so on." Also, having the subjects focus their attention on a single small point, or follow a moving object such as a pendulum, or stare at a bright shiny object, has the effect of bringing on fatigue or drowsiness. Drivers experience a great deal of eye fatigue when driving toward the sun. Glare from the sun, the road, and the hood of the car together can create a highly fatiguing pattern of stimulation. Similarly, after being awake all day and half the night, our eyes are fatigued, and in order to bring on sleep we take off our clothing (reduce skin stimulation), turn off the room illumination (reduce visual stimulation and provide a uniform monotonous pattern of blackness), lie down on a soft surface (further reduction of sensory stimulation), close our eyes (further reduction of visual stimulation), breathe slowly and deeply (encouraging relaxation, which further reduces stimulation from the external environment), and finally relax (reducing muscle stimulation and aiding in the reduction of body stimulation impulses to the brain).

In other words, we do the same things daily to bring on sleep that the hypnotist or the entrancer does to bring on hypnosis or trance. And interestingly, the result is the same: sleep! Anyone who has ever done an extensive number of hypnotic inductions is well aware of the fact that many clients who come to the experimental or therapeutic session arrive suffering from sleep deprivation. When they are then encouraged to close their eyes, relax, and fall asleep they do so readily. Some even snore. In order to communicate with these clients, you have to wake them up and figure out how to keep them awake long enough to carry out the therapy or experiment. Although it is seldom mentioned or ever discussed in most books and articles about hypnosis, the problem is a serious one. And it is of importance because of the simple fact that *nothing happens if the client or experimental subject is asleep, i.e., unaware of the external world.*

If the client or experimental subject does not apprehend the suggestion, the therapeutic message, or the metaphor, or any of the words being sent his way, then nothing of any consequence, either positive or negative, will occur. In any and every so-called hypnotic situation, the only tools any hypnotist has to work with are suggestion and relaxation. There is nothing else at work in the heterohypnotic or autohypnotic situation to bring about any effects whatsoever. There is no in-between condition—between being awake and aware and being asleep and unaware—called hypnosis that supposedly does something to or has some magical effect upon the client or subject. This is not to deny the obvious fact that many people can and do go back and forth and in and out of awareness and unawareness. During the states of unawareness, however, nothing is either apprehended or learned and consequently remembered. To retain something we must be awake and aware enough to apprehend it. Sleep learning works only to the extent that it takes place during a period when you are awake and aware enough to be exposed to and apprehend the material to be learned. This period can, of course, be a lot more extensive than one might believe. A bit of self-reflection will confirm the fact that all of us fluctuate between sleep and awareness several times every night. Although LaBerge (1985) and others have shown that there are more varieties of being "asleep" than the hypothetical condition in which we are experiencing nothing at all, the fact remains that if we are processing internal material—dreams for example—or if we are totally unaware of external events and stimuli during that time, we will not be learning.

It should be clearly recognized that sleep is not a unitary process. It consists, instead, of some three or four stages, ranging from drowsiness to deep sleep. One of the stages is relative wakefulness. If a pillow speaker is presenting some sort of material you could learn while awake, it is possible that you could learn some of it during the periods of light sleep. These periods, however, are so close to waking brain activity (alpha wave) periods that it does not appear correct or legitimate to call them sleep. In general, it appears that more learning and the most efficient sort of learning occurs when you are maximally alert, i.e., wide awake. (But as any college instructor can tell you, even then many people fail to learn anything at all.)

Since sleep-learning or unconscious learning has received a lot of attention in the past, and for a while was a multi-million dollar business, it is important to know whether or not such a thing is possible. In the mid-1950s, the heyday of claims for sleep-learning, Simon and Emmons (1955) became skeptical of the so-called evidence and ran several studies of their own. Using EEG records and defining as "awake" any subject showing the alpha rhythm on his record, even with highly intelligent volunteers they found no evidence that any material had been learned that was presented during periods of quiet deep sleep. As alpha rhythm diminished, so did learning. Simon and Emmons noted, however, that even though learning was impossible during deep sleep, it was feasible during periods of drowsiness and in other states of consciousness below maximal alertness. Since we move in and out of deep sleep all through the night, there are many opportunities, even though short-lived, for individuals, especially highly suggestible ones, to absorb and store items of information. It is now generally agreed that sleep learning is overrated, and if any learning does occur, it happens while we are awake (Simon and Emmons 1955, 1956).

What to Do with Sleeping Clients

Before leaving this topic, we would be remiss if we failed to elaborate a bit on the problem of the hypnotic client who falls asleep. In this case, the problem is not how to put the client to sleep but how to keep him awake. There are several approaches to this situation. First, you can make sure that your client is informed ahead of time that hypnosis is not sleep and that if he finds himself falling asleep he should try to concentrate on the hypnotist's voice and message. Or, you can give the client signals for waking up, such as, "If you find yourself falling asleep, don't worry, after exactly one minute you will wake up and attend to my voice," or, "Even if you do fall asleep, you will be able to hear and remember everything I am saying." Or you can tell him or her that if sleep comes it is perfectly natural and that you will wake him up when the time is ripe. If you find that after a few minutes your client is snoring loudly or is obviously asleep, you can use your good old common sense and do what most people do with sleepers: shake them gently and call their name. Of course, there are some people who are hard to arouse. For them, vigorous shaking, loud noises, a splash of cold water, etc., may be necessary.

The important point to remember is that if your client is asleep you are not communicating with him, and if you are not communicating with him you are doing him or her no good whatsoever, unless a good nap is really what your client needs. In this case, you are providing some excellent therapy even though it is purely unintentional. One of my own clients who was on medication that left him drowsy would appear for his therapy sessions complaining about not having gotten any sleep the night before. The instant he was seated and told to relax, after several deep breaths and a few suggestions about sinking into the easy chair he would drop off to sleep and start to snore. I would let him sleep for an hour while I carried on other tasks. After his snooze, I would wake him and proceed with our communication and suggestions.

Eric Greenleaf has a few words of wisdom in this regard,

> The pretense of hypnotist-operator is a sort of shared delusion which both patient and therapist participate in, even though therapists often report the experience of trance while doing inductions, and, of course, patients often report the absence of trance in similar circumstances. (Greenleaf 1986)

It is not surprising that therapists fall asleep while doing inductions. After you have done this sort of thing for a while it becomes truly boring, and if you did not have sufficient sleep yourself the night before, it is difficult to stay awake through it. Greenleaf also has an interesting commentary on the social aspects of this interpersonal game. In his words:

> Hypnosis is a human state, all right. People claim to know if they are "in it" or not, even if they can't characterize it. But it is not a state like Nebraska is a state; not is it a state like hypertension is a state. To be in hypnosis is more like being, say, in a state of confusion, or in love. And, if you please, the "methods of induction" of this state are more like following the rules of social procedure than they are like following the rules of chemical analysis. So that, to learn what to do in hypnotizing someone is like learning to play baseball or to chat at a cocktail party or to tell a joke. And to the extent that these learnings are shared by our patients, or that they can be instructed in them, we can mutually agree that hypnosis "has happened." (Greenleaf 1986)

Other therapists approach the question slightly differently, and think that any client falling asleep is doing so for a reason and that it is the therapist's business to determine what these reasons are. Others have raised the question whether the therapist should or should not arouse the sleeper and ask if the sleep is a means of avoiding the reality of treatment and clinging to the neurosis. Before entering the twilight zone of behavioral dynamics, however, one should first determine whether or not the client is on medication that causes drowsiness, or whether or not insomnia is a problem, or something has occurred—perhaps quite normal and logical— that has made ordinary sleep difficult or impossible.

It is often reported that even anaesthetized patients have reported what they heard while under anaesthesia. However, it is important to remember that even under anaesthesia people are awake some of the time. Our human ability to slip in and out of awareness, back and forth between consciousness and unconsciousness, has not been widely understood and this misunderstanding has added to the confusion about psychological phenomena and activities. Many have falsely assumed that once asleep always asleep, and once awake permanently awake.

Anthropologists have also marveled at a primitive tribe of Andean Indians, the Yahgans, who all show a remarkable talent for falling asleep effortlessly, remaining observant while supposedly asleep, and being able to ignore distractions. They sleep lightly, awaken rapidly and easily, at once fresh and alert, and after awakening are fully aware of what went on during their sleep. Neither do they seem to be annoyed or fatigued by repeatedly being aroused from their sleep, since they immediately and easily go back to sleep. All members of the tribe seem to be able to lie down and sleep no matter what the time of day or the amount of commotion going on around them. It is questionable, however, whether the members of this tribe are actually asleep. If they are not truly asleep they may need to do a considerable amount of resting day and night to compensate for their lengthy, enforced alertness.

We also know that there is a wide range of individual differences in the amount of sleep needed. Some individuals are able to get by on only two or three hours per night, whereas others require ten to twelve. These individual variations in the amount of sleep needed may be related to many different variables of both a physiological and psychological nature. But in addition to the amount needed it is clear from the anthropological evidence that there is a wide range of individual differences in the ease or difficulty with which we fall asleep and remain asleep. Moreover, even for the same individual the ease or difficulty of falling asleep varies considerably from night to night. Such considerations as these must be taken into account in any study of the relationship between so-called "hypnosis" and ordinary sleep. Hypnotizing a Yahgan would, or should, be no problem at all, since this seems to be their permanent mental condition, i.e., sleeping wakefulness.

Missing Time

This state of sleeping wakefulness also seems to characterize another interesting phenomena closely related to highway hypnosis, the "missing time" or "blanking out" experience reported by many drivers. Periods of amnesia or forgetfulness while driving are a familiar experience, especially to drivers who travel long distances over familiar routes. G. W. Williams (1963) tells of one case in which a woman driver had so many periods of amnesia while driving in New Jersey that she sought psychiatric help. She could remember stopping at traffic lights in the town preceding the one she was then in, but could recall nothing in between. Due to repeated experiences of this sort in which she could recall nothing of what had happened over stretches of twenty-five or thirty miles or more, and sometimes as long as an hour or two, she feared she was suffering from some sort of emotional instability.

This missing time phenomenon is really very common. Even automobile passengers report this sort of experience, but their reactions are more likely to pass unnoticed than those of the driver. Alternate drivers on long-distance trucking teams report that their alternates sometimes appear to be in a daze and operating the vehicle more or less mechanically. This, along with the driver's glassy stare, is a sign that it's time to switch drivers. Long-distance truck drivers suffer from these missing time experiences quite frequently. One long hauler reported:

> I discovered this fact (amnesia) while driving at night from Portland, Oregon, to San Francisco, California. The lights of a town approached and I realized that I had been in an almost asleep condition for about 25 miles. Inasmuch as I knew the road I had traveled was not straight, it was apparent that I had negotiated the road, making all the turns, etc. I did not remember the stretch of road at all.
>
> I purposely tried it several times after that and found that I could drive miles and miles without memory of it, and while resting. In each case whenever any driving emergency appeared, I became fully awake (Williams 1963).

Another driver reported the same sort of experience:

> We had started about 6:00 AM. . . . I had driven for about an hour and had passed through Chehallis, Washington. My mother was dozing beside me, there was little traffic, and I was feeling sleepy. I blinked my eyes to break the dazed feeling and found that I had just crossed the Cowlitz bridge leaving Toledo, Washington. The 20-mile gap between Chehallis and Toledo had vanished in that blink. The highway was US 99, the time elapsed was from a little past 7:00 AM to nearly 8:00 AM. . . . but there was absolutely no memory of the twenty miles. (Williams 1963, p. 147)

This same driver described several other experiences of a similar nature and reported that they always baffled and frightened him.

It is difficult enough when driving with someone else, but even more difficult when driving alone. As one solitary traveler reported:

I have noticed whenever I make a trip to New York City via the Merritt Parkway (Connecticut) that in spite of a good night's rest, I have to fight off going into a trance. . . . I have observed also that if I go to New York City via the Boston Turnpike which passes through many towns, I always find the trip interesting and am never in danger of a monotonous drive . . . . as well as I can recall, the only times the monotony of driving on a road like the Merritt Parkway has affected me have been when I have been driving alone. (Williams 1963, p. 148)

The trance and missing time experiences also seem to occur under two other conditions: first, when drivers are forced to follow trucks or other large vehicles for considerable distances; and second, when they drive at night and their range of vision is restricted to the area of their headlight beam.

Graham Reed in his *The Psychology of Anomalous Experience* (1974) discussed this missing time experience at length and explained it in terms of the level of mental organization or schematization required by a situation. While the task of driving a car is itself highly skilled, its component activities are all overlearned and habitual to the experienced driver. Steering, shifting gears, adjusting speed, giving signals, etc., all become automatic acts which do not require focused, conscious attention.

Furthermore, our experience of time and its passage is determined by events—either external or internal. When a person reports a "time gap," he is not saying that a piece of time has disappeared but that he failed to register a number of *events that normally serve as time-markers*. The experience that is reported and that seems so strange is actually "waking up" when one is already awake and being aware of a blank period in his recent past. Since most of us live our lives by the clock such that certain habits take place at certain times, we are disturbed when we find we have missed a period of time. A driver wakes up in New York and realizes that he remembers nothing since Boston. Although the driver describes his experience in terms of *time*, he could just as well describe it in terms of *distance*, or even more accurately in terms of *events*, i.e., in this case, *the absence of events*.

Even though there were events during the missing time, none of them represented anything in the way of a drastic change in the driver's situation—none of them had any alerting significance. The time gap is experienced when no events of significance occur, e.g., there is nothing unusual about traffic, there is clear visibility and smooth unchanging road surface, there are no warning signs, and the demands of the driving task are few and unchanging.

Moreover, when we learn and master a complex skill like walking or talking or driving a car, once we have perfected each component of the skill, its performance becomes automatic, in the sense that we can withdraw our attention from this level and focus on the next higher level. We do, however, have to attend to ways in which basic skills like driving must be organized in response to environmental demands—particularly when the demands are stressful or unfamiliar. The skilled tennis player cannot relax his concentration, because his opponent will be continually introducing changes in the environment. No matter how automatic his stroke or eye-hand coordination may be, he still must stay alert. But if all we are required to do is walk along a lonely beach for miles, we can do it and never know or notice we are doing it. It is possible to do two things at once as long as one of the activities is automatic and does not require focused attention.

The organization and integration of skills at one level can be achieved to a degree that functions at the next level are not impaired. A good example of this is our ability to hit the brakes and stop the car when a child suddenly and without warning darts in front of us. This we do without thinking, reflexively. The driver realizes that he has been driving *automatically* when the situation does change and events demanding his active attention "wake him up." He hits the brakes suddenly, or as he gets closer to New York, traffic increases, sirens intrude, highway signs appear and his automatic routines are now inadequate—he must reorganize his skills and pay attention to the constantly changing road and traffic conditions. When he "wakes up" he realizes, among other things, that he is now in New York before he supposes he should be. As Reed says, "In one sense he is correct in describing what has happened as a 'gap.' But the gap is not in time, but in alertness or his high level of conscious attention" (Reed 1974, p. 20).

In short, the experience of missing time is best considered in terms of the absence of events. Most of the time we cannot remember what took place simply because nothing of any importance occurred. Jerome Singer, in his *Inner World of Daydreaming* (1975), points out that the missing time experience is quite ordinary, common, and universal, and not restricted to driving on interstates. He asks:

Are there ever any truly "blank periods" when we are awake? It certainly seems to be the case that under certain conditions of fatigue or great drowsiness or extreme concentration upon some physical act we may become aware that we cannot account for an interval of time and have no memory of what happened for seconds and sometimes minutes. (Singer 1975)

The more one reflects upon the experience and its correlates and the circumstances surrounding its occurrence, the clearer it becomes that it has nothing whatsoever to do with either clinical or laboratory hypnosis.

Hypnogogic and Hypnopompic States

In 1861 a Frenchman, Alfred Maury, published a book entitled *Sleep And Dreams* that compared the hallucinations of the mentally ill with the kind of hallucinations or false perceptions that occur in normal people when they are falling asleep or waking up after having been asleep. Maury also tried to prove that dreams were caused by external stimuli.

To describe the vivid imagery that tends to occur in the drowsy or twilight state of consciousness just before falling asleep, Maury coined the term "hypnogogic imagery." If the images occur during the period while one is slowly waking up, they are called "hypnopompic images." When these images become particularly vivid and intense and result in dreamlike states of consciousness that seem to be quite real they are referred to as "hypnogogic and hypnopompic hallucinations." Such hallucinations are quite common in patients suffering from narcolepsy.

While there is nothing unusual about someone falling asleep after a heavy meal or during a boring lecture, frequent, irresistible, and repeated attacks of sleep during the day are another matter. Narcolepsy is, in fact, rather common. Its victims suffer from uncontrollable spells of sleep lasting minutes to hours at times other than when sleep is appropriate. Some victims fall asleep repeatedly during the day, some complain only of excessive sleepiness and dullness, and others do not complain at all until they discover they have extraordinary difficulty in staying awake, whereas previously they had had no such difficulties. Sufferers fall asleep while watching sports events, while taking dictation, during meetings, at plays, and one surgeon even reported falling asleep while he was performing major surgery. While the cause of naroclepsy may be due to a previous attack of encephalitis or a brain lesion, most of the time it seems to be constitutional or hereditary. It occurs in perfectly healthy people with no complaints other than that they have an uncontrollable compulsion to sleep at the most inappropriate times. The condition usually begins rather early in life and persists for many years. The frequency of attacks varies with the individual, and as many as fifteen to twenty attacks per day have been reported by some patients.

Accompanying the narcolepsy and as a part of this disordered sleep syndrome are sudden attacks of complete or partial muscular paralysis called "cataplexy." While the major symptom of narcolepsy is periods of irresistible sleepiness, it is cataplexy that is crucial for the diagnosis, since daytime sleep attacks could suggest other kinds of disorders. During a cataplectic seizure the victim is fully awake and aware of what is going on around him, but is simply unable to move. The attacks can occur at any time, but most often occur when the victim is emotionally aroused. People have fallen victim to cataplexy while playing baseball, making love, or watching television or a movie. While they are wide awake, they are unable to move a muscle. After a few minutes of relaxation and calm, however, they usually regain full muscular control.

Beside cataplexy and sleep attacks, narcoleptic patients also suffer from two other symptoms. These are sleep paralysis and hypnogogic and hypnopompic hallucinations. Sleep paralysis occurs most often when the individual is falling asleep or when he wakes and finds he is unable to move. Such paralyses are quite common and show up in people free from any symptom of narcolepsy. As for hypnogogic and hypnopompic hallucinations, they are very vivid and are actually waking dreams, and they are often smoothly continuous with the immediately prior waking events.

Prior to the work of William C. Dement and his collaborators at the Stanford University Sleep Disorders Clinic, many physicians tried to treat narcolepsy with psychotherapy, believing that the symptoms were all neurotic. In the early 1960s, however, Dement and his fellow researchers discovered that narcoleptic patients began their night's sleep by moving immediately from wakefulness into the rapid-eye-movement (REM) or dreaming phase of sleep, rather than into the non-rapid-eye-movement (NREM) phase (Dement 1976). Therefore, it is clear that the hypnogogic hallucinations are vivid dreams associated with periods of REM sleep.

Moreover, Dement was also able to explain the mysterious attacks of cataplexy and sleep paralysis. We have known for a long while that during REM periods of normal sleep the brain exerts a powerful inhibitory influence that paralyzes the arms, legs, and trunk of the sleeper. This paralysis allows us to have vivid dreams and still remain asleep. If the intense activity of the dreaming brain were not blocked at the level of the spinal cord by a strong inhibitory effect, the sleeper would literally jump out of bed and carry out his dream fantasies. Spinal inhibition has to be quite strong to keep the muscles in check. Usually all that occurs is an occasional twitch or spasmodic jerk. Another regulatory mechanism keeps the inhibitory force in check while we are awake, except in the narcoleptic victim. In these patients the inhibitory process breaks through and drops them like a rock.

Nightly, when the narcoleptic victim goes to sleep, the first thing he experiences is cataplexy, and the other REM processes soon follow. But if the victim tries to move before he is actually asleep, he will find that he is paralyzed. Then, if he is particularly imaginative, he will find himself caught up in some very realistic experiences and convinced that he is not asleep. In fact, although paralysis is the rule, many of the normal features of wakefulness may remain. The dreamer may be able to move his arms and legs or even to sit up in bed, with the images still persisting. As for the content of the hallucinations, it can be horrific or benign, and in many instances it may be related to the dreamer's current concerns. Christopher Evans reports the case of a scientist who had been struggling with a problem for months with little success. He was getting very discouraged until one morning he awoke to see the ghosts of the world's greatest scientists —Newton, Galileo, Darwin, et al.—marching past his bed, telling him not to give up, that he would win in the end. Similarly, most of the ghosts, monsters and aliens that visit sleepers in the middle of the night are creations of the dreaming brain having a hypnopompic experience (Evans 1985).

Although treatment of narcolepsy is difficult, the use of stimulant drugs such as amphetamines or methylphenidate helps keep the victim awake during the day. Compounds such as Tofranil (Imipramine), or vivactil (Protriptyline), or the MAO inhibitors have also been used to prevent cataplexy. Care must be taken, however, to insure that these drugs are not combined with an amphetamine.

Contrary to popular belief, narcolepsy is not a rare disorder. Dement and his co-workers found over two thousand sufferers in the San Francisco Bay area alone, and they have estimated that as many as 100,000 people in the nation may be afflicted with this conditon. The total number of people having hypnogogic and hypnopompic hallucinations must be sizable indeed, including so many narcoleptics as well as so many nonnarcoleptics who are also afflicted with the hallucinations. McKellar and Simpson made an attempt to identify hypnogogic experiences in college students and found as many as sixty-seven percent of them reporting such imagery (McKellar and Simpson 1954). Even this substantial figure is considered by McKellar to be an underestimate of the real number, and in 1979 he characterized hypnogogic imagery as a universal human phenomenon (McKellar 1979). McKellar also has made a very useful distinction between hypnogogic "sequences" and hypnogogic "episodes." Sequences are simply a group of rapidly changing images of object, persons, or places in apparently random order and lacking in any sort of coherence. Episodes, on the other hand, involve scenes or themes of longer duration, with clear definition and structure. The content may often be a mere continuation of recent perceptions and thoughts, or on other occasions, more symbolic or dreamlike, or fantastic, unreal, and totally foreign, and unrelated to the mental life of the person when awake.

Although these experiences occur during sleep and may appear to be somewhat hypnoidal in nature, they bear no relationship of any sort or kind to either laboratory or clinical hypnosis as it is commonly found in the world around us. In summary, there are a number of characteristic clues that indicate a hypnogogic or hypnopompic hallucination—clues that can help the person who experiences these events to discriminate the event from the perceptual reality it so closely mimics. First, the hallucinations always occur before or after falling asleep. Second, the hallucinator is paralyzed or has difficulty moving; or on the contrary, one may float out of one's body and have an out-of-the body experience. Third, the hallucination is usually bizarre; i.e., one sees ghosts, aliens, monsters, and such. Fourth, after a hallucination is over, the hallucinator typically goes back to sleep. And, finally, the hallucinator is unalterably convinced of the reality of the entire event. We will return to these experiences in a later chapter.

Hypnosis and Dissociation

The relationship between hypnosis and dissociation has a long history, dating back to Pierre Janet and Morton Prince, who, in the first two decades of this century, hypothesized that there are multiple layers of consciousness, that in certain individuals the mind can become disorganized into two or more mental systems, and that these systems may war with one another. Janet also felt that hysteria was a "dissociation of the personality." Even today, in the American Psychiatric Association's DSM-III manual of psychopathology, dissociative disorders are listed under the heading of "hysterical neuroses."

Psychologically, however, the term "dissociation" does not always imply a disorder or pathology. When used in a descriptive sense, dissociation indicates that there is a subsidiary mental activity operating more or less independently, i.e., dissociated from the primary or main mental activity making up the normal conscious personality. Dissociation can be seen in many ordinary everyday kinds of activities. In reading a book, for example, nearly everyone has had the experience of in the middle of a page beginning to think about something else. In this case, while the conscious mind follows the daydream, the eyes continue to read the words on the page line by line perhaps for several pages, until we suddenly realize we have no idea what we have been reading. The act of reading and the memory of what we read were dissociated from what we were concentrating upon in our reverie. Thinking about our work while driving a car, or in the case of a professional musician, reading and playing a complicated piece of music while carrying on a conversation, are other common examples. In the latter case, although the musician's conscious mind is focused on the conversation, another part of his mind is reading the notes and moving his fingers across the keys. Hilgard has been so fascinated by the phenomenon that he has written a book about it: *Divided Consciousness: Multiple Controls in Human Thought and Action* (1977).

Other examples of normal dissociation are provided by dreams, in which the higher elements of consciousness are temporarily out of action, while the lower centers take over and allow emotions and feelings to dominate and control our internal sleeping fantasies. Examples of abnormal dissociation include somnambulism, automatic writing, fugue states, sensory hallucinations, analgesias and anaesthesias, and the multiple personality syndrome.

Theoretically, it is assumed that the normal personality is made up of various mental factors or systems that have coalesced into one integrated, smoothly functioning unit. Under severe stress, however, especially during the formative stages of the personality, normal growth and development is retarded and abnormalities appear. Specifically, alternate or multiple personalities appear. Once the major or dominant personality has formed and is operating smoothly, things can go awry and dissociations show up in the form of sleep disturbances such as somnambulism (in which the sleeper gets out of bed, frequently talks, and may perform quite complex tasks, although he will have no conscious recollection of any of these things when he wakens. Or in automatic writing the writer can carry on an intelligent conversation while his hand writes highly creative sentences, without the speaker having any idea of what he is writing. Those unfortunate individuals suffering from fugue states find their normal personalities being suppressed for long periods of time. The fugue can involve the sufferer's forgetting his identity and his past, and totally unable to recall his name, address, occupation, or any other aspect of his prior existence. His intellect is perfectly normal in all ways except for the amnesia concerning his past.

Sensory hallucinations can also involve dissociation whenever normal consciousness is more or less set aside and the dissociated mental elements take control. While the main personality remains more or less intact, below the conscious level autonomous mental activity produces auditory and visual hallucinations that can often terrify the conscious mind. In the past, such spontaneous hallucinations were associated with witchcraft, possession states, divine intervention, and saintly visions. Hallucinations of this sort are also quite common in cases of severe hysterical neurosis. In the analgesias (or insensitiveness to pain) and anaesthesias (a loss of feeling in certain parts of the body) dissociation is at work again. Without any physiological changes whatsoever, many people show complete insensitivity to pain in certain body parts. A hand or arm, for example, can be burned, stabbed, pricked, or jabbed with a needle, and the individual seems totally unaware of it. As for the anaesthesias, it seems that although a part of the person's mind is subconsciously aware of being touched, these feelings never seem to reach the level of conscious awareness. Simple tricks can show that such individuals are actively repressing the stimulations and keeping themselves in the dark about them.

Related to the problem of pain acknowledgement is the use of hypnosis to suppress or control it. Hilgard has been one of the leaders in the use of hypnotic techniques to control pain. He has developed an ingenious theory to explain just how hypnosis does the job. Calling his ideas "neodissociation" theory to distinguish them from the older notions of Janet and Prince, Hilgard argues that in many individuals undergoing hypnosis a split or division of the mind occurs and the part of the mind that is responding to the hypnotic suggestions somehow or other is split off or becomes dissociated from the part associated with normal consciousness or awareness. The degree to which this splitting occurs varies widely among individuals. People who are easily hypnotized are capable of a large dissociation and respond easily to a wide range of suggestions, including suggestions for pain reduction. People who are difficult to hypnotize, on the other hand, do not dissociate or split at all, and consequently have only a small reduction in felt pain.

Hilgard also suggests that hypnotic pain reduction has two aspects or parts. The first part can be experienced by everyone regardless of their level of hypnotizability; it involves using relaxation and self-distraction to ease the pain. These procedures are not very effective, however, and give only a small reduction in felt pain. The second part is the truly effective component, since it involves dissociating the pain from conscious awareness. Easily hypnotized subjects separate or dissociate the felt pain from conscious awareness, although another part of the subject's mind continues to experience high levels of pain. The dissociated pain is separated from the conscious part of the mind by a "block" that prevents the conscious mind from feeling it. Hilgard's assumption is that individuals in this way continue to feel high levels of pain at an unconscious level, but no longer have conscious access to the dissociated pain. Hilgard has argued that with some highly hypnotizable subjects the experimenter can literally talk with the dissociated part of the subject's mind and obtain estimates of the pain's intensity. According to Hilgard, this talking part of the subject acts as a hidden observer, a sort of detached internal watcher or monitor of everything that is going on. A number of experimental studies carried out in Hilgard's lab and in the labs of several other investigators have confirmed this sort of dissociation or splitting phenomenon (Hilgard 1974, 1979; Laurence and Perry 1981).

Opposing Hilgard's dissociation hypothesis and his interpretation of his findings are social-cognitive theorists such as Spanos, de Groot, Chaves, Wagstaff, Coe, Steven Lynn, Judith Rhue, and others who offer a more parsimonious explanation. In their view, such notions as dissociation (borrowed from the files of abnormal psychology) are both unnecessary and superfluous. From their social-cognitive perspective, Hilgard's subjects are not helpless automatons but highly sensitive and intelligent people engaged in meaningful, goal-directed behavior tied to their understanding of the social context in which they are involved. Moreover, they are actively engaged in interpreting the communications they receive from the hypnotist and in presenting themselves in such a way as to meet and satisfy the prevalent social demands. In other words, Hilgard's subjects are role-playing and complying, rather than passive, involuntary, and helpless robots that have no control whatsoever over their own behavior.

Since key elements of the neo-dissociation theory involve the loss of conscious control of one's behavior, as well as arguments that hypnosis is something that happens to subjects rather than something they do, the question of volition or the subject's voluntary control of his behavior during hypnosis is a critical one. Hilgard states unequivocally that "one of the most striking features of hypnosis is the loss of control over actions normally voluntary" (1977, p. 115).

Because of the importance of hypnotic nonvolition in neo-dissociation thinking, Lynn, Rhue, and Weekes (1989) recently completed a long and exhaustive review of the experimental and theoretical literature dealing with this concept. Based upon the results from numerous studies, this survey clearly shows that hypnotic responding is in no way outside the realm of the hypnotic subject's control, nor is it in any sense automatic or involuntary. They explain the behavior in terms of social and cognitive psychology and show that: 1) all Hilgard's subjects' responses while they were supposedly hypnotized have all of the properties of behavior typically defined as voluntary, i.e., they are purposeful, goal-directed, and regulated in terms of the subject's intentions, and were progressively changed to better meet the subject's goals; 2) a considerable amount of evidence shows that subjects can resist suggestions when resistance is defined as consistent with the role of a "good" hypnotized subject; 3) evidence also shows that hypnotic behaviors are neither reflexive/automatic nor simply manifestations of innate stimulus-response connections; and 4) hypnotic performances consume attentional resources in a manner comparable to nonhypnotic performances. In summary, Hilgard's subjects were playing the role of "a good hypnotized and complying subject" to the best of their ability, and in the last analysis, their actions and responses were quite voluntary (Lynn, Rhue, and Weekes 1989).

As for the "hidden observer" concept, Spanos and his collaborators in a number of different studies attempted to replicate the findings of Hilgard and his supporters with no success. First, they tested subjects for their responses to both explicit and more ambiguously worded hidden observer suggestions, but failed to obtain a significant real/simulator difference in the frequency of hidden observer responding with either suggestion. Moreover, they failed to detect any associations between explicit or ambiguous hidden observer responding and either duality or incongruous writing during supposed age regressions. Spanos believes that the reason for his failure to replicate lies is the fact that whenever simulators are faced with an ambiguous or confusing situation and have little time to rehearse or to figure out what sort of response is called for, they do their best not to appear foolish or to give away the fact that they are faking, and they adopt a very conservative response pattern. Spanos's finding that real/simulator differences represent contextually bound phenomena does, therefore, call into serious question the validity of the hidden observer concept—particularly as an indicator of a dissociated cognitive subsystem during hypnosis (Spanos, de Groot, Tiller, Weekes, and Bertrand 1985, pp. 611–623; Gwynn, de Groot, and Spanos 1988).

With regard to the problem of hypnotic analgesia per se, Spanos and his coworkers over a period of several years have carried out over thirty separate studies dealing with the problem. In addition, Spanos has recently completed an exhaustive survey of the experimental research that has been carried out on the topic of hypnotic analgesia (Spanos 1989). Both the survey results and the experimental work demonstrate most convincingly the serious limitations inherent in viewing human subjects in hypnotic analgesia experiments as passive responders and in deemphasizing the importance of the contextual factors in guiding the subjects' understandings, the impressions they try to make, and the self-conceptions and roles they play as they interact with the hypnotist.

With regard to analgesia and hypnosis, Mark Twain, in his autobiography, has contributed, albeit unwittingly, a superb example of the hidden observer phenomena in action in his account of his boyhood experiences with a traveling mesmerist, one Professor Simmons. According to Twain,

> I was fourteen or fifteen years old, the age at which a boy is willing to endure all things, suffer all things short of death by fire, if thereby he may be conspicuous and show off before the public. . . . I had a burning desire to be a subject myself! (Twain 1962)

One of his friends, named Hicks, preceded Twain to the stage and was quickly mesmerized, and Twain became jealous of the attention Hicks was receiving. So after the mesmerist's first attempt to hypnotize Twain failed, Twain decided to play along and pretend to be sleepy and act out a number of the hypnotist's bizarre suggestions, including making love to imaginary girls, fishing in an imaginary lake, etc. . . . "I was cautious at first and watchful," Twain reports,

> being afraid the professor would discover that I was an impostor and drive me from the platform in disgrace; but as soon as I realized I was not in danger, I set myself the task of terminating Hicks's usefulness as a subject and of usurping his place.

When Twain found himself unable to imagine some of the things the mesmerist was suggesting, his fears of exposure returned and he reported feeling "ashamed and miserable." Fortunately, however, he was saved by carrying out some spectacular feats, including giving the appearance of insensitivity to having pins stuck in his arms. On this matter, Twain commented:

I didn't wince; I only suffered and shed tears on the inside. The miseries that a conceited boy will endure to keep up his "reputation". . . . That professor ought to have protected me and I often hoped he would, when the tests were unusually severe, but he didn't. It may be that he was deceived as well as the others, though I did not believe it nor think it possible. Those dear, good people . . . would stick a pin in my arm and bear on it until they drove it a third of its length in, and then be lost in wonder that by a mere exercise of willpower the professor could turn my arm to iron and make it insensible to pain. Whereas it was not insensible at all; I was suffering agonies of pain.

One of the most fascinating parts of Twain's account is of Professor Simmons standing behind him, staring at the back of his head, and "willing" him to carry out Simmons's silent "mental commands." On one of these occasions Twain spotted one of his teenaged enemies, a bully, in the audience. Having, of course, no idea what the hypnotist had in mind, Twain saw an old empty and rusty revolver among the props on a nearby table and decided to act. In his words,

I crept stealthily and impressively toward the table, with a dark and murderous scowl on my face, copied from a popular romance, seized the revolver suddenly, flourished it, shouted the bully's name, jumped off the platform and made a rush for him and chased him out of the house before the paralyzed people could interfere to save him. There was a storm of applause, and the magician, addressing the house, said, most impressively—"That you may know how really remarkable this is and how wonderfully developed a subject we have in this boy, I assure you that without a single spoken word to guide him he has carried out what I mentally commanded him to do, to the minutest detail. I could have stopped him at a moment in his vengeful career by a mere exertion of my will, therefore, the poor fellow who has escaped was at no time in danger" . . . .

I judged that in case I failed to guess what the professor might be willing me to do, I could count on putting up something that would answer just as well. I was right, and exhibitions of unspoken suggestion became a favorite with the public. Whenever I perceived that I was being willed to do something I got up and did something—anything that occurred to me—and the magician, not being a fool, always ratified it. When people asked me, "How can you tell what he is willing you to do?" I said, "It's just as easy," and they always said admiringly, "Well, it beats me how you can do it."

Here we have a classic example of a subject who not only surrendered to the pressures for compliance but also demonstrated beautifully the hidden observer phenomenon and showed us how some stage hypnotists plied their trade in days of yore. Dissociation? Hardly.

In sum, the dissociation hypothesis is simply unnecessary to account for the kinds and types of behavior shown in analgesia studies, and it is more parsimoniously explained by the social-cognitive, nonstate viewpoint. Because of its importance in hypnosis, the topic of hypnotic pain control will be discussed at length in a later section.

Dissociative Problems

It is generally agreed that most dissociative behavior is due to repression of one sort or another. By this we mean that there is a natural human tendency to reject and shove away from ourselves unpleasant and undesirable thoughts and experiences; we put them out of our mind and forget about them. For many highly traumatic and overpowering negative events the repressing is almost instinctive or automatic. The conscious personality finds the experience so emotionally disturbing that it must escape from it, and it does this by refusing to accept the reality of the experience or by deliberately forgetting it, i.e., willfully erasing it from conscious awareness. If, at times, experiences are so intense and traumatic that a large number of ideas and emotions are repressed simultaneously, or if these ideas and feelings tend to cohere or become integrated, the basis for a new or alternate personality is formed. If this repression occurs during early or formative stages in the development of the primary personality, an alternate personality may also come into being. This is known as multiple personality disorder, or MPD.

Among dissociative phenomena, MPD is perhaps the most fascinating. In nearly all cases of this disorder, the pathology, i.e., the dissociation, has been caused by severe abuse of the child in its formative stages. Beaten and mistreated by a warped or psychotic parent, the child concludes that if its main or primary personality is so evil or undeserving of love, then perhaps another completely different child or new personality would be deserving of love and affection. Therefore, a new personality is born. Cases of fugues and alternate personalities are relatively common in the clinical literature, and within the last decade cases of MPD have grown like wildfire. The growth has been so rapid that many investigators have become skeptical of many of the cases and have even raised doubt as to whether there is such a thing as MPD after all!

As far back as 1959, D. Rawcliffe argued most persuasively that not only are true cases of multiple personality quite rare, but that in nearly every so-called case of MPD, the therapist's own treatments and experiments have been mainly responsible for the emergence of the subsidiary personalities (Rawcliffe 1959). In other words, multiple personalities are iatrogenic, i.e., caused by the hypnotist himself! Since the hysterical neurotic is normally highly suggestible, and hypnosis is the standard method of treatment, it is easy to see why many many of the cases of MPD could be due simply to suggestion, i.e., they are artificially therapist-hypnotist created personalities. Since so many therapists are now extremely sensitive to possible cases of child abuse, and since child abuse is the clearly recognized cause of MPD, every case of early abuse is now seen as a possible cause of multiple personality. And if you look for something hard enough you are sure to find it. An ancient aphorism is applicable here: seek and ye shall find!

We have long known that good hypnotic subjects show exceptional talent for becoming imaginatively involved, and as Josephine Hilgard has shown, those unusually good hypnotic subjects were almost the same as the ones Wilson and Barber refer to as fantasy-prone. Such individuals not only have exceptional life histories, but also show an unusually high incidence of severe punishment or abuse in childhood (Hilgard 1970). Nash, Lynn, and Givens (1984) found these traits also among fifty percent of a large sample of highly hypnotizable college students.

When introduced to the hypnotic situation, such individuals often go into a deep trance-like state characterized by dissociation, extreme sensitivity to suggestion, heightened transference relationships, a loss in general reality orientation, and many cognitive distortions. Many of them then proceed to experience their fantasies as very real. Thus, their somatic or sensory hallucinations and dissociated imagery can be very frightening to them. Since they become very deeply absorbed in their experience and regard it as real, they also accept just about every hypnotic suggestion as real. During the routine hypnotic induction procedure, when these individuals begin to lose control over the hypnotic situation, over the direction of the events, and over their own repressions, this loss of control and the unpleasant revived memories can be very very disturbing. People who are already functioning at borderline levels can find the negative images unleashed by the hypnosis almost overpowering. Problems with negative imagery are fairly common in patients who suffer from sexual, physical, or emotional abuse. The same sort of problems have been reported by therapists working with rape victims, holocaust survivors, air crash victims, etc.

While as a psychologist I am prone to consider most examples of anomalous behavior pathological, there are many quite normal examples of dissociative phenomena that occur at various times in people who are in robust mental health. Three of these normal dissociative phenomena brought on primarily as a reaction to stress are: dissociation of affect, ego-splitting, and depersonalization.

Very traumatic events and situations can also bring about a temporary amnesia in perfectly normal, mentally healthy, individuals. People exposed to extreme danger often report a strange sense of detachment. It seems as if the threat is totally meaningless emotionally—as if the danger is really threatening someone else. This dissociation of affect, according to Reed (1988) and others, is most likely a biological defense mechanism which prevents the threatened person from being swamped by excessive emotions, and also allows him to continue to function. Later on, he may break down and be overcome by the trauma of the prior event. Many people report feeling "drugged" or "being in a daze" or behaving "like a robot." Individuals who are wounded or hurt report there is no pain at the time. Soldiers in combat report not even noticing they have been wounded until some time after the combat action is over. They then notice for the first time that they are bleeding, and then soon after, the pain. Milder threats to one's well-being can also bring on dissociative defense reactions at various levels. People facing examinations or job interviews who prior to the actual test or interview are terribly anxious, report feelings of extreme calm during the test or interview itself.

A second form of normal dissociation, another reaction to distress, is ego-splitting. In this case the subject not only feels calm but he has an even more extreme form of detachment—he feels that he is outside of himself, out of his own body. He seems to be watching his own performance from afar, with a sense of noninvolvement in the proceedings. Bereavement is a common situation in which ego-splitting is frequently encountered. Instead of being overcome with grief and loss, the survivor seems callous and emotionally numb. Relatives are often heard to remark, "She's taking it much better than I ever imagined." The ones having the experience often report both dissociation of affect and a sense of ego-splitting.

By far, perhaps, the most disturbing of the dissociative reactions is depersonalization. At its worst, the person undergoing the experience feels a loss of identity. Suddenly, he or she does not know who they are, and their loss of self-identity is sometimes accompanied by a feeling that their bodies are being controlled in a robotic fashion by a stranger or internal manipulator, and that they themselves have no control over their movements. All of this is accompanied by a sense of strangeness or unreality that is disturbing and frightening. This is not the same as the sensation people report when they are in love or win the lottery or have some sort of religious transcendental experience. Such experiences have a very positive affect, whereas the depersonalization experience is uniformly regarded as negative and unpleasant. Depersonalization also accompanies many pathological states and shows up frequently in syndromes of psychotic reactions. In such cases the patient may combine his experiences of depersonalization with or describe them as part of his hallucinations and delusions.

In normal, mentally healthy individuals, however, the loss of identity is usually accompanied by insight, that is, the individuals remain aware of the fact that their personal identity is still intact, and they understand that the sense of unreality is purely subjective. In general, when this happens to a normal, healthy person, while retaining his sense of personal identity, the person still feels he has changed, and this feeling is accompanied by an uncanny sense of unreality. In normal individuals the experience seems most often to be associated with stress situations involving social embarrassment or extreme physical fatigue. In some situations the feelings of depersonalization may also be accompanied by a sense of "derealization," that is, a feeling not so much that one has changed or has become unreal, but that the world around one has lost reality. The person is no longer convinced that what he is perceiving is real, and the quality of his perceptions is different.

Normally, we experience ourselves as a unity, and our convictions as to the reality of ourselves and the world around us is seldom questioned. This global experience operates automatically and we pay no attention to it until something goes awry. As Reed so succinctly explains,

> the disturbance of cognitive organizations brings into conscious awareness aspects of our experience which are normally "automatized". . . . What the sufferer from depersonalization is complaining about is the strange sensation caused by the breakdown of his normal integrated experience. (Reed 1988)

The breakdown is due to our shifting our attention to a single aspect of a complex, sequentially organized, automatic habit. If we concentrate on discrete features of this complex habit, this causes the smooth overall performance to disintegrate. For example, the millipede can walk just fine until someone asks him which leg he moves first. The attentional shifts occur, of course, because they are natural responses to trauma and stress.

To summarize, not all dissociation should be considered pathological. Much of it is normal, common, and can be found routinely in the mentally healthy. Moreover, this phenomenon has little to do with either clinical or laboratory hypnosis.

Hypnosis, Memory, and Confabulation

One of the most common fallacies about hypnosis is the belief that it somehow has the magical power to improve our memory and make the closed volume of the past an open book. Under certain conditions and in a specific context we can be assisted to remember more than we would ordinarily have thought. Hypnosis, however, has nothing to do with it. Many years ago, before I began to study memory, I was under the general impression from the literature on hypnosis that memory was improved under hypnosis. I was informed that everything that ever happened to us was retained and buried somewhere in the brain, and that all it took to bring it all back was a little hypnosis and being questioned by a clever hypnotist.

When I undertook research into both memory and memory under

hypnosis, however, it soon became clear that both the literature and my general understanding were incorrect. Research from the past two decades has clearly indicated that normal human memory is inexact—all our memories are flawed. Human memory is not like a tape or video recorder; rather, it is reconstructive.

All memory happens right now, in this immediate moment. When we remember something, we reconstruct the past in our brains. According to neurobiologists, when we think or undergo an experience, the specific stimuli of the experience are transformed by the nervous system into electrical impulses, which trigger a chemical chain reaction involving an enzyme, which rewires the connections between some of the brain's billions of nerve cells. It is this unique structure or pattern that is stored. What we experience as memory occurs when this electrical pattern is reactivated by later stimulation. It is also clear that during this process of reconstruction we never get it exactly right; we are always off a little. As a number of psychologists have phrased it, our memories are not like computers or phonograph records, but more like the village storyteller. Our brain doesn't passively store the facts and nothing but the facts; instead, it takes the facts and weaves them into a plausible and coherent story that, surprisingly enough, is re-created with each telling (Loftus 1980; Bolles 1988; Pettinati 1988; and Neisser 1982).

According to Magda Arnold, human memory is not an isolated process, since it depends upon perception, is influenced by emotion and imagination, and is embedded in the entire sequence from perception to action. Moreover, without memory there can be no perception as we experience it, no learning, nor any motivated action. In short, *memory is influenced by emotion and imagination.* And when we recall the important role imagination plays in the process of so-called hypnosis, it is clear we are going to find something very interesting when we look at the role imagination plays in hypnotic memories (Arnold 1984).

Shortly after I began to use hypnosis as a part of my teaching, a number of students came to me asking for my help in finding things they had lost. Their expectation was that if I hypnotized them they would remember what they had done with the thing they were missing. One student was particularly distraught because her father had given her a beautiful and expensive diamond ring for her birthday. In the past he had also accused her of being "scatter-brained" and "careless" about her possessions. She couldn't bear telling him that she had lost the ring within three weeks of receiving it.

My procedure then, and the one that I now use routinely, was to have her sit quietly in an easy chair and take several deep breaths and relax. Then I had her recall the last time she was absolutely sure she had the ring in her possession. Once this specific point in time was established, which happened to be on a date three nights earlier, I had her retrace step-by-step every movement she made and everything she did, moment by moment, until she reached the point that she realized the ring was gone. In this instance it proved to be very simple. After the date she went back to the dorm, undressed, put on her robe, studied for about an hour, then got her toilet articles and went down the hall to the bathroom, went to the lavatory, took off her ring and laid it on the shelf under the mirror, washed her face and hands, talked to a friend, dried herself, and went back to her room, leaving the ring on the shelf.

Unfortunately, possibly because she lived on a floor where the bath was shared with over twenty-five other students, she never regained the ring. Although she was relaxed, at no time was she ever hypnotized; she was able to retrace and remember every step and action and thus recall that she never picked up the ring from the shelf. Using this same "retracing one's steps" technique has been very useful over the years in helping a number of my friends and clients recover lost articles, and even, in one most interesting case, catch a thief who thought he had gotten away with his crime. At no time, however, and in none of my twenty-some cases did I use hypnosis—unless having someone sit down in an easy chair and relax and then "think back" is a definition of "hypnosis." As Pettinati stated in her recent comprehensive survey of hypnosis and memory,

> Memory can be enhanced and increased without hypnosis—an obvious comment in the context of the typical experience of suddenly remembering information that we thought we had totally forgotten. This ability is simply another characteristic example of how our memories work. It is interesting how this fact of nature can easily be overlooked when we are studying increases in memory through hypnosis. (Pettinati 1988, p. 279)

We also know that free association, fantasy, prolonged concentration, and even simple repeated recall efforts will often bring back supposedly forgotten material without having to resort to hypnosis (Erdelyi 1988).

To specifically answer the question, Does hypnosis improve memory? I carried out a number of laboratory studies over a period of three and a half years. Without going into details, my results in all cases showed no improvement in either memory or incidental memory as a result of hypnosis. Subsequent research has corroborated my results and has led Pettinati to conclude,

> At this juncture, it should be noted that the impressive body of work presented in this volume has not established a proven mechanism of action for hypnotic hypermnesia [improved memory] as distinct from nonhypnotic hypermnesia. However, it has been successfully demonstrated both by scien-

tific research and through selected case material that distortions of memories can occur when remembering is attempted during hypnosis. (Pettinati 1988; see also Baker, Haynes, and Patrick 1983; Baker and Patrick 1987)

At the moment we cannot tell whether a subject is telling the truth or is "confabulating," i.e., providing pseudomemories, during hypnosis without having or truly independent proof.

Because of the universality of the phenomenon of confabulation, it is surprising that it is not better known. Confabulation is a tendency of ordinary, sane individuals to confuse fact with fiction and to report fantasied events as actual occurrences. It has occurred in just about every situation in which a person has attempted to remember very specific details from the past. A classical and amusing example occurs in the movie *Gigi*, in the scene where Maurice Chevalier and Hermione Gingold compare memories of their courtship in the song "I Remember It Well." We remember things not the way they really were but the way we wished them to be. Our memories are both creative and recreative. We can and do easily forget. We blur, shape, erase, and change details of the events in our past. Many people walk around with their heads full of "fake memories." Moreover, the unreliability of eye-witness testimony is not only legendary but well documented. When all of this is further complicated and compounded by the impact of suggestions provided by the hypnotist, as well as the social-demand characteristics of the typical hypnotic situation, it is little wonder that the resulting recall bears slight resemblance to the truth.

Confabulation shows up without fail in nearly every context in which hypnosis is employed. In a well-publicized Arizona murder case in 1980, the wife of the victim, who was a witness to the crime, was hypnotized and asked to give details about what happened. During hypnosis the hypnotist suggested that the murderer's car was driving away so that she could see the rear license plate. He then asked the wife, "What was its number?" Even though the wife later reported she wanted to open her eyes and inform the hypnotist that she had not seen the car drive away, when he continued to suggest to her how clearly the departing car could be seen, it appeared on her mental television screen and the license plate came into sharp focus. Then, she heard herself describe the car, describe the license plate as green and white, and read off the license plates letters and numbers. Immediately after she was released from the hypnosis situation the wife informed the hypnotist that the information she had provided had to be mistaken. The police soon corroborated her statement when they found that the colors and number arrangements she reported did not fit those of any state in the union.

Forensic cases like this are far from rare. Many state courts have either begun to limit testimony from hypnotized witnesses or to follow guidelines laid down by the American Medical Association in 1985 to assure that witnesses' memories are not contaminated by the hypnosis itself. For not only do we translate beliefs into memories when we are wide awake, but in the case of hypnotized witnesses with few specific memories, the hypnotist may unwittingly suggest memories and create pseudomemories, i.e., vivid recollections of events that never happened. It may turn out that a recent U.S. Supreme Court decision allowing the individual states limited use of hypnotically aided testimony was unwise. In making their decision, however, the Supreme Court judges recognized that hypnosis may often produce incorrect recollections and unreliable testimony.

There have also been a number of clinical and experimental demonstrations of the creation of pseudomemories that have subsequently come to be believed as veridical. Bernheim and Janet went so far as to deliberately create such memories in order to successfully treat patients suffering from hysterical symptoms. More recently, Baker and Boas successfully treated a case of dental phobia by suggesting to the patient that a prior unpleasant dental experience was actually very pleasant. The pseudomemory was effective in permitting major dental surgery some months later with no emotional upset. Hilgard also implanted a false memory of an experience connected with a bank robbery that never occurred. His subject found the experience so vivid that he was able to select from a series of photographs a picture of the man he thought committed the robbery. In another instance Hilgard deliberately assigned to the same individual concurrent life experiences of two different people, and then regressed the individual at separate times to the times of those experiences. The individual subsequently gave very accurate accounts of both experiences, so that anyone believing in reincarnation would conclude that the man really had lived the two different lives (Hilgard 1981).

In a number of experiments designed to measure eye-witness reliability, Elizabeth Loftus (1979) found that details supplied by others invariably contaminated eye-witness memories. People's hair changed color, stop signs became yield signs, yellow convertibles turned to red sedans, the left side of the street became the right side, etc. The results of these studies led her to conclude, "It may well be that the legal notion of an independent recollection is a psychological impossibility." As for hypnosis, she believes,

> There's no way even the most sophisticated hypnotist can tell the difference between a memory that is real and one that's created. If you've got a person who is hypnotized and highly suggestible and false information is implanted in his mind, it may get imbedded even more strongly. One psychologist tried to use a polygraph to distinguish between real and phony memory but it didn't work. Once someone has constructed a memory, he comes to believe it himself. (Loftus 1979)

Orne heartily agrees. In my own work on hypnosis and memory the power of suggestion to evoke false memories was also clearly and dramatically evident (Baker, Haynes, and Patrick 1983). Sixty volunteers observed a complex display made up of pictures of a number of common objects, e.g., a television set, clock, typewriter, book, etc., and eight nonsense syllables, and were instructed to memorize the nonsense syllables in the center of the display. They were given two minutes to accomplish this. Nothing was said about the common objects. Following a forty minute delay, the students were questioned about the nonsense syllables and the other objects on the display. They were also asked to state their confidence in the accuracy of their answers. Some were questioned under hypnosis and others while they were wide awake. The students' suggestibility was studied by asking them to report on the common objects. They were also asked specific questions about objects that were not on the display. Their attention had not been directed at the objects specifically, and they were often unsure about what they saw and didn't see. When they were asked questions such as "What color was the sports car?" and "Where on the display was it located?" they immediately assumed there must have been a sports car present. A lawnmower and calendar were similarly suggested.

Although thirty-five subjects in the hypnoidal condition reported the color of the suggested automobile, thirty-four wide awake subjects reported the color. Similarly, although twenty-six subjects in the hypnoidal state reported the suggested lawnmower's color and position, twenty-seven who were awake reported its color and position. For the non-existent calendar, twenty-four hypnotized subjects reported the month and date, and twenty-three wide awake subjects reported them.

As for suggestibility per se under all conditions, fifty out of the sixty volunteers reported seeing something that wasn't there with a confidence level of 2 (a little unsure) or greater; forty-five out of sixty reported seeing something that wasn't there with a confidence level of 3 (sure) or greater; twenty-five out of sixty reported something that wasn't there with a confidence level of 4 (very sure) or greater; and eight out of the sixty reported something not there with a confidence level of 5 (absolute certainty). Interestingly, five of these eight who reported they were certain of the object's existence were wide awake. When they were allowed to see the display again, they were shocked to discover their error (Baker, Haynes, and Patrick 1983).

These matters are further complicated by so-called "hypnotic regression," i.e., taking the subject back to an earlier time in his existence, and "inadvertent cueing," i.e., having the hypnotist, as if unintentionally, reveal to the person being regressed exactly what response is wanted. How this complicates the situation is most clearly seen in an experimental study of hypnotic age regression carried out by R. M. True. True found that ninety-two percent of his subjects who had been regressed to the day of their tenth birthday could accurately recall the day of the week on which it fell. He also found the same thing for eighty-four percent of his subjects for their fourth birthday (True 1949). Other investigators, however, were not able to duplicate True's findings. When Martin Orne questioned True about his experiment he discovered that the editors of *Science*, in which True's report had appeared, had altered the procedure section without True's knowledge or consent. Orne discovered that True had inadvertently cued his subjects by following the unusual technique of asking them: "Is it Monday? Is it Tuesday? Is it Wednesday?" etc., and he monitored their responses by using a perpetual desk calendar that was in full view of all of his subjects.

Further evidence of the prevalence of and the importance of such cueing came from a study by O'Connell, Shor, and Orne (1970), in which they found that in an actual group of four-year olds, not a single one knew the day of the week. The hypnotic reincarnation or past-life regression literature is replete with examples of such inadvertent cueing. Wilson (1981), for example, has shown that hypnotically elicited reports of being reincarnated vary as a direct function of the hypnotist's belief about reincarnation. Finally, Laurence, Nadon, Nogrady, and Campbell (1986) have shown that pseudomemories were also elicited by inadvertent cueing in the use of hypnosis by the police.

As for advertent or deliberate cueing, one of my own studies offers a clear example of this. Sixty undergraduates, divided into three groups of twenty each, were hypnotized and age regressed to previous lifetimes. Before each hypnosis session, however, suggestions very favorable to and supportive of past life and reincarnation beliefs were given to one group; neutral and noncommittal statements about past lives were made to the second group; and skeptical and derogatory statements were made to the third group. The results clearly showed the effects of these cues and suggestions. Subjects in the first group showed the most past-life regressions and the most past-life productions, while subjects in the third group showed the least (Baker 1982). Regression subjects take cues as to how they are to respond from the person conducting the experiments and asking the questions.

In an excellent survey article of memory elicitation using hypnotic age regression techniques, Perry, Laurence, D'Eon, and Tallant (1988) point out that the characteristics most strongly related to hypnotizability are the subject's ability to create imagery and use his imagination. Both state and nonstate theorists are agreed that hypnosis involves the setting aside of critical judgment and indulgence in "make-believe" or fantasy on the part of the subject. It is also clear that hypnosis tends to increase the recall of both correct and incorrect material. Therefore, it is hardly surprising that hypnotic age regression is a rich and inexhaustible source of confabulation.

Every clinician and forensic hypnotist using regression techniques should be alert to the possibility that much of the material pulled from the patient's past—particularly tales of abuse, sexual molestation, infantile seductions, etc.—may well be products of the patient's imagination or responses to inadvertent cues supplied by the hypnotist. Suspect in this regard are a number of the hypnotic procedures advocated by Martin Reiser in his thirty-two-hour training course and in his textbook *Handbook of Investigative Hypnosis* (1980). Three procedures which may serve to increase the amount of confabulation are: (1) the technique of "affectless recall," in which the subject is asked to relive the events of the crime but not the emotions involved; (2) the practice of using metaphors derived from the television sports scene, such as asking the subject to "zoom in on" or to "watch in slow motion" the film of the crime stored in the subconscious; and (3) encouraging subjects to assume a separate identity and to refer to themselves as observers of the crime rather than as victims or participants. The first of these could well be a major source of distortion for recalling affect-laden material; the second is an invitation to confabulate if such images asked for were never stored in the first place; and, the third is, particularly for highly hypnotizable subjects, in Campbell Perry's words, "a free ticket to fantasy island" (Perry et al. 1988). Just how fantastic a creation some fantasy-prone individuals can concoct will be examined in detail in a later chapter.

A Note on Self-Hypnosis

Although many so-called experts in hypnosis treat the topic of self-hypnosis as something distinct and apart from ordinary or heterohypnosis, the only difference has to do with whether the subject or client relaxes himself and provides himself with internally generated suggestions or receives these stimuli from an external source. While many authorities argue that all hypnosis is self-hypnosis, others say that self-hypnosis is a myth and could not exist without a prior experience of heterohypnosis. Unless one knows how to play the game of hypnosis, it is extremely difficult to follow the rules and produce all of the hypnotic phenomena claimed as indicative of the true state of hypnosis. This is not to say, however, that individuals with vivid imaginations or fantasy-prone personalities could not, on their own, undergo cognitive experiences very similar to those produced by the hypnotist and his client or subject in the usual dyadic relationship. Many of the phenomena occurring in the heterohypnosis relationship, e.g., those due to the direct suggestions of the hypnotist, will not, of course, occur in the self-hypnosis situation. One cannot lift oneself by one's own bootstraps.

5.

Hypnosis and Pain

Hypnotically induced insensitivity to pain (analgesia) and general insensitivity (anesthesia) have been considered, by many, to be the most dramatic of all hypnotic phenomena.

Graham B. Wagstaff, *Hypnosis,
Compliance, and Belief*, 1981.

When relaxed and confident in the care of the hypnotist, subjects can appear to undergo painful stimulation that they would normally shrink from. Much of what we call pain is really a fear of harm, damage, or the persistence of an unpleasant stimulation. If we are told that something will not really hurt us (and if it does not), we stand much more of it than otherwise. Once the fear is removed (by suggestions of security), we can be quite heroic. A skillful dentist, sensitive to his or her patient's personality, can do a lot of tooth drilling without anesthesia. If he or she can convince his or her subject to relax and to believe that it will not hurt, it will not hurt as much.

B. Richard Bugelski and A. M. Graziano,
The Handbook of Practical Psychology, 1980.

Whenever it is argued that hypnosis does not exist or is nothing more than relaxation and suggestion, the other side responds: "Well, what about those people that have surgery without anaesthetics, using only hypnosis?" This entire chapter will be devoted to this matter.

The use of hypnosis or mesmerism as an anaesthetic can be traced back to a French surgeon named Cloquet, to John Eliotson at the University College Hospital in London in the 1830s, and to James Esdaile's use of mesmeric techniques in India. However, the reported pain-killing properties of hypnosis in those instances were by no means as clear-cut as advocates would have us believe. Wagstaff (1981) carried out extensive and careful review of the work of Eliotson and Esdaile, and has provided some alternative interpretations of mesmerism's so-called pain-killing powers. Also, according to the English historian H. B. Gibson (1977), Eliotson's painless operations were not quite as painless as reputed. Moreover, Esdaile's use of hypnotic or mesmeric surgery was not quite as easy or simple as we have been led to believe. In one of Esdaile's successful cases, attempts were made over a period of four days to mesmerize the patient, and at the end the patient fainted! Esdaile reported how he mesmerized men in law court without their knowledge and by making passes behind their backs. After he had put them in a trance, they supposedly walked away forgetting everything that had happened. If you are skeptical of this, then you should also be skeptical of his accounts of analgesia with mesmerism!

According to Wagstaff, a small proportion of the general population fails to experience pain when exposed to various kinds of unpleasant stimulation. While the number of people who could undergo painless surgery without anaesthetics is, obviously, quite small, it is important to point out that the number of people selected for surgery with hypnosis is equally small. Those who have studied the problem are in general agreement that the number is much less than the frequently reported ten percent. Two to three percent would be much more accurate. Additionally, total or complete analgesia under hypnosis is extremely rare, even though various writers on the subject would have you believe otherwise.

Many investigators have also pointed to cultural factors that affect the way people perceive and respond to pain. In Third World countries, people living in the midst of poverty, hunger, and disease develop an orientation to pain radically different from that of people in well-fed, hygienic America and Western Europe. Situations that would appear to be highly painful to Americans may be considered less painful in the more primitive cultures. In China, for example, children are conditioned from early childhood to accept surgery such as tonsillectomies with the full understanding that it will be successful and cause little or no pain. This cultural conditioning is very important in the determination of what is painful and the level of pain. As Wagstaff notes, just because Esdaile was able to carry out major surgery on the East Indians does not mean that he would have been as successful if he attempted this on Europeans.

Another factor that must be taken into account in any discussion of pain is the placebo effect. According to Shapiro (1973), until recently it is very probable that almost all medicines were placebos, i.e., sugar pills. In other words, it is not the medicine per se that brings about relief but the belief that you have ingested a magical potion that is curing you.

In the late eighteenth century a physician named Gerbi had a miraculous cure for toothaches. It consisted of crushing a worm between one's fingers and touching the tooth with it. Using this technique, 431 out of 629 toothaches ceased immediately. And from sixty-five to seventy percent reported immediate relief from pain when a ladybird was used (Gibson 1977). One cannot write a prescription without invoking the placebo effect. Space here does not permit the citation of the numerous studies showing the effectiveness of placebos in bringing about relief from symptoms. There have been well over 200 such studies to date. What is at work in placebo effects is suggestion. And suggestion alone—without hypnotic induction of any sort—has long been known to be highly effective for the relief of pain.

During World War II, two surgeons working in a prisoner-of-war camp without any access to drugs were forced to use hypnosis as an anaesthetic. Some of their patients couldn't be hypnotized, so the clever surgeons used placebos, i.e., they suggested anaesthesia from fake morphine pills. And it worked like a charm. Distraction also works well, as every general practitioner who has ever had to give shots to a child knows. A very simple technique for avoiding the pain of a shot in either the arm or the gluteus maximus is to make a fist and squeeze your hand as hard as you can just before the nurse hits you with the needle. You won't feel a thing!

Another form of distraction is what has been called acupuncture or acupressure. A Las Vegas dentist by the name of Dr. Norman Noorda, who specializes in working with children, developed an unusual formula for "painless dentistry" a few years ago. To insure that his oral efforts are devoid of pain, Noorda makes use of an ordinary household spring clothespin. As soon as his young patients climb into his chair, Noorda takes a small piece of cotton from a box and wraps it around his patient's left earlobe. Next he clamps the spring clothespin around the wrapped earlobe, and then proceeds to drill away. The clothespin and the cotton are the only painkillers employed, and apparently none of Noorda's patients suffer any pain. This type of acupressure turns out to be very successful on a large number of people, although it is not effective for everyone. The reason for Noorda's success involves the "gate control theory of pain," which we will get to a little later. Acupressure, like acupuncture, probably acts to impair the transmission of pain impulses to the brain either by altering the capacity of the nerve fibers which carry messages or by influencing the programming of the nervous system itself.

Other distractions include imagining pleasant scenes, imagining that one's body is numb in the area where the pain is coming from, concentrating upon one's breathing, or even singing a song. All of these activities serve well to reduce the amount of felt and reported pain. Many therapists use the technique of having the client imagine a television set with their favorite program on and describe the action as it occurs. Others have had their patients watch slides, count off the passing seconds on a clock, or talk about their sensations while experiencing painful dental or surgical procedures.

Experimenters have also reported that subjects report less pain when they listen to tape recordings or add numbers aloud. Investigators as far back as Liebault in 1885 have noted the role of distraction in alleviating pain and have argued that hypnotic suggestions help alleviate pain because they focus attention on ideas and thoughts other than the source of the pain. But we must go even further back than Liebault if we are to trace the use of distraction as a tool for dealing with pain. Avicenna, the eleventh century Arab physician and philosopher, described the use of "diversion" by means of soothing songs as a procedure for the lessening of pain. Thomas Aquinas, in the thirteenth century, wrote that pain could be relieved by meditating upon divine matters. Both Galen and Seneca also called attention to the role of emotional factors in the experience of pain. The former insisted that the physician consider the patient's fears, because fear influences reactions, and the latter wrote that young soldiers who were only slightly wounded were more afraid of the surgeon than the enemy, whereas veterans who were much more seriously wounded complained not at all. Dupuytren, an eighteenth century French surgeon, contrasted the reactions of civilians and soldiers to injuries and wounds, pointing out that soldiers who were used to forgetting themselves and familiar with the prospect of mutilation considered themselves lucky if they survived, and complained hardly at all. On the other hand, farmers and laborers moaned and groaned and were terrified at the slightest wound.

Studies carried out during World War II corroborated these claims. In one study comparing civilian patients undergoing surgery with soldiers wounded on Anzio Beachhead, even though the soldiers had extensive wounds, only thirty-two percent said the pain was severe enough to warrant asking for medication, whereas eighty-three percent of the civilians requested medication, though suffering less serious wounds. The intensity of suffering seems, therefore, largely determined by what pain means to the patient.

In general, our current society has a very low tolerance for pain as evinced by our penchant for pills and pain-relievers of every conceivable flavor and variety. For every ache and pain in the human corpus there are a dozen or more across-the-counter balms and analgesics, and if it really begins to hurt, there's always the friendly general practitioner whose relieving prescription can be quickly filled at the corner pharmacy. Pain is the single most common reason for seeing a physician and it is the number one reason why people take medication.

Pain, of course, is the body's alarm system. It alerts us to the fact that something is harming us and we need to do something about it. Many experts think that pain immobilizes us when we are injured, so that healing can occur. If we did not have any pain sensations, the result could be disastrous. Conversely, however, uncontrolled pain is also disastrous, and those who suffer from chronic pain are to be pitied, since they undergo an endless cycle of anxiety, depression, fatigue, sleeplessness, and despair. Primitive man, although he would have understood the acute pain of injury, must have been totally baffled by chronic pain, and attributed it to demons and evil spirits. The Egyptians believed it was due to spirits, gods and the dead. But by the sixteenth century B.C., steps were being taken to deal with it. Opium and hashish were used to induce anaesthesia. The Ebers Papyrus listed over a thousand prescriptions used during the reign of the Pharaoh Amenhotep. Some Roman physicians used an extract of mandrake roots containing belladonna to produce unconsciousness. Earlier, the Assyrians used partial strangulation and temporary unconsciousness for children undergoing circumcision. Concussions, obtained by simply hitting the patient on the head (sometimes covered with a wooden bowl), were another very popular method for producing unconsciousness. Opium and alcoholic beverages were also popular approaches to anaesthesia in days of yore, although these usually were not sufficient to stop the pain. With the advent of nitrous oxide and ether in the early 1800s, the dream of the complete elimination of pain during surgery was in sight.

Despite modern advances in surgical anaesthesia and improved analgesics it is unlikely that pain will ever be eliminated. Taking into account the thirty-six million arthritics, seventy million victims of back pain, twenty million migraine victims, one million cancer sufferers, and others who are afflicted by other painful disorders such as sciatica and gout, we need to recognize that pain will always be with us. Medical science is only beginning to understand it and has only recently come to the conclusion that pain is a very complex experience involving the emotions, previous experience with pain, and current attitudes toward pain. In other words, pain is a psychophysiological—mind-body—process that we are only slowly beginning to comprehend.

In addition to suggestion and the placebo effect, relaxation is useful in the alleviation of pain in a number of ways. For example, muscle relaxation is clearly related to pain responsiveness. H. K. Beecher (1959) showed that muscle-relaxant drugs had a powerful influence on pain. Also, relaxation is very effective in reducing fear and anxiety, which are inextricably linked with the pain response. The major difficulty with the use of relaxation techniques, however, is the fact that the person suffering from a traumatic wound and most in need of relief from fear and anxiety is also the most difficult to persuade to relax. Getting the recent victim to "Calm down, take slow deep breaths, let all of your muscles go soft and loose, etc." is not easy. Since what we call hypnosis also begins with the induction of relaxation, little wonder that so many therapists believe that it is the mysterious "state of hypnosis" that has relieved the pain rather than the relaxation.

Another part of the problem is that any psychological approach now used to alleviate pain is considered a hypnotic technique. Rather than being hypnotic, however, most use relaxation, suggestion, and distraction, and none of these are hypnosis! A classic example of this confusion is provided in Wester and Smith's *Clinical Hypnosis: A Multidisciplinary Approach* (1984), particularly Chapter 13, "Hypnosis in Surgery and Anesthesia," by Dabney M. Ewin. The purpose of that chapter is to instruct those unfamiliar with the treatment of burn patients how to go about hypnosis in a step-by-step fashion. The entire procedure, verbatim, is as follows:

When a newly burned patient arrives in the Emergency Room, his mind is concentrated and hypnosis is usually easy to induce. Since he may be a stranger to the physician, the first communication is an introduction and suggestion:

VERBALIZATION	COMMENT
Doctor: "I'm Dr. _____ and I'll be taking care of you [pause]. Do you know how to treat this kind of burn?"	This question is to bring to his immediate attention that he does not know and that he must put his faith in the medical team. Precise wording is important because if you ask "Do you know anything about treating burns?" he may know something and tell you about butter, Solarcaine, or kiss-it-and-make-it-well, which is a complete avoidance of recognizing the dependence.
Patient: "No."	The standard reply. In the rare instance of a physician or nurse who actually does know about burns, you simply use that knowledge to say, "Then you already know that you need to turn your care over to us and that we will do our best."
Doctor: "That's all right, because we know how to take care of this, and you've already done the most important thing, which was to get to the hospital quickly. You are safe now, and if you will do what I say, you can have a comfortable rest in the hospital while your body is healing. Will you do what I say?"	This exchange lets the patient know that he is on the team and has already done his biggest job, so he can safely lay aside his fight or flight response (he's already fled to the hospital), which mobilizes hormones that interfere with normal immunity and metabolism. It includes a prehypnotic suggestion (Abramson 1970) that he is safe and can be comfortable if he makes a commitment.

Patient: "Yes," or "I'll try."

With his affirmative answer he has made a hypnotic contract that is as good as any trance.

Doctor: "The first thing I want you to do is turn the care of this burn completely over to us, so you don't have to worry about it at all. The second thing is for you to realize that what you think will make a great deal of difference in your healing. Have you ever seen a person blush, or blanch white with fear?"

Frightened patients tend to constantly analyze each sensation and new symptom to report to the doctor. By turning his care over to us (the whole team), he is freed of this responsibility and worry. Next, his attention is diverted to something he had not thought of before.

Patient: "Yes."

Even dark-skinned patients are aware of this phenomenon in light-skinned people.

Doctor: "Well, you know that nothing has happened except a thought, an idea, and all of the little blood vessels in the face have opened up and turned red, or clamped down and blanched. What you think is going to affect the blood supply to your skin, and that affects healing, and you can start right now. You have had happy, relaxing, enjoyable thoughts to free up all of your healing energy. Brer Rabbit said 'everybody's got a laughing place,' and when I tell you to go to your laughing place, I mean for you to imagine that you are in a safe, peaceful place, enjoying yourself, totally free of responsibility, just goofing off. What would you do for a laughing place?"

The patient needs something he perceives as useful to occupy his time. The laughing place may be the beach, television, fishing, golfing, needlepoint, playing dolls, etc. It becomes the key word for subsequent rapid inductions for dressing changes, etc.—to simply "go to your laughing place."

Patient: "Go to the beach . . . or . . ."

It helps the doctor to know what the laughing place is and to record it, because he may enhance it later with some visual imagery. This simple, rapid induction usually produces a profound trance almost immediately.

Doctor: "Let's get you relaxed and go to your laughing place right now, while we take care of the burn. Get comfortable and roll your eyeballs up as though you are looking at the top of your forehead and take a deep, deep, deep breath and as you take it in, gradually close your eyelids and as you let the breath out, let your eyes relax and let every nerve and fiber in your body go [slow and cadenced] loose and limp and lazy-like, your limbs like lumps of lead. Then just let your mind go off to your laughing place and . . . [visual imagery of laughing place.]"

This short bit of conversation does not ordinarily delay the usual emergency hospital care. Most often, when the patient arrives in the Emergency Room an analgesic is given, blood is drawn, IV drips are started, and cold water applications are put in place by the time the doctor arrives. If not, these can proceed while the conversation takes place. A towel dipped in ice water produces immediate relief of the burning pain that occurs right after a fresh burn. Since frost bite is as bad an injury as a burn, the patient should not be packed in ice, but ice water towels are very helpful. In fact, Chapman (Chapman, Goodell, and Wolff, 1959) showed that applying ice water to a burn holds the inflammatory response in check for several hours, so there is ample time to call for the assistance of a qualified hypnotist if the primary physician is not skilled in the technique of hypnosis.

VERBALIZATION	COMMENT
Doctor: "Now while you are off at your laughing place, I want you to also notice that all of the injured areas are cool and comfortable. Notice how cool and comfortable they actually are, and when you can really feel this, you'll let me know because this finger (touch an index finger) will slowly rise to signal that all of the injured areas are cool and comfortable."	By this time, the patient has iced towels on and the analgesic is taking effect so that he actually is cool and comfortable. It is much easier hypnotically to continue a sensation that is already present than it is to imagine its opposite. The suggestion, "cool and comfortable," is anti-inflammatory, and if he accepts it, he cannot be hot and painful. From now on, the word injured is substituted whenever possible for the word burn, because patients use the word burning to describe their pain. (Do not specify a particular area, hand, neck, etc.,

because while these areas will do well, some spot you forgot may do poorly.)

Doctor: [after obtaining ideomotor signal] "Now let your inner mind lock-in on that sensation of being cool and comfortable and you can keep it that way during your entire stay in the hospital. You can enjoy going to your laughing place as often as you like, and you'll be able to ignore all of the bothersome things we may have to do and anything negative that is said."

I just leave the patient in trance, go ahead with his initial care, and get him moved to the Burn Unit. Often, he will drop off to sleep.

Doctor: "Go to your laughing place."

On subsequent days this is all the signal the patient usually needs to drop into a hypnoidal state and tolerate bed-side procedures, physical therapy, etc.:

In burns under 20% of the body surface, the single initial trance generally suffices, while in larger burns, repeated suggestion helps control pain, anorexia, and uncooperativeness (Crasilneck et al., 1955; Ewin, 1973; Knudson-Cooper, 1981; Schafer, 1975; Wakeman and Kaplan, 1978).

Since a thought can produce a burn (vide supra), continued feelings of guilt or anger can prevent healing, and should be dealt with during emotional countershock (Mattsson, 1975) a day or two after admission. If the patient is feeling guilty, I stress the fact that the injury was unintentional, he has been severely punished, and he has learned a lesson he will never forget or repeat. If he is angry, I point out that the goal is healing and that it does not interfere with his legal rights to get the best healing possible or to forgive the other person of evil intent. There is no place for anger at his laughing place, and he is instructed to postpone that feeling until healing has occurred. (Wester and Smith 1984, pp. 222-225)

From the foregoing it is obvious that the major therapeutic procedure here is anxiety reduction and the promotion of relaxation, and it is also patent that when these two things are achieved, the doctor is telling himself that his patient is in a trance. Medical personnel, psychologists, and others have known for many years that anxiety and tension amplify pain. Nevertheless, even today many doctors and dentists who use hypnotism in treatment and diagnosis are ignorant as to how and why it works. One of its effects—perhaps the most important—is the dispersal of tension and anxiety and the induction of relaxation, and a consequent reduction of pain.

If there is any one outstanding lesson that has been learned from the use of hypnosis it is that tension and anxiety accompany every human ailment. There is hardly any behavior disorder or nervous disturbance that is not grossly aggravated and made more complex by a heavy component of anxiety, and often fear as well. Illness, no matter what the cause, it always accompanied by some degree of anxiety. Even if the patient doesn't show it, there is still some concern or worry. Some of it may even be subconscious. We also know that it is impossible to be both relaxed and anxious at the same time. Therefore, one of the quickest ways to dispel anxiety is to get the patient to relax. And the use of hypnosis is using relaxation and suggestion to calm the patient down and distract him from the source of the anxiety.

Pain, certainly, is always accompanied by anxiety. The slightest wound —particularly if the wound is painful—is always a source of anxiety. "How serious is it? Will it get infected? When did I have my last tetanus shot? Am I going to die? Why did this happen to me?" These are the sort of questions that run through the mind of every victim—unless, of course, he is distracted by something of more importance, such as injury to a loved one, threats to something valued more than life itself, etc. In the latter instances pain may be totally ignored or suppressed until the crisis has passed.

We also know that there is a great deal of individual variation in susceptibility to pain. Some people seem to be able to tolerate major surgery without drugs or even hypnosis, whereas others will faint at a paper cut. Though it is difficult to believe, some rare individuals have even performed surgery upon themselves without the benefit of anaesthesia of any kind. Kalin (1979) reported an almost unbelievable case of a young man who successfully performed a bilateral orchiectomy (removal of both testicles), and then, two months later, attempted to denervate his adrenal glands. He quit during this second operation because he became tired and also had more pain than he anticipated while retracting his liver. He then went to the hospital for wound closure and postoperative care. Although there have been numerous cases of self-mutilation, this case was unique because of the young man's knowledge and skill.

Pankratz (1986) discovered an equally remarkable case that occurred during the 1880s. In this instance, a thirty-seven-year-old man performed a complete circumcision on himself, and then, "in order to see what was inside," slit his abdomen from the symphysis to the navel. He then went to the hospital with a prolapsed peritoneum and intestines, but shortly thereafter was discharged as cured. A year later, this same individual returned with his scrotum slit open and the testicles prolapsed. He recovered again in nine days. In 1880 he opened his abdomen a second time and recovered in two weeks. Next, he performed a castration of one testicle and carefully sutured the scrotum. As soon as the wound healed he removed the second testicle, but unfortunately suffered a hemorrhage. Nevertheless, he recovered. He probably performed these operations without the advantage of anaesthetics.

Related to the above instances are a few cases in which the patient has undergone surgery using only self-hypnosis. Although surgery under hypnosis is far from novel, serving as one's own anaesthesiologist is a bit unusual. In 1973 a psychiatrist named Bowen underwent a transurethral resection of the middle lobe of the prostate gland using only self-hypnosis as the anaesthesia both the night before and during the operation. Even though the urologist had an anaesthesiologist present in the operating room, he was never called upon. Neither was any post-operative medication required, though it was available. He was ambulatory the second day after surgery and had no complications (Bowen 1973).

A dentist named Rausch underwent major abdominal surgery using self-hypnosis as the sole anesthetic agent (Rausch 1980). During the cholecystectomy (removal of the gall bladder) only muscle relaxation and distraction were used to control the pain. Rausch managed this by focusing on Chopin's "Nocturne In E Flat," using time distortion and his own form of suggestion. He referred to "an interesting flowing sensation throughout my entire body." He also decided to use the initial incision as the "trigger" to force himself to go into "deep hypnosis." Even though he was able to get through the operation without any anaesthetics, and though he did not report any sensation of pain, it is evident from his own personal account that something unusual was happening. In his own words, at the precise moment the incision was made:

> I felt an interesting flowing sensation throughout my entire body. I was very aware of a definite change in my state of awareness. I felt as if my consciousness expanded or merged. Whatever happened, I was suddenly much more aware of my surroundings, people in the room and bodily sensations, than I had ever been before. . . . I was intently staring at the nurse to my immediate right and she later commented that I turned a funny color as if I were dead. . . . I heard and felt the music and dissociated very effectively, but almost instantly realized that if I dissociated completely I could not control my reflexes. I started reversing the process and again became aware that I needed a different approach if I hoped to successfully control the situation. I tried time distortion and quickly realized that neither was it enough. Up to this point I was desperately scrambling to find the answer, the approach that I knew had to be there. I again turned to the operating room nurse. . . . As soon as I had eye contact with her, I again felt the same kind of flowing sensation I had experienced when the initial incision was made. . . . (Rausch 1980)

Despite his subjective report, the hospital chart of his operation shows that at the moment of incision his pulse rate jumped from 82 beats per minute to 115, and his blood pressure immediately rose from 135 mm to 190. Both of these changes are good indicators of extreme physiological arousal.

Although these examples show that some few carefully selected individuals may be able to endure surgical pain with little or no distress, they do not in any way suggest that the average man or woman is capable of such feats. These events do, however, tend to show that surgical procedures may not actually be as painful as we previously supposed. It may well be that the major components of the pain are the fear and anxiety. Since so much of our pain is known to be psychological, the actual stimulation from the free nerve endings may be the least of the contributors to our overall misery.

It is interesting that the most sensitive part of the body as far as surgery is concerned is the skin, which is well supplied with free nerve endings, which are the sources of pain. As one moves deeper into the body's tissues and organs there are fewer and fewer free nerve endings, and consequently increasing insensitivity to the surgeon's scalpel. The anatomist T. Lewis in his book *Pain* (1942) provides a list of body parts which are totally insensitive (or almost so) to pain from the surgeon's knife. These parts include the subcutaneous tissue, compact bone, the articular surface of joints, the brain, the lungs and visceral pleura, the surface of the heart, the abdominal viscera, the oesophageal wall, the great omentum (the peritoneal fold that connects the abdominal viscera with the stomach), the stomach, lower portions of the alimentary canal, the uterus, and internal portions of the vagina. Lewis points out that solid organs such as the spleen, liver, and kidneys can be cut without the patient being aware of the incision. It is important to note, however, that these body parts are sensitive to stimulation coming from pulling, stretching, and drawing. Before the development and use of general anaesthetics, many patients underwent surgery using only a local pain killer to deaden the skin. Some authorities have suggested that simple superficial surgery involving the skin may actually be more painful than surgery on other major and deeper organs.

For such minor operations, however, the fear and anxiety is considerably less than that aroused when major organs are involved. Wagstaff (1981) has suggested that "the patient's belief in the efficacy of the technique (hypnotic surgery) may mean he will actually *allow* the surgeons to operate without a general anesthetic." This seems to be true in the cases of the two individuals who permitted operations to be performed while they used only self-hypnosis (Bausch 1980; Bowen 1973). Wagstaff has also suggested the possibility that many major operations conducted with hypnosis actually evoke little pain, not because of the hypnosis but because they would not be very painful anyway! Two additional points need to be made here: first, we need to remember that very few patients ever go under the knife using only hypnosis, so we are talking about a very small number of patients; second, even in such rare cases, hypnosis is seldom used alone, but in conjunction with analgesics primarily employed to anaesthetize the skin.

There is another aspect of the problem of pain we must consider. This is the fact that many people are simply not as sensitive to pain as others, as we have mentioned, and as a result, some people can subject themselves to various kinds of harsh stimulation and betray little or no discomfort. Jack Schwartz, a Dutchman who immigrated to the United States in 1957, has shown a startling insensitivity to pain over his entire lifetime (Schwartz 1978). In addition to sticking needles through his arm, Schwartz can hold burning cigarettes against his skin for periods of ten seconds or more. During these periods of self-torture Schwartz remains calm and relaxed, is able to control bleeding, and gives no physiological indicators of any pain. Similarly, a Peruvian national, one Ramon Torres, working with Gay Luce, has repeatedly shown his ability to master pain and control bleeding by routinely taking an ordinary bicycle spoke and sticking it through his cheeks from one side to the other—through his mouth and across his tongue—at the same time that he is carrying on an admittedly "lispy" conversation.

Vernon E. Craig of Wooster, Ohio, who is also known by his show business name of KOMAR, also has remarkable abilities to dominate and control pain. KOMAR, who currently holds the world's record for lying on a bed of nails, routinely walks up ladders made of the sharpened edges of sword blades, holds his hands in freezing water for two and a half minutes, runs nineteen-gauge needles through his biceps, endures the full voltage of cattle prods without pain, etc. According to KOMAR, he outthinks the pain and disciplines his mind to accept only one sensation at a time. "By filling the mind with another sensation, pain is displaced," KOMAR says, "and the body ceases to react to the painful stimulus. . . . Anyone who has attained self-mastery will know exactly what to do in any instance of pain. Usually, and in my case, particularly, I stop pain before it even occurs" (KOMAR and Steiger 1979, pp. 14 and 15).

Although such stunts or tricks are far from new, since Yogins and the Hindu fakirs have been carrying out similar feats for centuries, they are most impressive to anyone unaware of the simple fact that many spectacular feats like those described are simply not very painful to begin with, and for the few feats that are painful, an increased toleration for the pain can be learned with just a little courage and practice. Moreover, as every professional magician knows, kits for faking bloodless (or bloody, if desired) skin punctures, etc., can be purchased from any magic supply house. To understand exactly why so many of these tricks are not as painful as it would appear we need to know a little about the psychophysiological nature of pain itself.

The Psychophysiology of Pain

Although the mystery of pain is not completely solved, most of the pieces of the puzzle are now in place. For years psychologists thought there were four skin sensations: warmth, cold, pressure, and pain, and that for each of these there were specific skin receptors and centers in the brain where the experiences were interpreted. Research and study later showed that while there were skin receptors for temperature and pressure, none could be found for pain. Studies of the parietal lobes of the cortex of the brain also showed that electrical stimulation of certain areas gave rise to sensations of pressure and temperature, but no place could be found for sensations of pain. All other types of sensation—vision, hearing, taste, smell and touch—had both specific receptors and specific areas in the brain.

Nevertheless, it was well-known that pain sensitivity was localized in the spinal cord, since nerve pathways run back and forth through the cord to the brain. Diseases that involved the spinal cord were also known to cause excruciating pain, which could be relieved only by cutting some of the sensory pathways from the skin to and through the cord. Therefore, pain was obviously due to something traveling up the cord from the skin.

Looking at the nerve cells in the skin, physiologists noted that the axons of the basket cells in the skin had a special insulating sheath around them that insulated the electrical impulses passing along the axon, allowing them to flow faster. The insulated axons are called "fast fibers." Messages from the fibers flow about thirty times faster than messages from the other type of uninsulated or "slow fibers" or free nerve endings.

When the fast fibers in the spinal cord are stimulated directly, the individual reports feelings of pressure. On the other hand, if the slow fibers are stimulated, the person might report feeling pressure or temperature changes. If the stimulation of the slow fibers is intense enough, the individual will also report feeling pain. Yet, if both the fast and slow fibers are stimulated simultaneously, the individual experiences no pain whatsoever, no matter how intense the stimulation. Although slow fiber stimulation turns the pain on, fast fiber activity turns it off. The reasons for this are quite interesting, having to do with what Ronald Melzack and Patrick Wall, who discovered this phenomenon in 1965, call the "spinal gate" or "gate theory" of pain (Melzack and Wall 1988).

Since pain travels up the spinal cord by means of the slow fibers, when it arrives at the top of the spinal cord, depending upon what else is going on, it may or may not be able to get through the "gate" or "neural switch." If there is activity in the fast fibers, according to Melzack and Wall, the spinal gate is closed, and slow fiber activity is blocked and not allowed through the gate. When the gate is closed painful inputs never reach the cortex either by way of the straight-line system or by way of the reticular system—the body's two separate systems for pain control.

Experimental data from both humans and animals have confirmed Melzack and Wall's theory that the gate can be closed by fast fiber stimulation and that this type of input blocking seems to be built into fast fiber activity. Since the lower brain centers at the top of the spinal cord can only process so many inputs per second, the fast fiber activity overwhelms the centers and they turn the switch, screening out the slow fiber action and thus the pain. This explains why scratching an itch brings immediate relief. The greater fast fiber activity from the scratching overwhelms the slow fiber stimulation from the itch. It also explains the effectiveness of acupuncture, the painless dentistry that results from the clothespin on the earlobe, and the fact that making a fist before receiving a shot in the butt shuts down the pain.

Even more interesting, however, is the fact that the human brain can also learn and does learn to close this spinal gate. In an article in *Science*, Watkins and Mayer (1982) demonstrated that the body processes painful stimulation in two different ways, and therefore there must be two separate pain control systems. For example, if you accidentally burn your finger on a hot stove, the skin receptors in the finger send a signal up the spinal cord via the slow fibers that some harm has befallen your finger. When this signal gets to the top of the spinal cord it divides or splits, and the sensory information about the burn to the finger is passed right on through via the straight-line sensory system to the parietal cortex.

At the same time, however, your higher cortical centers are aware of the fact that you have done something stupid like touch your finger to a hot stove, and the consequent emotional knowledge of this fact is processed by the brain's reticular center. Fortunately, the stress resulting from this knowledge also serves to stimulate the cortex to release some of the body's own built-in pain killers, known as endorphins, which are chemically similar to morphine. It is this second pain-control system, which Watkins and Mayer call the "emotion-suppressing system," that explains the analgesic effects of hypnosis and other sorts of cognitive strategies. This second system is a stress-related general alarm mechanism for controlling pain, and we can learn to gain voluntary control over this mechanism.

When the pain from the burned finger reaches the reticular system, it triggers activity in the autonomic nervous system and the body releases epinephrin, norepinephrine, and the endorphins, as well as a number of other chemicals that cause reactions. The automatic release of the endorphins not only reduces neural activity in the reticular system and other emotional centers in the brain, but also slows down activity in the autonomic nervous system. We experience the reduced neural activity as a reduction in the emotional impact of the burn. For example, after receiving morphine, surgery patients often report, "The pain is still there, but it just doesn't seem important anymore." This emotion-suppressing system is easily conditioned via classical or Pavlovian techniques, according to Watkins and Mayer, whereas gaining voluntary control over the spinal gate comes about via operant or Skinnerian conditioning. Thus, if we are to achieve conscious control of pain, we need to develop techniques for dealing with these two separate systems. A number of researchers have attempted to do this. London and Engstrom (1982) suggested four techniques for pain control: one for activating the emotion-suppressing system and the others for stimulating the input-blocking system:

1. *Relaxation*—This is the simplest and most effective counter to stress, and anything reducing stress will also reduce pain. Learn how to relax, reduce tension in all the muscles of the body. Think peaceful pleasant thoughts, let all of the muscles go limp, take slow deep breaths, and let all of the tension drain out of your body.

2. *Use imagery as counter-conditioning*—Use pain as a stimulus to automatically evoke a pleasant mental image. For example, imagine yourself floating in a warm pool listening to soothing and peaceful music. Whenever you feel pain call up this pool image. Since it is impossible to experience *discomfort* and *warm* comfort simultaneously, you will have counter-conditioned yourself against the pain.

3. *Self-talk or self-instruction*—Another important cognitive technique for shutting off pain is *self-talk*, i.e., telling yourself that you can control the pain and turn it off whenever you wish. Zero in on the pain and try to make it hurt less, little by little, and reward yourself mentally when you succeed. Train yourself to be more positive in your approach to others and encourage them to help you in your attempts at self-control.

4. *Monitoring Yourself and Others*—Keep a chart or log of how effective you have been at controlling the pain. Try having someone else reward you for reducing your discomfort or merely take pride in your own success. Monitor carefully the response people around you are making to your symptoms—they may be rewarding you for suffering. Watch your own efforts to use pain as a way of controlling others, e.g., by avoiding work or avoiding facing important problems. Develop direct coping strategies.

For the past twenty years or so, Theodore X. Barber has taught a number of conscious strategies similar to the above for reducing the intensity of pain, and Barber has compared and contrasted these with the use of hypnosis. Some of these are much more effective than others, but the best of them seem to be just as effective or even more effective in reducing pain than so-called hypnosis. In one study, for example, Barber asked students to immerse their hands in extremely cold water. Some of the subjects were told to try the cognitive strategies used by London and Engstrom, while others were given similar instructions while hypnotized. The cognitive strategies proved in all cases and on all measures of painfulness to be just as effective in reducing pain as the hypnosis. Barber has concluded, with good reason, that hypnosis is no better as an analgesic than is "mental discipline," ergo, we have no need for the concept of hypnosis.

Finally, we need to look briefly at what pain experts have to say about the effectiveness of hypnosis as a pain-killer. Hilgard and Hilgard state flat out:

> Yet, despite a vast amount of excellent research on the effects of hypnosis on experimentally induced pain, there is virtually no reliable evidence from controlled clinical studies to show that it is effective for any form of chronic pain. (Hilgard and Hilgard 1986)

> Melzack and Wall also report:

> It remains to be shown that hypnotic suggestion is any better than a placebo pill or encouragement and moral support from the family physician or clergyman. (Melzack and Wall 1988)

These authors go on to state that hypnosis by itself does not have a sufficiently strong effect on clinical pain to be considered a reliably useful therapy. An even stronger opinion has been provided by Merskey, who concluded, on the basis of available clinical reports and his own personal experience, that hypnotism is not "worth using in anyone with pain of a physical origin and very rarely in patients with pain which is psychological in origin" (Merskey 1983).

All is not hopeless, however. Melzack and Wall have also suggested a number of cognitive coping strategies or skills for dealing with pain. Six that they strongly recommend include:

1. *Imaginative inattention*—You train yourself to ignore the pain by evoking imagery which is incompatible with the pain, e.g., you imagine you are at the beach, at a party, or in the country, or someplace else, depending on the image you can most vividly create.

2. *Imaginative transformation of the pain*—You interpret the subjective experience in terms other than "pain." For example, you might change it into tingling or warming. Or you might minimize the experience as trivial or meaningless or unreal.

3. *Imaginative transformation of context*—You acknowledge the pain but transform the setting or context. For example, if you have a sprained

arm you can picture yourself as a soldier who has been shot by a sniper who was trying to kill you.

4. *Attention diversion to external events*—You focus your attention on extenal objects in the environment or things around you such as pictures on the wall, the number of tiles in the ceiling, the texture of your clothes, and so on.

5. *Attention diversion to internal events*—You focus attention on internally or self-generated thoughts, such as your favorite poems, old familiar songs, mental arithmetic, pleasant memories, etc.

6. *Somatization*—You learn to focus attention on the painful area, but you do it in a detached manner. You analyze the pain sensations, for example, as if you were a news reporter and are writing a news story for a magazine article about the experience.

Although these are by no means foolproof, along with relaxation, biofeedback of some kinds, operant conditioning, stress inoculation training, and psychological counseling, such coping strategies can be most helpful in the reduction of pain. A note of caution however, is in order. As Melzack and Wall warn, these therapies rarely abolish pain entirely and they are not equally effective for everyone. Moreover, there are limits to the effectiveness of any given therapy. But we have also learned that the effects of two or more therapies in combination often prove to be cumulative, and for this reason "multiple convergent therapy," i.e., the use of a number of psychological procedures simultaneously, is rapidly becoming the treatment of choice for pain. Multiple convergent therapy is effective, perhaps, because each kind of therapy has its predominant effect on a different pain-causing mechanism. As for hypnosis per se, if it has any effects at all upon the reduction of pain, such effects are due to relaxation alone or relaxation in combination with the suggestions that excite the sufferer's imagination and divert his attention from the source of the pain and discomfort.

6.

The Abuses and Misuses of Hypnosis: Some Dangerous Games

All sciences alike have descended from magic and superstition but none has been so slow as hypnosis in shaking off the evil association of its origin.

Clark L. Hull, *Hypnosis and Suggestibility*, 1933

No mind-control technique has more captured popular imagination— and kindled fears—than hypnosis. Men have long dreamed they could use overwhelming hypnotic powers to compel others to do their bidding. And when CIA officials institutionalized that dream in the early Cold War days, they tried, like modern-day Svengalis, to use hypnosis to force their favors on unwitting victims.

John Marks, *The Search for the Manchurian Candidate: The CIA and Mind Control*, 1979.

There is a great deal of confused thinking among the general public in regard to the facts of hypnotism. To the uninformed hypnotism savors of a mysterious power of the mind with more than a hint of the supernatural. In actual fact, while our knowledge of hypnotism and suggestion is still incomplete, our understanding is more than sufficient to dispel any lingering belief in the operation of occult power.

D. H. Rawcliffe, *Illusions and Delusions of the Supernatural and the Occult*, 1959.

In the mail recently (June 1989) I received an invitation to subscribe to *The Journal of Borderline Research*, which from reading the flyer I discovered is

A Free-Thought Scientific Forum examining the living energy of our Creator and probing the parameters of Body, Mind, and Spirit. It is issued six times per year to members . . . who take an active interest in observations of their physical, mental, and spiritual environment—personally, globally, and universally. Subjects of inquiry on this Borderland between the Visible and the Invisible Manifestations of Reality include: Archetypal Forms and Forces of Nature and the Use of the Imagination and Intuition to perceive them, Light and Color and the Etheric Spectrum, Radionics and Radiesthesia, Dowsing, Ether Physics and Beneficial Technologies, Orgone Energy, Water Technology, Initiation Science, Nikola Tesla and the True Wireless, Electricity and the Evolving Soul, Hollow Earth Mysteries, Anomalies and Fortean Phenomena, Hypnosis, Photography of the Invisible, and Unidentified Flying Objects.

Somewhat taken aback at first to find hypnosis listed along with and in the company of pseudosciences such as dowsing, orgone energy, hollow earth, radionics, and ether physics, after a moment's reflection I thought, "Of course, of course, that's exactly where it belongs!" What is even more surprising is that after all these years hypnosis is still considered by many to be an "occult" practice and is closely identified with other mystical and paranormal (psi) phenomena. And, based upon reports printed in some of the current parapsychological literature, it is understandable why this is so. For example, believe it or not, this item was found in a 1974 publication titled *An Index of Possibilities* (Chesterman et al. 1974), in the section titled "Hypnotism."

In the 1920s the Russians confirmed reports of telepathic hypnosis in laboratory tests and concluded that if you can be hypnotised into the somnambulistic state (and 20% of us can) it is possible to be hypnotised telepathically. . . . Meanwhile, the Czech "psychic explorer" Bretislav Kafka, was busily sending his assistants into hypnotic trances lasting ten years or more; he then proceeded to train them in ESP until their clairvoyant abilities were perfected. He probably had the best overall picture of the progress made during World War II as his psyched up assistants delivered their clairvoyant pictures of what was happening around the globe.

Kafka also kept a man in hypnotic trance in one room for three weeks, without food, and told him that he was in a beautiful garden. He reported at the end of the three week period that not only was the man well, but that he had gained weight." (p. 171)

If you believe any of this then you also must believe in elves, the tooth fairy, and that the world is flat. Nevertheless, one of the primary reasons why hypnosis over the years has been and in some quarters is still linked with the paranormal is because in the minds of many it is considered to be "an altered state of consciousness," and all such altered states are associated with the mystical, the supernatural, and the unknown.

Prior to the nineteenth century there were only a few scattered attempts to examine supposedly supernatural phenomena objectively. Most of these attempts focused on Mesmer's animal magnetism. Louis XVI's two investigatory commissions reached highly skeptical conclusions concerning Mesmer's claims. Other investigators studying mesmerism in the eighteenth century and the early part of the nineteenth reached more favorable conclusions. Many of them became convinced that many of Mesmer's subjects showed various supernormal abilities, primarily telepathic and clairvoyant powers. By the middle of the nineteenth century the study of hypnosis, as it came to be called, led investigators to the study of other occult matters, such as spiritualism and apparitions, etc. Thereupon, the transition from the study of the occult to the study of the paranormal was easy, since, as Braid had surmised, changing the names of the phenomena, made them respectable. Theorists and researchers who before were afraid to soil themselves with superstition could now speculate and investigate without fear.

There was also a strong link between the mesmeric movement and the modern Spiritualist movement, which began around 1848. Subjects in the somnambulistic state not only could diagnose other people's ailments via clairvoyance but could also see when blindfolded, read the contents of sealed packages, and visualize distant scenes as if they were present at them. And if they could do such wondrous things, why not reach into the next world and contact people there. Quite early in the mesmeric movement Frederica Hauffe, known as the "Seeress of Prevorst," was made famous by her physician, Justinus Kerner, who wrote a book about her powers while she was in trance. While in the somnambulistic state, Frau Hauffe saw and talked with the spirits of the dead, some of whom gave her accurate accounts of their earthly careers. A Frenchman named A. Cahagnet published a book in 1847 called *The Celestial Telegraph*, describing details of the next world, which he had obtained while in a trance, and Dr. J. Haddock in 1849 in England published a similar sort of book titled *Somnolism and Psycheism*. Both of these gentlemen were followers of the mystic Swedenborg. Meanwhile, in 1847 in the United States, Andrew Jackson Davis, another follower of Swedenborg, published his 800-page spiritualistic classic *Principles of Nature*. According to Davis, this book was dictated by him at the age of nineteen while he was in a mesmeric trance.

Thus, from the very beginning of what Slater Brown (1970) has called "the heyday of spiritualism," the public was informed that certain gifted people while in an altered state of consciousness could make contact with the spirits of the departed and bring back information from the world beyond. What became known as the "mediumistic trance" clearly evolved out of the "mesmeric trance," and the concept of a magnetic flux from the operator to the subject was obviously extended to include the "control" exercised by the spirits. In this manner, the mesmeric movement merged with and became the Spiritualist movement. The first five chapters of Brown's book provide a delightful and informative review of the transition from animal magnetism and the supposedly paranormal antics of the magnetists to the spiritualists and their evocation of the dead.

In spite of the fact that hypnosis is now ultrarespectable, it still carries in many quarters the stigma of occult associations. Before Mesmer, people in a trance were suspected of being "possessed by the devil." Then they came to be seen as "magnetized," but still were considered to have psychic abilities. Such phenomena in Mesmer's day were a regular part of the somnambulist's powers, and Mesmer noted, "Sometimes through his inner sensibilities the somnambulist can distinctly see the past and the future!" (Ellenberger 1970). Mesmer also claimed that he could mesmerize from a distance. Puysegur also used hypnosis for medical diagnosis by clairvoyance. Both Esdaile and Eliotson reported incidents of apparent extrasensory perception while mesmerized. Although some skepticism existed (e.g., Bernheim wrote, "I have in vain tried to induce thought transmission in hundreds of persons. . . . "), others, such as Liebault, were convinced that clairvoyance was a feature of hypnosis. Janet, Charcot, and the psychic investigator Frederick Myers also believed in the telepathic induction of hypnosis (Fodor 1966).

Janet, in fact, carried out an experiment with one of his "good" subjects, Leonie. Leonie waited at his home under his housekeeper's eyes while Janet, from his office a quarter of a mile away, tried to hypnotize her. Janet sent his thoughts at random intervals, and the housekeeper recorded Leonie's waking and sleeping, i.e., hypnotic, states. The results, according to the investigators, were highly successful. Leonie also worked with the physiologist and Nobel Prize–winner Charles Richet to perform "traveling clairvoyance," in which the subject is given suggestions to observe and report events occurring in some distant location. While under hypnosis, Leonie "observed" Richet's laboratory and correctly reported fire there before news could possibly have reached her by normal means. Similarly, "traveling" incidents were reported from Sweden by A. Backman (1891), Eleanor Sidgwick (1891), and Azam and Dufay (1889). Besides clairvoyance, investigators also reported success with "community of sensations" experiments, in which, whenever the hypnotist was touched, his subject also reacted as if he had been touched (Podmore and Gurney 1884). Much later, another Swedish psychiatrist, John Bjorkhem (1942), reported a case of traveling clairvoyance. Under hypnosis one of Bjorkhem's clients was told to visit her home and describe what she saw. Shortly after the hypnotic session the client's parents anxiously called the psychiatrist because they were convinced they saw her apparition!

As with most such anecdotal reports, important and essential details are missing, and as with most verbal reports, exaggeration and confabulation are prevalent in the descriptions. Moreover, experiment protocols for these clinicians were far from acceptable by today's standards. All of these factors make the above claims highly suspect.

In his initial studies of extrasensory perception, J. B. Rhine tried to use hypnosis to promote telepathy. In the late 1930s, however, Rhine gave it up as hopeless, stating that "The general feeling we had at the Duke laboratory was that we did not know what to tell the hypnotized subject to do to increase his powers" (Rhine 1952). Honorton and Krippner (1969), in their review of ESP and hypnosis, found that nine out of twenty-two experimental studies reported significant differences between the waking and the hypnotic states. Yet sometimes the hypnotic state showed lower scores than the waking state. This was interpreted to mean that hypnosis affects not the direction, i.e., hitting or missing the target, but only the magnitude of the scores. Follow-up studies with better controls revealed that hypnotic performance was superior to that of groups motivated by suggestion and expectancy while wide awake. Yet, in view of the fact that we have no way of knowing whether any real differences exist between the waking state and the so-called hypnotic state, either in theory or in the laboratory, all such experimental differences are more than likely artificial.

The work of the Czech parapsychologist Milan Ryzl (1962) is a classic example. Through hypnosis, Ryzl trained groups of subjects to experience complex and vivid hallucinations and to move from the hallucinations into perceiving ESP targets. Ryzl claimed he was successful with approximately ten percent of his subjects. But he only reported the performance of one subject, Pavel Stepanek, who had already become something of an ESP celebrity (Ryzl and Ryzlova, 1962; Pratt 1973). Most interesting, however, is the fact that Ryzl was only successful in Czechoslovakia. Several replications of Ryzl's work failed to yield anything supportive, and even more damning was the fact that Ryzl himself failed to obtain any ESP results in the United States.

Another even more serious problem with such studies is that nineteenth-century hypnotists used "hysterics" as subjects, and by the mid-twentieth century hysteria was almost nonexistent as a diagnostic entity. As Adrian Parker (1975) and others have suggested, it is possible that what was called "hypnosis" in the nineteenth century may have been crucially different from laboratory and clinical hypnosis today. We can be almost certain that, because of the importance of the role assigned to the hypnotist in the past, suggestion, domination, and control played a much more important and significant role in the hypnotic sessions of the earlier twentieth century than they do today (Parker 1975).

A number of studies have attempted directly to link psi and internal attention states, e.g., hypnosis, meditation, relaxation, etc. A few years ago,

Charles Honorton, carried out an extensive review of this work (Honorton 1977). Honorton is a convinced believer in the reality of psi, and yet even he dismisses the work of the mesmerists and the spiritualists as irrelevant and inconsequential:

> Most of the cases supporting claims of "higher phenomena" are of little value when assessed by contemporary standards of experimental control. Rarely, for example, is it possible to feel confidence in the methods employed to eliminate sensory contact during demonstrations of "eyeless vision", in which the magnetizers eagerly encouraged the use of elaborate albeit easily manipulated blindfolds, while rejecting simpler methods which would have more effectively screened the somnambule from his target. . . . Similarly, reports of hypnosis at a distance suffer from the same problem encountered in contemporary hypnosis research in general; namely, what criteria were employed to assess the presence of the hypnotic state? Apparently most of the cases bearing on this claim were deemed successful if the subject "appeared" to be "asleep." (p. 443)

In his review of a number of contemporary psi guessing studies with hypnosis, Honorton also stresses the fact that they all suffer from *the lack of clear-cut objective correlates of the hypnotic state*. Since we do not have data on these studies, we are left with highly questionable research in general. Nevertheless, Honorton does review nearly all of the work carried out relating psi and hypnosis, psi and meditation, psi and progressive muscle relaxation, and psi and Ganzfeld (homogenous visual field or "sea of light" stimulation) and sensory deprivation studies—a total of eighty different experimental studies. Honorton concludes that "Psi functioning is enhanced (i.e., is more easily detected and recognized) when the receiver is in a state of sensory relaxation and is minimally influenced by ordinary perception and proprioception" (p. 466). Honorton points out, with regard to the most successful of the internal attention states, i.e., the Ganzfeld studies, that all of the successful studies originated in two laboratories, the Maimonides (his own laboratory) or a laboratory in Houston. Moreover, the most successful subjects were those who had had some prior involvement in psi research.

While at first glance the results seem to offer impressive evidence for the fact that people who are relaxed or hypnotized are able to guess or see more accurately than people at a higher level of muscular tension, we must remember that even though slightly more than fifty-five percent of the studies showed a "psi effect," we are dealing with very small performance differences that may well be statistical artifacts produced by the well-documented "experimenter" or "believer" effect. Equally as significant with regard to psi research is the finding that very few, if any, of the results are independent of the experimenter.

In the laboratory as in life, it seems, we find what we are looking for. Time after time, believers in psi find evidence for it, and disbelievers find no trace of it. As James Alcock (1981) and others have noted, despite the efforts made to show a diversity of replications in the area of psi research, most of the successful experiments are restricted to only a few names, and all of these names are believers. One critic noted that over half of the research articles published in the major psi research journal, *Journal of the American Society for Psychical Research*, are written by only five people. In addition, we have the spectacle of psi sympathizers—those who wish that it were true—bemoaning the failure of efforts to show its existence. Adrian Parker, for example, says,

> The present crisis in parapsychology is that there appear to be few if any finding which are independent of the experimenter. Indeed, it can be claimed that the experimenter effect is parapsychology's one and only finding. This is the impasse that parapsychology has reached today. (1978, p. 2)

And John Beloff, somewhat earlier, lamented

> I recently completed a seven-year programme of parapsychological research with the help of one full-time research assistant. No one would have been more delighted to obtain positive results than we, but for all the success we achieved ESP might just as well not have existed. . . . I have not found on comparing notes with other parapsychologists . . . that my experience is in any way out of the ordinary. (1973, p. 312)

Even earlier, D. J. West noted that even the "best" experiments on psi,

> fall short of the requirements for usual scientific conviction for several reasons, the chief one being that they are more in the nature of demonstrations than repeatable experiments . . . no demonstration, however well done, can take the place of an experiment that can be repeated by anyone who cares to make the effort. (1966, p. 17)

Ray Hyman (1977) made the important point that the issue with regard to psi research is not really replication or repeatability but rather respectability, that is, we need successful replications of psi effects made by skeptics and disbelievers rather than only by researchers who believe! Paul Kurtz has emphasized this as well, pointing out that,

> It is not enough for parapsychologists to tell the skeptic that he, the parapsychologist, on occasion has replicated the results. This would be like the American Tobacco Institute insisting that, based on its experiments, ciga-

rette smoking does not cause cancer. The neutral scientist needs to be able to replicate results in his own laboratory. Esoteric private-road-to-truth claims need to be rejected in science, and there needs to be an intersubjective basis for validation. (1978, p. 23)

Moreover, replication is more important in psi research than in other areas. As Alcock states, in regular science the dishonest researcher will eventually be found out when others are unable to reproduce his results. But in psi research, where replication by independent, impartial researchers seems difficult if not impossible, the possibility of fraud is even more likely and hence of greater concern.

In general, we must conclude along with Alcock (1981) and the National Academy of Science Committee report on parapsychology (Druckman and Swets 1987) that after a century or more of formal parapsychological inquiry there are no experiments or demonstrations that can be replicated by or in the presence of competent and skeptical scientists. There is also no independent way of demonstrating the existence of psi apart from statistical results, and it is still impossible to predict when psi should or will occur. Although psi proponents have made sweeping claims both for its existence and its applications, an evaluation of the evidence does not justify such optimism. There is, nevertheless, a discrepancy between the lack of scientific evidence and "the strength of many individuals' beliefs in paranormal phenomena" (Druckman and Swets 1987).

Over the years many of the world's most prominent scientists have concluded that such phenomena exist and have been verified. Yet in such cases subsequent investigation has shown that these convictions were unjustified. Arguments that the scientific method may not be the best tool with which to investigate the paranormal are not persuasive, since the use of alternate procedures merely increases the opportunities for deception and error. There is, thus, very little that can be learned about the nature of hypnosis and related phenomena by entangling it further in the morass of parapsychological research. If we learn anything from the century or so of research in this area, it is that we must be very wary of the "true believer," be he a scientist or otherwise.

In this regard, it is of interest that two of the psychologists who contributed to the 1987 NAS committee report, Rosenthal and Harris, felt that, on the basis of the statistical evidence available, a strong case could be made for the validity of some of the psi phenomena, e.g., the Ganzfeld studies that reported statistical significance of over a billion to one. The only reason the other members of the committee overruled their minority opinion was that all the confirming evidence came from the same true believers. Had the data come from neutral or unbiased sources, there is little doubt the results would have been accepted as legitimate.

Over and over, we find in the laboratory and in the field, as in daily life, that our biases, our preconceptions, and our expectations lead us to discover whatever it is we are seeking. Not only do human beings tend to observe what they have been conditioned to believe, but our experimental results—the ones we publish, at any rate—confirm what we were certain of at the outset. Most investigators do not publish the results of work that fails to support their theories and convictions, and, as many have pointed out, if one experimental approach or method fails to reveal data favorable to our position, we design ever more complex studies with ever more opportunity for unknown variables and systematic errors to creep in and further confuse the issue. We adopt abstruse statistical procedures by which the belief can be saved. The nature of human nature is difficult to change.

One final word before leaving this topic, we should be eternally grateful that if psi forces do exist they are fairly weak and inconsequential. Think what a horrible world it would be if psychokinesis were a fact and could be used at will by anyone. The slightest angry thought could propel a brick, a stone, a chair, a bottle, with deadly force. Cars would be washed from the highways and planes wiped out of the skies by someone's whim. If telepathy were common or universal, privacy would be a thing of the past and the mental effort we would be required to exert to monitor our own as well as other people's thinking processes would leave us little time for ordinary cognitive chores. We would be faced with a world made up of human monsters and creatures that would no longer be human. Rather than the boon and blessing that proponents of the paranormal have foreseen, universal access to such full-blown mental powers could destroy civilization as we know it and bring us down more quickly than the most deadly of our nuclear devices. There is much to be said for being as we are.

Hypnotic Regression and Progression

Another claim of the classical hypnosis theorists is that of hypermnesia or the ability to remember things we supposedly have forgotten. For a long while it was thought that hypnosis provided the person hypnotized with abnormal or unusual abilities of recall. The ease with which hypnotized subjects would retrieve forgotten memories and relive early childhood experiences was, astonishing. When told to go back to his fourth or fifth birthday, for example, a young man might begin to talk in the voice of a four- or five-year-old and proceed to talk about the presents he received, the people who were present at the party, the kind of ice cream that was served, and other specific details that had long been forgotten.

However, when the veridicality of such memories was examined, it was found that many of the memories were not only false but even outright fabrications. Confabulation seemed to be the norm rather than the exception. Hypnotized individuals taken back to childhood do not behave like real children. Rather, hypnotically age-regressed individuals behave the way they *believe* children of that age would behave. Silverman and Retzlaff (1986) demonstrated that age-regressed adults, when given the same cognitive and intellectual tasks as children of the age to which the subjects are regressed, usually outperform the children. Also, Barber, Spanos, and Chaves (1974) have shown that hypnotically age-regressed subjects in no way act like real children. They behave like adults playing at being a child. In other words, they are playing a game and acting out a fantasy—a fantasy they have been given permission to carry out while they are hypnotized.

By far the greatest misuse of hypnotic regression, however, is what is known as past-life regression. The fact that hypnotists were able to regress many of their subjects back to birth and even to the womb encouraged many of them to take it one step further and to look into preconception experiences. It was discovered that many individuals, if properly primed with suggestions, could report events that happened to them years before their birth, when they were supposedly living in another body in another time and place. These memories of other lifetimes, of having lived before, were not only intrinsically fascinating but became even more so when follow-up in a number of such cases provided corroborating evidence for some of the claims. To those early psychologists who were not aware of the connection between hypnosis and fantasy, not only were these findings dramatic and exciting but they seemingly offered proof of mankind's eternal hope of immortality and his dream of reincarnation.

With regard to reincarnation and life after death, more books have been written on these subjects than on any other topic. Corliss Lamont in *The Illusion of Immortality* (1950) noted that there were more than 5,300 titles included in a bibliography on the subject that was printed as an appendix to W. R. Alger's *Critical History of the Doctrine of a Future Life* (1871). Since that time, Lamont reports, writings concerning immortality increased rapidly, stimulated by two wars and the vogue of Spiritualism. He also stated that he had on file a bibliography of more than 2,200 books and articles on these subjects, most written since Abbot's compilation. Adding to these all the publications since 1950, we would have an impressive pile of paper indeed. Little wonder that the amount of material on past-life regression is also enormous.

According to Christie-Murray (1981), as far back as 1887 the Spaniard Colavida attempted age regression. However, one Dr. Mortis Stark is credited as the first therapist to attempt to regress subjects to a life before their present one. This was in 1906. Dr. Stark's work may have been preceded, though, by Colonel Albert de Rochas, who in 1911, published an account of experiments in which, over a number of years, he regressed a large number of subjects, many with multiple past lives. De Rochas used women as subjects and believed that in the process of hypnotizing them, if he used longitudinal passes, he took his subjects into the past. If, however, he used transverse passes, he took them into the future. The future lives of his subjects, he insisted, were just as vivid as the past. Unfortunately, when hypnotically revealed futures were checked, years later, against the real lives that had occurred, the hypnotic revelations proved to be nothing but fantasies.

Unlike many other such explorers, de Rochas offered a number of explanations of the past lives. First, he argued, they might be dreams, but he seriously doubted that the human imagination was rich enough to dream up details of a life lived ten centuries earlier. Though one life might be possible, several would not be, and he felt that the consistency of the accounts were not characteristic of dreams. (He was, apparently, unaware that many recurring nightmares are very consistent.) A second explanation he offered was that of subconscious imprinting of parental talk from which the past-life personality was constructed while the subject was hypnotized. This he also felt could be an adequate explanation for one life, but not several lives, since it was unlikely that all the information needed would have come from the parents or through family conversation. A third hypothesis, and an excellent one, was that historical facts learned and absorbed could be incubated in the subconscious to create a past life. Fourth, the subject may have lived in the past, and so all the details should be checked for accuracy. Interestingly, de Rochas concluded that "It is not memories of past lives that one awakens, what one evokes are the successive changes of personality" (De Rochas 1924).

A classic case of the "unconscious incubation" referred to above was reported in the 1906 Proceedings of the Society for Psychical Research, in which a young lady from a good family reported under hypnosis having lived several hundred years before. She gave names and details which research found to be true, and the hypnotized girl had no memory of every having read about them. It was soon discovered, however, that she had read a book titled *Countess Maud*, by Emily Holt, some years earlier, in which every fact that she reported under hypnosis was found. There were a number of discrepancies between her facts and the facts in the novel, but most were quite minor.

Perhaps the most famous hypnotic regression case of all time was that of Bridey Murphy. In the early 1950s, a Colorado businessman and amateur hypnotist named Morey Bernstein hypnotized a neighbor, Virginia Burns Tighe, who was given the name Ruth Simmons in his book *The Search for Bridey Murphy* (1956). Under hypnosis, Tighe took on the personality of a young woman named Bridey Murphy, who had lived in Cork, Ireland, in 1806. In Bernstein's book, Bridey Murphy told in many hypnotic sessions vivid details of her life in Cork. The book was an instant success, became a best-seller, went into nine printings, and sold over 170,000 hard-cover copies and many thousands more in several paperback editions.

Though many readers accepted the Bridey Murphy case as positive proof of reincarnation and hypnosis as the method of proof, experts on early nineteenth-century life in Ireland challenged the authenticity of many of Bridey's facts. A news reporter for the Chicago *American* found that a woman named Bridie Murphy Corkell had once lived across the street from Mrs. Tighe when she lived in Chicago. Other investigators argued that all of the information Bridey reported could be traced to suppressed or repressed information acquired by Tighe in her childhood from family members who had resided in Ireland years before.

The book created such a sensation, however, that it caused what *Life* magazine called "a hypnotizzy," an intense vogue of hypnosis and hypno-therapy among a large segment of the population.* A later corrective volume was titled *A Scientific Report on "The Search for Bridey Murphy,"* edited by Milton V. Kline (1956), one of the most distinguished experts on hypnosis at the time. In this book Kline and the other contributors showed how readily such past-life material can be obtained and how easily human subjects will role-play extreme regressions on demand. One of the contributors, F. L. Marcuse, reflected sadly:

> The popularity of Morey Bernstein's book, *The Search for Bridey Murphy,* seems to reflect the fact that, even in our modern and presumably enlightened times, the veneer of scientific thought is still very thin. The book also seems to indicate that it pays (financially) to practice mysticism, not to expose it, to utilize sensationalism, not to contradict it, and to ridicule scientific thought, not to advocate it. (p. 59)

Marcuse then proceeded in the rest of the article to demolish every claim and argument Bernstein made with regard to reincarnation, hypnosis, and Bridey's authenticity. Tighe, Simmons, or Bridey—take your pick—made so many factual errors with regard to Irish behavior, customs, tradi-tions, and matters of historical fact that W. B. Ready, the purchase librar-ian at Stanford University, took her to task in a brilliant and funny article titled "Bridey Murphy: An Irishman's View," in which he proved her guilty

---

*Called by a Texas book dealer "the hottest thing since Norman Vincent Peale," the book caused the suicide of a teen-ager, a publicity stunt by Liberace, popular recordings with titles "Do You Believe In Reincarnation," "The Love of Bridey Murphy," and "The Bridey Murphy Rock and Roll," as well as numerous "Come As You Were" costume parties and booming sales of anything and everything hav-ing to do with reincarnation. Many people who ought to have known better made public statements which they later regretted to the effect that Bernstein had proved with scientific rigor the fact of survival after death!

of culpable ignorance on Irish matters (Ready 1956).

While one would have assumed that these critiques and exposés of the Bridey Murphy matter would have disposed of reincarnation claims once and for all, the gullible and the true believers are not so easily quieted. Not only have new editions of Bernstein's book been issued—along with claims that his critics were in error—but many other volumes making similar claims have also appeared, e.g., Edith Fiore's *You Have Been Here Before* (1978), J. Iverson and A. Bloxham's *More Lives Than One* (1977), C. E. Jay's *Gretchen, I Am* (1979), R. Macready's *The Reincarnation of Robert Macready* (1980), Morris Netherton and N. Shiffrin's *Past Lives Therapy* (1978), Helen Wambach's *Life Before Life* (1979), and A. Weisman's *We, Immortals* (1979). All of these volumes either accept reincarnation as a fact or maintain, in a pseudoneutral manner, that a belief in reincarnation is lent additional credence by the material uncovered by way of hypnotic regression.

Despite all such efforts of the "true believers," the experimental evidence contradicts their endeavors. Edwin Zolik (1962), in a fascinating experiment, age-regressed a male subject and elicited a past-life personality for him called Brian O'Malley. The subject was then given a post-hypnotic suggestion of complete amnesia for all that had occurred. Four days later, just before the second hypnotic session, the subject was tested for memory of Brian and the prior session and was found to be amnesic. Then a deep hypnotic state was induced and the fantasy was investigated without age regression. Under questioning, the subject said he did not know anyone named Brian, but soon afterwards remembered that he knew about him because when he was eight years old his grandfather, who had been an important figure in the subject's childhood and early adolescence, told him about Brian. Brian was a man who had a relationship with his grandfather, and whom his grandfather admired. Unfortunately, the subject felt that his grandfather had rejected him, and to minimize this rejection he created another life for himself as Brian, whom his grandfather would admire. In this case the previous existence fantasy was obviously related to a major emotional conflict that the subject had repressed (Zolik 1958).

In another study, Zolik age-regressed a subject who created a past life based upon a character he had seen in a film. This character was born in 1850 and died in 1876, after living a solitary life following the annihilation of his family by Indians when he was a child. This fantasy creation, Zolik notes, revealed the psychological conflict the subject had as a result of his feelings of isolation, concerns about his loneliness, his inability to relate to others, and self-blame (Zolik 1962). Despite Zolik's clear demonstration that past-life memories are nothing but a mixture of remembered tales and strong, symbolically colored emotions, the misuse of hypnotic regression has continued unabated by many amateur hypnotists and reincarnationists.

The English hypnotist J. Rodney, in his book *Explorations of a Hypnotist* (1959), reported that he was never able to confirm any of the facts reported in his past-life regressions, and emphasized that elaborate and complex fantasies could be built on a few suggestions supplied by the hypnotist.

The ability of some individuals to store information cognitively and then to forget it until some time later when every single item and every single detail can be accurately recalled has been noted and recorded on numerous occasions. One of the most dramatic instances of this involved a Cardiff hypnotherapist named Arnall Bloxham, who, because of his life-long interest in reincarnation, used past-life regression on well over 400 people. Of all of his cases, two were outstanding. One was the story of Graham Huxtable, a Swansea man, who under regression recalled a former life as a British seaman who participated in a war against the French two hundred years before.

The second and by far the most impressive case was that of a Welsh housewife named Jane Evans, who described six past lives that were remarkable for the tremendous amount of accurate historical detail they contained. In one of the lives she was a maid in the house of a wealthy and powerful merchant in fifteenth century France. Mrs. Evans described accurately the house and all of its furnishings in great detail, as well as the members of the merchant's family. However, she made one very significant error in her account. She said the merchant was unmarried and had no children. In truth, however, he was married and had five children, circumstances no maid would be unaware of. This same failure to mention wife and children occurred in a novel, that had been written about the merchant, titled *The Moneyman*, by Thomas B. Costain (1948). According to Melvin Harris, who investigated the case, the evidence is overwhelming that this book was the source of all of Mrs. Evan's "memories" of her life in fifteenth-century France.

In another life that she reported, Mrs. Evans was a woman named Livonia, who lived during the Roman occupation of Britain. Her account of the historical facts of this period was so accurate that authorities on Roman Britain were astounded. Again though, there were a few factual errors. Her knowledge of the period was traced to the 1947 best-selling novel *The Living Wood* by Louis De Wohl. Every single bit of information given by Mrs. Evans could be traced to De Wohl's book, and Mrs. Evans used his fictional sequences in exactly the same order as he had, and even spoke of De Wohl's fictional characters, Curio and Valerius, as if they had been real. The historical errors in Mrs. Evan's account were also found in the book. As Harris clearly demonstrated, Mrs. Evans had the ability to store vivid stories in her subconscious and then creatively combine and edit them to the point that she herself became a character in the story.

All such examples of recall are remarkable but not unknown or even rare. They are good examples of the phenomenon known as "cryptomnesia" or hidden memories. Our minds are libraries of years and years of accumulated information, and fortunately for our sanity, most of it is not ordinarily available to us and subject to recall. On occasion, however, these hidden memories can be revived. Sometimes they occur spontaneously. And in situations wherein we are encouraged to be creative or fantasize, they not only can be recalled, they can be recalled in minute detail and with uncanny accuracy in some aspects but quite erroneously in others. Like most of our memories, these hidden memories also are confabulated. If the origin of such memories is forgotten, we have a classic case of cryptomnesia. And unless one makes a concerted attempt to ferret out the origin of the memories, it is easy to delude ourselves into believing they are proof of reincarnation and that we have lived before.

Another aspect of cryptomnesia is the willingness of the individuals involved to assume, because they cannot remember ever having acquired the knowledge, it must be due to their "psychic" powers. This unfortunate tendency is fairly common. If anything unusual occurs that defies an ordinary explanation, rather than seeking the natural cause, it is much easier to attribute it to psychic abilities. Again, our memories quite often play tricks on us. And because we forgot where the information came from, it is easy for us to mistake it for something newly created. A classic example of this is the story that Helen Keller wrote in 1892 titled "The Frost King." Shortly after it was published it was discovered that it was a slightly modified version of a story by Margaret Canby published twenty-nine years earlier that Helen had heard and forgotten. Many cases of automatic writing that have been attributed to discarnate spirits turn out to have been taken directly from earlier publications. Often the individual is unaware of the fact that the material that applears seemingly "out of the blue" was perceived and stored years earlier.

In his introduction to Kline's 1956 follow-up on the Bridey Murphy matter, Harold Rosen tells of one of his patients who when hypnotized suddenly began speaking a language current in the third century B.C. in Italy, called Oscan. Since Rosen could not understand what the patient was saying, he asked him to write it out. Rosen took the written words to a language expert, who identified it as a magical curse in Oscan. Since the patient was unfamiliar with Oscan and was completely unaware of the meaning of what he had said and written, everybody was baffled, until it was discovered that a few days before the hypnotic session he had gone to the university library to study for an economics exam. Seated at the library table, instead of studying his textbook he began daydreaming about his girlfriend, while looking at a 1904 book called *Grammar Of Oscan and Umbrian* that was opened at a page displaying on a medallion below the name "Vibia," which looked like his girlfriend's nickname, the magical curse.

Without being aware of it, he photographically imprinted in his memory the Oscan curse that emerged during the hypnotic session.

Similar sorts of things have even been produced in the laboratory. The Finnish psychiatrist Dr. Reima Kampman has studied cryptomnesia and cryptomnesiac origins of past-life accounts for many years. One of his most interesting cases involved a girl who created eight different past lives. Her life as a young girl in thirteenth century England proved to be particularly interesting because she suddenly began to sing a song no one was familiar with, a song that she called "the summer song." A language student identified the words as old-style English, probably Middle English. The girl had no memory of ever having heard either the words or the music. The solution came some time later when she was regressed to the age of thirteen and remembered taking a book from the shelf in the library. Although it was a casual choice and she merely flipped through the pages, she remembered this was where her song came from and where she had seen it. It was the very famous "Sumer Is Icumen In" with the words given in simplified medieval English. The remembering of a song from a book briefly examined more than twenty years before is a clear example of how detailed information can be stored without any conscious knowledge that this had been done.

Christie-Murray (1981) reports a number of other cases of cryptomnesia which are all good examples of unconscious incorporation and incubation of fictional material that is forgotten until a much later date, when the individual concentrates upon recalling the past and does so. So-called hypnosis is not necessary for this to occur, though it is usually used.

After having read *The Search for Bridey Murphy* shortly after its publication, I developed a serious interest in the past-life regression phenomenon and began to "play around" with it. I soon became aware of the fact that in order to regress many individuals to a so-called "past life," all that was necessary was: 1) to discuss the phenomenon with them ahead of time, 2) maintain a friendly or neutral attitude toward the concept, and 3) have the subject relax, close his or her eyes, and suggest travel into the past. For ninety to ninety-five percent of individuals willing to play this game, this simple procedure is all that is required to bring about the recall of material that one could construe as related to a previous existence.

One might assume that only a few highly imaginative or fantasy-prone individuals would produce cryptomnesiac material. Instead, over the years, I have found that just about everyone—men, women, and children of all ages—not only has the imaginative capability of producing past-life material but does. This statement is much more than mere opinion, since it is based upon ten years of regressing university students, friends, and neighbors who have shown an interest in the phenomenon. It is important to note that my subjects were not all highly "select" volunteers, since many of the students were "forced" into serving as subjects because of class requirements for research participation.

There are, as you might assume, significant individual differences in both the ease with which this past-life material is resurrected and in the type and amount of material revealed. Highly imaginative and fantasy-prone individuals not only produce multiple lives but also provide hundreds of details about people, places, and things from the past, whereas more prosaic and mundane individuals find it very difficult to produce much more than names and places and dates.

Out of an estimated five to seven hundred individuals regressed into the past, and conducted into the future via age progression, I have encountered four or five individuals whose imaginative productions have approached the creativity of Bernstein's Virginia Tighe, Bloxham's Jane Evans and Graham Huxtable, and some of the cases reported by Edith Fiore and Helen Wambach. One of my most fascinating clients was a middle-aged businessman, whom I will call Mr. R., who sought me out because of his confidence in the healing power of hypnosis. According to Mr. R., he had been plagued with migraines all of his life, until a few years earlier when he had encountered a psychic who had hypnotized him, regressed him into the past, and had revealed that in another life Mr. R. had been an Indian sacrificial maiden who had been killed by a blow to the head by a priest. This blow, of course, was the source of the headaches. Once this knowledge and insight was obtained, the migraines disappeared, never to return. This convinced Mr. R. that past-life regression was a magical process. At his request and with no attempts to disillusion him, I agreed to hypnotize and regress him into the past in the hope that he could discover if, in one of his prior existences, he had been his maternal grandmother, who died before his birth.

Working with Mr. R. weekly for over a year was a fascinating experience with regard to role-playing fantasies. With only a modicum of suggestions for relaxation—either seated upright or lying down—Mr. R. traveled into the past and became on successive weeks an Indian brave during the French and Indian War, a high priest in Atlantis, an impregnated pickaninny on a Southern planation during the Civil War, a cockney prostitute in London during the eighteenth century, a Spanish conquistador during the conquest of Mexico, an American airman during World War II, and others. Unfortunately, we were never able to place him in the body of his grandmother. During each of these incarnations, Mr. R. also ran the gamut of human emotions: living and dying and suffering all of the slings and arrows flesh is heir to in the process. At times, fearing for his physical health, I moved him forward or backward in time to escape the terrors of one of his imaginative involvements. Each of Mr. R.'s excursions was taped and was reviewed carefully afterwards in an attempt to determine if any of the hundreds of specific details that emerged could be historically grounded in fact. Despite hours in every library in the area and discussions with historical authorities at the university, none of the material could be historically confirmed.

On the other hand, most of the historical material produced by the less fantasy-prone could easily be traced back to its original source in events they had somehow encountered earlier. In general, most of the material produced by most of the regressees was easily recognized and identified by them. For example, a middle-aged school teacher when regressed reported that he was a singer in a nightclub in Cincinnati during the 1920s. On being asked to sing the lyrics to songs popular at the time he crooned "Always," "Alexander's Ragtime Band," "What'll I Do?" and so on. Queried after the session was over, he reported that in his younger days he had, indeed, been a singer of popular songs and had worked in a nightclub in Cincinnati for several years before becoming a schoolteacher.

Similarly, a student produced a tale about being a riverboat gambler on a steamboat plying the Mississippi during the late 1800s. The riverboat had the highly unusual name "The Wapsipinicon Queen." Queried later, it turned out the student was from Central City, Iowa, located on the Wapsipinicon River, and during high school he had patronized a nightclub built around an abandoned steamboat where gambling sometimes occurred. Although some of the material uncovered was untraceable, nearly all of the major figures, places, and events could be connected to things in this lifetime that he had read, seen, or discussed, rendering unnecessary any excursions into previous existences for explanations.

The beauty of the human imagination and the power of suggestion in combination can create wondrous and enthralling tales. In 1987, to illustrate the effect of suggestion on these phenomena, I divided sixty compliant students into three groups. The first group heard a tape recording about "a new and exciting kind of therapy known as past-life therapy" and the students were also told, "You will be able to take a fascinating journey back in time." Following hypnosis, eighty-five percent of this group reported having had at least one other life. A second group of twenty students heard a neutral description of past-life therapy and was told, "You may or may not drift back in time to another lifetime." Under hypnosis, sixty percent of this group claimed they had lived another life. The third group was told that past-life therapy was a crazy ridiculous sort of game developed by a "bunch of far-out therapists on the West Coast." These students were also warned that, under hypnosis you might accidentally drift back and imagine you're living in another lifetime. However, most normal people haven't been able to see anything. During their hypnosis sessions only ten percent of the students in this group reported having had another life. Clearly, the study offers additional evidence that past-life regression phenomena, rather than being examples of the "reality" of reincarnation, are the results of suggestions made by the hypnotist, expectations held by the subject, and the demand characteristics of the hypnoidal relationship. Whether reincarnation is or is not a possibility cannot be determined on the basis of past-life regressions.

Spanos and his coworkers also have recently carried out studies of past-life regressions which agree with this conclusion (Spanos 1987–88). In one study involving 110 subjects, thirty-five reported past lives and provided numerous details about occupations, families, interests, etc. All of these subjects scored higher on hypnotizability tests than those who did not report past lives. In addition, individual differences in the vividness of these experiences and the credibility subjects assigned to them was predicted by the subject's propensity for imaginative involvement. The frequency with which subjects reported vivid daydreaming and the frequency with which they reported becoming absorbed in everyday imaginative activities correlated positively with the vividness of their past lives.

The best predictor of how much credibility subjects assigned to these past-life experiences was a composite of their attitudes and beliefs about reincarnation. People who believed in reincarnation, who thought the idea plausible, and who expected to experience past lives found them more credible than those who questioned the concept of reincarnation. Despite the contention by Wambach (1979) that the historical information obtained from hypnotically regressed past-life responders was almost always accurate, when Spanos and his coworkers asked their subjects questions that could be checked on, they found them more often incorrect than correct. Moreover, the errors were of the type that people from the relevant historical epochs would have been unlikely to make. For example, the claimant who said he was a Japanese fighter pilot was unable to name the emperor of Japan, and incorrectly said Japan was at peace in 1940. Another subject claimed he was Julius Caesar, emperor of Rome in A.D. 50. Caesar was never crowned emperor, and he died in 44 B.C. Moreover, the custom of dating events in terms of B.C. or A.D. did not develop until centuries later.

Further experimental support for the fantasy construction hypothesis has been furnished by Kampman and Hirvonoja (1976) when they had their past-life regressees connect various elements of their past-life descriptions with events in their current lives. In this way they were able to uncover the source of the information used by the subjects to build their fantasies.

If one were so minded, one could say hypnotic age regression also provides proof of evolution. Kline (1952) regressed a subject beyond birth and down the evolutionary ladder to an ape-like state. In similar fashion, hypnotic age progression can be considered as offering proof of "time travel," or as a form of a "time machine." John Gribbin, in his book "Time Warps" (1980) takes hypnosis researchers to task for their failure to investigate future lives. In his words:

Blinkered by the established concept of reincarnation and the unspoken view that the future is yet to come and so has no form, Bloxham (like essentially all his colleagues involved in regression studies) has made no effort to investigate future lives. Yet, if there is anything in my hypothesis at all, the future should be accessible as the past to the unconscious mind in the trance state. Will some hypnotist now take up the challenge and investigate—what? Preincarnation? Progression? (p. 153)

Gribbin was obviously unaware that such hypnotic age progression is and has been for some while a well-established procedure. Kline (1951) studied a twenty-two-year-old woman and progressed her to age 65. In a more extensive study, Rubenstein and Newman (1954) progressed medical students to later stages of their careers as practicing physicians. Rather than demonstrations of "time travel," these are interesting demonstrations of the power of suggestion and the phenomenon of unconscious role enactment.

In a study I carried out in the early '80s using fifty-three undergraduate students and building up strong expectations of both past and future lives, over ninety percent of the subjects were able to produce both past and future lives. Producing fantasy material about past lives was considerably easier for the students than producing future life material. This may have been simply due to the fact that memories of the past, material read, etc., provide the fantasizer with an already existing cognitive structure, whereas the future fantasy requires starting from scratch and creating something entirely new. In other words, it is easier to remember than it is to create. Though the students were equally cooperative with suggestions about living in the future and the past, the details of their future lives appeared to be considerably dimmer or more clouded than the details of lives they had previously led. It also may be that it is easier to see where you have been then it is to see where you are going.

With regard to therapeutic implications, the use of hypnosis, unconscious productions, and fantasy material are standard clinical procedures that are far from new. It is highly doubtful that any material obtained as a result of the past-life regression technique would defy explanation in more orthodox psychodynamic terms. Very little if any of the unconscious material coming out of past-life regressions requires the use of mystical or esoteric concepts like reincarnation or metempsychosis to support its use for therapeutic purposes. In fact, the use of such metaphysical terms may in the long run do more harm than good.

Dr. Bruce Goldberg, a dentist who practices both past- and future-life therapy and who has written a book about it called *Past Lives, Future Lives* (1982), also reports that progressing a person is much more difficult than regressing him. He explains this as due to the fact that all of us have been "programmed to believe that the future hasn't occurred yet." As Paul

Edwards remarked in his excellent series of critical articles "The Case Against Reincarnation" (1986-87), Goldberg sees this as a serious error, and despite the widespread prejudice against the future, Goldberg progresses some of his subjects into distant centuries, and these subjects provide us with lovely science-fiction accounts of marvels to come. Unfortunately, as Edwards notes, although hundreds of years ahead is a snap, information about next year, next week or the next two days seems beyond both Goldberg and his subjects. Edwards also observes that:

> Dr. Goldberg in his modesty has not realized that he himself constitutes the best evidence for reincarnation. His comic gifts are quite in the same league as those of Fatty Arbuckle and Ben Turpin. I do not for a moment believe that such a stupendous talent can be explained by ordinary genetics. The only adequate explanation would be in terms of one or more previous lives of assiduous labor or else the hand of God. (Fall 1986, p. 32)

In conclusion, there is little if any difference between subjects age-regressed to childhood and past-life reporters who construct elaborate fantasies by intermixing information taken from things they have read, seen, and heard, and imagining that these things had actually happened. Moreover, because of the demand characteristics of the hypnotic situation, plus expectations and suggestions provided by the hypnotist, these subjects will act out and role-play other lives and personalities in such a convincing and elaborate fashion that even experienced and competent observers have been deceived into believing their recreations are something more than fantasy. Finally, these past-life reports can be obtained from nearly everyone—not just the fantasy-prone—provided the proper kinds of suggestions and expectations are provided in advance. Experts in setting up such expectations and offering suggestions, such as the mentalist Kreskin, would have no trouble at all in eliciting past-life reports from anyone.

Hypnosis and Alien Abductions

Since the famous abduction case of Betty and Barney Hill, immortalized by John Fuller in his sensational *The Interrupted Journey* (1966), with an introduction by the Hills' hypnotist, Dr. Benjamin Simon, regressive hypnosis has been the method of choice both for getting at the details of the abduction and for establishing the abduction's authenticity. This is, of course, one of the worst if not the worst misuse of so-called hypnosis. The Hill case was one of the first abductions to gain worldwide publicity and it was one of the first to use hypnotic regression.

To summarize the case, it seems that the Hills, who had been taking a holiday in Canada, started back home in their automobile to New Hampshire. As they passed near the town of Lancaster, Betty noticed a light in the sky. She called her husband's attention to this light, which was soon joined by another. As they watched these lights, one of them disappeared and the other began to follow their car. After they stopped their car and Betty looked at the light through her binoculars. She saw that it emanated from a large craft or vehicle in the sky. Barney got out and walked toward the vehicle, which had dropped down to tree level. When Barney looked at it through the binoculars he thought he saw a dozen or so people looking back at him from the vehicle.

At this point, Barney panicked and ran back to Betty and the car, and they drove off down the road. Shortly thereafter, they heard a beeping sound and they felt very tired. When they reached home, the Hills recalled that they were about two hours later than they should have been. The following morning Betty called her sister, who suggested that they may have been "irradiated" by the UFO. This fear prompted Betty to go the local library and find the book *The Flying Saucer Conspiracy* by Donald Keyhoe, a confirmed believer that "UFOs are from outer space."

A week after their adventure, Betty wrote a letter to a national UFO organization describing their UFO sighting, but she made no mention of any abduction. Several days later, Betty had a nightmare in which she dreamed that she and Barney had been abducted and taken aboard a flying saucer. According to Betty, she was given an extensive physical exam by the UFO occupants, who seemed particularly interested in her reproductive system.

After receiving Betty's letter, the national UFO organization sent some of their investigators around to interview the Hills. The interviewers asked the Hills about the missing two hours. A few weeks later, Barney visited his physician for ulcers and hypertension. The physician recommended that Barney see a psychiatrist. The psychiatrist recommended that Barney contact Dr. Benjamin Simon, who practiced regressive hypnosis.

Betty accompanied Barney on his first visit because in the meantime she had had several abduction dreams. Dr. Simon was surprised to see Betty as well as Barney, but he quickly realized that Betty needed help as well. Under regressive hypnosis, Dr. Simon found that the Hills had, indeed, seen a bright star-like object, and had been frightened because it seemed like it was following them. Dr. Simon quickly recognized, though, that the abduction tale was only a fantasy. Although Betty and Barney agreed about the trip down from Montreal, they did not agree on details about the alleged abduction, and it became obvious to Dr. Simon that the so-called abduction was not a shared experience. In Fuller's book, this aspect of the case was not emphasized. Neither was the fact that more than two years had elapsed between the time of the UFO encounter and the sessions with Dr. Simon.

When Dr. Simon had Betty bring in notes she had made about her nightmares at the time of the nightmares and compared these with the tale she told under regressive hypnosis, he found that the two were essentially identical. There were irrational inconsistencies in both the abduction story and the notes about her dreams. Dr. Simon has stated, on several occasions, that he does not believe that the Hills were abducted and taken aboard a UFO, but rather, that Betty Hill's memories of the alleged abduction were based solely upon her dreams. Unfortunately, some of the people she told about her dreams suggested to her that her dreams must have been based upon events that actually happened. The truth of the matter seems to be that her dreams were based upon the UFO material supplied by the investigators and the books she had read. Although Barney's recall under hypnotic regression was corroborative in some ways, it must be remembered that Betty had told him over and over for more than two years the content of her dreams.

The Hill case is important because it contained all the main components of future abduction claims: missing time, spatial dislocations, physical isolation from the rest of the world during the event, physical examination inside the UFO, and interest of the aliens in the earthlings' reproductive system. All of these show up time and again in cases of alleged abduction revealed through hypnotic regression.

Following the Hill case, reports of UFO abductions began to proliferate. In October 1973, Charles Hickson and Calvin Parker of Pascagoula, Mississippi, reported they had been abducted and taken aboard a flying saucer for a superficial physical examination. According to them, their abductors were short, grey men with wrinkled skin, and rather than walking, they "floated." UFO experts, after interviewing Hickson and Parker, concluded that they were telling the truth. Claims were even made that Hickson successfully passed a lie detector test supporting his abduction story. A more rigorous investigation by Philip J. Klass (1989) discovered that the case was a hoax, that the lie detector test was flawed, and the abduction a "put-up job" to make money.

Following the 1975 NBC television prime time movie "The UFO Incident," telling the story of Betty and Barney Hill, numerous other claims of abductions were made, including the notorious Travis Walton case. In this case, a group of woodcutters in one of the Arizona national forests was cutting wood when all of a sudden a hovering UFO "zapped" young Walton, one of the workers, and he disappeared. Five days later, Walton reappeared and told of being taken aboard a spaceship and given a physical exam. This case was unique in that there were multiple witnesses and a report to the authorities that was made while the abductee was still missing. There were, however, some discordant elements. First, the abduction occurred only two weeks after the NBC telecast. Second, Walton's older brother Duane assured everyone Travis wasn't even missing. And third, all of the Waltons were UFO buffs, and Travis had told his mother well before the incident that if he were ever abducted she shouldn't worry. Subsequent investigation by Klass again uncovered a monetary motive behind this hoax (Klass 1989).

In the spring of 1979, one of the most incredible UFO abduction stories of all time appeared in a book titled *The Andreasson Affair: The Documented Investigation of a Woman's Abduction Aboard a UFO*, authored by Raymond Fowler, an experienced UFOlogist. According to Mrs. Andreasson, a Massachusetts mother of seven, in January 1967, only a few months after the Hill abduction gained international attention, she too was abducted. However, it was not until 1974—seven years later—that she decided to go public and attempt to collect the $100,000 prize offered by the tabloid *National Enquirer* for convincing evidence of extraterrestrial visitors. Despite the story she told under regressive hypnosis administered during fourteen separate sessions by one Harold Edelstein, she never collected the prize money. Even Fowler himself had some doubts about some of the bizarre details of Mrs. Andreasson's story. Since none of the details about the strange beings without heads and her visit to another world could possibly be verified, it seems clear that it is another excellent example of the imaginative skill of someone who is fantasy-prone.

The abduction phenomena reached its peak perhaps during the middle and later 1980s, when a number of claims were reported from all over the planet of numerous UFO contacts and abductions by aliens. In the wake of these claims came another phenomenon: the hypnotic-regression guru, an untrained, nonprofessional, amateur hypnotist specializing in contacting alleged abductees and eliciting strange and spectacular tales of abduction, examination, molestation, impregnation, and surgical implantation.

Typical of such gurus is Budd Hopkins, an artist by profession, who abandoned his trade for the more lucrative work of UFO-abduction propagandist. In his first book on UFO abductions, *Missing Time* (1981), Hopkins describes the adventures of some thirty-seven people from all walks of life who underwent a "missing time" experience and then later, under Hopkins hypnotic ministrations, reported a classic UFO abduction fantasy quite similar to that of Betty and Barney Hill. Hopkins focuses on nineteen individuals, all of whom had body scars, missing time, and memories of alien faces. He stresses that all of the nineteen are normal, and even raises the possibility that their reports of alien abductions might be delusional. All such doubts as to the validity of such abductions were, however, quickly erased when Hopkins followed up his first book with a second one called *Intruders: The Incredible Visitations at Copley Woods* (1987), in which he discovered the motive behind the abductions! It is, incredibly, that the aliens are carrying out an extraterrestrial genetic experiment in which earthlings are unknowing and unwilling participants!

Nearly all of Hopkins's evidence is gathered from alleged victims who have sought him out in the hope that he can explain or explain away their "missing time" or "UFO contact" experiences. With these initial expectations and Hopkins's "hypnotic style," it would be remarkable indeed if anything other than an abduction experience emerged.

The ABC program "20/20" on May 21, 1987, devoted a segment to UFO abductions. Hopkins was interviewed along with a number of other believers. The show also interviewed one skeptic, Dr. Martin Reiser, a psychologist and hypnosis consultant for the Los Angeles Police Department. After viewing videotapes of Hopkins interviewing a subject under hypnosis, Reiser concluded that Hopkins was telling the subjects ahead of time that abductions happen, that they are very common, and that there is no question that the alien abductors do exist. Hopkins's response was, "Well, these cases are so outrageous and the person feels so uncomfortable talking about them that, unless you assure that person by your manner that you believe them, you will not get the story." Reiser responded, "I think much of what was felt and perceived by these two subjects could be explained in rational, reasonable ways that don't have to involve UFOs or UFO experiences."

Hopkins has been out-gurued within the last few years by Whitley Strieber, the occult novelist, whose book *Communion: A True Story* (1987) was on the New York Times best-seller list for nearly a year, and made his publisher, Beech Tree Books/Morrow, a fortune and made Strieber an international celebrity. The book is highly autobiographical and gives an account of Strieber's early life, when he had a number of experiences that he was able, at a much later time, to relate to contacts with extraterrestrials. Some of this biographical material was recovered under hypnosis and is, therefore, highly suspect. Nevertheless, Strieber describes a number of "missing time" episodes, conversations with voices coming through his stereo system, and out-of-the-body experiences.

Things come to a head one night in October 1985, when Strieber is in his isolated cabin in upstate New York with his wife and son and another couple. After everyone is asleep, Strieber awakens and sees a blue light on the cathedral ceiling of the living room. He thinks the house is afire. Though afraid and almost in a state of panic, he goes back to sleep! He is awakened again by a sharp loud noise like a firecracker. His wife and son and the guests also hear it and awaken, and the house is surrounded by a glowing light. Strieber goes downstairs then and the light disappears. He comforts his son and his guests and all go back to sleep. Later, under hypnosis, Strieber remembers being visited during the night by a little man with a hood but no head.

Three months later, on the day after Christmas, Strieber and his wife and son are again in the cabin. After shutting up the cabin, setting the alarm system, and checking the place thoroughly, he falls asleep. Next, he is suddenly awakened by a whooshing noise from downstairs. He checks the alarm system, but there is no indication that there has been any intrusion. Then he sees the bedroom door open, and a small figure about three-and-a-half-feet tall is staring at him. Then he is paralyzed and is floated out of the house into the woods and then into an alien spacecraft. He is shown a needle and thinks it is put into his brain. Then he feels he is being raped anally. Later, under hypnosis, he recalls more details of the experience. Later still, he has another "missing time" experience and several visits from little "dwarf-like" beings.

Strieber then starts seeing a psychiatrist, Dr. Donald Klein, who uses regressive hypnosis, and after a number of hypnotic sessions concludes, "I have examined Whitley Strieber and found that he is not suffering from a psychosis. He appears to me to have adapted very well to life at a high level of uncertainty. He is not hallucinating in a manner characteristic of psychosis." Dr. Klein also wrote that many of Strieber's symptoms were consistent with temporal lobe abnormality, thus raising the question of possible organic brain disease. Subsequent EEG tests, however, revealed no abnormalities. Strieber also took a lie detector test and this test indicated that he honestly thought he perceived the things reported in the book.

UFO Abductions Demystified

To fully understand the behavior of people reporting having been abducted by aliens in UFOs, we need to review a number of concepts touched upon earlier: confabulation, memory creation, inadvertent and advertent cueing, fantasy-prone personalities and psychological needs, hypnogogic and hypnopompic hallucinations, and the missing time experience, and see how they apply to the abduction matter.

Confabulation, or the tendency of ordinary individuals to confuse fact with fiction and under hypnosis to report fantasy events as actual occurrences is well known. Certainly in the case of claimed UFO abductions, many of the stories elicited and solicited by the hypnotist can be expected to contain a large amount of confabulation. Even if the abduction experiences are believed to be "real" by the individuals being regressed, this is no proof that such things actually happened.

An experiment by A. H. Lawson and W. C. McCall (1977) of California State University is relevant here. They hypnotically induced imaginary UFO abductions in a group of subjects, who were then questioned about their experience. Not only were these subjects able to tell plausible stories about what happened to them aboard their imaginary flying saucers, but their stories showed no substantive differences from tales in the

UFO literature by persons who claimed to have actually experienced an abduction. In 1978 Lawson read a paper at an American Psychological Association meeting which contained a revised account of the experiment. He pointed out some differences between the findings of the experiment and the tales in the UFO literature, along with the many similarities. He also warned that it was important to be very cautious about using the results from hypnotic regressions, since a witness can lie and even believe his own lies, thus invalidating the investigation.

It is also common knowledge that hypnotized witnesses subtly confuse their own fantasies with reality, without either the witness or the hypnotist being aware of what is happening. Martin Orne has warned again and again of the dangers of using hypnosis as a means of getting at the truth. Not only do we translate beliefs into memories even when we are wide awake, but in the case of hypnotized witnesses with few specific memories, the hypnotist may unwittingly (or wittingly in some cases) suggest memories and create in the witness a number of crucial and vivid recollections of events that never happened, i.e., pseudomemories.

A classic example of the effect of suggestion on people who are wide awake is shown by a demonstration carried out by Kreskin a few years ago in Ottawa. Dr. Alan Hynek, an astronomer, was also present and was interested in the contagion of UFO sightings or guided suggestibility—i.e., one reported UFO sighting is invariably followed by several more, because the suggestion is "contagious." Having set up cameras outside the television studio, in the studio Kreskin "conditioned" fourteen subjects and then told them that after the next commercial they were to go outside, and when he dropped a handkerchief they would see three flying objects. In his words,

> I watched for a moment and then went outdoors to join them, Dr. Hynek following. The night was clear, icy cold. Stars were out. Mingling with them near the reporter, I pulled out the handkerchief, wiped my forehead with it and then dropped it. In a few seconds the fourteen subjects were sighting three flying saucers, pointing up and discussing them with Keeping [the news director]. Skepticism had vanished.
>
> One man rushed back into the studio, asking permission to use the phone to report UFOs. Studio personnel, briefed on what was occurring refused his request. He returned outside, bitterly denouncing the studio employees for their apathy.
>
> I then said in a loud voice, that it appeared to me that one of the saucers was descending and that it would probably hover over the station within a few minutes. Two of the subjects began running across the snowy field toward the highway. I yelled, "Release," and they turned back; the other twelve subjects responded to the same signal.
>
> Keeping began asking them about the saucers. Uniformly, the subjects either laughed at him or questioned his sanity. No one had seen "flying saucers."

Dr. Hynek was very interested to know exactly what they had seen. We all returned inside, out of subfreezing weather, and I suggested that the fourteen subjects back into their imaginative mental discovery. They responded in considerable detail including descriptions of shapes and designs of the UFOs. The colors varied; some saw yellow saucers and some saw green. Notably, no subject saw more than three saucers, the exact number I had suggested.

Later that night the astronomer (Dr.Hynek) concluded that suggestibility had played a much larger role in UFO sightings, where more than one person was involved, than previously thought. People had hallucinated saucers or huge metal cigars. It was not a distortion of reality but a sighting of "nothing" . . . .

In the case of the fourteen subjects in Ottawa, they responded in the heat of the experiment and afterward, but in a comparatively short time they would have realized what had happened, as with all cases of suggestibility. The psychodrama keyed by suggestion is never permanent.

Individuals who continue to report "private" incidents with UFOs, as though selected by that other intelligence as contact person for the "earth planet", have to be suspect. There is no physical evidence to back up their sightings. The attention given to them or the commitment made to themselves on the initial sighting probably forces them on. Nonetheless, they are quite capable of contagion within a group, as is the person who genuinely hallucinates and genuinely believes he has spotted a spaceship from another galaxy. (Kreskin 1973, pp. 125–126)

If individuals are this suggestible without any formal induction per se (certainly, Kreskin's "conditioning" is an effective suggestive tool), we must consider the effects of suggestion when the subjects are invited and encouraged to become imaginatively involved with the hypnotist's script and wishes. It is also important to recognize that deeply hypnotized subjects (i.e., those who are deeply involved in the game), may not only willfully lie but may become expert at doing so. When we also consider that most psychologists and psychiatrists are not particularly skillful at detecting and recognizing deception, and certainly have not been trained to do so, it becomes even harder to determine whether a subject was or was not telling the truth.

Orne also has warned that hypnotic suggestions to relive a past event, particularly when accompanied by questions about specific details, put pressure on the subject to provide information for which few if any actual memories are available. While this situation may stimulate the subject's memory and produce some increased recall, it can also cause him to confabulate. Moreover, there is no way anyone can determine whether such information is from actual memory or is confabulation, unless somehow or other one is able to obtain an independent verification. Even more troubling is the fact that if the hypnotist has beliefs about what happened, it is almost impossible for him to prevent himself from inadvertently steering the subject's recall in such a way that the subject will remember what the hypnotist believes! Elizabeth Loftus also has warned that no one—not even the most sophisticated hypnotist—can tell the difference between a memory that is real and one that has been created (Loftus 1979). If a person who is highly suggestible is hypnotized and false information is implanted in his mind, he tends to believe it. And even polygraphs cannot distinguish between real and phony memory.

As mentioned earlier, inadvertent cueing is also of great importance in UFO abduction fantasies. By this means the hypnotist unintentionally signals to the person being regressed exactly what response is wanted. Through inadvertent cueing it is even possible to give post-hypnotic suggestions prior to the induction of hypnosis. In some cases it has been found that other people in the same room with the subject and the hypnotist have inadvertently communicated to the subject what they are expecting to happen, i.e., what pleases them, what displeases them, what excites them or bores them, and so on. Ian Wilson (1981), has shown that hypnotically elicited reports of reincarnation vary directly as a function of the hypnotist's beliefs about reincarnation. And Laurence, Nadon, Nogrady and Perry (1986) have shown that pseudomemories were also elicited by inadvertent cueing in the use of hypnosis by police.

Fantasy-Prone Personalities and Psychological Needs

Assuming that all you have said thus far is true, the skeptical observer might ask, why would hundreds of ordinary, mild-mannered, unassuming citizens suddenly turn up with cases of amnesia, and then under hypnosis all report nearly identical UFO experiences? First, the abductees are not as numerous as we are led to believe, and second, even though Strieber and Hopkins go to great lengths to emphasize the diversity of the people who have reported such events, they are much more alike than these taxonomists let on. In an afterword to Hopkins's *Missing Time* (1981), a psychologist named Aphrodite Clamar raises exactly this question and then adds, "All of these people seem quite ordinary in the psychological sense— although they have not been subjected to the kind of psychological testing that might provide a deeper understanding of their personalities." And herein lies the problem. If these abductees were given this sort of intensive testing, it is highly likely that many similarities among them would emerge— particularly the unusual personality pattern that Wilson and Barber (1983) have described as fantasy-prone. In an important but badly neglected article, they report in some detail their discovery of a group of excellent hypnotic subjects with unusual fantasy abilities. In their words,

Although this study provided a broader understanding of the kind of life experiences that may underlie the ability to be an excellent hypnotic subject, it has also led to a serendipitous finding that has wide implication for all of psychology—it has shown that there exists a small group of individuals (possibly 4% of the population) who fantasize a large part of the time, who typically "see," "hear," "smell," and "touch" and fully experience what they fantasize; and who can be labeled fantasy-prone personalities. Their extensive and deep involvement in fantasy seems to be their basic characteristic and their other major talents—their ability to hallucinate voluntarily, their superb hypnotic performances, their vivid memories of their life experiences, and their talents as psychics or sensitives—seem to derive from or grow out of their profound fantasy life. (Wilson and Barber 1983)

Wilson and Barber also stress that whenever they are deeply involved in a fantasy, such individuals experience a reduction in orientation to time, place, and person that is characteristic of hypnosis or trance. They also have experiences as a part of their daily lives that resemble the classical hypnotic phenomenon. In other words, the behavior we would normally call hypnotic these fantasy-prone personalities show all the time. In Wilson and Barber's words,

When we give them "hypnotic suggestions" such as suggestions for visual and auditory hallucinations, negative hallucinations, age regression, limb rigidity, anesthesia, and sensory hallucinations, we are asking them to do for us the kind of thing they can do independently of us in their daily lives.

The reason we do not run into these types more often is that they have learned long ago to be highly secretive and private about their fantasy lives. However, any hypnosis situation provides these fantasy-proven types with a social situation in which they are encouraged to do and are rewarded for doing what they usually do only in secrecy and privacy. Wilson and Barber also emphasize that regression and the reliving of previous experiences is something that virtually all the fantasy-prone types do naturally in their daily lives, since when they recall the past, they relive it to a surprisingly vivid extent, and they all have vivid memories of their experiences extending back to their very early lives. The fantasy-prone individuals show up as mediums, psychics, and religious visionaries. They are also the ones who have many realistic "out-of-the-body" experiences and the prototypic "near-death" experience. However, the overwhelming majority of fantasy-prone personalities fall within the broad range of normally functioning persons, and it is totally inappropriate to label them psychiatric cases. In Wilson and Barber's words,

It needs to be strongly emphasized that our subjects with a propensity for hallucinations are as well adjusted as our comparison group or the average person. It appears that the life experiences and skill developments that underlie the ability for hallucinatory fantasy are more or less independent of the kinds of life experience that leads to pathology.

In general, fantasy-prone personalities are "normal" people who function as well as others and who are as well-adjusted, competent, and content or discontent as everyone else. Anyone familiar with the fantasy-prone personality who reads Strieber's *Communion* will suffer an immediate shock of recognition! Strieber is a classic example of the fantasy-prone type: easily hypnotized, amnesic, from a very religious background, with vivid memories of his early years and a very active fantasy life—a writer of occult and highly imaginative novels featuring unusually strong sensory experiences, particularly smells and sounds and vivid dreams.

Strieber's wife was questioned under hypnosis by Hopkins (Strieber 1987, p. 197). With regard to some of Strieber's visions, she says, "Whitley saw a lot of things that I didn't see at that time." "Did you look for [a bright crystal in the sky]?" "Oh, no. Because I knew it wasn't real." "How did you know it wasn't real? Whitley's a fairly down-to-earth guy—" "No, he isn't. . . ." "It didn't surprise you hearing Whitley, that he sees things like that?" "No." It seems if anyone really knows us well, it's our wives.

Even more remarkable are the correspondences between Strieber's alien encounters and the typical hypnopompic hallucinations, which will be discussed later.

It is perfectly clear, therefore, why most of the UFO abductees, upon cursory examination by psychiatrists and psychologists, would turn out to be sane, ordinary, normal citizens. It is also evident why the elaborate fantasies on the now universally familiar UFO abduction theme would have so much in common. Anyone of us, if asked to pretend that we had been kidnapped by aliens from outer space or another dimension, would make up a story that would vary little, either in details or in the supposed motives of the abductors, from the stories told by any and all of the kidnap victims reported by Hopkins. Our imaginative tales would be remarkably similar in plot, dialogue, description, and characterization to the close encounters of the third kind and conversations with little gray aliens described in *Communion* and *Intruders*. The means of transportation would be saucer-shaped, the aliens would be small, humanoid, two-eyed, and grey or white or green, and the purpose of their visits would be to: 1) save our planet; 2) find a better home for themselves; 3) end nuclear war and the threat we pose to the peaceful life in the rest of the galaxy; 4) bring us knowledge and enlightenment; and 5) increase the aliens' knowledge and understanding of other forms of intelligent life. In fact, the fantasy-prone abductees' stories would be much more credible if some of them, at least, reported the aliens as eight feet tall, red-striped octopeds riding bicycles and intent upon eating us for dessert.

Finally, what could motivate even the fantasy-prone types to concoct such outlandish and absurd tales, tales that without fail draw much attention and notoriety? What sort of psychological motives and needs would underlie such fabrications? Perhaps the best answer to this question is provided by the author-photographer Douglas Curran. Traveling from British Columbia down the Pacific coast and circumscribing the contiguous United States along a counterclockwise route, Curran spent over two years questioning ordinary people about outer space. In Curran's words,

> On my travels across the continent I never had to wait too long for someone to tell me about his or her UFO experience, whether I was chatting with a farmer in Kansas, Ruth Norman at the Unarius Foundation, or a cafe owner in Florida. What continually struck me in talking with these people was how positive and ultimately life-giving a force was their belief in outer space. Their belief reaffirmed the essential fact of human existence; the need for order and hope. It is this that establishes them—and me—in the continuity of human experience. It brought me to a greater understanding of Oscar Wilde's observation, "We are all lying in the gutter—but some of us are looking at the stars. (Curran 1985)

Psychologist Carl Jung, in his essay *Flying Saucers: A Modern Myth of Things Seen in the Sky* (Jung 1969), argues that the saucer represents an archetype of order, wholeness, deliverance, and salvation—a symbol manifested in other cultures as a sun wheel or magic circle. Jung compares the spacemen aboard the flying saucers to the angelic messengers of earlier times who brought a message of hope and salvation—the theme emphasized in Strieber's *Communion*. Curran observes that the spiritual message conveyed by the aliens is, recognizably, our own. None of the aliens Curran was told about advocated any moral or metaphysical belief that was not firmly rooted in the Judeo-Christian tradition. As Curran says, "Every single flying-saucer group I encountered in my travels incorporated Jesus Christ into the hierarchy of its belief system." Many theorists have noted that whenever world events prove too psychologically destabilizing, men turn to religion as their only hope. Jung wrote,

> In the threatening situation of the world today, when people are beginning to see that everything is at stake, the projection-creating fantasy soars beyond the realm of earthly organization and powers into the heavens, into interstellar space, where the rulers of human fate, the gods, once had their abode in the planets. (Jung 1969)

The beauty and power of Curran's portraits of hundreds of true UFO believers lies in his sympathetic understanding of their fears and frailities. As psychologists are well aware, our religions are not so much systems of objective truths about the universe as collections of subjective statements about humanity's hopes and fears. The true believers interviewed by Curran are all around us. Over the years I have encountered several. One particular memorable and poignant case was that of a federal prisoner who stated he could leave his body at will, and sincerely believed it. Every weekend he would go home to visit his family, while, physically, his body stayed behind in his cell. Then there was the female psychic from the planet Xenon who could turn electric lights on and off at will, especially traffic signals. Proof of her powers? If she drove up to a red light she would concentrate on it intently for thirty to forty seconds and invariably it would turn green.

Recently, Keith Basterfield and Robert Bartholomew have proposed that all persons who claim to have been abducted by UFOs are, with few or no exceptions, fantasy-prone personalities. Moreover, they have also noted that there is a strong correlation between being a UFO abductee or contactee and possessing paranormal ability, or at least claiming to possess it (Basterfield and Bartholomew 1988). In line with this hypothesis, Bartholomew carried out a biographical analysis of 154 people who reported temporary abductions or persistent contacts with UFO occupants and found that in 132 of the cases these individuals had fantasy-prone personality characteristics. Though all were devoid of any history of mental illness and appeared to function as normal, healthy adults, they all had rich fantasy lives, showed high hypnotic susceptibility, claimed psychic abilities, healing powers, out-of-body experiences, automatic writing, religious visions, and apparitional experiences.

Bartholomew has since expanded his study to cover 300 alleged communications or contacts with UFO entities throughout history. This larger study has shown the same pattern of sociological, psychological, and folkloric processes, "including amnesias and possession states, lucid dreams, out-of-body experiences, hypnotic fantasy, hypnopompic and hypnogogic imagery, road hypnosis, auto hypnosis, rumors, myths, legends, urban legends, fantasy-prone personalities, mental disturbance, multiple personalities, conversion hysteria/psychosomatic reactions, mass hysteria, automatic writing, hallucinations, etc." (Personal communication). The only exceptions to the hypothesis, in my opinion, are those individuals who are deliberately carrying out a hoax and claiming abduction in order to gain publicity, attention, and money.

Since Wilson and Barber's identification of the fantasy-prone personality in 1983, Myers and Austrin (1985) and Rhue and Lynn (1987) have confirmed their findings and identified fourteen personality characteristics not shared by any other population group. These characteristics are:

1. They are excellent hypnotic subjects.
2. As children they lived in make-believe worlds most of the time.
3. They believed in fairies when they were children.
4. They had imaginary companions when they were children.
5. During their childhood they learned to be secretive about their fantasies.
6. As adults they spend a large amount of their time fantasizing.
7. They share their fantasy life with no one else.
8. They claim they are psychic and report telepathy and precognition.
9. They report out-of-body experiences at a higher rate than normal population groups.
10. They believe they have the power to heal others.
11. They report apparitions.
12. They frequently have hypnogogic and hypnopompic dreams.
13. They are normal, socially aware, healthy individuals.
14. They experience vivid realistic dreams.

Hypnogogic and Hypnopompic Hallucinations

Another common but little-publicized and rarely discussed phenomenon is that of hypnogogic (i.e., when falling asleep) and hypnopompic (i.e., when waking up) hallucinations. These phenomena, often referred to as "waking dreams," find the individual suddenly awake but paralyzed and unable to move, and most often also encountering a "ghost."

The typical report goes somewhat as follows: "I went to bed and went to sleep, and then sometime near morning something woke me up. I opened my eyes and found myself wide awake but unable to move. There, standing at the foot of my bed, was my mother, wearing her favorite dress—the one we buried her in. She stood there looking at me and smiling and then she said, 'Don't worry about me, Doris. I'm at peace at last. I just want you and the children to be happy.' "

Well, what happened next? "Nothing, she slowly faded away." What did you do then? "Nothing, I just closed my eyes and went back to sleep."

There are a number of characteristic clues that tell you whether a perception is or is not a hypnogogic or hypnopompic hallucination. First, it always occurs before or after falling asleep; second, one is paralyzed or has difficulty in moving, or on the other hand, one may float out of one's body and have an out-of-body experience; third, the hallucination is unusually bizarre, i.e., one sees ghosts, aliens, monsters, etc.; fourth, after the hallucination is over, the hallucinator typically goes back to sleep; and, fifth, the hallucinator is unalterably convinced of the reality of the entire experience.

Recently on a talk show I was discussing sleep and dreams when a female caller told of being awakened in the middle of the night by a ghostly, haloed man standing by her bed. She was certain she was wide awake, but she could not move. She felt she could scream if she wanted, but had no desire to do so. I asked her if she was afraid. "No," she replied. I then asked her what the man did. "Nothing, he just walked around, and then disappeared." I asked her what she did next. "Nothing. I just closed my eyes and went back to sleep." I then asked what did she think her friends would do if they were to awake in the middle of the night to find a strange man standing by their bed? "They'd scream bloody murder, I'm sure." Well, I told her the mere fact that she didn't is positive proof that it was what we call a hypnopompic dream, not reality.

Strieber's *Communion* contains a classic, textbook description (pp. 172–175) of a hypnopompic hallucination, complete with the wakening from a sound sleep, the strong sense of reality and of being awake, the paralysis (due to the fact that the body's neural circuits keep our muscles relaxed to help preserve our sleep), and the encounter with strange beings. Following the encounter, instead of jumping out of bed and going in search of the strangers, Strieber, typically, goes back to sleep. He even reports that the burglar alarm had not gone off—proof again that the intruders were mental rather than physical. On another occasion Strieber reports awakening and believing that the roof of his house is on fire and that aliens are threatening his family. Yet his only response to this is to go peacefully back to sleep—again, clear evidence of a hypnopompic dream.

Strieber, of course, is convinced of the reality of these experiences. This, too, is expected. If he were not convinced of their reality, the experience would not be hypnopompic nor hallucinatory. The point cannot be more strongly made that ordinary, perfectly sane and rational people have these hallucinatory experiences, and such individuals are in no way mentally disturbed or psychotic. But neither are such experiences to be taken as incontrovertible proof of some sort of objective reality. Subjectively they may be real, but objectively they are nothing more than dreams and delusions. They are called "hallucinatory" because of their heightened subjective reality.

Leaving no rational explanation unspurned, Strieber is nevertheless forthright enough to suggest the possibility that his experiences could, indeed be hypnopompic. Moreover, in a summary chapter he speculates, correctly, that the alien visitors could be "from within us" and/or "a side effect of a natural phenomenon . . . a certain hallucinatory wire in the mind causing many different people to have experiences so similar as to seem to be the result of encounters with the same physical phenomena." Interestingly, these hypnopompic and hypnogogic hallucinations show individual differences in content and character as well as a lot of similarity: ghosts, monsters, fairies, friends, lovers, neighbors, and even little gray men and golden-haired ladies from the Pleiades. Do such hallucinations appear more frequently to highly imaginative and fantasy-prone people than to other personality types? There is evidence that they do (McKellar 1957; Tart 1969; Reed 1972; Wilson and Barber 1983), and there can certainly be no doubt that Strieber is a highly imaginative personality type.

Missing Time

As for the so-called "missing time" or lacunae experienced by all the UFO abductees, these experiences, too, are quite ordinary, common, and universal. Jerome Singer in his *Inner World of Daydreaming* (1975) comments:

> Are there ever any truly "blank periods" when we are awake? It certainly seems to be the case that under certain conditions of fatigue or great drowsiness or extreme concentration upon some physical act we may become aware that we cannot account for an interval of time and have no memory of what happened for seconds and sometimes minutes. . . . Some people may say that their day-to-day experience is much more full of blank spots than I seem to be suggesting. Introspection tells me that may seem to be the case when a person is not actively attending to the fact that the stream of thought is running along and he has not developed a labeling system for the stream of thought. . . . All too often we do not have already developed labels for many of our emotional reactions in particular situations and without them we may be led to threatening or frightening interpretations of our own feelings and experiences.

Reed (1972) has also dealt with the "time-gap" experience at great length. Typically, motorists will report after a long drive that at some point in the journey they woke up to realize they had no awareness of a preceding period of time. With some justification, people will describe this as a "gap in time," a "lost half-hour," or a "piece out of my life." In Reed's words,

> The strangeness of the experience springs partly from "waking up" when one is already awake. But mainly it is due to the knowledge of a blank in one's temporal awareness. Doubtless the uneasiness associated with such a realization is largely culturally determined.
>
> For in our culture our everyday lives are sharply structured by time requirements. For most of us there are conventional times for commencing and finishing work, for taking breaks, for eating, sleeping and enjoying leisure pursuits. We talk about "wasting time" as opposed to "spending time profitably." We are continually consulting our watches or turning on the radio to check our subjective estimates of the passage of time, and in many jobs "clock-watching" has a very real significance. Only when we are on holi-

day can most of us indulge in the luxury of ceasing to bother about clock time. But furthermore, our consciousness of self is closely related to the sense of continuity in the passage of time. To miss a period of time can be very disturbing; it has been used as the theme of several stories and films, as in the alcoholic's "lost weekend."

A little reflection will suggest, however, that our experience of time and its passage is determined by events, either external or internal. What the time-gapper is reporting is not that a slice of time has vanished, but that he has failed to register a series of events which would normally have functioned as his time-markers. If he is questioned closely he will admit that his "time-gap" experience did not involve his realization at, say, noon that he had somehow "lost" half an hour. Rather, the experience consists of "waking up" at, say, Florence and realizing that he remembers nothing since Bologna. . . . To understand the experience, however, it is best considered in terms of the absence of events. If the time-gapper had taken that particular day off, and spent the morning sitting in his garden undisturbed, he might have remembered just as little of the half-hour in question. He might still describe it in terms of lost time, but he would not find the experience unusual or disturbing. For he would point out that he could not remember what took place between eleven-thirty and twelve simply because nothing of note occurred.

In fact, there is nothing recounted in any of the abduction literature that cannot be easily explained in terms of normal, though somewhat un-usual, psychological behavior we now term "anomalous." Different and unusual? Yes. Paranormal or otherworldly and requiring the presence of extraterrestrials? No.

One of the most recent and most fascinating developments among the abduction gurus is their belated recognition of the dangers of depending wholly upon hypnotic regression as proof of their pudding. In a recent issue of the periodical *UFO* published by an organization called California UFO and devoted to the topic of "Hypnosis In UFO Research," both Strieber and Hopkins urged caution in the use of hypnosis and hypnotic regression. Strieber titles his article "Technique Out-of-Control," and for an individual who has in the past relied so heavily on hypnotic regression to prove his abduction claims, it is extraordinary indeed to hear him now make the following statements:

Abduction research may not even be possible utilizing hypnosis; even highly trained hypnotists cannot use the technique reliably for retrieving basic factual information. Until there is a base of information gained from unhypnotized subjects, it must properly remain a therapeutic tool, not an investigative one. The so-called "abduction narrative," which has been gained primarily from hypnotically-induced recall, probably does not reflect actual experience, but rather the application of the subject's worst fears to their most enigmatic experiences. (Streiber 1989, p. 22)

And in another part of the article Strieber observes,

> There is a tendency among abduction researchers—largely untrained in the scientific method and unrestrained by licensing—to be less-than-objective in their treatment of witnesses and to summarily dismiss evidence not consistent with their previous findings. I have come to believe that many techniques used by amateur investigators are not just suspect but disastrous. They amount to a form of unintentional but devastatingly effective brainwashing that denies witnesses access to the truth of their experiences as they originally perceived them. (p. 23)

Finally, Strieber comes down firmly on the side of respectability with the recommendation that

> nobody except a professionally trained hypnotist—preferably one with the credentials and ethical considerations of a mental health professional—should hypnotize any UFO witness for any reason, and then only for therapeutic purposes. Both free and regressed narratives should be interpreted by behavioral psychologists and other professionals skilled in the process. (p. 25)

Hopkins, too, has undergone a conversion, and while he still supports the use of hypnosis as an investigative tool, he is, he claims, extremely sensitive to the difficulties and dangers of using regressive hypnosis. In Hopkins's words in his article in *UFO*, titled "One UFOlogist's Methodology,"

> Perhaps the most basic misconception about hypnosis holds that one's hypnotically-recalled memories and one's normal memories are somehow innately different. They are not. Normal recollection, obviously can be inaccurate, so can hypnotic recall. *All testimony*, hypnotically elicited or otherwise, is affected to some extent the the questioner. In a court trial, a calm, non-leading judge can elicit one kind of information, a bullying prosecutor another. A lover sharing one's bed may inquire with a special kind of intimacy, eliciting yet another kind of recollection. All of this is self-evident with regard to hypnosis, but it is not so easily recognized that with normal recall exactly the same problems exist. (Hopkins 1989, p. 27)

Just a few paragraphs earlier Hopkins dramatically declares that it is not hypnosis that establishes the truth or falsity of the abduction, because the true believers nowadays proudly declare that many of the abduction tales are recounted while abductees are wide awake and prior to hypnosis. In Hopkins's words, "In roughly one-fourth of the abduction cases I've investigated, the subject has recalled virtually all of his or her basic abduction scenario prior to hypnosis" (p. 27).

Hopkins also wants us to know that he is aware of the existence of "screen memories," that is, memories that soften or cover up the horror of the true meaning of a person's recollection. An example would be recalling a beautiful deer with large soulful eyes instead of the horrible alien with his slanted eyes. But the fact of such screen memories clearly establishes the need for hypnosis if one is to ever know the whole truth about any abduction. Hopkins is also aware that the aliens probably use some form of "alien hypnotic suggestion" to block abductees' memories in the first place. And Hopkins also assures us that he is aware of the existence of fantasy-prone individuals—he ran into one once—but since he now has established contact with the proper professionals, everything is hunky-dory. In his words,

> The network of psychiatrists, psychologists, therapists and investigators which I have slowly been assembling [very slowly, I'll bet!] now encompasses 22 cities in 14 states, Canada and the District of Columbia. In addition to this network, three psychiatrists have come to me for hypnosis because of their own apparent abduction experiences, as well as four psychologists and a number of therapists. . . . Unfortunately, unqualified practitioners abound, with and without the necessary academic and medical degrees. (Hopkins 1989, p. 30)

Hopkins is indeed correct in this last regard!

By far the most scholarly and sober of the abduction gurus is Dr. Thomas Bullard, who has a Ph.D. in folklore from Indiana University. Bullard has gained considerable attention and has built up a following primarily on the basis of his attack upon the use of hypnosis in UFO abduction research, which he incidentally takes very very seriously. He believes in the reality of abductions. According to Bullard, who has catalogued and compared over 300 reports of abductions or abduction-like events, 104 of his cases qualified high in both reliability and information content. A careful analysis on his part has lead him to conclude:

> Weighed and found wanting time and again, hypnosis cannot shoulder nearly as much responsibility for abductions as the skeptics have proposed. None of their appeals to confabulation, influence by the hypnotist, and experiments with non-abductees stand up under a comparative examination. In light of these findings, the burden of proof now drops on the skeptics. They can no longer repeat their old claims as meaningful answers. For any future rebuttals the skeptics must look deeper into the phenomenon itself rather than simply deduce the hazards of hypnotic testimony from scientific studies of hypnosis, or read theoretical interpretations into abduction reports from a safe distance. The skeptical argument needs rebuilding from the ground up. (Bullard 1989a, p. 36)

Bullard's efforts would be much more acceptable and credible were it not for several considerations. First, the database he used to arrive at his conclusions is certainly highly questionable, and much of it is based on hearsay. Maybe in folklore circles such data are acceptable and de rigeur. In the hard sciences they are not. Second, nothing he has said in his analysis contradicts the fact that all of the contactees and abductees are, more than likely, either fantasy-prone or perpetrators of a hoax. Third, with regard to differences he found between stories of experimental subjects and those of "real" abductees, Bullard failed to consider that the narratives themselves are quite different. One group of stories is told by normal, ordinary, students, while the other group of stories is told by experienced fantisizers— the fantasy-prone. Fourth, most damaging to Bullard's cause are his own words:

Contrary to popular belief, hypnosis cannot guarantee truthful testimony, and in that sense, hypnosis is a disappointment. . . . The potential for misuse of hypnosis is undeniable, yet an examination of abduction evidence points to a reassuring conclusion: what might happen according to theory seems not to have happened in fact. . . . Carefully worked out programs of abduction investigation now under development promise far tighter control over hypnotic procedures in the future, leading to even more reliable testimony. . . . One cloud still darkens this otherwise bright vista: the negative scientific reputation associated with hypnosis. . . . For UFOlogists hypnosis will remain an indispensable tool, but attention to conscious testimony, multiple-witness cases, and physical evidence holds out better hope than hypnosis for gathering the kind of evidence no one can ignore. (Bullard 1989b)

It certainly does not take a clinical psychologist to interpret the above remarks and conclude which side Dr. Bullard is on. He is a "true believer," and it is a dirty shame that people are still doubting the truth of the abductees' claims! Just you wait. Soon we will have the "kind of evidence no one can ignore," and then all of those skeptics will eat their words! With regard to hypnosis per se, it is high time indeed that the UFOlogists recognize its inherent limitations and that hypnosis is not a "truth serum." "Hypnosis no 'truth serum,' " incidentally, is the title of Bullard's essay (1989b).

At this point, many readers might feel compelled to ask, Well, what is so bad about people having fantasies anyway? What harm do they do? They are entertaining. And as far as psychiatric patients are concerned, whether the fantasies are true or false is of little matter—it's the patient's perception of reality that matters, and it is this that you have to treat.

True. If the client believes a thing is so, you have to deal with that belief. The only problem with this procedure lies in its potential for harm. Too many people's lives have been negatively affected and even ruined by well-meaning but tragically misdirected persons who believe the fantasies of children, the alienated, the fantasy-prone, and have charged innocent people with rape, child molestation, assault, Satanic practices, and other sorts of abusive crimes. Nearly every experienced clinician has encountered such claims and then later has discovered to his chagrin that none of the fantasized events ever happened.

Law enforcement officials are also quite familiar with the products of response expectancies and overactive imaginations of fantasy-prone persons who confess to murders that never happened or to murders that did happen but with which they have no connection. Other problems with the UFO and abduction literature is that it is false, misleading, rabble-rousing, sensationalistic, and opportunistically money-grubbing—taking advantage of people's hopes and fears and diverting them from more scientific studies and endeavors. Our journeys to the stars will be made on spaceships created by determined, hardworking scientists applying the principles and laws of science, not flying saucers piloted by little gray aliens from some other dimension.

Flying saucers and spaceships from beyond? Unlikely. Those lights in the sky are much more likely to be ball lightning, normal lightning, meteors, auroras, auroral meteors, weather balloons, experimental aircraft, phenomena related to the murky problems of human perception, or just plain hoaxes.

Need we be concerned about an invasion of little gray kidnappers? Amused, yes. Concerned, no.

Should we take Strieber, Hopkins, et al., seriously? Not really. They are a long way from furnishing reliable and replicable data, and their shaky hypotheses are miles from obtaining anything resembling proof.

In their way, though, the UFOnaut creations may be of some redeeming value. Besides their value as entertainment, they provide the useful albeit unintended service of directing our attention to the extremities of human belief and the perplexing and perennial problem of detecting deception. In spite of all our scientific accomplishments, we have today no absolutely certain, accurate, or reliable means for getting at the truth—for simply determining whether or not someone is lying. Not only are the polygraph and voice-stress analyzer notoriously unreliable and inaccurate, the professional interrogators, body language experts, and psychological testers are also the first to admit their lack of absolute predictive skill. If the abduction claims do no more than stimulate greater efforts toward the development of better "truth detectors," they will have made an important contribution.

In the meantime, no matter how skillfully the fabulists present their cases, it is important to remember that no authoritative news source has published detailed reports of contacts with aliens backed by proof in the form of nonfantasy-prone multiple witnesses initially freely reporting these contacts *without the benefit of regressive hypnosis*. When one man has a private conversation with an angel in the corner, we consider it hallucinatory; when twenty people simultaneously see and talk with this angel, then we would have good reason to suspect it might not be hallucinatory. When one man never sees an angel in the corner until and unless he is hypnotized and regressed, even then such reports are not hallucinatory. They are merely confabulations. Nor do we classify such a person as psychologically disturbed or even a liar. Most likely, he is as normal and mentally healthy as any of us, and if he has been properly primed with powerful suggestions, might sincerely believe in the truth of his confabulations. If fantasy-prone types tell us about their fantasies, again, we are justified in questioning the validity of their imaginings.

Lack of tangible artifacts or evidence, such as photographs made simultaneously by different photographers, raises additional questions. But most disturbing is the failure of the aliens to either contact or abduct any people whose status or position would make them more easily subject to definitive questioning and investigation—scientists, political officials, ministers, or military officers of field grade or higher. If, as is claimed, the visitors are intelligent, why hasn't at least one of them screamed: "Take me to your leader—or at least to Ollie North?" Why is it that they do not communicate and commune with those who are in a position to foster and foment change toward a better, safer, more peaceful world? Why must they insist on communicating only with certain fringe elements, such as the uneducated, the mentally distraught, the alienated, or those who by profession make their living weaving fanciful, emotion-arousing, exotic tales. And why does it take a recognizedly unreliable process like hypnotic regression to produce such implausibilities?

Hypnosis and Channeling

Accompanying the so-called "New Age" movement in America has been the phenomenon of "channeling." Perhaps the best definition of this behavior is the one given by Jon Klimo in his book *Channeling: Investigations on Receiving Information from Paranormal Sources* (1987). According to Klimo,

> Channeling is the communication of information to or through a physically embodied human being from a source that is said to exist on some other level or dimension of reality than the physical as we know it, and that is not from the normal mind (or self) of the channel. (p. 2)

Klimo is careful to rule out communication from one's own normal mind as a source, as well as communication from other physically embodied minds. In other words, the information has to come from beings who inhabit a higher dimension of reality than our own. Over the years these mysterious contacts have been known by a number of names including "discarnate entities," "spirits," "spirit guides," "soul partners," etc. Around the beginning of the twentieth century, during the age of Spiritualism, individuals who gained contact with such beings were referred to as "mediums." Today, they are called "channels," and operating in the same manner as their earlier counterparts, they are said to serve as conduits for information and teachings from the spiritual dimension or other higher planes of being and reality.

Although much if not most of the material channeled is of a religious or spiritual nature and seems to be emanating from transcendent sources, little if any of it is of an orthodox religious nature. Little wonder that most members of the clergy find the channeling phenomenon disturbing, and most scientists or skeptics find it ridiculous or outright fraudulent. The psychologist Ray Hyman does not see the channels as conscious frauds, but rather as split personalities or fantasy-prone types (Hyman 1986). He notes that everyone has the potential to be a channel, since we all have enough information that we can act out hundreds of personalities quite convincingly.

While many, like Hyman, see the phenomenon as harmless, others believe it is potentially dangerous. Louis J. West, director of UCLA's Neuropsychiatric Institute, sees it as "a New Age confidence game that can aggravate psychiatric illness. . . . and a force drawing [the psychiatric patient] further away from his already poorly grasped relationship with reality."

Other critics have called attention to the shallowness and vapidity of the messages that supposedly emanate from the channeled entities, as well as the lack of personal enlightenment and achievement among the channelers and their followers.

Klimo (1987) notes that:

> a disturbing lack of agreement can often be found among the channels and their material, giving rise to mutually contradictory claims. Intellectual limitations, grammatical incompetence, and historical and scientific inaccuracies also appear in the expressions of the channels and their purported sources. All of this makes it much more difficult—if not impossible—for the logical mind to accept channeling outright, or to believe that authentic channeling is actually taking place on all the fronts where it is reported. . . . Trickery and lies have clearly been exposed in many who claimed the channel's skills. (p. 14)

Most of the material that is channeled from worlds beyond or the higher planes by such master channelers as J. Z. Knight and her Ramtha, Kevin Ryerson and his John, and Jach Pursel and his Lazaris harps on the same basic themes:

Everything is one, the universe is a unity. The universe is basically spiritual and each of us is in tune with it. We are all spiritual and immortal beings within. We are all like gods or we are God, part of him, yet unconscious of this identity. We must all work to overcome our debilitating negative self-image and we must love one another because love is the most powerful force in the universe. We must contact and align ourselves with our higher self. (Klimo 1987, p. 70)

This is also essentially the message of Helen C. Schuchman's A *Course In Miracles* (1976), a three-volume set that has now sold hundreds of thousands of copies. Readers are impressed with its sincerity and simplicity of language, and most readers feel that the words on the page are meant for them personally and that the message is the truest words they have ever heard. This message is that our vision of ourselves is false and that our ordinary, day-to-day ego is not our true self. Each of us is part of a larger spiritual reality within which our true identity resides and within which the ego is only an artificial and transient presence. Heaven is awareness of the perfect oneness of which you are a part. The course also provides a series of exercises, one for each day of the year, to help the students get over all their past negative programming. Even though Schuchman professed to be an atheist, the material in the course quite clearly seems to have come from the Holy Spirit, and most readers are convinced that the true author of the words is Christ himself. In her later years Helen apparently shared this belief.

The experiences that all of these channels undergo in order to bring their messages to a waiting world is well understood by the Czechoslovakian psychologist Peter D. Francuch, who in his book *Principles of Spiritual Hypnosis* (1982) provides a possible way of bridging the traditional notions of hypnosis with the channeling phenomenon. According to Francuch, hypnosis is,

a vital link between different spheres of the human mind and of the human personality through which the higher modes of awareness of these spheres is possible, attainable, and approachable within and without temporal-spatial categories of the so-called objective reality. . . . Spiritual hypnosis deals with that part of hypnosis that enables man to perceive, to realize, and to experience events and happenings out of a spatial-temporal context and in different dimensions than that of matter and the natural world. (Francuch 1982)

Spiritual hypnosis is apparently hypnosis that is out of this world, and in Francuch's terms, when channels put themselves into a trance, they are utilizing spiritual hypnosis. If you are skeptical of these phenomena, you are not alone.

Anyone experienced with hypnosis and self-hypnosis could argue very convincingly that all of these so-called trance channels are not one whit different from their medium precursors, and that, without exception, they are playing a role and behaving exactly in the manner that they think channels in a trance should behave. Some skeptics, willing to give these gamesters the benefit of the doubt, argue that some of them are sincere and not consciously aware they are being deceptive. In a few rare cases this well may be true, since many cryptomnesiacs do, most sincerely, believe that the voices they hear from within are not from their own subconscious but from "the great beyond" or "out of the blue."

The phenomenon of cryptomnesia is, itself, so fascinating it needs to be treated in depth. Without retreating too far from the present topic of hypnosis, it can be said that relaxation and suggestion can easily trigger the release of hundreds of buried memories that are connected in complex associative chains, and that, once revived, appear to come from "out of the blue," since the original stimulus and storage has long since been forgotten. Once these subconscious or unconscious sources have been tapped and the creative wellsprings have released the flood of fantasy material that is organized and made semilogical by the conscious cognitive processes, even the individual undergoing the experience is astounded. To onlookers and bystanders the channel does appear to speak with the tongues of angels and bring messages from the gods.

Anyone who has read the works of some of the New Age channels or has attended any of their costly channeling sessions would readily agree with James Randi's assessment of channeling as

> "the latest supernatural fad" and of channels as a group of "wild-eyed persons who ranted about entities who said they were "speaking through channels into this world". . . . I could extract not one bit of sense from them about evidence for the reality of these "entities" other than one lady's enthusiastic observation that "if it happens in my head, then its real!" That was a statement I could hardly accept. (Randi 1986, p. 13)

We should be very suspicious of many things that happen inside our heads, particularly of those entities or godlings of the depth of the psyche, whether we call them Seth or Ramtha or Lazaris or John or even Christ. It is much too easy to shift the responsibility for our own lives and our own decisions onto one or more of such discarnate entities, abdicating responsibility for improving the material world we live in. One lesson all channels need to learn and remember is: Gods help those who help themselves! On second thought, some of the channels seem to have learned this very well. J. Z. Knight, for example, has become a millionairess from channeling her Ramtha. Many others have reaped—and are currently reaping—similar profits. Seems that Barnum was right.

Forensic and CIA Abuses of Hypnosis

In our discussion of memory in Chapter 4, it was pointed out that there is no guarantee that information recalled during hypnosis is true. The so-called hypnotized person is uncritical and compliant, and at the hypnotist's suggestions will supply any and all requested details to the best of his ability. And if he can't remember them, he will obligingly make them up. Then they will often become thoroughly incorporated into his memory and he will swear on a stack of bibles they are real.

Moreover, people can pretend to be hypnotized and use the fact that they are supposedly hypnotized as an excuse for letting their imaginations and fantasy-production abilities run wild. The result is that any testimony elicited by hypnotic means for forensic purposes is suspect.

Orne, more than anyone else, has urged extreme caution in the legal use of hypnosis and has prescribed a set of guidelines he believes would make the forensic use of hypnosis far more reliable than it currently is. Orne's first recommendation is that only a specially trained psychologist or psychiatrist—who has received no prior information about the case—should be used as the hypnotist. Second, the entire proceedings and especially the dialogue between the hypnotist and the subject should be videotaped, so that any suggestions inadvertently given to the subject by the hypnotist can be detected. Third, there should be no one else present—no observers of any sort—during the hypnotic session, because reactions of observers to the subject's statements can shape the subject's recall of events. Finally, videotapes of any and all interrogations should be made available to all parties in the legal action to permit them to check for information that might have been implanted during interrogations. Under these conditions and these conditions only would Orne recommend the use of hypnosis in the courtroom (Orne 1979). Orne and others have been adamant in their condemnation of the widespread use of hypnosis in police investigative work by untrained and/or poorly trained law enforcement personnel who are not sensitive to the errors that can be made when hypnotic procedures are used indiscriminately.

Martin Reiser, on the other hand, who has been a staunch defender and trainer of hundreds of police officers in the use of hypnotic procedures, insists that to deny the police officer the use of this valuable tool is a serious mistake (Reiser 1976). Reiser and others point out that many cases that might never have been solved have been salvaged through the use of hypnosis. They give as examples the Chowchilla school bus kidnapping, the New York Opera House murder, and the Ted Bundy sorority house slayings in Tallahassee. Hypnosis played a critical and significant role in all three of these highly publicized cases. They stress that there is no contention that hypnosis is a truth-finding technique. They see it, correctly, as merely an interview technique that uses deep relaxation to help improve recall. The information retrieved by this method is not claimed to be factual, and the hypnosis proponents are well aware that people can lie, fantasize, and confabulate while hypnotized. But, they argue correctly, this also happens in the case of witnesses who have not been hypnotized. Similarly, with regard to witnesses' production of fantasy, confabulation, attempts to please the interrogator, etc., the same problems exist without the use of hypnosis. Although most states have refused to admit as evidence information gained by hypnosis, its use in legal situations has continued to grow.

In 1983 the state of Massachusetts established stringent guidelines for the use of hypnosis. These guidelines are very similar to those recommended by Orne:

1. A record must be established of what the witness knew prior to the use or attempted use of hypnosis.
2. A witness will be allowed to testify to his or her present memory of events prior to hypnosis only if that record has been made.
3. The court defines "hypnotically aided testimony" as testimony by a witness to a fact that became available following hypnosis.
4. Hypnotically aided testimony not remembered before hypnosis will not be admissible unless corroborated by tangible evidence and a case for independent reliability can be made.
5. The party that uses hypnosis must make disclosure that hypnosis or its attempted use was employed.
6. The court also recognizes that on occasion the hypnotist need not be a licensed psychiatrist or psychologist. He must, however, be qualified in the use of hypnosis and independent of the investigation of the crime. In some situations a person other than the hypnotist and the subject, for example a parent of a child, may be present before, during and after the hypnosis.

If, in addition to these guidelines, hypnosis is only resorted to after all preliminary investigation has been accomplished and the case is dead-ended, and if each hypnosis session is audiotaped and videotaped, it is hard to see that much harm can possibly be done. Unfortunately, these conditions have not been adhered to in the past and are not being adhered to at the moment. Currently, hypnosis is used primarily to enhance memory—the memory of the defendant whose recall of certain facts or details could help to prove his innocence; the memory of the victim whose recall might identify a culprit; or the memory of an eyewitness whose accurate recall might establish guilt or innocence.

Once the dangers and possible misuses are attended to, it is hard to see how any harm can be done. But be that as it may, in June 1987 the United States Supreme Court ruled that states may not absolutely bar criminal defendants from testifying about details they are able to recall only after hypnosis. While noting that hypnosis may often produce incorrect recollections and unreliable testimony, they struck down the Arkansas Supreme Court's absolute ban on hypnosis, saying it was an arbitrary restriction on a defendant's "constitutional right to testify in her own defense." The court denied that it was expressing an opinion of the "admissibility of testimony of previously hypnotized witnesses other than criminal defendants."

The Supreme Court decision overturned the manslaughter conviction and prison sentence of Vicki L. Rock in the fatal shooting of her husband. Rock had been barred from testifying that she had not had her finger on the trigger of the gun and that it had discharged accidentally. She had not recalled this, until she was hypnotized. The Arkansas Supreme Court argued that since hypnosis was inherently unreliable, the hypnotist could have planted misleading suggestions. The Supreme Court decided that the prosecution failed to show "that hypnotically enhanced testimony is always so untrustworthy and so immune to the traditional means of evaluating credibility that it should disable a defendant from presenting her version of the events for which she is on trial."

In a dissenting opinion, four of the Supreme Court judges said that the states should be able to ban hypnotically enhanced testimony because of its inherently unreliable nature. There is little doubt that such information is untrustworthy, they said. On this last point it seems, everyone agrees— even the majority justices, who were more concerned with defendant rights than with the validity of hypnosis.

Other governmental officials, however, have shown precious little if any concern about citizens' rights—personal, civil, or otherwise. These officials worked for the Central Intelligence Agency during the period 1951–1964. They believed they could use the powers of hypnosis to compel others to do their bidding. They were aided and abetted in these efforts by a group of so-called "professional experts in hypnosis," who argued that hypnosis could and would lead to major breakthroughs in the art of spying. Although the agency officials did not fully trust the academic experts, they felt that hypnosis offered such promise that it had to be formally and systematically pursued.

The CIA engaged in a program of behavioral research on hypnosis designed to take maximum advantage of its alleged powers. The first head of this program, Morse Allen, was so intrigued by hypnosis that in 1951 he went to New York and took a four-day course in hypnotic techniques from a stage-hypnotist. This enterprising con man persuaded Allen that hypnosis could be used to seduce young women and the technique was so effective that he, the hypnotist, "spent five nights a week away from home engaged in sexual intercourse" (Marks 1979).

Allen returned to Washington and received permission from his superiors to try out hypnotic techniques in his office on members of his staff. To prove to his own satisfaction that hypnosis could make people do whatever he wanted, Allen asked young CIA secretaries to stay after work and undergo hypnotic inductions, after which he had them steal files and pass them on to total strangers, thus violating fundamental CIA security rules. He also got them to steal from each other and even to start fires. He made one of them report to the bedroom of a strange man and then go into a deep sleep. Allen wrote, "This activity clearly indicates that individuals under hypnosis might be compromised and blackmailed" (Marks 1979).

In 1954 Allen carried out a Manchurian Candidate, or programmed assassin, type of experiment. The "victim" was a secretary that Allen put into a deep trance and who was told to keep sleeping until he ordered her to do otherwise. The "assassin" was another secretary who was told that if she could not wake up her friend, her rage would be so great she would pick up a nearby pistol and kill her. Under hypnosis, even though she said she was afraid of guns, the "assassin" did pick up the gun and "shoot" her sleeping friend, except that blank rounds were used.

Allen was not, however, completely naive. All he felt he had proved was that impressionable young volunteers would accept commands from legitimate authority figures and do things they were sure would not end in tragedy. The subjects, obviously, trusted Allen well enough to believe he would not let them do anything wrong. The experimental setting was enough to legitimate the secretary's behavior in her eyes. Although Allen wanted to carry out a field test under operational conditions with an involuntary and unwitting subject, no one could come up with an effective way of hypnotizing such a person. Also, the experimenters would have only limited custody of their subject. Moreover, since the subject was likely not to respond after just one command, and probably months of preparation for such an operation would be needed, the project was abandoned.

Control of this project was later taken from Allen and given to a Dr. Sidney Gottlieb, who felt that the agency's purposes could be accomplished using a combination of psychedelic drugs and hypnosis. Gottlieb also was fascinated by hypnosis and strongly believed the creation of a Manchurian Candidate was possible if it was approached properly. To insure it was done right Gottlieb recruited a distinguished member of the American Society of Clinical and Experimental Hypnosis to create the "sleeper-killer." This hypnotist was called "Dr. Fingers" by the agency team because of the theatrical way he used his hands to put the subject into a trance. When Dr. Fingers was told that the intended victim was to be Fidel Castro, he had no qualms about carrying out the potentially lethal experiment.

From here on the experiment took on all of the characteristics of a Marx Brothers comedy. Moving to Miami, the research team sought poten- tial candidates for the assassin's role among jobless immigrants in the large

Cuban community. After selecting one that appeared to be an "ideal sub-ject," Dr. Fingers took him to a motel room, and with a display of hand-waving, put him into a trance. Dr. Fingers then told the Cuban that Castro had to be killed and that doing so was not a crime, but was the only way to liberate Cuba. When the man nodded, Dr. Fingers set about implanting in his subconscious a key word that, when the Cuban heard it in the pres-ence of Castro, would cause him to draw his weapon and shoot. The word chosen was "cigar."

To test how effective his technique had been, Dr. Fingers ordered the Cuban to imagine he was at Castro's side. As the other team members watched, Dr. Fingers uttered the key word. Nothing happened. Dr. Fingers tried again. Again, nothing. Finally, Dr. Fingers gave up and brought the man out of the trance. Then once more he said "cigar." This time the man looked at Dr. Fingers blankly and said, "No, thanks, I don't smoke."

A second candidate refused to wake on command and was driven back to the Cuban quarter and dumped unceremoniously on a street corner still asleep. A third became violent after being hypnotized, and whenever Castro's name was mentioned tried to break up the motel room. Perplexed and frustrated, the agency dismissed Dr. Fingers and returned to Washington (Thomas 1989).

Despite this setback, though, the farce went on. The agency continued to carry out studies involving the use of drugs, electroshock, and sex—in-cluding keeping a brothel—as means of investigating how brainwashing tech-niques could be used and countered. The investigation into the use of hyp-nosis as a practical mind-altering technique apparently was discontinued in 1966. According to CIA-watchers, the agency's efforts to come up with a practical Manchurian Candidate, involving a dozen or more projects, cost the taxpayers almost $2 million. These efforts produced no useful results, but only a large number of classified reports to justify their failure and ration-alize a number of serious breaches of medical ethics and the use of treatment methods that were reckless and dangerous to people's lives.

In the process of trying to create a hypnotically programmed assassin, a number of so-called hypnotic experts were pressed into service. Many of these made all sorts of rash and ridiculous claims, not only about their skill but also about the power of hypnosis in general. One of them, Milton Kline, told the CIA he could program a "patsy," i.e., he could walk an individual through a series of seemingly unrelated events—a visit to a store, a talk with the mailman, picking a fight at a political rally, etc. The subject would remember everything that happened and would be amnesic only about the fact that the hypnotist ordered him to do these things. The purpose of this exercise would be to "set up" the patsy so that he would leave a circumstantial trail that would make the authorities believe he had committed a particular crime. Even if the amnesia didn't hold up and the victim told the police he was hypnotized, it is highly unlikely they would believe such a preposterous story. Kline told the CIA he could create a patsy in three months and create a Manchurian Candidate in six months. Both these assertions fall in the category of wishful thinking on Kline's part.

It is most important that we recognize how far afield and misguided this effort really was. Apart from the total misunderstanding and planned misuse of so-called hypnosis, the entire effort was dim-witted from the outset. Why bother to capture, hypnotize, and/or brainwash some poor unwary soul in the first place? Why go to all this trouble if all that is desired is the assassination of some one or two dictators in a foreign country? Wouldn't it be simpler, much more reliable and more convenient, to contact the Mafia or some similar organization and hire a professional "hit man" on a "half of the payment now and half when the job is finished" basis? Not only are such professionals trained, experienced, and capable, they also know how to get the job done with a minimum of fuss and bother.

The only real gain in employing a hypnotized killer would be, in theory, that he would not remember who ordered him to pull the trigger. Such total amnesia, however, is highly unlikely, even in a Manchurian Candidate. As some of the CIA officials noted, a large number of professional killers already have a built-in amnesia mechanism that has nothing to do with hypnosis. As for the targets, most of them already know who their enemies are and who might be likely to try to assassinate them. It is highly unlikely that Castro or Ghaddafi, is unaware that people are out to get them.

Despite this CIA fiasco, the legend of the Manchurian Candidate refuses to die. A 1989 episode of the television show "MacGyver," titled "Brainwashed," dealt with this theme. Jack Dalton, a flyer and one of MacGyver's buddies, is hypnotized and programmed to assassinate a visiting East-African president. Everyone connected with the story takes it for granted that such matters are routine—easily and readily accomplished. It seems that really good stories die hard.

Is Hypnosis Dangerous?

The above question might be better phrased: Are relaxation, suggestion, and freeing the individual's imagination dangerous? Or we might as well ask: Is water dangerous? Are automobiles dangerous? Is salt dangerous? Are aspirins dangerous? Is life dangerous? (It certainly is. No one ever gets out of it alive!)

The answer to all of these questions is—well, yes and no. While water is necessary to life, too much of it at the wrong time and place can cause drowning. Just because hundreds of people are killed every year in auto accidents doesn't mean that we will stop using them. Just because if we take too many aspirins at once we will poison ourselves doesn't mean we should ban this painkiller. Just about anything and everything can be dangerous if it is misused or misapplied or amassed in such quantities that it threatens life and limb.

Of all the things mentioned above, hypnosis is perhaps the least dangerous. There are no deaths on record due specifically to hypnosis. In spite of this fact, a number of years ago Harold Rosen launched a nationwide campaign against hypnosis, on the premise that it could endanger a patient's physical and emotional health and life through serious adverse sequelae such as incapacitating substitute symptoms, suicidal depression, and psychotic episodes. In an article in the *American Journal of Clinical Hypnosis*, A. Meares (1961) pointed out nine possible areas of difficulty the hypnotist or his client might encounter. These were:

1. Perverse motivation; either the patient or the physician may misuse the situation to satisfy ulterior needs.
2. Untoward personality effects; hypnosis can increase a subject's suggestibility and overdependence; conversely, continued use of hypnosis may exaggerate unfortunate facets of the physician's own personality.
3. Traumatic insight; sudden confrontation with repressed material intolerable to the subject.
4. Precipitation of a psychosis.
5. Development of disabling substitute symptoms when the original symptoms have been removed by hypnotic suggestion.
6. Sudden panic reactions occasioned by the experience of hypnosis.
7. Complications arising from misunderstandings of communication.
8. Possible unscrupulous use of hypnosis.
9. Difficulty in waking a subject and unfortunate effects of incomplete waking.

Meares concluded that the use of hypnosis by an unskilled person can represent a real danger, but the dangers, he felt, are minimal in the hands of a trained physician. It is obvious, however, that most of the dangers listed above are by no means peculiar to hypnosis. They are intrinsic to all intimate interpersonal relationships that develop during any type of psychotherapy. In fact, if there is any danger at all with regard to the use of hypnosis, it resides almost wholly in its use as a therapeutic tool, and the danger in that case is primarily to the hypnotist rather than the client!

Sydney Pulver (1963) called attention to the fact that many patients suffer from delusions following a hypnotic session, and the delusions are usually the result of the interplay of three factors: 1) the heightening of transference fantasies due mainly to the regression of the hypnotic state; 2) the presence of major ego defects, projective defenses, or other predisposing factors in the patient's character; and 3) countertransference reactions on the part of the hypnotist which touch on a specific area of conflict within the patient.

The delusions most commonly take the form of the patient accusing the hypnotist of violating the patient's person, property, or privacy, of unduly influencing him, of rendering him helpless against the sexual or financial influence of others, etc. Pulver recommends that anyone using hypnosis should be careful to conduct a good preliminary evaluation and select patients who are free from dispositions to delusions, and also be aware of his own emotional responses to the patient. These precautions, Pulver says, are more useful than taping the entire treatment session and having a third party present at every hypnosis session. Nevertheless, all these techniques and precautions are helpful if the hypnotist wants to avoid charges of rape, sexual molestation, etc.

As for hypnosis being of any danger to the client, other than in a few rare and isolated instances, hypnosis has proven to be one of the safest tools in the armamentarium of the healing professions. This was the conclusion of a special symposium devoted to hypnotic complications that was published in the January 1987 *American Journal of Clinical Hypnosis*. J. H. Conn (1972), among others, has also minimized the complications related to the use of hypnosis and concluded it is a very safe procedure. According to Conn, "There are no significant dangers associated with hypnosis *per se* and the actual dangers are those which accompany every psychotherapeutic relationship." Hilgard also concluded that

> On the whole, hypnosis is not at all dangerous. . . . Still, there are some people who have a very slight hold on reality and for whom too much playing with fantasy might conceivably release tendencies toward psychotic behavior that they have shown under other circumstances as well. If such discordant behavior follows hypnosis, the hypnotist is likely to be blamed for it, even though there can usually be found many instances of similar behavior by the subject prior to any attempted hypnosis. (Hilgard 1971)

In his book *Hypnotism: Its Powers and Practice*, Peter Blythe (1971) notes that even trained professionals make mistakes in their use of hypnotherapeutic procedures. In his words, "my intention has been to illustrate that there are no dangers inherent in hypnosis itself, and any dangers which do arise are created by the hypnotist, and not hypnosis" (pp. 124–125).

In fact, almost no one believes the use of hypnosis constitutes any danger. Here is a smorgasbord of quotes from "experts" over the centuries, assembled by the Hypnotist's Examining Council of Glendale, California, in 1987:

> Pierre Janet: "The only danger in hypnotism is that it is not dangerous enough."
> Leslie LaCrone: "As to self-induction, many thousands have learned it; and

I have yet to hear a report of any bad results of its use."

David Cheek, M.D.: "We can do more harm with ignorance of hypnotism than we can ever do by intelligently using hypnosis and suggestion constructively."

William S. Kroger: "Platonof, an associate of Pavlov, who used hypnosis over fifty years in over fifty-thousand cases, reports as follows: 'We have never observed any harmful influences on the patient which could be ascribed to the method of hypno-suggestion therapy, or any tendency toward the development of unstable personality, weakening of the will, or pathological urge for hypnosis.' "

Dr. Julius Grinker: "The so-called dangers from hypnosis are imaginary. Although I have hypnotized many hundreds of patients, I have never seen any ill effects from its use."

Rafael Rhodes: "Hypnotism is absolutely safe. There is no known case on record of harmful results from is therapeutic use."

Dr. Louie P. Thorpe: "Hypnotism is a natural phenomena, and there are no known deleterious effects from its use."

Gil Boyne: "In almost thirty years of clinical practice and teaching, I have never seen a single documented case of harm from hypnosis."

Cheek and LeCron: "The best indication that dangers are minimal is the fact that thousands of lay hypnotists and many stage hypnotists who know little about hypnosis other than how to induce it use it indiscriminately, yet bad results are rarely reported."

It is time to remember the words of William C. Coe, quoted in an earlier chapter, that because of the public and professional prejudices and misunderstandings about hypnosis, its greatest danger is probably to the hypnotist, not the subject. As Coe notes, even though there is no definitive evidence that hypnosis is harmful, it may be used as an explanation for unfortunate complications. This is exactly what has been done by Dr. Frank J. MacHovec, whose book *Hypnosis Complications* (1987) is a collection of cases of individuals who suffered from various sorts of personality and emotional disorders prior to hypnotherapy, and then after hypnotherapy blamed the therapy for their problems.

Hypnosis is blamed for headaches, nausea, increased nervousness, and other sorts of neurotic manifestations including depressed mood, shakiness, cold hands, sweating, frequent urination, feelings of impending doom, a choking or smothering feeling, etc., ad nauseam. Kreskin described the book as "the re-introduction of witchcraft into science" (personal correspondence). My own reaction was that a similar book could be written about the complications some people have with aspirin or coffee or chocolate, e.g., upset stomach, hives, nervousness, difficulty in sleeping, and so on. What is particularly amusing about the entire question of hypnosis and its dangers is that only those who consider hypnosis to be some sort of altered state ever raise the issue. If we phrase it properly—is there anything dangerous about an individual relaxing, using his imagination, and mentally following along with a therapist's suggestions?—the answer is a resounding NO!

Yet for every general rule it seems there is always at least one exception or qualification. The only thing dangerous about hypnosis is its attractiveness for naive or self-seeking individuals like Budd Hopkins and other abduction gurus who convince incipient paranoids and/or the fantasy-prone that their worst fears have been realized and that they were victims of alien monsters who abducted them, invaded their bodies, and are still monitoring their behavior. As Philip Klass (1989) has observed, such alleged UFO abductions are "a dangerous game," and grievous mental harm is being done to many innocent and trusting individuals in need of skilled professional help who instead receive treatment at the hands of fanatics like Hopkins.

Before concluding this chapter mention must be made of a recent attempt on the part of the parapsychologist R.A. McConnell to persuade students of hypnosis and of parapsychology that hypnosis is a "psychokinetic process." After reading the work of Vasiliev, the Soviet parapsychologist, McConnell concluded that

> psychokinesis is almost certainly the essence of hypnosis. . . . Psychokinesis has been the subject of intensive research by psychology for many years under the guise of hypnosis. We are faced with the possibility that hypnosis is an ubiquitous psi-mediated "brain washing" process that enters to a greater or lesser extent into all interpersonal relationships. (McConnell 1983, p. 163)

McConnell is convinced that the essential element of hypnosis is the psychokinetic control of the brain of the subject by the hypnotic operator. He submitted a paper making these claims to both T. X. Barber and E. R. Hilgard, as well as to six psychological journals, including the *Journal of Parapsychology* and the *Journal of the American Society for Psychical Research*. All readers, reviewers, and journals—without exception—rejected both the paper and the hypothesis. Sadly, McConnell still does not understand why and has accused the entire world of practicing scientific repression (McConnell 1983, p. 164).

7.

The Future of Hypnosis: Unsettled Issues

Evidence is gradually accumulating to suggest that *there is one measurable personality trait related to hypnotizability: imagination.* . . . We seem to have come full circle from Mesmer's encounter with the French Academy of Science to contemporary discoveries regarding the role of imagination in hypnosis . . . in this regard . . . the editors state their belief that all contributors to their volume [Fromm, E. and Shor, R., eds., *Hypnosis: Developments in Research and New Perspectives,* 1979] would now agree that hypnosis is essentially a *profoundly compelling imaginal fantasy.*

Steven Starker, *Fantastic Thought,* 1982.

Know thyself!

Socrates

Practice, data, and theory—all three—now seem to agree that hypnosis, rather than some unusual altered state of consciousness, is exactly what King Louis's commissioners said it was: imagination. And all the rest of the hypnotic phenomena are due to relaxation, suggestion, expectation, and compliance. Steven Starker (1982) a few years ago called attention to the similarity between hypnotic induction procedures and other techniques designed to stimulate imagery and fantasy. Certainly evidence is at hand to show that the ability to daydream and hallucinate at will is not confined to persons in a hypnotic trance. People asked to try hard to imagine hypnotic phenomena experience them just as profoundly as people put through the hypnotic induction procedure—in fact there is good reason to believe the two conditions or approaches are essentially one and the same. Certainly the outcome is the same, i.e., people become imaginatively involved. Those individuals who have the ability to become immersed or deeply involved in fantasies or imaginative pursuits are, of course, better subjects.

If you are a fantasy-prone personality type, then the reach of your fantasy creations is unbounded. Like Robert Lindner's Kirk Allen in "The Jet-Propelled Couch," included in Linder's *The Fifty-Minute Hour* (1955), one can create an entire new world and then move into it and live there most of the time if the requirements of existence on planet Earth are too demanding.

Or like T. Flournoy's Helene Smith, in *From India to the Planet Mars: a Study of a Case of Somnambulism with Glossolalia* (1900). Helene, a pleasant and intelligent young woman who was an excellent worker and conscientious and efficient on the job, was possessed of a phenomenal memory for past details. When placed in a hypnotic trance, she showed a number of unusual behaviors, including automatic writing, glossolalia, auditory hallucinations, and somnambulistic phenomena. Helene would act out her fantasies and run the gamut of intense emotional experiences as a young woman living in medieval India and on the planet Mars under the guidance and tutelage of a benevolent spirit named Leopold. On Mars, Helene spoke and wrote in the Martian language. Through a careful analysis of Helene's past, Flournoy was able to explain her spiritualistic visions and communications in orthodox psychological terms. His book still makes for fascinating reading.

Such people as Kirk Allen and Helene Smith are at the extreme end of the fantasy spectrum. What about the average or ordinary citizen? A number of behavior theorists have recently come to the conclusion that one of the deepest, most powerful, and all-pervasive of human motivations is the desire to alter consensual reality. For most human beings, it seems, reality is never good enough and it must be changed. And change it we do, through daydreaming and fantasy, through poetry, drama, and fiction, through alcohol and drugs, and through religions and belief systems of one sort or another.

A few years ago Andrew Malcolm in his survey of drugs and drug use *The Pursuit of Intoxication* (1972) pointed out that intoxicating substances have been used by humans for thousands of years in nearly every part of the world to alter consciousness, to heal the body, to stimulate the mind and body, and to create pleasure and euphoria and escape from mental distress. According to Malcolm, the general threshold for physical and mental discomfort seems to be diminishing steadily in recent years, and to endure pain of any sort is no longer regarded as a virtue. To alleviate progressively more minor states of tension or emotional upset has become a significant trend of our time. Chemists and members of the pharmaceutical industry are doing their best to meet this demand. Their drugs and the illegal drugs marijuana, cocaine, and heroin make the alteration of consciousness on a daily basis easy and affordable.

All drugs—including caffeine, nicotine, and alcohol—are treated with diminished respect because of their familiarity. We have become so habituated to popping pills and ingesting one sort of drug or another on a daily and nightly basis that we have already unwittingly created a chemophilic society and an entire addicted nation. Although many who are addicted to one or more of these drugs would vehemently deny addiction, they could not give up their eight to ten caffeinated colas or their twenty to forty cigarettes a day. They do not consider their daily doses of aspirin, Tylenol, Ibuprofen, Anacin, etc., "drugs." "Because I drink six to ten beers every night, whaddayuh mean I'm an alcoholic? You're out of your mind, bub!"

Recently psychologists and students of addictive behavior like Ronald Siegel of UCLA's School of Medicine have gone on record to predict that the federal government's current "War on Drugs" can never be won. In his book *Intoxication: Life in Pursuit of Artificial Paradise* (1989), Siegel agrees with Malcolm that the desire to alter one's state of consciousness is a drive as elemental as hunger, thirst, or sex. If chemical intoxicants are not available, human beings resort to fantasizing, daydreaming, dancing, drumming, music, fasting, prayer, flagellation, and a variety of other means to escape from ordinary reality. According to an aphorism very popular in the '60s, "Reality is a nice place to visit, but I wouldn't want to live there."

Malcolm and Siegel both have called attention to the fact that today more people from every level of society seem inclined to solve their personal problems by seeking an altered state of consciousness and temporary oblivion. Malcolm notes that we are inundated by chemical drugs that are either legal or easy to come by. Siegel argues that society would be best served if we accept the fact that, like it or not, people are going to drink and use consciousness-altering drugs. In his opinion, we should launch an all-out effort to come up with less damaging, nonaddictive substitutes for alcohol, cocaine, heroin, and the like. Since today's drugs of choice are too dangerous and seductive for safe use, we need to invent a class of intoxicants that will provide pleasure or stimulation within limits, but not cause the user to lose control or be dangerous in terms of potential for overdose.

Harvard psychiatrist Dr. Lester Grinspoon and drug researcher Dr. Andrew Weil of the University of Arizona also support Malcolm's and Siegel's views. Grinspoon says, "I have come to the view that humans have a need—perhaps even a drive—to alter their state of consciousness from time to time," and Weil has opined, "There is not a shred of hope from history or from cross-cultural studies to suggest that human beings can live without psychoactive substances" (Beaty 1989).

Neither Weil nor Malcolm, however, believes that the better drugs that Siegel envisions ever *can* or *should* be made. Weill believes there is a real danger in thinking that there will ever by a perfect drug—one that will not interfere with psychological and spiritual growth and will also lack the potential for dependence and damage. Malcolm warns against the ultimate mind-altering drug—Panaceazine. In his words, "Its precursors surround us today, and they are held to be decidedly useful. In the near future it will be crucially important for us to discover ways of preventing Panaceazine from becoming not merely useful but utterly essential for a very large dependent population. The chemists will not oblige. It is the society that must present a thousand convincing alternatives" (Malcolm 1972, p. 256).

Malcolm's suggestion may be the light at the end of the tunnel. If there is a fundamental need or drive to alter one's ordinary linear state of consciousness, then nonchemical ways and means of satisfying this need must be sought. If the path that Siegel prescribes is too perilous—and the chance of merely adding new classes of psychoactive and addictive substances to our present oversupply seems the most likely outcome—then other solutions are needed. This raises the question: are there any safe ways of altering consciousness, ways that are as satisfying and fulfilling as the highs obtained from cocaine or heroin or even alcohol? Perhaps training people to use meditative or autogenic or cryptomnesiac techniques could reduce the need for the chemical depressants (heroin, alcohol, cannabis) and stimulants (cocaine, amphetamines) and hallucinogens (LSD, psilocybin, et al.).

From one point of view, it seems that seeking less dangerous and destructive but still psychoactive substances is not the answer. In the past, morphine was used to treat opiate addiction, and heroin was used to treat morphine addiction, etc. As one of Drug Enforcement Agency head William Bennett's deputy directors has noted, "If the drug Siegel envisions were too good, people would just want more of it" (Beaty 1989). However, there may be something in what Siegel is saying. There is already on the market a number of drugs that have some very positive and beneficial mood-altering effects and as far as anyone can determine the side effects are nil. In fact, it is doubtful that they should be called "drugs" at all, since they are amino acids and more properly fall in the category of food or nutritional supplements. Called DL-phenylalanine, or DLPA, they can be taken before meals on an empty stomach and have an invigorating effect and increase one's feeling of well-being. Six 400-mg tablets or capsules per day seem sufficient to produce a positive salutary effect with no known side effects.

The phenylalanines are amino acids found in milk, cheese, and other high protein foods. Under clinical tests they have been found to be a very quick and effective remedy for a wide variety of depressions—including the depressive phase of manic-depressive illness, and endogenous, schizophrenic, and post-amphetamine depressions. When doses of 100 to 500 mg of pure phenylalanine per day were taken on an empty stomach for two weeks, most depressed people were entirely relieved of their depressions. Faster results were obtained when the dosages were increased to 1 to 1½ grams all at once, which could be taken provided the patient had no history of hypertension or heart disease or was not pregnant. Only a day or two at these dosage is required in order to obtain significant improvement. In fact, phenylalanine has been shown to be twice as effective as imipramine—the current drug of choice in treating depression (Barchas 1978; Erdmann and Jones 1987).

Neither phenylalanine nor any other drug has the power to change reality or bring back the dead, but it can reduce the time required for sufferers to regain the ability to enjoy living again. There are two forms of the drug: D-phenylalanine and L-phenalalanine which are mirror images of each other. The D form has been found effective against physical pain, and the L form effective against depression. A mix of the two forms seems to work best. The L form has been found to be the natural precursor for the neurotransmitters dopamine and norepinephrine, and the increase in the supply of these chemicals in the brain is the reason why L-phenylalanine works as an antidepressant. Known as DLPA when used together, the substance has no toxic side effects to metabolically normal people in normal antidepressant dosages. In excessive amounts DLPA can cause headaches, insomnia, and irritability, but merely reducing the dosage will clear up these symptoms.

D-phenylalanine has recently been discovered to be very effective for severe pain because it inhibits the enzymes that break down the body's natural painkillers, the enkephalins. By producing and activating the endorphins D-phenylalanine intensifies and prolongs the body's own natural pain-killing response to injury, accident, and disease. DLPA effects often equal or exceed those of morphine and other opiate derivatives, but DLPA differs significantly from other prescribed and over-the-counter medicines in that it is nonaddictive and the pain relief becomes more effective over time, without the development of any tolerance. DLPA has strong antidepressive action and can provide continuous pain relief for up to a month without additional medication. It is also nontoxic and can be combined with any other medication or therapy to increase benefits without any adverse interactions.

Why isn't this substance better known? Because it is cheap, doesn't require a doctor's prescription, and is available at any food health store! Another reason is that the average M.D. is not well-trained in nutrition, and what he hasn't heard of he can't recommend. Finally, people who do not respond to conventional pain-killers like Empirin or codeine do respond to DLPA. Certainly, there may be a number of other benign nutritional substances that can have similar beneficial psychological effects and yet not prove to be addictive and destructive.

But there is a catch here, just about anything and everything can be addictive. Milkman and Sunderwirth in their *Craving for Ecstasy: The Consciousness and Chemistry of Escape* (1987) define addiction as "self-induced changes in neurotransmissions that result in behavior problems," and they emphasize that most any stress-reducing activity may be subject to compulsive overuse and the escalating consequence of loss of control. Moreover, any distinction between internally or externally induced alterations of mood, thought, or behavior is both arbitrary and misleading. They point out that humans pursue three avenues of experience to cope with psychic pain: satiation, arousal, and fantasy, and they start down these pathways in the first years of life. Childhood experiences combined with genetic predisposition are the foundations of adult compulsions.

People do not become addicted to drugs or mood-altering activities as such, but rather to the satiation, arousal, or fantasy experiences that can be had through the drugs and activities. The satiation addicts binge on food, or television, or use depressant drugs like heroin or alcohol. They want to shut off negative feelings from the internal or external world. Like children in the first year of life, the mouth and skin are the primary receptors, and well-being depends upon food and warmth. The biochemical effects of these acts are very similar to the effects of the opiates.

Satiation addicts tend to avoid stimulation and confrontation. Arousal addicts, on the other hand, actively seek stimulation. The behavior associated with their addiction includes crime, gambling risk-taking, and the use of stimulant drugs such as cocaine and the amphetamines. They want to feel powerful and in control and cocaine provides this feeling. They boast about their intellect, their talent, their sexual prowess, and their physique and physical skills. They also spend vast amounts of mental and physical energy denying their underlying feelings of helplessness. They often use magical denial as a defense, and they sometimes will posture like three-year-olds coping with a world of grownups.

Fantasy addicts favor the hallucinogenic drugs—LSD, psilocybin, ecstasy. Since a number of these psychotropic drugs like indole and phenylethylamine occur naturally in the brain as neurotransmitters, some individuals of this type may come by their addiction naturally. It is possible that all artistic, romantic, or spiritual activities may be brought about by the conversion of the brain's own hallucinogenic compounds into hallucinogenic drugs. Differences in neurotransmission, influences from the limbic and cortical centers of the brain, and the effects of the various brain enzymes all interact with powerful social forces to push susceptible individuals toward activities that have a high dependency potential. Lotteries, computer games, sex games, and role-playing are all good examples of their methods of escape from the real world.

According to Denise Kandel of Columbia University, the most reliable finding in drug research is the strong relation between a person's drug use and concurrent use by friends. It is very easy indeed to get imprisoned in a deviant role if you are a slum or ghetto dweller. It is also very difficult to change one's lifestyle if status and esteem are gained from deviant activities. Bars, pool rooms, pornography parlors become islands of comfort and refuge for the alienated. With such complex social and psychological forces at work, no wonder that sixty to eighty percent of all addicts who attempt abstinence relapse within six months.

The problem of addiction is more than just drugs. Each of the behaviors listed below can and may become an agent for addiction, subject to compulsion, loss of control, and long-term continuation despite numerous harmful consequences:

Drug ingestion—Includes ingestion of nicotine, caffeine, pot, valium, aspirin and all the other psychoactive substances.

Overeating—Includes overindulgence in various foods, such as sugar, soft drinks, salt, meat, etc.

Sex—Includes autoeroticism (masturbation), pornography, sado-masochistic acts, etc.

Gambling—Includes betting on horses, dogs, cards, dice, roulette, lotteries, numbers, and sports.

Physical Activity—Includes work, exercise, and sports of all kinds.

Pursuit of Power—Includes spiritual, physical, and material power.

Media Fascination—Includes television, movies, and music.

Isolation—Includes sleep, fantasy, and dreams.

Risk Taking—Includes excitement related to danger.

Cults—Includes groups using brainwashing or other techniques of psychological restructuring.

Crime and Violence—Includes crimes against people and property.

Bonding-Socializing—Includes any excessive dependence on relationships or social gatherings.

Institutionalization—Includes any excessive need for environmental structure, such as prisons, mental hospitals, religious sanctuaries, and any institutional use of psychoactive medication.

Milkman and Sunderwith state,

If you have never been enslaved by an irresistible impulse, it is difficult to appreciate a person's apparent inability to captain his own ship. Whatever the seductive agent—substances, services, or sweets—addicts repeat time and time again: "Whenever it's right there in front of me, I have no choice. I've never been able to turn down a . . . . " (p. 177)

All is not lost however. Recovery-oriented self-help groups like Alcoholics Anonymous or Narcotics Anonymous are very effective, and one-on-one forms of psychotherapy can also be very helpful. So can cognitive therapy. And to combat addictions hypnotherapy can also be of great value, provided it is combined with behavioral approaches, and provided the psychodynamics of the patient's anger, depression, and frustration are discovered, explored, and made conscious, and the patient's inner resources for coping are developed. If properly applied in this context, suggestion can be a very powerful tool. Even though Franklin and the rest of King Louis's commissioners recognized the fallacy of Mesmer's contentions and the errors in his assumptions about animal magnetism, they and others were aware that some sort of powerful force was at work and that this force possessed properties that would be useful to the medical establishment. Down through the years, this force—relaxation and suggestion—has proved beneficial in literally thousands of therapeutic situations. Suggestion—not hypnosis—is a powerful therapeutic tool and there is every reason to believe it would be even more powerful and effective in the hands of the modern clinician if he would give up the fallacious notion that he is dealing with some sort of mysterious force called "hypnosis" and recognize and admit that he really doesn't understand exactly what he is doing or what is happening to his patients. It's all a great mystery, this mysterious altered state called "hypnosis!"

Weitzenhoffer (1963) inveighed against this blind fumbling in the dark and the crude misapplications of medicine man mumbo-jumbo in therapeutic situations calling for precise and subtle use of tried and tested therapeutic principles. Little in the way of systematic and effective research has been done on the topic of suggestion per se because it has never been identified as the essential and critical variable in the hypnotic situation. Every clinician planning to use hypnosis as a therapeutic tool should go back and read and study Coué, look into the practical literature of the stage hypnotist, and even follow some of the better masters of applied suggestion about as they ply their trade. Moreover, they should study social psychology, especially works like Robert Cialdini's *Influence: The New Psychology of Modern Persuasion* (1984) and Ernest Dichter's *The Strategy of Desire* (1960).

Most practitioners are not very effective applicants of the art of suggestion, and the reason for this is very simple: few if any are students of suggestion, influence, or persuasion. The lame excuse that is usually heard, "Psychotherapy is an art, not a science," will not suffice. If it is not a science then it is high time that it became one, and that the critical variables in the client-therapist relationship be identified and measured and their effects explored and understood in the traditional scientific manner. This has not been done in the case of what has been fallaciously called "hypnosis." Until it is done, hypnosis has no future, and rightfully and thankfully so. It is high time we get on with how we can more effectively communicate with and influence the minds and behaviors of our clients and assist them in solving their problems, healing their illnesses, optimizing their health, and improving their lives.

We also need to do more research into the nature of imagination and the image-making capabilities of human beings. Not only is the imagination necessary for adaptive living, but those with impoverished fantasy lives tend to be tied directly to external stimulation, and consequently are less able to cope with the complexities of modern living. They are more prone to alcohol and drug abuse, overeating, compulsions, and delinquency.

Through our ability to make images in our heads, we can plan ahead, look back into the past, connect the past with the future, work through the consequences of our actions ahead of time, and create things which have never before existed. There is also good reason to believe that our imagination has an even more important adaptive function—that of keeping us well. We have long known that eighty-five percent or more of the illnesses physicians are called upon to treat are self-limiting, i.e., without any help at all, the human body can prescribe for, treat, and heal itself.

We have known for a long time that the mind and the body interact, that our emotions affect our biology, that the nervous system, the endocrine system, and the immune system are related to each other. In the past this relationship was called "psychosomatic medicine" or the mind-body relationship. More recently, however, better understanding of exactly how these various systems interact has led to the newer science of "psychoneuroimmunology." We now know that psychological factors can play a part in causing diseases of all sorts—everything from colds to cancer. Physicians who are active in this new specialty are unanimous in stating that our emotions and our health are closely and intimately related.

Like stress, panic, negative attitudes, and a pessimistic outlook can cause a breakdown in our immune system, can interfere with effective treatment, and can hinder recovery. Conversely, positive emotions, humor and laughter, and an optimistic outlook can slow the progress of disease, aid in and speed recovery, and in some cases even bring about remission of otherwise terminal disorders. Although the full details of mind-body interaction have yet to be worked out, evidence for a clear-cut connection is now overwhelming. Although the picture is far from complete, the general principles are somewhat as follows:

There are three parts: the mental or cognitive part, the immune system, and the nervous system. The immune system is made up of a trillion or more individual cells manufactured by a number of organs and glands. These work in close concert with the brain and peripheral nerves. The brain, which is the control center of the nervous system, secretes four hundred or more complex chemical substances which include the neurotransmitters, hormones, and endorphins or enkephalins—opiate-like substances which suppress bodily pain. These substances work like molecular messengers and are called neuropeptides. Not only do they cause reactions in the brain, they also travel throughout the entire body and carry chemical messages to all of the organs and glands—the thyroid, liver, spleen, heart, kidneys, digestive tract, and sex organs. Moreover, they serve to activate, instruct, and regulate the immune system.

Some of the immune cells are sensitive to certain neurotransmitters, and when these cells and neurotransmitters meet in the bloodstream they are stimulated to produce interferon or interleukin-2, which serve as immune system boosters. Vasopressin, a brain chemical, for example, stimulates gamma interferon production. In the brain certain peptides affect our moods and pain perceptions, while others in the bloodstream attract the immune scavenger cells—the microphages—to damaged tissue cells. Biochemical messengers from the hypothalamus and pituitary glands stimulate the thymus gland to produce immune system fighting cells known as T-cells. Prolactin, another brain peptide, helps to regulate the branch of the immune system that builds the antibodies for the B-cells. In fact, there is an entire range of substances—sex hormones, corticosteroids, growth hormones—secreted by the brain that are accepted and acted upon by the immune system. In turn, the immune system manufactures its own peptide molecules and sends messages back to the central nervous system. Since the cells of both the immune and nervous systems receive and transmit information via these chemical messengers, the body's defenses are maximized.

These same chemicals play an important role in our moods and emotions. Radical changes in our affective life, consequently, cause the brain to undergo specific biochemical changes, thus altering the messages sent to the organs and to the immune system. Negative emotions such as rage, anxiety, depression, and grief affect organs throughout the body in a negative fashion. Conversely, techniques such as meditation, positive mental imagery, humor, and optimism, along with a strong will to live, can realign the chemical balance and stimulate the immune system to increase its attack upon cancer, infectious diseases, allergies and other life-threatening invasions.

Meditation techniques, including visualization, when used as complements to traditional medicine, have proved successful in treating gastrointestinal disorders, high blood pressure, chronic headaches and pain, arthritis, and cancer. In addition most any sort of morale-boosting activities, pet therapy, group activities to reduce isolation, and laughter can be very effective in the treatment of all gerontological disorders.

As practiced today, what is called "mental medicine" is based primarily upon a procedure called "imaging." This procedure is amazingly like what has been called "hypnosis." First, the patient is relaxed, then the therapist gives suggestions or guides the patient in the production of warm, positive, concrete images. Patients are encouraged to envision their desired state of being or goals as strongly and clearly as they can. While some clients combine their visualization with prayer, others may repeat over and over to themselves the Coué-type suggestions, "I am getting stronger. I am feeling better every day. I feel happy and relaxed. My tumor is disappearing."

Perhaps the most famous of all attempts to use imagery to fight cancer has been the work of Carl and Stephanie M. Simonton, who were able to achieve several dramatic recoveries and remissions among cancer patients they treated with visualization and relaxation (Simonton, Simonton, and Creighton 1978). The Simontons are the first to admit their treatment procedure is not a panacea, and they recommend it be used along with standard oncological treatment, never as a substitute for the standard treatment.

Visualization therapy has also proved effective in many cases of hypertension. The mind's attention can be focused through relaxation and suggestion, and if it is focused upon what is going on inside the body, and if we use mental images to produce specific biological effects, and visualize these effects strongly enough, will some physical change occur in the area visualized? Apparently so, in some people, in some particular situations, at some times. Howard Hall, a Penn State psychologist, inspired a few years ago by the efforts of the Simontons, taught twenty healthy people aged twenty-two to eighty-five self-hypnosis (i.e., relaxation and concentrated visualization), telling them to imagine their white blood cells as "strong and powerful sharks" attacking any germ cells roaming through their bodies.

He took blood samples before the session and also an hour afterward. The group was then sent home and told to practice self-hypnosis and the shark hunting exercises on their own. Two weeks later the group returned to Hall and a third blood sample was taken. Interestingly, a few of them had significantly more active immune systems. Those that did proved to be younger and more suggestible (Hall 1982). Although the lack of close experimental control in this instance is obvious, the results are intriguing enough to warrant more research in this direction.

Dr. Barbara Peavey (1982) studied the effect of a biofeedback-assisted relaxation program on immune function in sixteen people who were under high levels of stress and had low levels of immunity as measured by white blood cell counts and a test of the ability of the neutrophils to ingest debris through phagocytosis. Half made up the control group and half the biofeedback group. The latter group was given biofeedback instructions and taught how to use the biofeedback equipment—both an EMG muscle monitor and a temperature device. Cassette tapes of stress and muscle relaxation exercises were also provided to train them in how to relax and how to reduce the physical effects of stress.

Blood samples were collected before the training began, at the beginning of the biofeedback sessions, and after the subjects met the criteria for relaxation. Comparisons were made of the subjects' pretreatment and posttreatment neutrophil levels and those of the control group. The comparisons revealed that the neutrophil functioning was significantly enhanced by the treatment. The effect was related to functioning only, since there were no differences in total numbers of white blood cells. There was also a direct but selective effect upon immunity. Other research has shown that relaxation alone is not sufficient to change the immune system, but that some imagery or visualization procedure is also required (Smith et al. 1981). In neither the Hall nor Peavey studies was any attempt made to control any type or activity of the white blood cells. Nevertheless, these studies demonstrate that through conscious effort the immune system can be stimulated to function more efficiently. This finding is in no way new.

Basmajian (1963) found evidence that subjects could gain voluntary control over a single cell. When tiny electrodes were inserted into a single motor nerve cell so that the cell's electrical activity could be measured, and auditory feedback was provided to the subject whenever the cell would fire, the subject quickly learned to fire the cell at will. Subjects even learned how to signal with the firing, i.e., produce long bursts, short bursts, or patterns of long and short bursts (Basmajian 1963).

The work of Barbara Brown (1975), Joe Kamiya (1968), and others has shown that brain waves can be similarly controlled if feedback is provided. Smith and Schneider have repeatedly shown that imagination, in and of itself, without years of meditational training or any biofeedback can control some of the functions of the neutrophils. White blood cells were visualized as garbage collectors that picked up the trash and dumped it outside the body. Before the imagery sessions began the subjects were shown slides of the neutrophils which were to be incorporated into their imagery.

Suggestions for effective imagery were also given, and the subjects drew pictures of their imagery and were coached in improving it. Relaxation tapes were played and the subjects were told to be playful with their images and to change their imaging techniques at any time it seemed sensible to do so. Articles describing white blood cell function were also sent home with the participants. Blood samples taken before and after the six twenty-minute imagery sessions were compared by raters who had no prior knowledge of the bloodwork. The results were very clear: the total white blood cell count dropped significantly from pre-to post-session, and all sixteen subjects showed a drop in count—the average percent of neutrophils that left the bloodstream was sixty percent, and the imagery was highly specific to the neutrophils.

Similar results were obtained in later studies with tighter controls. Replications of these findings have been made in several other laboratories. The conclusion seems unavoidable that imagery seems to have a direct effect upon the functioning of the neutrophils *for those who believe it will.* The emphasis is most important because in all of the foregoing studies only subjects who believed they might be able to consciously control their immune system were accepted as subjects. Again, the factor of belief enters into the picture (Schneider, Smith, and Whitcher 1983).

Clearly, this is the direction that future research in laboratory hypnosis, at least, should go. Suggestion, belief, imagination, attitudes, emotions, and imagery, and their relations to and impact upon the body's biological and physiological mechanisms need to be fully understood if clinical science is to make any major advance in helping people solve their psychological problems. Works such as Jeanne Achterberg's *Imagery in Healing: Shamanism in Modern Medicine* (1985), Steven Locke and Douglas Colligan's *The Healer Within: The New Medicine of Mind and Body* (1986), or Norman Cousins's *Anatomy of an Illness* (1979) and his newer *Head First: The Biology of Hope* (1989), on the healing powers of hope, are all well-written, popular introductions to the topic of mind-body interactions and the place to begin for those unfamiliar with the topic. (Most of the information in Cousins's *Head First, The Biology of Hope* is reliable and valid, but his statements on page 179 that hypnosis is dangerous and that firewalking is the result of group hypnosis are naive and inaccurate.)

With regard to the topic of hypnosis in general, what is needed most of all is not that old familiar standby "more research." What is needed is "more scholarship," that is, more reading, training, and education on the part of therapists and clinicians who have such a poor and rudimentary understanding of normal human functioning and normal human behavior that whenever they encounter anything the least bit unusual they, like their nondegreed fellow citizens, jump to the conclusion that something supernatural or uncanny is at work. Many therapists, unfortunately, have the degrees but lack the knowledge—particularly knowledge of anomalistic psychology—or an understanding of and familiarity with the many twists and turns that the normal human mind takes in trying to make sense out of our perceptual world. When we add to this difficulty the problems created by the number and variety of neurological ailments and impairments— things that go wrong with the most complex mechanism in the known universe, the human brain and nervous system—it is easy to understand why so many clinical errors and misdiagnoses are made on the part of psychologists, psychiatrists, and neurologists. Complexity, however, is no excuse for perversity or failure to keep oneself informed and loyal to the principles of science and consensual reality.

Therapists of whatever persuasion who see little green men or believe in the little green men their clients see, or who believe that because one of their clients has a déjà vu experience it is proof positive he has lived before are doing little to help either their clients or society. Even more reprehensible are those so-called mental healers who because their patients show an unusual pattern of neurotic symptoms convince themselves and their clients they are possessed by demons. Or those who use hypnosis to probe their client's memory and upon encountering fantasies of childhood sexual abuse immediately conclude the child is a victim of satanists and proceed to ruin the reputations and lives of many innocent citizens. Who can possibly measure the harm done by licensed and degreed individuals who publish alarmist and sensationalistic tracts pandering to the fears and fantasies of the ignorant and uninformed merely to inflate their egos and pocketbooks?

Thoughtless or poorly informed healers and helpers who aid and abet gurus of the occult or purveyors of extraterrestrial myths should remember the fundamental therapeutic ground rule: First, do no harm.

At present, considerable grievous harm is being done by too many individuals in the mental health profession who are using their power and prestige to foment and promote belief in and allegiance to medieval superstitions: demonic possession; abduction by spirits, fairies, elves, and other little aliens; the power of amulets and talismen (e.g., crystals) to heal; ability to communicate with the spirit world (e.g., through channels); the ability of the soul to leave the body and return; the ability of the dead to return to life; communication between people using extrasensory means; etc. Unfortunately, hypnosis is still considered by many of these individuals as the tool and technique for bringing these occult mysteries to life. As in the case of liberty, it seems that eternal vigilance on the part of the rationalists is required if such nonsense is to be met and defeated, and the many fallacies surrounding hypnosis exposed.

In summary, although people think of hypnosis as a special state of consciousness involving some sort of trance, during which people can remember past lives and every minute detail of their childhood, and during which they become insensitive to pain—none of this is true. What we call "hypnosis" is nothing more than compliant behavior on the part of people who relax and follow along with the suggestions provided by the hypnotist. The hypnotist is possessed of no special talents or powers. Anyone can be hypnotized and anyone can be a hypnotist. Although the newspapers and the media imply that hypnotists have special powers and abilities, such as to cause people to do things against their will or relive past lives, all such claims are, in the words of Bugelski and Graziano (1980):

pure drivel designed to titillate unknowledgeable readers. We can dismiss the reincarnation nonsense as just that—sheer nonsense, unworthy of disproof—since there is nothing to disprove. There has been no evidence presented beyond some idle claims that someone today is reliving incidents of some earlier life. . . . stories of people speaking foreign languages they never learned are just that—stories.

Under controlled laboratory conditions, unhypnotized subjects can do anything that supposedly hypnotized subjects can do. "Hypnosis," though it comes from the Greek word meaning "sleep," is not sleep unless during the course of interaction with the hypnotist the subject falls asleep. In all such instances (and the instances are fairly common) the subject is asleep and not hypnotized. Physiological measures show clearly there is no difference between a hypnotized subject and someone who is awake. There is no way to tell whether or not a person is hypnotized unless he says he is. Because all such verbal reports are untrustworthy and no altered or special states of consciousness can be identified, and because each and every phenomenon believed to be unique to hypnosis has been duplicated in unhypnotized people, most authorities in the field believe hypnosis per se does not exist. It is a fallacy—a false or mistaken idea based on faulty reasoning.

As for suggestibility, some people are much more suggestible than others. Some are so suggestible they can fantasize easily while awake, fully conscious, and without bothering to relax. People who are fantasy-prone live very active fantasy lives and on occasion act out fantasies of visiting distant planets, being abducted by extraterrestrials, traveling out of the body, and living past lives. Such fantasies are, for the most part, harmless. In Bugelski and Graziano's words again:

When hypnosis is defined as a heightened state of suggestibility, it implies that we are in a special state. Actually, we can be no more suggestible than we are, once we have let down the safeguards that might normally prevent us from doing whatever anyone tells us to do. If we have agreed to let someone hypnotize us, we have agreed to cooperate and to follow instructions. We are not in any different state of suggestibility; we are merely less critical. Those who worry about all the harm that hypnotists might cause are misplacing their worries. There are enough persuaders around to cause all the trouble we need. Popular leaders such as Hitler could get others to do all sorts of horrible things without relaxing them and telling them that they were falling asleep. All they had to do was to promise to satisfy strong yearnings of their willing followers. The followers wanted to believe, and so they believed. Similarly, the hypnotized subject wants to believe; he or she does not dispute or argue, and does what he or she is told to do. He or she cannot do, however, anything that he or she could not do without the help of hypnosis. If someone wants to quit smoking, for example, he or she can quit.

If the subject does not really want to quit, a hypnotist might be able to make him or her believe what is essentially true and what no one can deny: that smoking is a filthy habit, disease promoting, a public nuisance, and so on. The additional support to the belief may help the subject quit. (Bugelski and Graziano, pp. 123–124)

As a clinical tool, hypnosis in the hands of a competent psychotherapist can be very useful. It is not, however, the hypnosis that does anything; it is the skill on the part of the therapist in using suggestions to help his client confront and more effectively cope with the problems he is facing. Based on current research in mind-body relationships, perhaps the best and most effective use of suggestion and the imagination is yet to come. All conscientious and dedicated therapists would do well to hone their suggestion-making and influencing skills if they hope to do a better job of helping their clients.

It is, perhaps, expecting a bit too much to believe that a better under-standing of how human beings behave and function in the hypnotic interrelationship will also lead to a diminution in the use of the misnomer "hypnosis." Two hundred years ago the term "mesmerism" and the term "animal magnetism" were in common use, just as "hypnosis" is today. As our knowledge about both the nature of the universe and human beha-vior grew, we abandoned "mesmerism" and "animal magnetism" as antiquated and inappropriate. If we are lucky it will not require another two hundred years for: 1) a full understanding of what takes place when human beings turn their thoughts inward and use their imaginations, and 2) all of us to abandon the anachronism that the word "hypnosis" is today.

Recapitulation—Questions and Answers

Q: Is there such a thing as "hypnosis"?

A: No. Not as a unique state of awareness or consciousness.

Q. But why do people close their eyes and act like they're in a trance?

A: Because of their desire to cooperate with the hypnotist, i.e., social compliance.

Q: But why do they do it if there isn't a hypnotist around? What about self-hypnosis?

A: Closing our eyes helps us focus our attention and helps us focus on our internal images, our imaginings, our daydreams. And everyone can and does do this. If we're controlling the flow of our images, this is daydreaming. If we fall asleep and it happens automatically, this is called just plain dreaming. Everybody—without exception—dreams and daydreams.

Q: Then everybody *can* be hypnotized *if* they want to be?

A: Yes.

Q: And nobody can be hypnotized if they don't want to be?

A: Correct. If you don't want to listen to or follow someone else's suggestions, you don't have to.

Q: Then concentrating on our own internal imagery and using our own
imagination, or daydreaming, is all that self-hypnosis is?

A: Yes. Intense concentration on our internal images is what we seen by
"self-hypnosis."

Q: Then everybody can be hypnotized, that is, if they follow the images
that the other person supplies them with. But nobody can be hypnotized against their will.

A: Yes. No one can be hypnotized unless they want to be.

Q: But why have there been all these claims about the mysterious powers
and abilities people supposedly acquire under hypnosis?

A: Because some unscrupulous or naive people like to deceive or impress
others and make them believe things that aren't true. Salesmen do it
all the time in order to sell us things.

Q: Then people under hypnosis don't become extraordinarily strong, are
not able to remember accurately everything that ever happened to them,
and are not able to have surgery without pain?

A: They *do not* and *are not* able to do these things under hypnosis *any
more than they can* do them when they are wide awake. In other words,
motivated people who are wide awake are *just* as strong; our memories
are improved a little when we, wide awake, close our eyes, relax and
concentrate. But we do mix fact with fiction anytime we remember
anything; and being *distracted* from the cause of the pain and *reducing
the anxiety* surrounding the pain does reduce its intensity when we are
wide awake. Moreover, most of the pain in surgery comes from the
cuts made in the surface of the skin. In this situation (and in nearly
all cases) local anesthetics are used along with the hypnosis. In fact,
most of the hypnosis is nothing but *reassurance* and *distraction*.

Q: What you're saying then, is that most of the things about ordinary
human behavior that we think are due to the so-called power of hypnosis
are things that people *can do* and *do* all the time anyway?

A: Yes.

Q: Then are people wasting their time and money when they go to a
hypnotist—a psychiatrist or psychologist—for help in stopping smoking,
losing weight, getting rid of phobias, and so on?

A: No, not at all. Relaxation and suggestion and belief are powerful
therapeutic tools. But it is *these* things, not the nonexistent hypnosis,
that brings about the relief and the cure. Any therapist worth his salt
knows this.

Q: What about so-called "highway hypnosis?" Is this *true* or *classical* hypnosis such as we find in the laboratory or clinic, or is it something else?

A: Something else. Monotonous repetitive stimulation to our eyes and ears —our bodies—can cause us to lose awareness of the external world, i.e., fall asleep, and we do. We are *asleep*—even with our eyes open.

Q: But people can still drive their cars and perform automatically like robots, like they're in a trance. Are they really hypnotized or in a trance?

A: Consciously, we're asleep, i.e., we are not aware of the meaning of the signals we're receiving from the external world. Because of habit and conditioning our bodies are still performing the well-learned behavior like robots, i.e., mechanically. But these movements are without meaning. As far as awareness or meaning is concerned about signals from the external world, we're either *asleep* or *awake*. As far as our awareness is concerned, it's like a light switch—it is either "off" or "on." There's no in-between condition.

Q: But people say that they're "half-awake" or "half-conscious" of what is happening when they're in a trance or a hypnotized state. How do you explain this?

A: Well, when we're asleep we are not dead. That is, we are not permanently unaware. Sleep, as you know, is not continuous. We drift in and out of awareness all night long. But if something loud enough or *important* enough happens, we awaken instantly. If the signal from the external world is not important, then we go right back to sleeping and dreaming. Of course, there are also times when we have real difficulty determining whether something really happened or whether we dreamed it.

Q: What you're saying is that there are many things about ordinary human behavior that we overlook or ignore or don't know about that can account for all the things that we have been calling "hypnosis?"

A: Right. Moreover, this is also true about all of those weird and odd kinds of occult or paranormal behavior we hear about, such as seeing ghosts, talking with the dead, being abducted by aliens, having lived before, and so on. There is a branch of psychology called anomalistic psychology that studies such things. Anyone interested in the so-called supernatural or paranormal should become more familiar with it.

Q: Well, how do we do this?

A: There are a number of excellent books on the subject that you can find at your local library or bookstore. There is even one publisher: Prometheus Books, Inc., 700 East Amherst Street, Buffalo, New York, 14215, that specializes in such books. If you write them they will be happy to send you their latest catalog.

Q: What are some of these books that you particularly recommend?

A: Some that immediately come to mind are: *Science: Good, Bad and Bogus* by Martin Gardner; *Flim Flam!: The Truth About Unicorns, Parapsychology and Other Delusions* by James Randi; *The Psychology of Anomalous Experience* by Graham Reed; *Science and Supernature: A Critical Appraisal of Parapsychology* by James Alcock; and *Extrasensory Deception* by Henry Gordon. All of these are published by Prometheus Books. Two other books that are also excellent are *The Psychology of Transcendence* by Andrew Neher (Prentice-Hall 1980) and *Anomalistic Psychology: A Study of Extraordinary Phenomena of Behavior and Experience* by Leonard Zusne and Warren Jones (Lawrence Erlbaum Associates 1982). All of them are excellent.

References

Introduction

Araoz, D. L. 1984. Foreword to *A Clinical Hypnosis Primer*, by G. J. Pratt, D. P. Wood, B. M. Alman. La Jolla, Calif.: Psychology & Consulting Associates Press.

Barber, T. X. 1969. *Hypnosis: A Scientific Approach*. New York: Van Nostrand, Reinhold.

Jastrow, J. 1935. *Error and Eccentricity in Human Belief*. New York: Dover Publications, Inc.

Kusche, L. D. 1975. *The Bermuda Triangle Mystery—Solved*. New York: Harper & Row.

Lankton, S. and Lankton, C. 1983. *The Answer Within: a Clinical Framework of Eriksonian Hypnotherapy*. New York: Brunner/Mazel.

Moss, C. S. 1965. *Hypnosis in Perspective*. New York: Macmillan Publishing Company, Inc.

Pattie, F A. 1937. "The genuineness of hypnotically produced anesthesia of the skin," *Am. J. Psychol.* 49: 435–443.

Sarbin, T. 1950. "Contributions to role-taking theory: I. Hypnotic behavior." *Psychol. Review* 57: 255–270.

Sheehan, P. W. 1979. "Hypnosis and the process of imagination," in *Hypnosis: Developments in Research and New Perspectives*, ed. by E. Fromm and R. E. Shor. New York: Aldine Publishing. Co..

Spanos, N. P. and Chaves, J. F. 1989. *Hypnosis: The Cognitive-Behavioral Perspective*. Buffalo: Prometheus Books.

Udolf, R. 1984. *Forensic Hypnosis*. Boston: Lexington Books.

Wagstaff, Graham R. 1981. *Hypnosis, Compliance, and Belief*. New York: St. Martin's Press.

Weitzenhoffer, A. M. 1985. "In search of hypnosis," in *Modern Trends In Hypnosis*, ed. by D. Waxman, P. C. Misra, M. Gibson, and M. A. Basker. New York: Plenum Press.

Chapter 1

American Journal of Clinical Hypnosis. January 1985. Editorial, "Are Hypnotherapy Patients Hypnotized?" 27(3):152.

Andrewski, S. 1972. *Social Science as Sorcery.* New York: St. Martin's Press.

Blythe, P. 1980. *Self-Hypnotism.* Toronto: Coles Publishing Co.

Bogan, M., and Bogan, D. 1984. *Hypnosis and the Christian.* New York: Bethany House.

Caprio, F. S., and Berger, J. R. 1968. *Helping Yourself With Self-Hypnosis.* New York: Warner Books.

Gill, M. M. and Brenman, M. 1959. *Hypnosis and Related States: Psychoanalytical Studies in Regression.* New York: International Universities Press.

Glaskin, G. M. 1974. *Windows of the Mind.* London: Wildwood House, Ltd., Arrow Books.

———. 1978. *Worlds Within.* London: Wildwood House, Ltd., Arrow Books.

———. 1979. *A Door to Eternity.* Sydney, Australia: Wildwood House, Bookwise.

Hassan, Steven. 1988. *Combatting Cult Mind Control.* New York: Park Street Press.

LeCron, L. and Bordeaux, J. 1947. *Hypnotism Today.* New York: Grune and Stratton.

Ludwig, A. M. 1963. "Hypnosis in fiction." *Int. J. Clin. & Exp. Hypnosis* 11:71–80.

Mahoney, M. J. 1987. "Scientific publication and knowledge politics." *J. Soc. Behav. and Personality* 2(2): 26–33.

———. 1977. "An experimental study of confirmation bias in the peer review system," *Cognitive Therapy & Research* 1(1) 18–29.

Merriam-Webster Pocket Dictionary. 1964. New York: Pocket Books.

Moss, C. S. 1965. *Hypnosis in Perspective.* New York: Macmillan Publishing Company, Inc.

Salter, A. 1944. *What Is Hypnosis?* New York: Richard R. Smith.

Sykes, Charles J. 1988. *Profscam: Professors and the Demise of Higher Education.* Washington, D.C.: Regnery Gateway.

Van Pelt, S. J. 1954. *Hypnotism and the Power Within You.* New York: Wehman Brothers.

Weitzenhoffer, A. M. 1963a. "The Nature of Hypnosis, I." *Am. J. Clin. Hypnosis* 5:295–321.

——— 1963b. "The Nature of Hypnosis, II." *Am J. Clin. Hypnosis* 6:40–72.

——— 1978. "Hypnotism and altered states of consciousness," in *Expanding Dimensions of Consciousness,* ed. by A. A. Sugerman and R. E. Tarter. New York: Springer Publishing Company.

Chapter 2

Allison, R., with T. Schwarz. 1980. *Minds in Many Pieces.* New York: Rawson, Wade Publishers, Inc.

Baudouin, C. 1920. *Suggestion and Autosuggestion.* New York: Dodd, Mead & Co.

Berger, S. M. 1988. *What Your Doctor Didn't Learn in Medical School.* New York:

William Morrow & Co., Inc.

Binet, A., and C. Feré. 1888. *Animal Magnetism*. New York: Appleton-Century-Crofts.

Coe, W. C. 1989. "Hypnosis and the role of sociopolitical factors in a paradigm clash," in *Hypnosis: The Cognitive-Behavioral Perspective*, ed. by N. P. Spanos and J. Chaves. Buffalo: Prometheus Books.

Coué, Emile. 1922. *Self-Mastery through Conscious Autosuggestion*. New York: American Library Service.

———. 1923. *My Method*. New York: American Library Service.

Crabtree, A. 1985. *Multiple Man: Explorations in Possession and Multiple Personality*. New York: Praeger Publishers.

Fiore, E. 1987. *The Unquiet Dead*. New York: Doubleday and Co.

Freud, S. 1925. "The origin and development of psychoanalysis," in *An Outline of Psychoanalysis*, ed. by J. Van Teslaar. New York: Modern Library.

Freud, S. and Breuer, J. 1950. *Studies in Hysteria*. Boston, Beacon Press.

Guirdham, A. 1982. *The Psychic Dimensions of Mental Health*. Wellingborough, England: Thurston Press.

Hull, C. L. 1933. *Hypnosis and Suggestibility: An Experimental Approach*. New York: Appleton-Century.

Jacobson, E. 1929. *Progressive Relaxation*. Chicago: University of Chicago Press.

Kline, M. V. 1958. *Freud and Hypnosis: the Interaction of Psychodynamics and Hypnosis*. New York: Julian Press.

Lenox, J. R. 1970. "Effect of hypnotic analgesia on verbal report and cardiovascular responses to ischemic pain." *J. Abnorm. Psychol.* 75: 199–206.

Luthe, W. 1969. *Autogenic Therapy*. Vols. 1–6. New York: Grune & Stratton.

MacKay, C. 1869. *Memoirs of Extraordinary Popular Delusions and the Madness of Crowds*. London: Routledge.

Munthe, A. 1929. *The Story of San Michele*. New York: E. P. Dutton.

Myerson, A. 1936. "Error in Psychiatry," in J. Jastrow. *The Story of Human Error*. New York: Appleton Century Company.

Pattie, F. A. 1989. *Mesmer and Animal Magnetism: A Chapter in the History of Medicine*. Unpublished manuscript. Lexington, Ky.

Read, G. D. 1984. *Childbirth Without Fear*. New York: Harper and Row.

Schultz, J. 1959. *Autogenic Training: a Psychophysiological Approach in Psychotherapy*. New York: Grune and Stratton.

Thornton, E. M. 1976. *Hypnotism, Hysteria, and Epilepsy: An Historical Synthesis*. London: Heinemann.

Wagstaff, G. B. 1981. *Hypnosis, Compliance, and Belief*. New York: St. Martin's Press.

Wolberg, Louis. 1945. *Hypnoanalysis*. New York: Grune and Stratton.

Chapter 3

Allison, R. B., with Schwarz, T. 1980. *Minds In Many Pieces*. New York: Rawson and Wade Publishers, Inc.

Araoz, D. 1984. Foreword to *A Clinical Hypnosis Primer*, by G. J. Pratt, D. P. Wood, B. M. Alman. La Jolla, Calif.: Psychology & Consulting Associates Press.

Baker, R. A., Haynes, B., and Patrick, B. 1983. "Hypnosis, memory, and incidental memory." *Am. J. Clin. Hypnosis* 25(4):253–262.

Barber, T. X., and Hahn, K. W. 1963. "Hypnotic induction and 'relaxation': An
√   Experimental Study." *Arch. Gen. Psychiatry* 8: 295–300.

Barber, T. X.. 1964. "Hypnotizability, suggestibility and personality: V. A critical review of research findings." *Psychological Report* 14 (Monogrophic Supplement 3).

Barber, T. X., Spanos, N., and Chaves, J. F. 1974. *Hypnotism, Imagination, and Human Potentialities.* New York: Pergamon Press.

Barber, T. X. 1986. "The realities of stage hypnosis," in *Hypnosis Questions and Answers*, ed. by B. Zilbergeld, M. G. Edelstien and D. L. Araoz. New York: W. W. Norton & Co.

Barrett, D. 1979. "The hypnotic dream: Its relation to nocturnal dreams and waking fantasies." *J. Abnorm. Psychology* 88:584–591.

Beahrs, John O. 1971. "The hypnotic psychotherapy of Milton H. Erickson." *Am. J. of Clinical Hypnosis*, 14(2): 73–90

Benson, Herbert. 1975. *The Relaxation Response.* New York: Wm. Morrow & Co.

Bernheim, H. 1886. *Suggestive Therapeutics.* New York: G. P. Putnam's Sons.

Bolles, E. P. 1988. *Remembering and Forgetting.* New York: Walker & Co.

Bryan, Dr. W. J., Jr. 1962. *Religious Aspects of Hypnosis.* Springfield: C. C. Thomas.

Clawson, T. A., and Swade, R. H. 1975. "The hypnotic control of blood flow and pain: the cure of warts and the potential for the use of hypnosis in the treatment of cancer." *Am. J. Clin. Hypnosis* 17:160–169.

Coe, W. C. 1989. "Hypnosis: The role of sociopolitical factors in a paradigm clash," in *Hypnosis: The Cognitive-Behavioral Perspective*, ed. by N. P. Spanos and J. F. Chaves. Buffalo: Prometheus Books.

Coe, W. C., and Buckner, L. 1975. "Expectation, hypnosis, and suggestive methods," in *Helping People Change*, ed. by F. H. Kanfer and A. P. Goldstein. New York: Pergamon Press.

Coe, W. C. and Ryken, K. 1979. "Hypnosis and risks to human subjects." *Am. Psychologist* 34(8):673–681.

Crailsneck, H. B., and Hall, J. A. 1959. "Physiological changes associated with hypnosis: a review of the literature since 1948." *Int. J. Clin. & Exp. Hypnosis* 7:9–50.

Damaser, E. C. 1964. *Experimental Study of Long-term Post-hypnotic Suggestion.* Unpublished doctoral dissertation, Harvard University, Cambridge, MA.

Davies, P. 1988. "Some considerations of the physiological effects of hypnosis," in *Hypnosis: Current Clinical, Experimental and Forensic Practices*, ed. by M. Heap, London and New York: Croom Helm.

De Groot, H., and Gwynn, I. 1989. "Trance logic, duality, and hidden-observer responding," in *Hypnosis: The Cognitive-Behavioral Perspective*, ed. by N. P. Spanos and J. F. Chaves. Buffalo: Prometheus Books.

Edmonston, W. 1979. "The effects of neutral hypnosis on conditional responses: Implications for hypnosis as relaxation," in *Hypnosis: Developments in Research and New Perspectives* (2nd ed.), ed. by E. Fromm and R. E. Shor. New York: Aldine.

————. 1980. *Hypnosis and Relaxation: Modern Verification of an Old Equation*. New York: John Wiley & Sons.

Edmonston, W. E., and Pessin, M. 1966. "Hypnosis as related to learning and electrodermal measures." *Am. J. Clin. Hypnosis* 9:31–51.

Ewin, D. M. 1974. "Condyloma acumination: Successful treatment of four cases by hypnosis." *Am. J. Clin. Hypnosis* 17:73–78.

Fromm, E., and Shor, R. 1979. *Hypnosis: Development, Research, and New Perspectives*. Chicago: Aldine.

Gilligan, S. G. 1987. *Therapeutic Trances: Cooperative Principles in Ericksonian Psychotherapy*. New York: Brunner/Mazel.

Glass, L. B., and Barber, T. X. 1961. "A note on hypnotic behavior, the definition of the situation, and the placebo effect," *J. Nerv. & Mental Diseases*. 132:539–541.

Gorton, B. E. 1949. "The physiology of hypnosis," *Psychiat. Quarterly* 23:317–343 and 457–485.

Hammond, D. C. 1986. "Evidence of Erickson's effectiveness," in *Hypnosis: Questions & Answers*, ed. by B. Zilbergeld, M. G. Edelstien, and D. L. Araoz. New York: W. W. Norton and Co. Inc.

Heller, S., and Steele, L. 1987. *Monsters and Magical Sticks: There's No Such Thing As Hypnosis*. Phoenix: Falcon Press.

Hilgard, E. R. 1965. *Hypnotic Susceptibility*. New York: Harcourt, Brace, & World.

————. 1971. "Hypnotic phenomena: the struggle for scientific acceptance," *Am. Scientist* 59 (Sept.–Oct.): 567–577.

————. 1977. *Divided Consciousness. Multiple Controls in Human Thought and Action*. New York: John Wiley & Sons.

————. 1984. "Review of the collected papers of Milton H. Erickson on hypnosis." *Int. J. Clin. and Exp. Hypnosis* 32:257–265.

Hilgard, E. R., and Hilgard, J. R. 1975. *Hypnosis in ihe Relief of Pain*. Los Altos, Calif.: Wm. Kaufman Publishing Co.

Hilgard, J. 1970. *Personality And Hypnosis: A Study of Imaginative Involvement*. Chicago: University of Chicago Press.

Hull, C. L. 1933. *Hypnosis And Suggestibility: An Experimental Approach*. New York: Appleton-Century Crofts.

Jacobson, E. 1929. *Progressive Relaxation*. Chicago: University of Chicago Press.

Johnson, R. F. Q. 1972. "Trance logic revisited: a reply to Hilgard's critique." *J. Abnorm. Psychol.* 79:234–238.

Johnson, R. F. Q., Maher, B. A., and Barber, T. X. 1972. "Artifact in the 'essence of hypnosis': an evaluation of trance logic." *J. Abnorm. Psychol.* 79:212–220.

Kanfer, F. H., and, Goldstein, A. P., 1975. *Helping People Change*. New York: Pergamon Press.

Kirsch, I. 1985. "Response expectancy as a determinant of experience and behavior." *Am. Psychologist* 40:1189–1202.

Knox, V. J., Morgan, A. H., and Hilgard, E. R. 1974. "Pain and suffering in ischemia." *Arch. Gen. Psychiatr.* 30:840–847.

Kreskin. 1973. *The Amazing World of Kreskin*. New York: Random House.

———. 1981. "On hypnosis," letter to the editor, *Omni*, May 1981, 3(8):131.

Kubie, L. S., and Margolin, S. 1942, "A physiological method for the induction of states of partial sleep, and securing free association and early memories in such states." *Trans. Amer. Neurol. Assoc.* 2: 136–139.

———. 1943. "The use of induced hypnogogic reveries in the recovery of repressed amnesia data." *Bull. Menninger Clinic* 7:172–182.

———. 1944. "The process of hypnotism and the nature of the hypnotic state." *Amer. J. Psychiat.* 100:611–622.

Kusche, L. D. 1975. *The Bermuda Triangle Mystery—Solved*. New York: Harper & Row.

Lunde, D. T. 1975. *Murder and Madness*. Stanford, Calif.: The Portable Stanford.

Lynn, S. J., and Rhue, J. W.. 1988. "Fantasy proneness: hypnosis, developmental antecedents, and psychopathology." *Am. Psychologist* 43(1):35–44.

McGill, O. 1947. *The Encyclopedia of Genuine Stage Hypnotism*. Colon, Michigan: Abbot's Magic Novelty Company.

Meeker, W. B., and Barber, T. X. 1971. "Toward an explanation of stage hypnosis." *J. Abnorm. Psychol.* 77:61–70.

Memmesheimer, A. M., and Eisenlohr, E. 1931. "Untersuchungen uber die suggestive-behandlung der warzen." *Dermatologie Zietshrift* 62:63–68, cited by T. X. Barber, 1969, in *Hypnosis: A Scientific Approach*, New York: Van Nostrand.

Milgram, Stanley. 1974. *Obedience to Authority*, New York, Harper & Row.

Moll, A. 1889. *The Study of Hypnotism*. Reprinted 1958. New York: Julian Press.

Moss, C. S. 1965. *Hypnosis in Perspective*. New York: The Macmillan Co.

Nelson, R. A. 1965. *A Complete Course in Stage Hypnotism*. Columbus, Ohio: Nelson Enterprises.

O'Brien, D. 1985. *Two of a Kind: The Hillside Stranglers*. New York: New American Library.

Orne, M. T., Whitehouse, W. G., Dinges, D. F., and Orne, E. C. 1988. "Reconstructing memory through hypnosis," in *Hypnosis and Memory*, ed. by Helen M. Pettinati. New York: Guilford Press.

Orne, M. T. 1961. "The potential uses of hypnosis in interrogation," in *The Manipulation of Human Behavior*, ed. by A. D. Biderman and H. Zimmer. New York: John Wiley & Sons.

Reiser, M. 1976. "Hypnosis as a tool in criminal investigation." *Police Chief* 43(76):39–40.

———. 1980. *Handbook of Investigative Hypnosis*. Los Angeles, Calif.: Lehi Publishing Co.

Reveen, P. 1987. *The Superconscious World*. Montreal: Eden Press.

Sarbin, T. R., and Slagle, R. W. 1972. "Hypnosis and psychophysiological outcomes," in *Hypnosis: Research Developments and Perspectives*, ed. by E. Fromm, and R. E. Shor. Chicago: Aldine-Atherton.

Sarbin, T. R., and Coe, W. C. 1972. *Hypnosis: a Social Psychological Analysis of Influence Communication*. New York: Holt, Rinehart and Winston.

Sears, Robert R. 1932. "An experimental study of hypnotic anesthesia." *J. Exp. Psychol.* 15:1–22.

Sidis, Boris. 1910. *The Psychology of Suggestion.* New York: Appleton-Century Co.

Spanos, N. P. 1982. "A social psychological approach to hypnotic behavior," in *Integrations of Clinical and Social Psychology,* ed. by G. Weary and H. L. Mirees. New York: Oxford University Press.

Spanos, N. P., and Chaves, John F. 1989. *Hypnosis: The Cognitive-Behavioral Perspective.* Buffalo: Prometheus Books.

Spanos, N. P., de Groot, H. P., and Gwynn, M. I. 1987. "Trance logic as incomplete responding." *J. Person. & Soc. Psychol.* 53(5):911–921.

Spanos, N. P., and McPeake, J. 1977. "Cognitive strategies, reported goal-directed fantasy, and response to suggestion in hypnotic subjects." *Am. J. Clin. Hypnosis* 20:114–123.

Spanos, N. P., Weeks, J. R., and Bertrand, L. D. 1985. "Multiple-personality: a social psychological perspective." *J. Abnorm. Psychol.* 9:362–376.

Starker, S. 1982. *Fantastic Thought.* Englewood Cliffs, N.J.: Prentice-Hall.

Stattman, J. 1980. "The creative trance: a unitive approach toward the phenomena of mental imagery in therapy," in *Studies in Non-Deterministic Psychology,* ed. by Gerald Epstein. New York: Human Sciences Press.

Sutcliffe, J. P. 1960. " 'Credulous' and 'skeptical' views of hypnotic phenomena." *Int. J. Clin. Exp. Hypnosis.* 8:73–101.

———. 1965. "The relations of imagery and fantasy to hypnosis." Final report on Natural Institute of Mental Health Project, United States Public Health Service, Washington, D.C.

Telegen, A., and Atkinson, G. 1974. "Openness to absorbing and self-altering experiences, a trait related to hypnosis," *J. Abnorm. Psychol.* 83:268–277.

Thigpen, C. H., and Cleckley, H. M. 1957. *The Three Faces of Eve.* New York: McGraw-Hill Publishing Co.

Wagstaff, G. F. 1981. *Hypnosis, Compliance and Belief.* New York: St. Martin's Press.

———. 1989. "Forensic aspects of hypnosis," in *Hypnosis: The Cognitive-Behavioral Perspective,* ed. by N. P. Spanos and J. F. Chaves. Buffalo: Prometheus Books.

Wells, W. R. 1923. "Experiments in waking hypnosis for instructional purposes," in *Hypnosis in Perspective.* 1965. Ed. by C. S. Moss. New York: Macmillan Publishing Co.

Weitzenhoffer, A. M. 1963. "Credulity and skepticism in hypnotic research: a critical examination of Sutcliffe's thesis and evidence, Part I." *Am. J. Clin. Hypnosis* 6(1):137–162.

———. 1964. "Credulity and skepticism in hypnotic research: a critical examination of Sutcliffe's thesis and evidence, Part II." *Am. J. Clin. Hypnosis* 6(3):241–268.

White, Robert W. 1941. "A preface to the theory of hypnotism." *J. Abnorm. & Soc. Psychol.* 4(36):477–505.

Wilson, S. C., and Barber, T. X. 1983. "The fantasy-prone personality: implications for understanding imagery, hypnosis, and parapsychological phenomena," in *Imagery: Current Theory, Research, and Application,* ed. by A. A. Sheikh. New York: John Wiley & Sons.

Young, P. C. 1926. "An experimental study of mental and physical function in the normal and hypnotic states." *Am. J. Psychol.* 37:345–356.

Chapter 4

Arnold, M. B. 1984. Memory and the Brain. Hillsdale, N.J.: Lawrence Erlbaum Associates.

Baker, R. A. 1982. "The effect of suggestion on past-lives regression." Am. J. Clin. Hypnosis, 25(1):71–76.

Baker, R. A., Haynes, B., and Patrick, B. 1983. "Hypnosis, memory, and incidental memory." Am. J. Clin. Hypnosis 25(4):253–262.

Baker, R. A., and Patrick, B. 1987. "Hypnosis and memory: The effects of emotional arousal." Am. J. Clin. Hypnosis, 29(3):177–184.

Baker, S. R., and Boas, D. 1983. "The partial reformulation of a traumatic memory of a dental phobia during trance: a case study." Intl. J. Clin. & Exp. Hypnosis 31:14–18.

Bolles, E. B. 1988. Remembering and Forgetting. New York: Walker & Co.

Dement, W. C. 1976. Some Must Watch While Some Must Sleep: Exploring the World of Sleep. New York: W. W. Norton & Co. Inc.

Erdelyi, M. H. 1988. "Hypermnesia: the effect of hypnosis, fantasy and concentration," in Hypnosis and Memory, ed. by Helen Pettinati. New York: Guilford Press.

Evans, C. 1985. Landscapes of the Night. New York: Washington Square Press, Pocket Books.

Gilligan, S. G. 1987. Therapeutic Trances: The Cooperation Principle in Ericksonian Hypnosis. New York: Brunner/Mazel.

Greenleaf, E. 1986. "What to do when a patient falls asleep," in Hypnosis: Questions and Answers, ed. by B. Zilbergeld, M. B. Edelstein, and D. L. Araoz. New York: W. W. Norton & Co.

Gwynn, M. L., de Groot, H. P., and Spanos, N. P. 1989. "Hidden observer responding and its relationship to tests of trance logic." Unpublished manuscript. Carleton University, Ottawa, Canada.

Haley, J. 1963. Strategies of Psychotherapy. New York: Grune & Stratton.

Hilgard, E. R. 1974. Toward a neo-dissociation theory: multiple cognitive controls in human functioning. Perspectives in Biology and Medicine, 17:301–316.

———. 1977. Divided Consciousness: Multiple Controls in Human Thought and Action. New York: John Wiley & Sons.

———. 1979. Divided consciousness in hypnosis: the implication of the hidden observer, in Hypnosis: Developments in reverse and new perspectives, ed. by E. Fromm and E. E. Shor 2nd ed. Chicago: Aldine.

———. 1981. Hypnosis gives rise to fantasy and is not a truth serum. Skeptical Enquirer, 5(3) Spring.

Hilgard, J. R. 1970. Personality and Hypnosis: A Study of Imaginative Involvement. Chicago: University of Chicago Press.

Janet, P. 1920. Major Symptoms of Hysteria. New York: Macmillan Publishing Co., Inc.

LaBerge, S. 1985. Lucid Dreaming. Los Angeles: J. A. Tarcher.

Laurence, J. R., and Perry, C. 1981. "The 'hidden observer' phenomenon in hypnosis. Some additional findings." Journal of Abnormal Psychology 90:334–394.

Laurence, J., Nadon, R., Nogrady, H., and Campbell, P. 1986. "Duality, dissociation, and memory creation in highly hypnotizable subjects." *Intl. J. Clin. Exp. Hypnosis* 34(4):295–310.

Loftus, E. 1979. *Eyewitness Testimony.* Cambridge: Harvard University Press.

———. 1980. *Memory.* Boston: Addison-Wesley.

Lynn, S. J., Rhue, J., Weekes, J. R. 1989. "Hypnosis and experienced nonvolition: a social cognitive integrated model," in *Hypnosis: The Cognitive-Behavioral Perspective,* ed. by N. P. Spanos, and J. F. Chaves. Buffalo: Prometheus Books.

Maury, A. 1861. *Sleep And Dreams.* Paris: Didier.

McKellar, P. 1979. "Between wakefulness and sleep: hypnogogic fantasy," in *The Potential of Fantasy and Imagination.* New York: Random House.

McKellar, P., and Simpson, L. 1954. "Between wakefulness and sleep: hypnogogic imaging," *Brit. J. Psychol.* 45:266–276.

Nash, N. R., Lynn, S. J., Givens, D. L. 1984. "Adult hypnotic susceptibility, childhood punishment and child abuse." *Intl. J. Clin. Exp. Hypnosis* 32:6–11.

Neisser, U. 1982. *Memory Observed: Remembering in Natural Contexts.* Ithaca, N.Y.: Cornell University Press.

O'Connell, D. N., Shor, R. E., Orne, M. T. 1970. "Hypnotic age regression: an empirical and methodological analysis." *J. Abnorm. Psychol. Monographs* 76 (3, part 2):1–32.

Perry, C., Laurence, J. R., D'Eon, J., Tallant, B. 1988. "Hypnotic age regression techniques in the elicitation of memories: applied uses and abuses," in *Hypnosis and Memory,* ed. by Helen M. Pettinati. New York: Guilford Press.

Pettinati, H. M. 1988. Editor, *Hypnosis And Memory.* New York: Guilford Press.

Prince, M. 1908. *The Dissociation of a Personality.* New York: Longmans, Green & Co.

Rawcliffe, D. 1959. *The Psychology of the Occult: Illusions and Delusions of The Supernatural and the Occult.* New York: Dover Publications, Inc.

Reed, G. 1974. *The Psychology of Anomalous Experience.* Boston: Houghton-Mifflin Co.

———. 1988. *The Psychology of Anomalous Experience.* Rev. ed. Buffalo: Prometheus Books.

Reiser, M. 1980. *Handbook of Investigative Hypnosis.* Los Angeles: Lehi Publishing Co.

Simon, C. W., and Emmons, W. H. 1955. "Learning during sleep." *Psychol. Bull.* 52:328–342.

———. 1956. "EEG, consciousness, and sleep." *Science* 124:1066–1069.

Singer, Jerome. 1975. *Inner World of Daydreaming.* New York: Harper & Row.

Spanos, N. P., de Groot, H. P., Tiller, D. K., Weekes, J. R., Bertrand, L. D. 1985. "Trance logic, duality, and hidden observer responding in hypnotic imagination control, and simulating subjects." *J. Abnorm. Psychol.* 94:611–623.

Spanos, N. P. 1989. "Experimental research on hypnotic analgesia," in *Hypnosis: The Cognitive-Behavioral Perspective,* ed. by N. P. Spanos and J. F. Chaves. Buffalo: Prometheus Books.

True, R. M. 1949. "Experimental control in hypnotic age regression states." *Science* 110:583–584.

Twain, M. 1962. *The Autobiography of Mark Twain.* New York: Washington Square Press, Inc.

Udolf, R. 1984. *Forensic Hypnosis.* Lexington, Mass.: Lexington Books.

Van der Walde, P. H. 1965. "Interpretation of hypnosis in terms of ego psychology." *Arch. Gen. Psychiatr.* 12:438–447.

Weitzenhoffer, A. M. 1953. *Hypnotism.* New York: John Wiley & Sons.

———. 1985. "In search of hypnosis," in *Modern Trends in Hypnosis,* ed. by D. Waxman, P. C. Misra, M. Gibson, and M. A. Basker. New York: Plenum Press.

Williams, G. W. 1948. "Do highways hypnotize you while you drive?" *Science Illustrated* 3(8):108–109.

———. 1949. "Highway hypnosis: Our newest hazard." *Parade* (August 28), pp. 6–7.

Williams, G. W. 1963. "Highway hypnosis: an hypothesis." *Intl. J. Clin. Exp. Hypnosis* 11(3):143–151.

Wilson, Ian. 1981. *Mind Out of Time.* London: Gollancz Publishers.

Chapter 5

Abrahamson, M. 1970. "Self-hypnosis for hemophiliacs," paper presented at American Society for Clinical Hypnosis Workshop, University of Minnesota, Minneapolis (October).

Beecher, H. K. 1959. *Measurement of Subjective Responses.* New York: Oxford University Press.

———. 1966. "Pain: One mystery solved." *Science* 151:840–841.

Bowen, D. E. 1973. "Transurethral resection under self-hypnosis." *Am. J. Clin. Hypnosis* 16(2):132–134.

Bugelski, B. R., and Graziano, A. M. 1980. *The Handbook of Practical Psychology.* Englewood Cliffs, N.J.: Prentice-Hall.

Chapman, L. E., Goddell, H., and Wolf, H. G. 1959. "Changes in tissue vulnerability induced during hypnotic suggestion." *J. Psychosom. Research* 4:99.

Crailsneck, H. B., Stirman, J. A., Wilson, B. J., McCranie, E. J., Fogelman, M. J. 1955. "Use of hypnosis in the management of burns." JAHA 158:103.

Ellenberger, H. F. 1970. *The Discovery of the Unconscious.* New York: Basic Books.

Ewin, D. M. 1973. "Hypnosis in industrial practice," *J. Occup. Medicine* 15:586.

———. 1984. "Hypnosis in surgery and anesthesia," in *Clinical Hypnosis: A Multidisciplinary Approach,* ed. by W. C. Wester and A. H. Smith. Philadelphia: J. B. Lippincott Co.

Fodor, Nandor. 1966. *Encyclopedia of Psychic Science.* New York: University Books Inc.

Gibson, H. B. 1977. *Hypnosis: Its Nature and Therapeutic Benefits.* London: Peter Owen Publishers.

Hilgard, E. R., and Hilgard, J. 1986. *Hypnosis in ihe Relief of Pain.* Los Altos, Calif.: William Kaufman Co., Publishers.

Kalin, N. H. 1979. "Genital and abdominal self-surgery: a case report." JAMA, 241:2188–2189.

Knudson-Cooper, M. S. 1981. "Relaxation and biofeedback training in the treatment of severely burned children." *J. Burn Care Rehab.* 2:102.

KOMAR and Steiger, B. 1979. *Life Without Pain.* New York: Berkeley Books.

Lewis, T. 1942. *Pain.* New York: Macmillan Publishing Co.

London, P., and Engstrom, D. 1982. "Mind Over Pain." *American Health* 1(4):62–67.

Mattson, E. L. 1975. "Psychological aspects of severe physical injury and its treatment." *J. Trauma* 15:217.

Melzack, R., and Wall, P. D. 1988. *The Challenge of Pain.* New York: Penguin Books.

Merskey, H. 1983. "The psychological treatment of pain," in *Relief of Intractable Pain,* ed. by M. Swerdlow. Amsterdam, Netherlands: Elsevier Publishing Co., Inc.

Pankratz, L. 1986. "Do it yourself section: Surgery." JAMA, 255(3):324.

Rausch, V. 1980. "Cholecystectomy with self-hypnosis." *Am. J. Clin. Hypnosis* 22(3):124–130.

Schafer, D. W. 1975. "Hypnosis use on a burn unit." *Int. J. Clin. Exp. Hypnosis* 23:1–14.

Shapiro, A. K. 1973. "Contributions to a history of the placebo effect," in *Biofeedback and Self Control,* ed. by Neal E. Miller, et al. Chicago: Aldine Publishing Co.

Schwartz, J. 1978. *Voluntary Controls.* New York: E. P. Dutton.

Wagstaff, G. F. 1981. *Hypnosis, Compliance and Belief.* New York: St. Martin's Press.

Wakeman, R. J., and Kaplan, J. Z. 1978. "An experimental study of hypnosis in painful burns." *Am. J. Clin. Hypnosis* 21:3–11.

Watkins, L. R., and Mayer, J. D. 1982. "Organization of endogenous opiate and nonopiate pain control systems." *Science* 216:1185–1192.

Wester, W. C., and Smith, A. H. 1984. *Clinical Hypnosis: A Multidisciplinary Approach.* Philadelphia: J. B. Lippincott Co.

Chapter 6

Adverse reactions in the use of hypnosis. 1987. Special issue of *The American Journal of Clinical Hypnosis* 29 (3) (January).

Alcock, James. 1981. *Parapsychology: Science or Magic.* New York: Pergamon Press.

Alger, W. R. 1871. *Critical History of the Doctrine of a Future Life.* London: W. J. Widdleton.

Azam, R. and Dufay, P. 1889. "Observations on clairvoyance." *Proceedings of the Am. Soc. for Psychical Research* 6(16).

Backman, A. 1891. "Experiments in clairvoyance." *Proceedings of the Am. Soc. Psychical Research* 7(19).

Brown, S. 1970. *The Heyday of Spiritualism.* New York: Hawthorn Books.

Bjorkhem, J. 1942. *De Hypnotiska Halluciantionetna.* Goteberg, Sweden: Lunde.

Beloff, J. 1973. *Psychological Sciences.* London: Crosby, Lockwood Staples.

Barber, T. X., Spanos, N. P. and Chaves, J. F. 1974. *Hypnosis, Imagination and Human*

Potentialities. New York: Pergamon Press.

Bernstein, Morey. 1956. *The Search for Bridey Murphy.* New York: Doubleday and Co.

Basterfield, K. and Bartholomew, R. 1988. "Abductions: the fantasy-prone personality hypothesis." *Intn. UFO Review* 13(3) (May–June):9–11.

Bullard, T. 1989a. "Hypnosis and UFO abductions: a troubled relationship." *J. UFO Studies* 1:3–40.

Bullard, T. 1989b. "Hypnosis no 'truth serum.' " *UFO* 4(2):31–35.

Blythe, P. 1971. *Hypnotism: Its Powers and Practice.* New York: Taplinger Publishing Co.

Chesterman, J., et al. 1974. *An Index of Possibilities: Energy and Power.* New York: Pantheon Books, Random House.

Christie-Murray, D. 1981. *Reincarnation: Ancient Beliefs and Modern Evidence.* London: David and Charles, Newton Abbot.

Curran, D. 1985. *In Advance of the Landing: Folk Concepts of Outer Space.* New York: Abbeville Press.

Conn, J. H. 1972. "Is hypnosis really dangerous?" *Intl. J. Clin. Exp. Hypnosis* 20:61–69.

Druckman, D., and Swets, J. A. 1987. Eds. of *Enhancing Human Performance: Issues, Theories, and Techniques.* Washington, D.C.: National Academy Press.

De Rochas, A. 1924. *Les Vies Successives.* Paris: Chacornac Frères.

Edwards, P. 1986–1987. "The case against reincarnation." *Free Inquiry* (four parts: Fall 1986, Winter 1986–87, Spring 1987, and Summer 1987).

Fiore, E. 1978. *You Have Been Here Before.* New York: Coward, McCann & Gohegan.

Fuller, J. 1966. *The Interrupted Journey.* New York: Dial Press.

Fowler, R. 1979. *The Andreasson Affair: The Documented Investigation of a Woman's Abduction Aboard a UFO.* Englewood Cliffs, N.J.: Prentice-Hall.

Francuch, P. D. 1982. *Principles of Spiritual Hypnosis.* Santa Barbara, Calif.: Spiritual Advisory Press.

Gribbin, J. 1980. *Time Warps.* New York: Dell Publishing Co., Delta Books.

Goldberg, B. 1982. *Past Lives, Future Lives.* New York: Newcastle Publishing Co. Inc., Ballantine Books, Random House.

Hull, C. L. 1933. *Hypnosis and Suggestibility: an Experimental Approach.* New York: Appleton Century.

Honorton, C. 1977. "Psi and internal attention states," in *Handbook of Parapsychology,* ed. by Benjamin B. Wolman. New York: Van Nostrand, Reinhold Co.

Honorton, C., and Kripner, S. 1969. "Hypnosis and ESP performance: a review of the experimental literature," *J. Am. Soc. Psychical Research* 63:214–252.

Hopkins, B. 1981. *Missing Time.* New York: G. P. Putnam's Sons.

———. 1987. *Intruders: The Incredible Visitations at Copley Woods.* New York: Random House.

———. 1989. "One UFOlogist's methodology," *UFO,* 4(2):26–30.

Hyman, R. 1977. "The case against parapsychology," *The Humanist* 37(6):47–49.

———. 1986. Quoted in Lynn Smith's "The new chic metaphysical fad of channeling." *Los Angeles Times* (December 5).

Hilgard, E. R. 1971. "Hypnotic phenomena: The struggle for scientific acceptance."

Am. Scientist 59 (Sept.–Oct.):567–577.

Hypnotist's Examining Council of California. 1987. Newsletter and Legal Defense Kit. Glendale, California.

Iverson, J., and Bloxham, A. 1977. *More Lives Than One.* New York: Warner Books.

Jay, C. E. 1979. *Gretchen, I Am.* New York: Avon Books.

Jung, C. 1969. *Flying Saucers: A Modern Myth of Things Seen in the Sky.* New York: Signet Books, New American Library.

Kampman, R., and Hirvonoja, R. 1976. "Dynamic relation of the secondary personality induced by hypnosis to the present personality," in *Hypnosis at its Bicentennial,* ed. by F. H. Frankel and H. S. Zamansky. New York: Plenum Press.

Keyhoe, D. 1955. *The Flying Saucer Conspiracy.* New York: Holt, Rinehart and Winston.

Klass, P. J. 1989, *UFO Abductions: a Dangerous Game.* Buffalo: Prometheus Books.

Klimo, J. 1987. *Channeling: Investigations on Receiving Information from Paranormal Sources.* Los Angeles: J. P. Tarcher.

Kline, M. V. 1951. "Hypnosis and age progression: a case report." *J. Genet. Psychol.* 78:195–206.

———. 1952. "A note on primate-like behavior induced through hypnosis." *J. Genet. Psychol.* 81:125–131.

———. 1956. Editor of *A Scientific Report on the Search for Bridey Murphy.* New York: Julian Press.

Kreskin 1973. *The Amazing World of Kreskin.* New York: Random House.

Kurtz, P. 1987. "Is parapsychology a science?" *The Skeptical Inquirer* 3(2):14–32.

Lamont, C. 1950. *The Illusion of Immortality.* New York: Philosophical Library.

Laurence, J. R., Nadon, R., Nogrady, H., and Perry, C. 1986. "Duality, dissociation, and memory creation in highly hypnotizable subjects." *Int. J. Clin. Exp. Hypnosis* 34:295–310.

Lawson, A. H., and McCall, W. C. 1977. "What can we learn from the hypnosis of imaginary abductees?" MUFON UFO Symposium Proceedings, Seguin, Texas; Mutual UFO Network. Pp. 107–135.

Loftus, E. 1979. *Eyewitness Testimony.* Cambridge, Mass.: Harvard University Press.

MacHovec, F. J. 1987. *Hypnosis Complications.* Springfield, Illinois: C. C. Thomas.

Macready, R. 1980. *The Reincarnation of Robert Macready.* New York: Zebra Books, Kensington Publishing Co.

Marks, J. 1979. *The Search for the Manchurian Candidate: the CIA and Mind Control.* New York: Quadrangle Books.

McConnell, R. A. 1983. *An Introduction to Parapsychology in the Context of Science.* Pittsburgh: Geological Sciences Department, University of Pittsburgh.

McKellar, P. 1957. *Imagination and Thinking.* London: Cohen and West Publishers.

Meares, A. 1961. "An evaluation of the dangers of medical hypnosis." *Am. J. Clin. Hypnosis* 4:90–97.

Myers, S. A. and Austrin, H. R. 1985. "Distal eidetic technology: further characteristics of the fantasy-prone personality." *J. Mental Imagery* 9(3):57–66.

Netherton, M. and Shiffrin, N. 1978. *Past Lives Therapy.* New York: Wm. Morrow & Co.

Orne, M. T. 1979. "The use and misuse of hypnosis in court." *Intl. J. Clin. Exp. Hypnosis* 27:311–341.

Parker, A. 1975. *States of Mind: ESP and Altered States of Consciousness.* New York: Taplinger Publishing Co.

——. 1978. "A holistic methodology in psi research." *Parapsychol. Review* 9(2):1–6.

Podmore, F., and Gurney, E. 1884. "Third Report of the Committee on Mesmerism." *Proc. Soc. Psychical Research,* Vol. 2, Part 5.

Pratt, J. G. 1973. "A decade of research with a selected ESP subject: an overview and reappraisal of the work with Pavel Stepanek." *Proc. Am. Soc. Psychical Research* 30.

Pulver, S. E. 1963. "Delusions following hypnosis," *Int. J. Clin. Exp. Hypnosis* 11(1):11–22.

Randi, J. 1986. "On channeling." Letter to Jeremy P. Tarcher, December 8.

Rawcliffe, D. H. 1959. *The Psychology of the Occult: Illusions and Delusions of the Supernatural and the Occult.* New York: Dover Publications Inc.

Ready, W. B. 1956. "Bridey Murphy: an Irishman's View," *Fantasy & Science Fiction* 11(2) (August):81–88.

Reed, G. 1972, *The Psychology of Anomalous Experience.* Boston: Houghton Mifflin Co.

Reiser, M. 1976. "Hypnosis as a tool in criminal investigation." *The Police Chief* 43(11):39–40.

Rhine, J. B. 1952. "Hypnosis and ESP," in *Experimental Hypnosis,* ed. by L. LeCron. New York: Macmillan Publishing Co.

Rhue, J. W., and Lynn, S. J. 1987. "Fantasy proneness: developmental antecedents." *J. of Personality* 55(1):121–137.

Rodney, J. 1959. *Explorations of a Hypnotist.* London: Elek Publications.

Rubenstein, R., and Newman, R. 1954. "The living out of 'future' experiences under hypnosis." *Science* 119:472–473.

Ryzl, M. 1962. "Training the psi faculty by hypnosis." *J. Soc. Psychical Research* 41:234–252.

Ryzl, M., and Ryzlova, J. 1962. "A case of high-scoring ESP performance in the hypnotic state." *J. of Parapsychol.* 26:153–171.

Schuchman, H. 1976. *A Course in Miracles,* three volumes. Tiburon, Calif.: The Foundation for Inner Peace.

Sidgwick, E. 1891. "On evidence for clairvoyance," *Proc. Soc. Psychical Research* Vol. 7, Part 18.

Silverman, P. S. and Retzlaff, P. D. 1986. "Cognitive stage regression through hypnosis: are earlier cognitive stages retrievable?" *Int. J. Clin. Exp. Hypnosis* 34:192–204.

Singer, J. 1975. *The Inner World of Daydreaming.* New York: Harper & Row.

Spanos, N. P. 1987–88. "Past-life hypnotic regression: a critical view." *Skeptical Inquirer* 12(2) (Winter): 174–180.

Strieber, W. 1987. *Communion: A True Story.* New York: Beach Tree Books, Wm. Morrow Co.

——. 1989. "Technique Out-of-Control." *UFO* 4(2):22–25.

Tart, C. 1969. Editor of *Altered States of Consciousness: A Book of Readings.* New York: John Wiley & Sons.

Thomas, G. 1989. *Journey Into Madness: the True Story of Secret CIA Mind Control and Medical Abuse.* New York: Bantam Books.

Wambach, H. 1979. *Life Before Life.* New York: Bantam Books.

Weisman, A. 1979. *We Immortals.* New York: Pocket Books.

West, D. J. 1966. "The strength and weakness of the available evidence for extra-sensory perception," in *Extrasensory Perception*, ed. by G. E. W. Wolstenholme and E. C. P. Miller. New York: Citadel Press.

West, L. J. 1987. Quoted in Carol McGraw, "Seekers of Self Recall New Age." *Los Angeles Times*, February 17.

Wilson, I. 1981. *Mind Out of Time.* London: Gollancz Publishers.

Wilson, S. C., and Barber, T. X. 1983. "The fantasy-prone personality: implications for understanding imagery, hypnosis, and parapsychological phenomena," in *Imagery: Current Theory, Research and Application*, ed. by A. A. Sheikh. New York: John Wiley & Sons.

Zolik, E. S. 1958. "An experimental investigation of the psychodynamic implications of the hypnotic 'previous existence.' " *J. Clin. Psychol.* 14(2):179–183.

———. 1962. "Reincarnation phenomena in hypnotic states." *Intl. J. of Parapsychol.* 4(3):66–78.

Chapter 7

Achterberg, J. 1985. *Imagery in Healing: Shamanism in Modern Medicine.* Boston: New Science Library, Shambala.

Barchas, J. et. al. 1978. "Behavioral neurochemistry, neuroregulation, and behavioral states." *Science* 200 (May 26):964–973.

Basmajian, J. V. 1963. "Control of individual motor units." *Science* 141:440–441.

Beaty, J. 1989. "Do humans need to get high?" *Time*, Aug. 21, p. 58

Brown, B. 1975. *New Mind, New Body.* New York, Harper & Row.

Bugelski, B. R. and Graziano, A. M. 1980. *Handbook of Practical Psychology.* Englewood Cliffs, N.J.: Prentice-Hall.

Cialdini, R. 1984. *Influence: the New Psychology of Modern Persuasion.* New York: Quill, Wm. Morrow & Co.

Cousins, N. 1979. *Anatomy of An Illness.* New York: W. W. Norton & Co.

———. 1989. *Head First: The Biology of Hope.* New York: E. P. Dutton.

Dichter, E. 1960. *The Strategy of Desire.* Garden City, N.Y.: Doubleday & Co.

Erdmann, R., and Jones, M. 1987. *The Amino Revolution.* New York: Simon & Schuster, Inc., Fireside Books.

Flournoy, T. 1900. *From India to the Planet Mars: a Study of a Case of Somnambulism.* New York: Harper & Bros.

Hall, H. R. 1982. "Hypnosis and the immune system: a review with implications for cancer and the psychology of healing." *J. Clin. Hypnosis* 25(2–3):92–103.

Kamuya, J. 1968. "Conscious control of brain waves." *Psychology Today* 1:57–60.

Kandel, D., and Maloff, D. 1983. "Commonalities in drug use: a sociological perspective," in *Commonalities in Substance Abuse & Habitual Behavior,* ed. by P. Levinson, D. Gerstein, and D. Maloff. New York: Brunner/Mazel.

Lindner, R. 1955. "The jet-propelled couch," in *The Fifty-Minute Hour.* New York: Rinehart & Company.

Locke, S., and Colligan, D. 1986. *The Healer Within: the New Medicine of Mind and Body.* New York: E. P. Dutton.

Malcolm, A. 1972. *The Pursuit of Intoxication.* New York: Pocket Books, Washington Square Press.

Milkman, H., and Sunderwith, S. 1987. *Craving for Ecstasy: The Consciousness and Chemistry of Escape.* Lexington, Mass.: Lexington Books.

Peavey, B. S. 1982. *Biofeedback Assisted Relaxation: Effects on Phagocytic Immune Function.* Unpublished Ph.D. dissertation, North Texas State University, Denton, Texas.

Schneider, J., Smith, C. W., Whitcher, S. 1983. "The relationship of mental imagery to white blood cell (neutrophil) function: experimental studies of normal subjects." Mimeograph. Michigan State University College of Medicine, East Lansing, Michigan.

Siegel, R. 1989. *Intoxication: Life in Pursuit of Artificial Paradise.* New York: E. P. Dutton.

Simonton, O. C., Simonton, S. M., and Creighton, J. L. 1978. *Getting Well Again.* Los Angeles, Calif.: J. P. Tarcher.

Smith, C. W., Schneider, J., Minnin G. C., and Whitcher, S. 1981. "Imagery and neutrophil function studies: a preliminary report." Prepublication Report. Michigan State University, Department of Psychiatry, East Lansing, Mich.

Starker, S. 1982. *Fantastic Thought.* Englewood Cliffs, N.J.: Prentice-Hall.

Weitzenhoffer, A. M. 1963. "Credulity and skepticism in hypnotic research: a critical examination of Sutcliffe's thesis and evidence, Parts I & II." *Am. J. Clin. Hypnosis* 6(1 and 3):137–162 and 241–268.

Index